Lecture Notes in Computer Science 14359

Founding Editors

Gerhard Goos
Juris Hartmanis

The series Lecture Notes in Computer Science (LNCS), including its subseries Lecture Notes in Artificial Intelligence (LNAI) and Lecture Notes in Bioinformatics (LNBI), has established itself as a medium for the publication of new developments in computer science and information technology research, teaching, and education.

LNCS enjoys close cooperation with the computer science R & D community, the series counts many renowned academics among its volume editors and paper authors, and collaborates with prestigious societies. Its mission is to serve this international community by providing an invaluable service, mainly focused on the publication of conference and workshop proceedings and postproceedings. LNCS commenced publication in 1973.

Huchuan Lu · Wanli Ouyang · Hui Huang ·
Jiwen Lu · Risheng Liu · Jing Dong · Min Xu
Editors

Image
and Graphics

12th International Conference, ICIG 2023
Nanjing, China, September 22–24, 2023
Proceedings, Part V

Springer

Editors
Huchuan Lu 🆔
Dalian University of Technology
Dalian, China

Hui Huang 🆔
Shenzhen University
Shenzhen, China

Risheng Liu 🆔
Dalian University of Technology
Dalian, China

Min Xu 🆔
University of Technology Sydney
Sydney, NSW, Australia

Wanli Ouyang 🆔
University of Sydney
Sydney, NSW, Australia

Jiwen Lu 🆔
Tsinghua University
Beijing, China

Jing Dong 🆔
Institute of Automation, CAS
Beijing, China

ISSN 0302-9743   ISSN 1611-3349 (electronic)
Lecture Notes in Computer Science
ISBN 978-3-031-46316-7   ISBN 978-3-031-46317-4 (eBook)
https://doi.org/10.1007/978-3-031-46317-4

This Springer imprint is published by the registered company Springer Nature Switzerland AG
The registered company address is: Gewerbestrasse 11, 6330 Cham, Switzerland

Paper in this product is recyclable.

Preface

These are the proceedings of the 12th International Conference on Image and Graphics (ICIG 2023), which was held in Nanjing, China, on September 22–24, 2023. The Conference was hosted by China Society of Image and Graphics (CSIG), organized by Nanjing University of Posts & Telecommunications, co-organized by Nanjing University of Science & Technology and Nanjing University of Information Science and Technology, supported by Springer.

ICIG is a biennial conference that focuses on innovative technologies of image, video, and graphics processing and fostering innovation, entrepreneurship, and networking. ICIG 2023 featured world-class plenary speakers, exhibits, and high-quality peer-reviewed oral and poster presentations.

CSIG has hosted the series of ICIG conference since 2000. Details about the past conferences are as follows:

Conference	Place	Date	Submitted	Proceedings
First (ICIG 2000)	Tianjin, China	August 16–18	220	156
Second (ICIG 2002)	Hefei, China	August 15–18	280	166
Third (ICIG 2004)	Hong Kong, China	December 17–19	460	140
4th (ICIG 2007)	Chengdu, China	August 22–24	525	184
5th (ICIG 2009)	Xi'an, China	September 20–23	362	179
6th (ICIG 2011)	Hefei, China	August 12–15	329	183
7th (ICIG 2013)	Qingdao, China	July 26–28	346	181
8th (ICIG 2015)	Tianjin, China	August 13–16	345	170
9th (ICIG 2017)	Shanghai, China	September 13–15	370	172
10th (ICIG 2019)	Beijing, China	August 23–25	384	183
11th (ICIG 2021)	Haikou, China	December 26–28	421	198

For ICIG 2023, 409 submissions were received and 166 papers were accepted. To ease the search for a required paper in these proceedings, the accepted papers have been arranged into different sections according to their topic.

We sincerely thank all the contributors, who came from around the world to present their advanced work at this event. We would also like to thank all the reviewers, who carefully reviewed all submissions and made their valuable comments for improving the accepted papers. The proceedings could not have been produced without the invaluable efforts of the members of the Organizing Committee, and a number of active members of CSIG.

September 2023

Huchuan Lu
Wanli Ouyang
Hui Huang
Jiwen Lu
Risheng Liu
Jing Dong
Min Xu

Organization

Organizing Committee

General Chairs

Yaonan Wang	Hunan University, China
Qingshan Liu	Nanjing University of Posts & Telecommunications, China
Ramesh Jain	University of California, Irvine, USA
Alberto Del Bimbo	University of Florence, Italy

Technical Program Chairs

Huchuan Lu	Dalian University of Technology, China
Wanli Ouyang	University of Sydney, Australia
Hui Huang	Shenzhen University, China
Jiwen Lu	Tsinghua University, China

Organizing Committee Chairs

Yuxin Peng	Peking University, China
Xucheng Yin	University of Science and Technology Beijing, China
Bo Du	Wuhan University, China
Bingkun Bao	Nanjing University of Posts & Telecommunications, China

Publicity Chairs

Abdulmotaleb El Saddik	University of Ottawa, Canada
Phoebe Chen	La Trobe University, Australia
Kun Zhou	Zhejiang University, China
Xiaojun Wu	Jiangnan University, China

Award Chairs

Changsheng Xu   Institute of Automation, CAS, China
Shiguang Shan   Institute of Computing Technology, CAS, China
Mohan Kankanhalli   National University of Singapore, Singapore

Publication Chairs

Risheng Liu   Dalian University of Technology, China
Jing Dong   Institute of Automation, CAS, China
Min Xu   University of Technology Sydney, Australia

Workshop Chairs

Yugang Jiang   Fudan University, China
Kai Xu   National University of Defense Technology,
                                 China
Zhu Li   University of Missouri, USA
Oliver Deussen   Universität Konstanz, Germany

Exhibits Chairs

Qi Tian   Huawei Cloud, China
Wu Liu   JD.COM, China
Weishi Zheng   Sun Yat-sen University, China
Kun Xu   Tsinghua University, China

Tutorial Chairs

Weiwei Xu   Zhejiang University, China
Nannan Wang   Xidian University, China
Shengsheng Qian   Institute of Automation, CAS, China
Klaus Schöffmann   Klagenfurt University, Austria

Sponsorship Chairs

Xiang Bai   Huazhong University of Science and Technology,
                                 China
Mingming Cheng   Nankai University, China

Finance Chairs

Lifang Wu	Beijing University of Technology, China
Yubao Sun	Nanjing University of Information Science & Technology, China
Miao Hong	CSIG, China

Social Media Chairs

Zhenwei Shi	Beihang University, China
Wei Jia	Hefei University of Technology, China
Feifei Zhang	Tianjin University of Technology, China

Local Chairs

Jian Cheng	Institute of Automation, CAS, China
Xiaotong Yuan	Nanjing University of Information Science & Technology, China
Yifan Jiao	Nanjing University of Posts & Telecommunications, China

Website Chairs

Rui Huang	Chinese University of Hong Kong, Shenzhen, China
Jie Wang	Nanjing University of Posts & Telecommunications, China

Area Chairs

Yuchao Dai	Xi Peng	Yong Xia
Yulan Guo	Boxin Shi	Shiqing Xin
Xiaoguang Han	Dong Wang	Feng Xu
Tong He	Lijun Wang	Jia Xu
Gao Huang	Limin Wang	Kun Xu
Meina Kan	Nannan Wang	Yongchao Xu
Yu-Kun Lai	Xinchao Wang	Junchi Yan
Li Liu	Xinggang Wang	Shiqi Yu
Huimin Lu	Yunhai Wang	Jian Zhang
Jinshan Pan	Baoyuan Wu	Pingping Zhang
Houwen Peng	Jiazhi Xia	Shanshan Zhang

Additional Reviewers

Bingkun Bao
Yulong Bian
Chunjuan Bo
Zi-Hao Bo
JIntong Cai
Zhanchuan Cai
Mingwei Cao
Jianhui Chang
Yakun Chang
Bin Chen
Guang Chen
Hongrui Chen
Jianchuan Chen
Junsong Chen
Siming Chen
Xiang Chen
Xin Chen
Ziyang Chen
Jinghao Cheng
Lechao Cheng
Ming-Ming Cheng
Jiaming Chu
Hainan Cui
Yutao Cui
Enyan Dai
Tao Dai
Jisheng Dang
Sagnik Das
Xinhao Deng
Haiwen Diao
Jian Ding
Wenhui Dong
Xiaoyu Dong
Shuguang Dou
Zheng-Jun Du
Peiqi Duan
Qingnan Fan
Yongxian Fan
Zhenfeng Fan
Gongfan Fang
Kun Fang
Sheng Fang
Xianyong Fang

Zhiheng Fu
Wei Gai
Ziliang Gan
Changxin Gao
Qing Gao
Shang Gao
Zhifan Gao
Tong Ge
Shenjian Gong
Guanghua Gu
Yuliang Gu
Shihui Guo
Yahong Han
Yizeng Han
Yufei Han
Junwen He
Mengqi He
Xiaowei He
Yulia Hicks
Yuchen Hong
Ruibing Hou
Shouming Hou
Donghui Hu
Fuyuan Hu
Lanqing Hu
Qiming Hu
Ruimin Hu
Yang Hu
Yupeng Hu
Bao Hua
Guanjie Huang
Le Hui
Chengtao Ji
Naye Ji
Xiaosong Jia
Xu Jia
Chaohui Jiang
Haoyi Jiang
Peng Jiang
Runqing Jiang
Zhiying Jiang
Leyang Jin
Yongcheng Jing

Hao Ju
Yongzhen Ke
Lingshun Kong
Jian-Huang Lai
Yu-Kun Lai
Xingyu Lan
Yang Lang
Wentao Lei
Yang Lei
Baohua Li
Bocen Li
Boyang Li
Chao Li
Chenghong Li
Dachong Li
Feng Li
Gang Li
Guanbin Li
Guorong Li
Guozheng Li
Hao Li
Hongjun Li
Kunhong Li
Li Li
Manyi Li
Ming Li
Mingjia Li
Qifeng Li
Shifeng Li
Shutao Li
Siheng Li
Xiaoyan Li
Yanchun Li
Yang Li
Yi Li
Ying Li
Yue Li
Yunhao Li
Zihan Li
Dongze Lian
Jinxiu Liang
Junhao Liang
Tian Liang

Zhengyu Liang
Zhifang Liang
Bencheng Liao
Zehui Liao
Chuan Lin
Feng Lin
Qifeng Lin
Weilin Lin
Wenbin Lin
Xiaotian Lin
Yiqun Lin
Jingwang Ling
Qiu Lingteng
Aohan Liu
Chang Liu
Cheng-Lin Liu
Haolin Liu
Jingxin Liu
Jinyuan Liu
Kenkun Liu
Lei Liu
Long Liu
Meng Liu
Min Liu
Qingshan Liu
Risheng Liu
Shengli Liu
Shiguang Liu
Shuaiqi Liu
Songhua Liu
Wei Liu
Wenrui Liu
Wenyu Liu
Xuehu Liu
Yiguang Liu
Yijing Liu
Yipeng Liu
Yong Liu
Yu Liu
Yunan Liu
Zhenguang Liu
Zilin Lu
Weiqi Luo
Yong Luo
Zhaofan Luo

Zhongjin Luo
Yunqiu Lv
Junfeng Lyu
Youwei Lyu
Chunyan Ma
Fengji Ma
Huimin Ma
Tianlei Ma
Xinke Ma
Qirong Mao
Yuxin Mao
Wei Miao
Yongwei Miao
Weidong Min
Jiawen Ming
Weihua Ou
Jinshan Pan
Yun Pei
Zongju Peng
Hongxing Qin
Liangdong Qiu
Xinkuan Qiu
Yuda Qiu
Zhong Qu
Weisong Ren
Nong Sang
Guangcun Shan
Linlin Shen
Zhiqiang Shen
Jiamu Sheng
Jun Shi
Zhenghao Shi
Zhenwei Shi
Chengfang Song
Jiechong Song
Jifei Song
Yong Song
Zhengyao Song
Qingtang Su
Jiande Sun
Long Sun
Xuran Sun
Zhixing Sun
Gary Tam
Hongchen Tan

Jing Tan
Jiajun Tang
Jin Tang
Shiyu Tang
Minggui Teng
Yao Teng
Yanling Tian
Zhigang Tu
Matthew Vowels
Bo Wang
Dong Wang
Dongsheng Wang
Haiting Wang
Hao Wang
Jingyi Wang
Jinjia Wang
Jinting Wang
Jinwei Wang
Junyu Wang
Lijun Wang
Longguang Wang
Meng Wang
Miao Wang
Peizhen Wang
Pengjie Wang
Rui Wang
Ruiqi Wang
Ruotong Wang
Shengjin Wang
Shijie Wang
Tao Wang
Xiaoxing Wang
Xin Wang
Xingce Wang
Yili Wang
Yingquan Wang
Yongfang Wang
Yue Wang
Yun Wang
Zi Wang
Hongjiang Wei
Shaokui Wei
Xiu-Shen Wei
Ziyu Wei
Shuchen Weng

Zhi Weng
Qian Wenhua
Jianlong Wu
Lianjun Wu
Tao Wu
Yadong Wu
Yanmin Wu
Ye Wu
Yu Wu
Yushuang Wu
Di Xiao
Yuxuan Xiao
Jin Xie
Jingfen Xie
Jiu-Cheng Xie
Yutong Xie
Jiankai Xing
Bo Xu
Hongming Xu
Jie Xu
Xiaowei Xu
Yi Xu
Mingliang Xue
Xiangyang Xue
Difei Yan
Xin Yan
Yichao Yan
Zizheng Yan
Bin Yang
Cheng Yang
Jialin Yang
Kang Yang
Min Yang

Shuo Yang
Shuzhou Yang
Xingyi Yang
Xue Yang
Yang Yang
Yiqian Yang
Zhongbao Yang
Chao Yao
Chengtang Yao
Jingfeng Yao
Chongjie Ye
Dingqiang Ye
Jingwen Ye
Yiwen Ye
Xinyu Yi
Xinyi Ying
Di You
Bohan Yu
Chenyang Yu
Jiwen Yu
Runpeng Yu
Songsong Yu
Danni Yuan
Yang Yue
Lin Yushun
Qingjie Zeng
Qiong Zeng
Yaopei Zeng
Yinwei Zhan
Dawei Zhang
Guozhen Zhang
Jianpeng Zhang
Jiawan Zhang

Jing Zhang
Mingda Zhang
Pengyu Zhang
Pingping Zhang
Xiao-Yong Zhang
Xinpeng Zhang
Xuanyu Zhang
Yanan Zhang
Yang Zhang
Ye Zhang
Yuanhang Zhang
Zaibin Zhang
ZhiHao Zhang
Jie Zhao
Sicheng Zhao
Yuchao Zheng
Shuaifeng Zhi
Fan Zhong
Chu Zhou
Feng Zhou
JiaYuan Zhou
Jingyi Zhou
Tao Zhou
Yang Zhou
Zhanping Zhou
Minfeng Zhu
Mingli Zhu
Mingrui Zhu
Xu Zhu
Zihao Zhu
Shinan Zou

Contents – Part V

Color and Multispectral Processing

Computational Imaging

Multi-view and Stereoscopic Processing

Multimedia Security

Surveillance and Remote Sensing

Virtual Reality

Biological and Medical Image Processing

An Efficient Medical Image Fusion via Online Convolutional Sparse Coding with Sample-Dependent Dictionary

Chengfang Zhang[1,2(✉)], Ziliang Feng[3], Chao Zhang[1], and Kai Yi[1]

[1] Intelligent Policing Key Laboratory of Sichuan Province, Sichuan Police College, 186 Longtouguan Road, Luzhou 646000, Sichuan, China
chengfangzhang@scpolicec.edu.cn
[2] National Key Laboratory of Fundamental Science on Synthetic Vision, Sichuan University, South 1st Ring Road, Chengdu 610065, Sichuan, China
[3] College of Computer Science, Sichuan University, South 1st Ring Road, Chengdu 610065, Sichuan, China

Abstract. Convolutional sparse coding (CSC) as an interpretable signal representation and decomposition model has achieved promising performance in medical image fusion by virtue of translation-invariant dictionary. CSC-based compensates for the limited detail preservation capability and high sensitivity to misregistration of SR-based fusion methods. However, existing CSC-based fusion methods have high time consumption due to batch mode. The online convolutional sparse coding (SCSC) model of Sample-Dependent dictionary borrows the idea of separable filters with much lower time cost than CSC. In this paper, SCSC is introduced to medical image fusion to balance fusion performance and time consumption. The proposed method adopts classical 'decomposition-fusion-reconstruction' framework. Firstly, source images are decomposed into base and detail layers using two-scale image decomposition (Fast Fourier Transform). Secondly, average strategy is applied to base layer and detail layer uses SCSC to obtain fused detail components. Finally, two-scale image reconstruction (inverse Fast Fourier Transform) is used to reconstruct fused image. The analysis of subjective and objective results shows that our method improves efficiency while ensuring excellent fusion performance.

Keywords: medical image fusion · online convolutional sparse coding · sample-dependent dictionary · separable filters · time consumption

1 Introduction

Iterative improvements in medical imaging technology have given rise to many types of medical brain images, such as computed tomography (CT) and magnetic resonance imaging (MR). Multiple types of medical images provide physicians with sufficient data for clinical diagnosis and assessment of medical conditions. Restricted by different imaging mechanisms, relying on only a single type of medical images tend to presents misjudgment or discrimination difficulties. CT accurately captures dense structures, such

4   C. Zhang et al.

as bones and implants (Fig. 1(a)); MRI focuses on soft tissue information (Fig. 1(b)). To alleviate the limitations of unimodal medical images, medical image fusion technology uses algorithmic strategies to integrate information from different modal images, which helps physicians reduce misclassification and diagnostic costs.

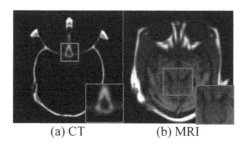

(a) CT   (b) MRI

Fig. 1. Examples of medical images.

Scholars have proposed various medical image fusion methods due to continuous improvement of signal representation theory. Based on signal representation and decomposition, fusion methods are mainly: traditional fusion methods and deep learning-based fusion methods. As classic traditional fusion framework, image fusion methods based on multi-scale transform (MST) consist of 3 steps: (1) image decomposition; (2) fusion of coefficients using specific rules; (3) image reconstruction using an inverse transform similar to decomposition. Benefiting from the excellent mathematical interpretation and outstanding signal representation capability of MST, MST-based medical image fusion methods [1–5] have been continuously proposed and achieved remarkable performance. Deep learning solves shortcomings of traditional signal representation methods that are limited by manual operations, and various neural network-based medical image fusion methods [6–10] have been proposed and achieved surprising results.

Convolutional sparse coding (CSC), which can be regarded as a 1-layer convolutional neural network, was first introduced to medical image fusion by Yu Liu [11] rely on its unique signal representation capability. Subsequently various advanced CSC models were successfully applied to medical image fusion [12–18]. CSC outperforms MST as far as fusion performance, time cost is yet expensive. With advantage of low time complexity of online convolutional sparse coding (OCSC) [19], researchers introduced OCSC to image fusion [20] and results showed that fusion performance and time efficiency are better than CSC. The OCSC has smaller time complexity and space complexity compared to CSC. However, number of filters still constrains OCSC, especially in the stage of dictionary update.

The non-separable filters trained by CSC lead to slow dictionary and coding updates. Rigamonti et al. [21], Sironi et al. [22] used separable filters to improve speed. Inspired by studies, Wang et al. extended idea of sample adaptive training filtering to OCSC, using base filter to approximate filter, and proposed online convolutional sparse coding (SCSC) using Sample-Dependent dictionary [23]. Compared with OCSC, SCSC maintains excellent reconfiguration ability and reduces operation cost. In this paper, SCSC is applied to medical image fusion by drawing on excellent reconstruction ability of

SCSC to provide new ideas for fusion. The proposed fusion method adopts classical 'decomposition-fusion-reconstruction' framework. Specifically, medical source images are decomposed into base and detail layers; then base layer uses 'average' fusion rule while SCSC is applied into detail layer; the fused image is finally reconstructed using fused base and detail layers. 8 pairs of medical images and 7 classical comparison methods are used to verify superiority of proposed method.

The rest of this paper is organized as follows. CSR-based and OCSC-based medical image fusion and theory of SCSC is described in Sect. 2. In Sect. 3, we present proposed fusion method. Section 4 is experimental results and analysis. Finally, Sect. 5 concludes this paper.

2 Related Work and Theory

2.1 CSC-Based Medical Image Fusion

Liu et al. [11] abandoned sparse representation using local image patch to represent source images and introduced CSC to image fusion, which was successful in medical image. The CSC can be represented by the following model.

$$\arg \min_{D \in D, \{Z_i\}} \frac{1}{2} \sum_{i=1}^{N} \left\| \sum_{k=1}^{K} D(:, k) * Z_i(:, k) - x_i \right\|_2^2 + \lambda \|Z_i\|_1 \tag{1}$$

where, x is source images, D denote convolution filter and Z is sparse coefficient maps. Similar to SR-based image fusion, CSC-based fusion continues to use l_2- and l_1-paradigms. However, CSC is optimized for global signal, so fused images have more advantages in terms of detail preservation and global representation. In addition, convolutional dictionary and CSC contribute to robustness of misalignment and insensitivity to noise by virtue of shift-invariance [11, 24, 25]. The filters have non-separable properties and convolution operation leads to slow dictionary and coefficient updates, which in turn reduces fusion performance [23].

2.2 OCSC-Based Medical Image Fusion

Wang et al. [19] used online learning to propose a scalable online convolutional sparse coding (OCSC) that reconstructs CSC objective to alleviate high space and time complexity of traditional CSC algorithms. Subsequently, scholars successfully applied OCSC to image fusion [20]. Given input signal x_t, after observing tth sample, the OCSC model The OCSC model is shown in Eq. 2.

$$\arg \min_{D \in D, \{Z_i\}} \frac{1}{t} \sum_{i=1}^{t} \frac{1}{2} \left\| \sum_{k=1}^{K} D(:, k) * Z_i(:, k) - x_i \right\|_2^2 + \lambda \|Z_i\|_1 \tag{2}$$

OCSC is superior to CSC in time performance, but its spatial complexity is still limited by the size of filters. For OCSC-based fusion method, increasing number of filters indefinitely not only cannot alleviate time efficiency, but also degrades fusion performance.

2.3 SCSC

Sironi, A. et al. [22] used separable filters for post-processing and approximation to speed up. Inspired by this idea, Wang et al. [23] learned dictionary directly during signal reconstruction. Moreover, more filters are learnt by combining up filters from base filters in sample-dependent manner to reduce learning consumption. Given base filters $B \in \mathbb{R}^{M \times R}$ ($\{B(:, r)\}$ is columns), samples $\{x_1, x_2, \ldots, x_N\} \in \mathbb{R}^P$ and filter combination weights matrix $W_i \in \mathbb{R}^{R \times K}$, the model of SCSC is defined as Eq. 3.

$$\min_{B, \{W_i, Z_i\}} \frac{1}{N} \sum_{i=1}^{N} f_i(B, W_i, Z_i) + \lambda \|Z_i\|_1$$

$$s.t. \quad BW_i \in D \ i = 1, \ldots, N, B \in \mathcal{B} \qquad (3)$$

$$f_i(B, W_i, Z_i) = \frac{1}{2} \left\| \sum_{k=1}^{K} (\sum_{r=1}^{R} W_i(r, k) B(:, r)) * Z_i(:, k) - x_i \right\|_2^2$$

where, $\mathcal{D} = \{D : \|D(:, k)\|_2 \leq 1, \ \forall k = 1, \ldots, K\}$ normalize filters and $\mathcal{B} = \{B : \|B(:, r)\|_2 \leq 1, \forall r = 1, \ldots, R\}$. Equation 3 can be decomposed into update B and $\{W, Z\}$, where B is updated using alternating direction method of multipliers (ADMM) [26], and nonconvex and inexact accelerated proximal gradient (niAPG) [27] is solved for $\{W, Z\}$.

3 Proposed Fusion Method

Similar to fusion methods based on convolutional sparse coding, SCSC-based medical image fusion methods in this paper can be divided into: decomposition, fusion and reconstruction. However, difference is that convolutional filter dictionary and detail layer fusion used online convolutional sparse coding with sample-dependent dictionary. The fusion framework is shown in Fig. 2. b_{CT} and d_{CT} denote base layer and the detail layer

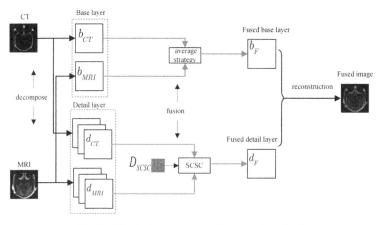

Fig. 2. The fusion structure of proposed method.

for CT source image. The MRI source image are decomposed into b_{MRI} and d_{MRI}. b_F and d_F are base layer and detail layer for fused image. D_{SCSC} is trained filter dictionary.

4 Experimental Results and Discuss

4.1 Experiment Settings

Datasets. Figure 3 shows medical brain images used in our experiment from Harvard dataset (http://www.med.harvard.edu/AANLIB/home.html). All methods are implemented in MATLAB 2019 on a PC with a Core (TM) i7-9750H, 2.60 GHz and 16G RAM.

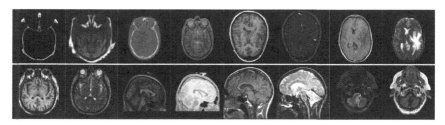

Fig. 3. 8 pairs medical images used in our experiments.

Comparison Methods. 7 medical image fusion methods (CSR [11], CNN [6], NSST_PAPCNN [3], source_NSCT [4], INS [28], joint_three_layer [29], NSST_MSMG_PCNN [5]) are used to verify the performance of our framework.

Objective Evaluation. 4 metrics (Q^P [30], PSNR [31], RMSE [31], SSIM [32]) are evaluated fusion effect.

4.2 Fused Results with Medical Brain Image

Figures 4, 5 and 6 show visual fusion results of 7 comparison methods and the proposed framework on medical brain images. Compared with the comparison methods, our method has clear advantages. 1) The functional information of CT and MRI images is clearly expressed. 2) The rich textural details of MRI images are preserved. 3) Information reflecting dense structures such as bone in MRA is clearly presented.

CT/MRI Brain Image. Figure 4 shows fusion results of CT/MRI. CSR, joint_three_layer, NSST_PAPCNN and NSST_MSMG_PCNN have poor performance in describing the functional information. CNN, INS and source_NSCT cannot capture the texture details of the source image. Combined with the above analysis, our method obtains fusion results with structural and functional information that is closest to source images.

8   C. Zhang et al.

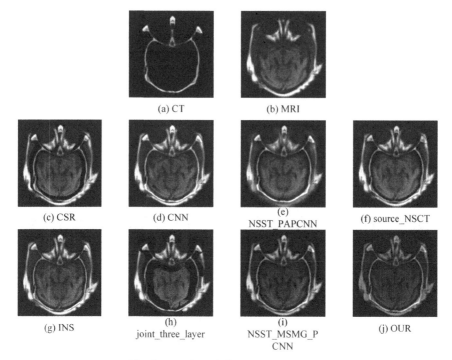

(a) CT

(b) MRI

(c) CSR

(d) CNN

(e)
NSST_PAPCNN

(f) source_NSCT

(g) INS

(h)
joint_three_layer

(i)
NSST_MSMG_P
CNN

(j) OUR

Fig. 4. Fused result for 'CT/MRI' image.

T1-MRI/MRA Brain Image. Figure 5 is the fusion results of T1-MRI/MRA. CSR, joint_three_layer and INS methods are adversely affected by energy loss, and the fusion results show information loss. CNN, NSST_PAPCNN and NSST_MSMG_PCNN have low detail extraction ability. The source_NSCT method images appear as noise artifacts. In contrast, our method preserves functional information while presenting clear texture details and no loss of structural information.

Other Brain Images. To highlight superiority of proposed method, Fig. 6 shows fusion results of other 6 images. Combining subjective analysis of Figs. 4 and 5, Fig. 6 corroborates performance of our method with respect to retention of functional and structural information.

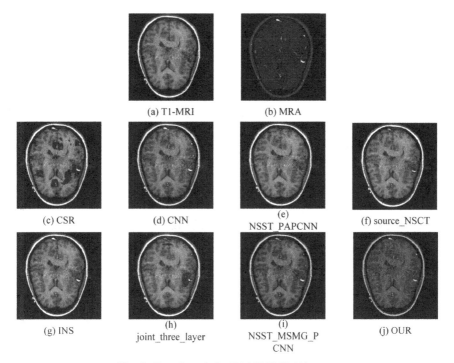

Fig. 5. Fused result for T1-MRI/MRA' image.

4.3 Objective Evaluation with Medical Brain Image Fusion

Section 4.2 depicts fused results of 8 pairs of medical brain images. To further demonstrate performance of proposed method, objective evaluation averages are listed in Table 1 to support subjective analysis (the best are marked by red bolded). Moreover, to visually show dominance of objective evaluation, fused metrics are summarized in Fig. 7. From Table 1 and Fig. 7, we can clearly visualize that proposed method obtains excellent results on vast majority of dataset. Our method achieves the best average values in Q^P, RMSE, SSIM and PSNR. Combining subjective fusion results and quantitative evaluation analysis, it can be demonstrated that our method achieves promising results in preserving structural, detailed and functional information.

4.4 Comparison of Running Cost

Table 2 is average running time for all methods. Observing Table 2, running time of our method is significantly better than CSR, CNN and joint_three_layer. NSST_PAPCNN, source_NSCT and INS have shorter running time than the proposed method, but fused image quality is not as good as ours. We analyze that main reason is image decomposition and reconstruction. The subsequent work will use more efficient decomposition methods to reduce time consumption.

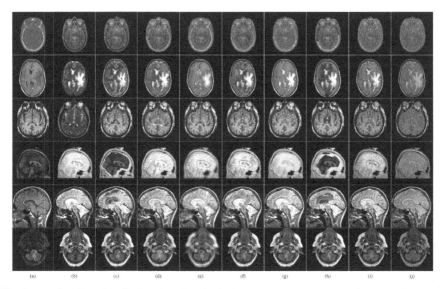

Fig. 6. The fused results of other 6 medical brain images. (a) source medical image 1; (b) source medical image 2; (c) result of CSR; (d) result of CNN; (e) result of NSST_PAPCNN; (f) result of source_NSCT; (g) result of INS; (h) result of joint_three_layer; (i) result of NSST_MSMG_PCNN; (j) result of our method.

Table 1. Objective fusion assessment of medical brain images (average values of 8 images).

Methods	Q^P	PSNR	RMSE	SSIM
NSST_PAPCNN[3]	0.4250	56.0895	0.1661	1.2735
source_NSCT[4]	0.4484	56.1441	0.1625	1.3174
NSST_MSMG_PCNN [5]	0.4230	56.5022	0.1499	1.2879
CNN[6]	0.4590	56.0786	0.1657	1.2563
CSR[11]	0.4758	55.8518	0.1770	1.2936
INS[28]	0.4758	56.0249	0.1667	1.3197
joint_three_layer[29]	0.4494	55.8848	0.1748	1.3275
OUR	0.4974	56.8352	0.1390	1.3535

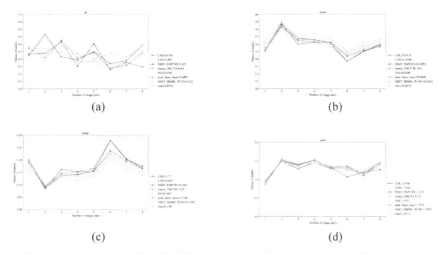

(a)   (b)

(c)   (d)

Fig. 7. Comparison of all medical brain images on fusion methods by using 4 metrics.

Table 2. The average running time from all fusion methods for medical brain images.

	CSR	CNN	NSST_PAPCNN	source_NSCT	INS	joint_three_layer	NSST_MSMG_PCNN	OUR
Times(second)	18.2	13.3	4.0	1.9	0.4	53.3	9.4	6.3

5   Conclusion

We design medical image fusion method using online convolutional sparse coding with sample-dependent dictionary in this paper. Compared to convolutional sparse coding, online convolutional sparse coding based on sample-adaptive dictionaries reduces time and space complexity using an online learning approach. Therefore, we use SCSC which can improve the time efficiency of fusion. Low frequency using the mean strategy can extract the core region of the source image. The maximum value rule is used for detail layer fusion to maximize the preservation of edge information. The subjective and objective results show that our method outperforms some advanced fusion methods.

Acknowledgments. This work is supported by Sichuan Science and Technology Program(2023NSFSC0495), Si-chuan University and Luzhou Municipal People's Government Strategic cooperation pro-jects(2020CDLZ-10) and Colleague Project of Intelligent Policing Key Laboratory of Sichuan Province (ZNJW2022ZZMS001, ZNJW2023ZZQN004).

References

1. Xu, X., Wang, Y., Chen, S.: Medical image fusion using discrete fractional wavelet transform. Biomed. Sig. Process. Control **27**, 103–111 (2016)
2. Chavan, S.S., Mahajan, A., Talbar, S.N., Desai, S., Thakur, M., D'cruz, A.: Nonsubsampled rotated complex wavelet transform (NSRCxWT) for medical image fusion related to clinical aspects in neurocysticercosis. Comput. Biol. Med.. Biol. Med. **81**, 64–78 (2017)
3. Yin, M., Liu, X., Liu, Y., Chen, X.: Medical image fusion with parameter-adaptive pulse coupled neural network in nonsubsampled shearlet transform domain. IEEE Trans. Instrum. Meas.Instrum. Meas. **68**(1), 49–64 (2018)
4. Zhu, Z., Zheng, M., Qi, G., Wang, D., Xiang, Y.: A phase congruency and local Laplacian energy based multi-modality medical image fusion method in NSCT domain. IEEE Access **7**, 20811–20824 (2019)
5. Tan, W., Tiwari, P., Pandey, H.M., Moreira, C., Jaiswal, A.K.: Multimodal medical image fusion algorithm in the era of big data. Neural Comput. Appl. 1–21(2020)
6. Liu, Y., Chen, X., Cheng, J., Peng, H.: A medical image fusion method based on convolutional neural networks. In 2017 20th International Conference on Information Fusion, pp. 1–7 (2017)
7. Huang, J., Le, Z., Ma, Y., Fan, F., Zhang, H., Yang, L.: MGMDcGAN: medical image fusion using multi-generator multi-discriminator conditional generative adversarial network. IEEE Access **8**, 55145–55157 (2020)
8. Li, B., Hwang, J.N., Liu, Z., Li, C., Wang, Z.: PET and MRI image fusion based on a dense convolutional network with dual attention. Comput. Biol. Med.. Biol. Med. **151**, 106339 (2022)
9. Yousif, A.S., Omar, Z., Sheikh, U.U.: An improved approach for medical image fusion using sparse representation and Siamese convolutional neural network. Biomed. Sig. Process. Control **72**, 103357 (2022)
10. Liu, Y., Shi, Y., Mu, F., Cheng, J., Chen, X.: Glioma segmentation-oriented multi-modal MR image fusion with adversarial learning. IEEE/CAA J. Automatica Sinica **9**(8), 1528–1531 (2022)
11. Liu, Y., Chen, X., Ward, R.K., Wang, Z.J.: Image fusion with convolutional sparse representation. IEEE Sig. Process. Lett. **23**(12), 1882–1886 (2016)
12. Liu, Y., Chen, X., Ward, R.K., Wang, Z.J.: Medical image fusion via convolutional sparsity based morphological component analysis. IEEE Sig. Process. Lett. **26**(3), 485–489 (2019)
13. Wang, L., Shi, C., Lin, S., Qin, P., Wang, Y.: Convolutional sparse representation and local density peak clustering for medical image fusion. Int. J. Pattern Recogn. Artif. Intell. **34**(07), 2057003 (2020)
14. Liu, F., Chen, L., Lu, L., Ahmad, A., Jeon, G., Yang, X.: Medical image fusion method by using Laplacian pyramid and convolutional sparse representation. Concurr. Comput. Pract. Exp. **32**(17) (2020)
15. Wang, L., et al.: Multimodal medical image fusion based on nonsubsampled shearlet transform and convolutional sparse representation. Multimedia Tools Appl. **80**, 36401–36421 (2021)
16. Zhang, C.: Medical brain image fusion via convolution dictionary learning. In 2020 4th Annual International Conference on Data Science and Business Analytics, pp. 292–294 (2020)
17. Zhang, C., Feng, Z.: Medical image fusion using convolution dictionary learning with adaptive contrast enhancement. In: The 4th International Conference on Information Technologies and Electrical Engineering, pp. 1–5 (2021)
18. Veshki, F.G., Vorobyov, S.A.: Coupled feature learning via structured convolutional sparse coding for multimodal image fusion. In: ICASSP 2022–2022 IEEE International Conference on Acoustics, Speech and Signal and Processing, pp. 2500–2504 (2022)

19. Wang, Y., Yao, Q., Kwok, J.T., Ni, L.M.: Scalable online convolutional sparse coding. IEEE Trans. Image Process. **27**(10), 4850–4859 (2018)
20. Zhang, C., Zhang, Z., Feng, Z.: Image fusion using online convolutional sparse coding. J. Ambient Intell. Human. Comput. 1–12 (2022)
21. Rigamonti, R., Sironi, A., Lepetit, V., Fua, P.: Learning separable filters. In: IEEE Conference on Computer Vision and Pattern Recognition, pp. 2754–2761 (2013)
22. Sironi, A., Tekin, B., Rigamonti, R., Lepetit, V., Fua, P.: Learning separable filters. IEEE Trans. Pattern Anal. Mach. Intell.Intell. **37**(1), 94–106 (2015)
23. Wang, Y., Yao, Q., Kwok, J.T.Y.: Online convolutional sparse coding with sample-dependent dictionary. In: International Conference on Machine Learning, pp. 5209–5218 (2018)
24. Wohlberg, B.: Efficient algorithms for convolutional sparse representations. IEEE Trans. Image Process. **25**(1), 301–315 (2015)
25. Garcia-Cardona, C., Wohlberg, B.: Convolutional dictionary learning: a comparative review and new algorithms. IEEE Trans. Comput. Imaging **4**(3), 366–381 (2018)
26. Boyd, S., Parikh, N., Chu, E., Peleato, B., Eckstein, J.: Distributed optimization and statistical learning via the alternating direction method of multipliers. Found. Trends Mach. Learn. **3**(1), 1–122 (2011)
27. Yao, Q., Kwok, J., Gao, F., Chen, W., Liu, T.-Y.: Efficient inexact proximal gradient algorithm for nonconvex problems. In: International Joint Conferences on Artificial Intelligence, pp. 3308–3314 (2017)
28. Li, X., Zhou, F., Tan, H., Zhang, W., Zhao, C.: Multimodal medical image fusion based on joint bilateral filter and local gradient energy. Inf. Sci. **569**, 302–325 (2021)
29. Li, X., Zhou, F., Tan, H.: Joint image fusion and denoising via three-layer decomposition and sparse representation. Knowl.-Based Syst..-Based Syst. **224**, 107087 (2021)
30. Zhao, J., Laganiere, R., Liu, Z.: Performance assessment of combinative pixel-level image fusion based on an absolute feature measurement. Int. J. Innov. Comput. Inf. Control **3**(6), 1433–1447 (2007)
31. Jagalingam, P., Hegde, A.V.: A review of quality metrics for fused image. Aquatic Procedia **4**, 133–142 (2015)
32. Wang, Z., Bovik, A.C., Sheikh, H.R., Simoncelli, E.P.: Image quality assessment: from error visibility to structural similarity. IEEE Trans. Image Process. **13**(4), 600–612 (2004)

Multimodal Medical Image Fusion Based on Multichannel Aggregated Network

Jingxue Huang[1], Xiaosong Li[1(✉)], Haishu Tan[1], and Xiaoqi Cheng[2]

[1] School of Physics and Optoelectronic Engineering, Foshan University, Foshan, China
lixiaosong@buaa.edu.cn

[2] School of Mechatronic Engineering and Automation, Foshan University, Foshan, China

Abstract. As a powerful and continuously sought-after medical assistance technique, multimodal medical image fusion integrates the useful information from different single-modal medical images into a fused one. Nevertheless, existing deep learning-based methods often feed source images into a single network without considering the information among different channels and scales, which may inevitably lose the important information. To solve this problem, we proposed a multimodal medical image fusion method based on multichannel aggregated network. By iterating different residual densely connected blocks to efficiently extract the image features at three scales, as well as extracting the spatial domain, channel and fine-grained feature information of the source image at each scale separately. Simultaneously, we introduced multispectral channel attention to address the global average pooling problem of the vanilla channel attention mechanism. Extensive fusion experiments demonstrated that the proposed method surpasses some representative state-of-the-art methods in terms of both subjective and objective evaluation. The code of this work is available at https://github.com/JasonWong30/MCAFusion.

Keywords: Multimodal medical image fusion · multiple channels and scales · multispectral channel attention

1 Introduction

It is often challenging for a single type of medical image to provide comprehensive diagnostic information owing to different imaging mechanisms [1–5]. Magnetic resonance imaging (MRI) can generate a high-resolution image of soft tissue but cannot detect information on human metabolic activity. Positron emission tomography (PET) images provide rich information on tumor function and metabolism. Single-photon emission computed tomography (SPECT) images reflect tissue and organ blood flow. However, both resolutions are relatively low. Fortunately, these difficulties can be overcome by multimodal medical image fusion (MMIF) technology, which can fuse different modal images into a fused image, providing a more synthetic, trustworthy, and excellent description of lesions. Therefore, MMIF is helpful for biomedical study and clinical diagnosis, e.g., in surgical navigation and radiotherapy planning [6].

H. Lu et al. (Eds.): ICIG 2023, LNCS 14359, pp. 14–25, 2023.
https://doi.org/10.1007/978-3-031-46317-4_2

Convolutional neural networks (CNN) excel at feature extraction and data representation, which has increased the use of deep learning (DL) in MMIF. For example, Ma et al. [7] proposed DDcGAN, which can fuse visible and infrared images or multimodal medical image pairs with different resolutions. Xu et al. [8] proposed an image fusion method called FusionDN. Xu et al. added an elastic weight consolidation (EWC) as a regularization item in U2Fusion [9] to avoid the forgetting problem of the fusion framework in the training of multiple fusion tasks. In 2021, Li et al. [10] designed a multiscale residual pyramid attention network for MMIF and obtained satisfactory results. Ma et al. [11] proposed SDNet, which greatly differs from other DL methods in that it aims to decompose the fusion result and approximate the source images from the fused image. Tang et al. [12] proposed MATR, using the powerful ability of CNN to capture short-distance information and the advantage of Transformer being able to achieve long-distance modeling, and achieved promising results.

The above studies achieved promising performance, but existing DL-based methods still have a few drawbacks: (a) Source images are usually fed into a single network without considering information between scales. This leads to loss of information across different scales; (b) little attention has been paid to designing strategy to save fine-grained features from source images, resulting in loss of details; (c) Information loss due to the use of the global average pooling (GAP) channel attention mechanism.

A novel MMIF method called MCAFusion, which has multiple channels and scales, is proposed to address the above shortcomings. The proposed method extracts image features at three scales by iterating a different number of residual dense blocks (RDBs), and then extracts spatial domain information, channel information, and fine-grained feature information of source images at each scale. We used multispectral channel attention (MCA) to avoid information loss caused by the use of GAP in the vanilla channel attention mechanism. Finally, structural similarity index measurement (SSIM) and spatial frequency (SF) are proposed as loss terms to save more important information from source images.

The contributions of this work include the following two aspects:

- An MMIF method based on a multichannel aggregated network is proposed, using a multispectral attention mechanism to retain important information in source images. To the best of our knowledge, this is the first time a multispectral attention mechanism has been applied to image fusion.
- Gradient RDBs (GRDBs) are introduced to preserve fine-grained texture and details from source images and realize feature reuse, which helps improve the descriptiveness of CNNs and the extraction of recognition information.

In the remainder of this paper, we concretely introduce the proposed MCAFusion framework in Sect. 2. Section 3 contains the results of the proposed method, a comparison with other algorithms, and a comprehensive analysis. Finally, we summarize our work and present future directions in Sect. 4.

2 Proposed Method

2.1 Network Architecture

The popular "RGB → YUV → RGB" color channel scheme was used in the proposed method. As shown in Fig. 1(a), our model is divided into three main channels, each of which has three different channels; each main channel is equipped with a different number of RDBs, extracting source image features at different scales. Then, we connected three channels with different functions in parallel to complete the extraction of three types of information from feature maps at each scale, including information at the spatial domain scale, information at the channel scale, and fine-grained image feature information. Finally, all the different types of information are integrated to obtain the fused image.

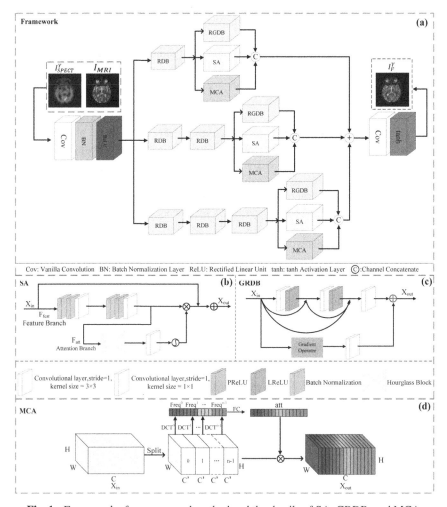

Fig. 1. Framework of our proposed method and the details of SA, GRDB, and MCA.

We used numerous RDBs [13] to replace vanilla convolutions in the proposed method. Compared with ordinary convolution, RDB is better at extracting features with the same network parameters owing to its complex but reasonable network structure. The convolution kernel used by RDB in this work is completely consistent with the GRDB convolution kernel shown in Fig. 1(c).

Fine-grained features reflect the details of source images. GRDB is used to extract fine-grained features from source images [14]. As shown in Fig. 1(c), GRDB is a variant of RDB. The GRDB module is expressed as follows:

$$F = Cov^n(x) \oplus Cov(\nabla x) \tag{1}$$

where x is the input feature maps, ∇ represents the Sobel gradient operator, $\oplus$ represents elementwise addition, $Cov(\cdot)$ indicates the convolutional layer, $Cov^n(\cdot)$ represents n cascaded convolutional layers, and F represents the output result of GRDB.

Visual attention was first proposed in [15] to simulate the importance of features in image caption tasks. The key idea of the attention mechanism is to use the weight map to reweight the features, highlight important information, and suppress useless feature information. In this study, we introduce a spatial attention (SA) module [16] that the convolutional layer can use to adaptively guide the model to focus on a feature-rich area in feature maps. As shown in Fig. 1(b), the SA module uses a residual connection to prevent the gradient from disappearing. Feature maps are input into the SA module, which includes attention and feature branches. In the attention branch, we use an hourglass block to extract multiscale features from source images. The SA formula is as follows:

$$f = F_{feat}(X_{in}) \tag{2}$$

$$a = \sigma(F_{att}(f)) \tag{3}$$

$$X_{out} = X_{in} \oplus a \otimes f \tag{4}$$

where f represents the output results of the feature branch F_{feat}, F_{att} represents the attention branch, σ represents the sigmoid function, and $\otimes$ represents elementwise multiplication.

Because GAP cannot capture complex information from different inputs, Qin et al. proposed FraNet, which mathematically proves that GAP is a special case of feature decomposition in the frequency domain [17] and generalizes the compression of the channel attention mechanism in the frequency domain. To introduce a wealth of useful information from source images, we used MCA [17], and 2D DCT was used to fuse multiple frequency components, including the lowest frequency component, namely GAP. As shown in Fig. 1(d), we related the 2D DCT index to the one-dimensional format for simplicity. The specific workflow is as follows: first, the input X_{in} is divided into n parts according to the channel dimension. We denote $[X^0, X^1, \ldots, X^{n-1}]$ as parts, in which $X^i \in \mathbb{R}^{C' \times H \times W}$, $i \in \{0, 1, \ldots, n-1\}$, $C' = C/n$, C is the number of channels, and n must be divisible by C. For each part, the corresponding 2D DCT frequency component B is allocated. The MCA formula is as follows:

$$Freq^i = \sum_{h=0}^{H-1} \sum_{w=0}^{W-1} X^i_{:,h,w} B^{u_i,v_i}_{h,w} \tag{5}$$

where H and W represent the height and width of feature images, respectively, and $[u_i, v_i]$ is the 2D index of the frequency component corresponding to X^i.

Then, the whole compression vector $Freq$ is obtained by merging

$$Freq = cat([Freq^0, Freq^1, \ldots, Freq^{n-1}]) \tag{6}$$

Finally, the whole MCA att can be written as

$$att = sigmoid(fc(Freq)) \tag{7}$$

where fc represents the fully connected layer. The final output characteristic diagram can be expressed as

$$X_{out} = X_{in} \otimes att \tag{8}$$

2.2 Loss Function

We proposed an unsupervised DL fusion method; the loss function is essential to the fusion effect. However, the critical link is how to comprehensively extract the unique features of the source images, such as the rich structural information of the MRI images or the accurate functional information of the SPECT images. In this study, to preserve the complementary information in medical images as much as possible, a loss function composed of two terms is proposed:

$$L = L_{SSIM} + L_{SF} \tag{9}$$

L_{SSIM} and L_{SF} represent structural and SF loss, respectively.

The structural loss term is usually used to ensure the fused image contains enough structural detail for source images. To constrain the similarity between the fused image and the source image, L_{SSIM} is defined as follows:

$$L_{SSIM} = 1 - SSIM(I_F^Y, I_1) + \alpha(1 - SSIM(I_F^Y, I_2)) \tag{10}$$

where I_1, I_2 are source images, I_F^Y is the Y-channel component of fused image, and α is the weight. SSIM can be expressed as follows:

$$SSIM(I_1, I_F^Y) = \frac{(2\mu_{I_1}\mu_{I_F^Y}+C_1)(2\sigma_{I_1 I_F^Y}+C_2)}{(\mu_{I_1}^2+\mu_{I_F^Y}^2+C_1)(\sigma_{I_1}^2+\sigma_{I_F^Y}^2+C_2)} \tag{11}$$

where μ_{I_1} and $\mu_{I_F^Y}$ represent the intensities of I_1 and I_F^Y, respectively. To avoid instability when $\mu_{I_1}^2 + \mu_{I_F^Y}^2$ or $\sigma_{I_1}^2 + \sigma_{I_F^Y}^2$ is close to 0, $C1$ and $C2$ are constants. $\sigma_{I_1}^2$ and $\sigma_{I_F^Y}^2$ denote the variances of I_1 and I_F^Y, respectively. $\sigma_{I_1 I_F^Y}$ represents the covariance of I_1 and I_F^Y.

For another loss term, L_{SF}, the formula is as follows:

$$L_{SF} = \beta \cdot ||SF(I_f) - SF(I_1)||_2 + \gamma \cdot ||SF(I_f) - SF(I_2)||_2 \tag{12}$$

$|| \cdot ||_2$ represents the L2 norm. SF is the spatial frequency of the image. β and γ are weights. SF is calculated by calculating the gradient in the vertical and horizontal directions to reflect the gray level transformation of the image. The formula is as follows:

$$SF = 1 - \sqrt{Hor^2 + Ver^2} \qquad (13)$$

where Hor and Ver represent the horizontal and vertical gradients, respectively. The horizontal gradient formula is defined as follows:

$$Hor = \sqrt{\frac{1}{HW}\sum_{i=1}^{H}\sum_{j=2}^{W}|I(i,j) - I(i,j-1)|^2} \qquad (14)$$

where H and W represent the height and width of the image I, respectively. The vertical gradient formula is defined as follows:

$$Ver = \sqrt{\frac{1}{HW}\sum_{i=1}^{H}\sum_{j=2}^{W}|I(i,j) - I(i-1,j)|^2} \qquad (15)$$

3 Experiments

3.1 Data and Training Details

We selected 742 pairs of 256×256 pixel registered medical images from the Harvard Dataset for training and chose the overlapping cropping strategy for data enhancement. The training set was split into 19704 pairs of 120×120 medical images and then normalized to [0, 1]. It was not used for validation or testing because the cropping strategy was used for data enhancement. Nineteen pairs of PET-MRI images and 35 pairs of SPECT-MRI images from the remaining dataset were selected for testing.

The experiment was performed using two NVIDIA GeForce RTX 3090 GPUs and the PyTorch framework. The Adam optimizer was used in the training phase. The learning rate was fixed at 1×10^{-3}, and the batch size was 64. The training epochs was set to 35.

The weights in the loss function was set to $\alpha = 1, \beta = 5 \times 10^{-4}$, and $\gamma = 5.6 \times 10^{-4}$. In the MCA, n was set to 16. For each part, the corresponding 2D DCT frequency component, B, was allocated. We selected the "Top16" with the best performance provided by the work [17] as the frequency component.

3.2 Comparison Methods and Fusion Evaluation Metrics

Seven state-of-the-art methods were used as comparison methods, including two traditional methods, LDR [1] and MSMG [18], and five DL methods, U2Fusion [9], DDc-GAN [7], MATR [12], MSRPAN [10], and SDNet [11]. For all the above methods, the parameters were fixed at their default values, as given in the original publications, for comparison. For better comparison, two local regions in each image were magnified as close-ups.

Eight widely-used metrics were employed to objectively evaluate the fused results: Q_{NCIE} [19], Q_{CB} [20], VIF [21], SSIM [22], SF [23], Q_s [24], average gradient (AG), and SCD [25]. Q_{NCIE} is used to measure the nonlinear correlation information preserved in

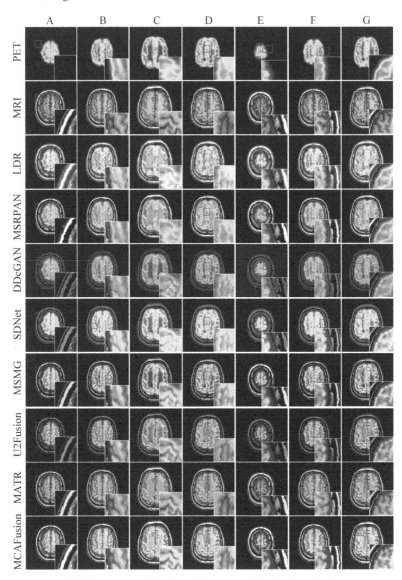

Fig. 2. PET/MRI fused results generated by eight methods.

the fused image. VIF was designed to quantify the information fidelity between source images and the fused image based on human visual perception. Q_s is used to calculate the similarity between the source and fused images. AG is based on the features of the fused images. SCD enables quantifying the quality of fused images. Q_{CB} is an objective index based on human visual system modeling. The larger the value of these objective indicators, the better the effect of the above indicators on the fused image.

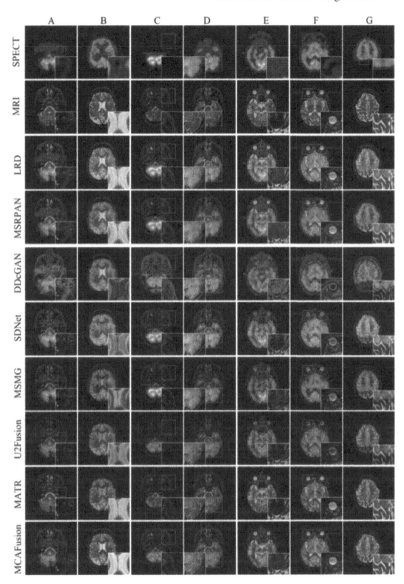

Fig. 3. SPECT/MRI fused results generated by eight methods.

3.3 Results and Discussion

As shown in Figs. 2 and 3, the seven methods obtained relatively good results. However, compared to the proposed methods, they still have some shortcomings. This section provides a detailed analysis of groups A and B in Figs. 2 and 3. Specifically, LRD had color distortion in both fusion types; therefore, much of the functional information was lost in this method. MSMG had a bluish phenomenon, such as the skeletal part in PET/MRI fusion. The MSRPAN fusion method was not capable of preserving MRI information. The corresponding local amplification region from the PET/MRI fusion type can be seen, and the edge part appears jagged. The results of both fusion types of DDcGAN differ from the source MRI image in the exoskeleton portion, which can be considered as a loss of exoskeleton information from the MRI image. The fused image of U2Fusion had low contrast, especially in the exoskeleton part of the MRI image. By contrast, SDNet had high contrast in MRI-PET fusion. The fusion performance of MATR was excellent and was also the closest to that of MCAFusion. For example, in PET/MRI fusion, the color and details of the fusion effect were very close to the input images. Either the structural information of the input MRI image or the functional information of SPECT and PET was saved, and the fusion effect was superior. However, in SPECT/MRI image fusion, the magnified view of local areas shows that the MCAFusion results have more detail than those of MATR. Therefore, our proposed method is better than MATR.

Table 1. Average quantitative evaluation of SPECT/MRI and PET/MRI fusions. Red, orange, and green represent the best, second, and third places, respectively.

Fusion types	Methods	Q_{NCIE}	Q_S	Q_{CB}	VIF	AG	SSIM	SF	SCD
PET/MRI	MCAFusion	0.80626	0.9290	0.6921	0.3009	7.8434	0.8155	28.1277	1.4507
	U2Fusion	0.80504	0.6562	0.2949	0.2327	5.6260	0.5689	19.1421	0.7797
	DDcGan	0.80446	0.3544	0.2448	0.1808	5.6319	0.2553	20.3668	0.5333
	LDR	0.80496	0.8507	0.6079	0.1986	6.2679	0.7633	21.1770	1.3543
	MATR	0.80757	0.9165	0.7040	0.3424	7.0538	0.8074	24.7307	0.6643
	MSRPAN	0.80726	0.8606	0.6447	0.1815	6.8412	0.7956	27.9082	1.1578
	SDNet	0.80507	0.4693	0.2924	0.2252	6.8084	0.3535	24.8116	1.4509
	MSMG	0.80483	0.8297	0.5830	0.1924	7.0467	0.7406	26.6026	0.9788
SPECT/MRI	MACFusion	0.80706	0.9539	0.7802	0.3474	5.6709	0.8761	22.1251	1.2257
	U2Fusion	0.80520	0.6691	0.2906	0.3074	3.3892	0.5854	13.2088	0.3885
	DDcGan	0.80422	0.2834	0.2024	0.1468	4.8413	0.2074	17.9991	0.4514
	LDR	0.80542	0.9001	0.6631	0.2882	4.2273	0.7997	16.5170	1.5933
	MATR	0.80723	0.8820	0.7365	0.3590	4.0985	0.8015	16.4613	0.1827
	MSRPAN	0.80721	0.8342	0.6427	0.1973	3.1753	0.8051	14.4096	1.1153
	SDNet	0.80555	0.5867	0.3024	0.2921	4.8952	0.4714	19.0665	1.4901
	MSMG	0.80327	0.9287	0.6650	0.3275	2.3444	0.8651	11.7987	0.7556

Table 1 and Fig. 4 show the average values of the six methods in 35 pairs of SPECT-MRI images and 19 pairs of PET-MRI images and the average values of each method under each index of the two types of fusion. In Fig. 4, M1–M8 represent MCAFusion, U2Fusion, DDcGAN, LDR, MSRPAN, MATR, SDNet, and MSMG methods, respectively. As shown in Fig. 4, our fused images achieved the best scores in terms of AG, Q_S, SSIM, and SF. Therefore, the high value of the AG reflects that the edges and details of our fused image are superior to those fused by the comparison methods.

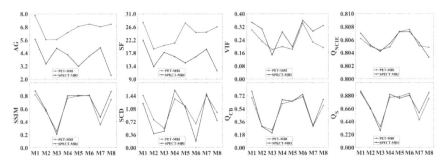

Fig. 4. Average score of different methods for PET/MRI and SPECT/MRI fusions.

3.4 Ablation Experiment

We performed ablation experiments for six combinations of modules to test the effectiveness of each of our channel modules. As shown in Table 2, it is intuitive to see that most of the objective indicators of MCAFusion were higher than those of the six combinations, especially in terms of VIF and SSIM. VIF shows that the fused image was superior to other combinations in terms of visual effects, whereas SSIM reflects that the three-channel module improved the structural information of the source images.

Table 2. Average quantitative evaluation of three kinds of models. Red means best.

Fusion types	Methods	Q_{NICE}	Q_S	Q_{CB}	VIF	SSIM	SF	AG	SCD
PET/MRI	MCAFusion	0.8063	0.9290	0.6921	0.3009	0.8155	28.1277	7.8434	1.4507
	GRDB+CA	0.8054	0.8928	0.6751	0.1990	0.7950	32.8704	7.7627	1.2104
	GRDB+SA	0.8054	0.8314	0.6226	0.1249	0.7424	52.8374	10.7540	0.9527
	SA+CA	0.8056	0.4253	0.2965	0.2563	0.2852	26.4922	7.3390	0.9691
	GRDB	0.8055	0.9242	0.6318	0.2691	0.8010	26.8666	7.4200	1.5102
	CA	0.8054	0.9024	0.6738	0.2357	0.8056	27.8753	7.3104	1.3141
	SA	0.8056	0.9148	0.6725	0.2374	0.8115	28.7129	7.5878	1.3876
SPECT/MRI	MCAFusion	0.8071	0.9539	0.7802	0.3474	0.8761	22.1251	5.6709	1.2257
	GRDB+CA	0.8052	0.8607	0.7039	0.2585	0.7978	21.9499	4.2281	0.5929
	GRDB+SA	0.8050	0.8337	0.6804	0.2247	0.7677	30.0926	5.4174	0.5631
	SA+CA	0.8052	0.3980	0.2454	0.2842	0.2756	16.8185	4.0408	0.0619
	GRDB	0.8053	0.9002	0.6482	0.2927	0.8061	17.6306	4.2943	1.2018
	CA	0.8051	0.8439	0.6947	0.2748	0.8011	16.9522	3.7140	0.8501
	SA	0.8052	0.8666	0.6997	0.2883	0.8089	16.6723	3.8494	1.728

4 Conclusion

In this study, MCAFusion was proposed, characterized by multiscale and multichannel features. Three convolutional channels composed of different numbers of RDB modules were proposed to form three scale feature maps, then three modules were developed that can extract different information under each channel, and finally, all the information were integrated to fuse important information from input images. Numerous experiments showed that MCAFusion is better than some representative state-of-the-art methods in terms of visual effects and objective metrics. Moreover, ablation experiment proved that the three-channel modules are important for both subjective and objective effects. In the future, we will focus on unregistered and low-quality medical image fusion problems to increase their applicability in medical applications.

Acknowledgements. This research was supported by the National Natural Science Foundation of China (Grant Nos. 62201149, 62271148, 62201151).

References

1. Li, X., Guo, X., Han, P., Wang, X., Li, H., Luo, T.: Laplacian redecomposition for multimodal medical image fusion. IEEE Trans. Instrum. Meas.Instrum. Meas. **69**(9), 6880–6890 (2020)
2. Li, X., Zhou, F., Tan, H.: Joint image fusion and denoising via three-layer decomposition and sparse representation. Knowl.-Based Syst..-Based Syst. **224**, 107087 (2021)
3. Jie, Y., Zhou, F., Tan, H., Wang, G., Cheng, X., Li, X.: Tri-modal medical image fusion based on adaptive energy choosing scheme and sparse representation. Measurement **204**(30), 112038 (2022)
4. Li, X., Wan, W., Zhou, F., Cheng, X., Jie, Y., Tan, H.: Medical image fusion based on sparse representation and neighbor energy activity. Biomed. Sig. Process. Control **80**, 104353 (2023)
5. Zhu, Z., He, X., Qi, G., Li, Y., Cong, B., Liu, Y.: Brain tumor segmentation based on the fusion of deep semantics and edge information in multimodal MRI. Inf. Fusion **91**, 376–387 (2023)
6. Li, X., Zhou, F., Tan, H., Zhang, W., Zhao, C.: Multimodal medical image fusion based on joint bilateral filter and local gradient energy. Inf. Sci. **569**, 302–325 (2021)
7. Ma, J., Xu, H., Jiang, J., Mei, X., Zhang, X.-P.: DDcGAN: a dual-discriminator conditional generative adversarial network for multi-resolution image fusion. IEEE Trans. Image Process. **29**, 4980–4995 (2020)
8. Xu, H., Ma, J., Le, Z., Jiang, J., Guo, X.: FusionDN: a unified densely connected network for image fusion. In: Proceedings of the AAAI Conference on Artificial Intelligence, New York, pp. 12484–12491 (2020)
9. Xu, H., Ma, J., Jiang, J., Guo, X., Ling, H.: U2Fusion: a unified unsupervised image fusion network. IEEE Trans. Pattern Anal. Mach. Intell.Intell. **44**(1), 502–518 (2020)
10. Fu, J., Li, W., Du, J., Huang, Y.: A multiscale residual pyramid attention network for medical image fusion. Biomed. Sig. Process. Control **66**, 102488 (2021)
11. Zhang, H., Ma, J.: SDNet: a versatile squeeze-and-decomposition network for real-time image fusion. Int. J. Comput. VisionComput. Vision **129**, 2761–2785 (2021)
12. Tang, W., He, F., Liu, Y., Duan, Y.: MATR: multimodal medical image fusion via multiscale adaptive transformer. IEEE Trans. Image Process. **31**, 5134–5149 (2022)
13. Zhang, Y., Tian, Y., Kong, Y., Zhong, B., Fu, Y.: Residual dense network for image restoration. IEEE Trans. Pattern Anal. Mach. Intell. **43**, 2480–2495 (2021)
14. Tang, L., Yuan, J., Ma, J.: Image fusion in the loop of high-level vision tasks: a semantic-aware real-time infrared and visible image fusion network. Inf. Fusion **82**, 28–42 (2022)
15. Xu, K., et al.: Show, attend and tell: neural image caption generation with visual attention. In: International Conference on Machine Learning, pp. 2048–2057. PMLR, Lille (2015)
16. Chen, C., Gong, D., Wang, H., Li, Z., Wong, K.-Y.K.: Learning spatial attention for face super-resolution. IEEE Trans. Image Process. **30**, 1219–1231 (2020)
17. Qin, Z., Zhang, P., Wu, F., Li, X.: FCAnet: frequency channel attention networks. In: Proceedings of the IEEE/CVF International Conference on Computer Vision, Montreal, QC, Canada, pp. 783–792 (2021)

18. Tan, W., Tiwari, P., Pandey, H.M., Moreira, C., Jaiswal, A.K.: Multimodal medical image fusion algorithm in the era of big data. Neural Comput. Appl. 1–21 (2020)
19. Wang, Q., Shen, Y., Zhang, J.Q.: A nonlinear correlation measure for multivariable data set. Physica D D **200**(3–4), 287–295 (2005)
20. Chen, Y., Blum, R.S.: A new automated quality assessment algorithm for image fusion. Image Vis. Comput.Comput. **27**(10), 1421–1432 (2009)
21. Han, Y., Cai, Y., Cao, Y., Xu, X.: A new image fusion performance metric based on visual information fidelity. Inf. Fusion **14**(2), 127–135 (2013)
22. Wang, Z., Bovik, A.C., Sheikh, H.R., Simoncelli, E.P.: Image quality assessment: from error visibility to structural similarity. IEEE Trans. Image Process. **13**(4), 600–612 (2004)
23. Eskicioglu, A.M., Fisher, P.S.: Image quality measures and their performance. IEEE Trans. Commun.Commun. **43**(12), 2959–2965 (1995)
24. Liu, Z., Blasch, E., Xue, Z., Zhao, J., Laganiere, R., Wu, W.: Objective assessment of multiresolution image fusion algorithms for context enhancement in night vision: a comparative study. IEEE Trans. Pattern Anal. Mach. Intell.Intell. **34**(1), 94–109 (2012)
25. Aslantas, V., Bendes, E.: A new image quality metric for image fusion: the sum of the correlations of differences. AEU-Int. J. Electron. Commun. **69**(12), 1890–1896 (2015)

Multi-path Feature Fusion and Channel Feature Pyramid for Brain Tumor Segmentation in MRI

Yihan Zhang, Zhengyao Bai^(✉), Yilin You, Xuheng Liu, Xiao Xiao, and Zhu Xu

School of Information Science and Engineering, Yunnan University, Kunming 650500, China
baizhy@ynu.edu.cn

Abstract. Automated segmentation of gliomas in MRI images is crucial for timely diagnosis and treatment planning. In this paper, we propose an encoder-decoder network for brain tumor MRI image segmentation that can address the problem of imbalanced data classification in brain tumors. Our method introduces a multi-path feature fusion module and a multi-channel feature pyramid module into the U-Net architecture to alleviate the problems of low segmentation accuracy for small targets and insufficient use of multi-scale information. The output feature maps from each level of the encoder are fed into the multi-path feature fusion module to achieve multi-scale feature fusion. Both the encoder and decoder parts of the proposed method use cascaded dilated convolutional modules, which can effectively extract additional feature information without increasing the number of parameters.

In the BraTS'2019 training dataset of 50 samples, our method achieved Dice values of 0.8551, 0.8728, and 0.7906, and Hausdorff values of 2.5693, 1.5845, and 2.7284 for the entire tumor, tumor core, and enhanced tumor, respectively. The proposed encoder-decoder network shows significant performance advantages in brain tumor MRI image segmentation, especially in addressing the problems of low segmentation accuracy for small targets and insufficient use of multi-scale information. Moreover, our method can extract additional feature without increasing the number of parameters, demonstrating good practicality and versatility. These results suggest that our method can provide an effective solution for automated segmentation of MRI brain tumors.

Keywords: Brain tumor segmentation · Feature fusion · Feature pyramid · High-Resolution prediction

1 Introduction

Glioblastoma is a prevalent primary malignancy with a high fatality rate. For modern clinical medicine, precise and safe resection of glioblastoma within a secure margin is of paramount importance. Magnetic resonance imaging (MRI), as a non-invasive and non-intrusive imaging modality, provides high-contrast and high-resolution brain imaging information, enabling physicians to accurately diagnose tumors and devise tailored treatment strategies. However, due to equipment-related constraints, imaging

© The Author(s), under exclusive license to Springer Nature Switzerland AG 2023
H. Lu et al. (Eds.): ICIG 2023, LNCS 14359, pp. 26–36, 2023.
https://doi.org/10.1007/978-3-031-46317-4_3

results may suffer from noise artifacts, and the shape and position of tumors may exhibit interpatient variability. Therefore, the development of rapid and accurate automatic brain tumor segmentation techniques holds significant implications for practical applications. The annual MICCAI BraTS Brain Tumor Segmentation Challenge serves as a platform for identifying optimal segmentation methodologies.

To address the automatic brain tumor segmentation problem, deep learning has shown promise in medical imaging [1]. Methods based on Fully Convolutional Networks (FCN) have achieved good results but may lack fine details. Convolutional Neural Networks (CNNs) can also achieve good results, with most current methods using either 2D-CNNs or 3D-CNNs. While 3D-CNNs can fully utilize three-dimensional information, they greatly increase computational costs. Previous studies [2, 3] have identified the limitations of 3D-CNNs in medical image applications. To reduce the computational cost of the model, 2D-CNNs are widely used in medical image segmentation. To address the problem of feature loss during the convolution process, the U-Net [3] has been proposed to complement low-level features that are rich in detail but lack semantic information with high-level features that have rich semantic information. However, the simple fusion of high and low-level features is not efficient [4], as low-level features may contain a significant amount of noise and continuous down-sampling operations may cause loss of important edge information. Variants of the 2D U-Net model have been proposed in [5, 6], which improve model performance through multiple skip connections and convolutional layers, but also lead to significant computational costs. The V-Net is a network designed for 3D medical image segmentation, which utilizes 3D convolutions to capture inter-slice relationships. However, due to the high computational cost of 3D CNNs, they are not practical for real-world applications. In recent years, many lightweight networks have been proposed [7, 8] to achieve efficient image segmentation. However, these lightweight networks overlook the input data and sacrifice segmentation accuracy for efficiency. Moreover, they cannot adapt to different input sizes.

To address these issues, we propose a multi-resolution feature fusion brain tumor segmentation algorithm. Our method fuses the multi-resolution images of the encoder through a multi-path feature fusion module, which complements the lost spatial information in the decoder. To enable adaptive adjustment of different input sizes, we use iterative feature pyramid modules in both the encoder and decoder to extract features and contextual information at multiple scales, greatly reducing the number of parameters.

Our main contributions are as follows:

- we propose a novel end-to-end encoding-decoding segmentation network for medical image segmentation. Our method fully utilizes the information in the down-sampling process to achieve high-resolution prediction, providing a lightweight and efficient segmentation network, which is essential for clinical medicine.
- To further improve the performance of our segmentation network, we introduce multi-path feature fusion module and channel feature pyramid module to comprehensively utilize the multi-scale and multi-resolution information for prediction and capture information from any size feature maps, respectively.
- Experimental results on the BraTS2019 dataset demonstrate that our network significantly improves the accuracy of medical image segmentation. Our detailed methodology is presented in Sect. 2, and the experimental process and results are discussed

in Sect. 3. Finally, we draw conclusions and provide directions for future research in Sect. 4.

2   Method

In this paper, we propose a new network that fuses multi-scale and multi-resolution images at the encoding end through multiple paths. We first describe the multi-path feature fusion module in Sect. 2.1 and then the iterative feature pyramid module in Sect. 2.2. Finally, we introduce the proposed network in Sect. 2.3.

2.1   Multi-path Feature Fusion

In U-Net, the high-resolution low-level features of the encoder contain rich semantic information, while the low-resolution high-level features contain more spatial information. To effectively utilize multi-level features, we propose a novel module that can make full use of all available information during down-sampling and achieve high-resolution predictions through long skip connections. Generally, low-level features and high-level features are complementary, and the effectiveness of multi-scale feature fusion relies on the overlap of semantic information and resolution between them. Simple fusion of multi-level features can only achieve marginal improvements because there is a semantic and resolution gap between low-level and high-level features. We believe that features at each level should be reasonably utilized.

As shown in Fig. 1, the module consists of three parts: multi-resolution fusion module, chain feature pooling module, and adaptive module. Firstly, the adaptive convolution generates feature maps of the same size as the input. The small feature maps are up-sampled to the maximum resolution, and all feature maps are added together to fuse them. Then, the output feature map is inputted into the chain feature pooling module, which consists of multiple pooling blocks. Each pooling block consists of a max pooling layer and a convolutional layer. The convolutional output of the pooling layer is used as the weighted layer, and the output of the previous pooling block is used as the input of the next pooling block. Each pooling block fuses with the input feature map through residual connections. The purpose of using residual connections is to promote gradient propagation during training. Different sizes of pooling kernels are used for max pooling to extract features and increase the network's receptive field. Different pooling paths can highlight feature information and suppress irrelevant feature responses. This module aims to capture background context from large image regions, collect features from different sized windows effectively, and merge them using learnable weights. Finally, the output of the chain feature pooling module is inputted into the adaptive module, which adaptively adjusts the size of the feature map to be concatenated with the up-sampled feature map from the decoder.

2.2   Multi-channel Feature Pyramid

Many studies have proven the effectiveness of dilated convolutions [9, 10] in extracting large-scale features without increasing the total number of parameters. Moreover,

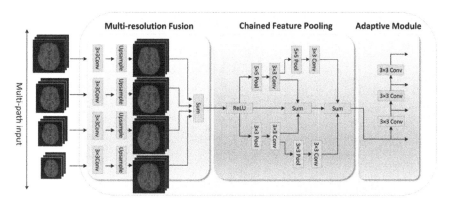

Fig. 1. Multi-path Feature Fusion Module

the Inception module has utilized multi-scale convolutions, and their potential has been demonstrated in previous works [11, 12]. Multi-scale convolutions can capture receptive fields of different scales and integrate features of various sizes. However, both methods have their limitations. Dilated convolutions increase the receptive field without losing feature map size but suffer from the checkerboard effect [13] caused by the gap between convolutional filters, which hinders learning by (1) reducing local information and (2) introducing irrelevant long-range information. Inception modules, on the other hand, contain numerous parameters and may miss local information due to their fixed dilation rates. To address these issues, we propose a multi-channel feature pyramid module (MCFP) that combines the advantages of dilated convolutions and Inception modules to effectively extract local dense features. The MCFP module is composed of several feature pyramid (FP) channels, each of which consists of multiple groups of asymmetric convolutions with residual connections. This approach significantly reduces the number of parameters while preserving the ability to learn features. The MCFP module consists of four groups of FP channels with different dilation rates, as shown in Fig. 2. The high-level feature maps are first mapped to lower dimensions using 1×1 convolutions and then input into the four parallel FP channels. Before each convolution, batch normalization and PReLU (Parametric Rectified Linear Unit) activation functions are applied. Compared with ReLU, PReLU can improve model fitting ability without adding additional parameters, reduce the risk of overfitting, and improve accuracy. Although asymmetric convolution structures can effectively reduce training parameters and increase network depth, they also make the network difficult to train. Therefore, we adopt a cascading approach to train deep networks and provide additional feature information.

2.3 3M-FF Net

We propose a multi-scale, multi-channel, and multi-resolution feature fusion network, called the 3M-FF Net, which combines a multi-channel feature extraction module and a multi-path feature fusion module. This network effectively utilizes information from various resolution and scale feature maps, as shown in Fig. 3. We use U-Net as the basic network and replace some of the normal convolution blocks with MCFP modules to

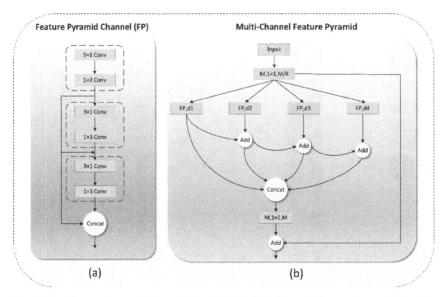

Fig. 2. (a) Feature Pyramid Channel Module (b) Multi-Channel Feature Pyramid Module

extract local dense features, especially small tumor features. In addition, the original U-Net structure uses skip connections to directly connect the encoded feature maps with the up-sampled feature maps in the decoding stage. This direct connection results in redundant information, and we believe that feature maps of different resolutions contain useful information. Therefore, we design a multi-path feature fusion module to fully utilize all scale feature maps. In the encoding stage, we use the ECA channel attention module [14] to realize the interaction of information from four modalities of brain tumor images, extract features using a 3×3 convolution kernel, and extract dense features, especially small tumor features, using MCFP Blocks. In the decoding stage, we fuse the feature maps from the encoder and the MPFF Block output, and then concatenate them with the up-sampled feature maps from the decoder. Finally, we use the SoftMax activation function to output the classification results.

3   Experiments

3.1   Dataset and Pre-processing

In this study, we employed the BraTS2018 and BraTS2019 datasets for training and testing. The BraTS2018 dataset contains 280 samples, including 210 cases of high-grade glioma (HGG) and 70 cases of low-grade glioma (LGG) in the training set. We randomly divided the training set into 75% for training and 25% for validation. The BraTS2019 dataset has 50 more samples in the training set than BraTS2018, with 49 HGG and 1 LGG sample, which we used as the test set. Each sample in the datasets includes four MR images: T1-weighted, T1 contrast-enhanced, T2-weighted, and fluid-attenuated inversion recovery (FLAIR) sequences. T1 and T2 are two different sequences

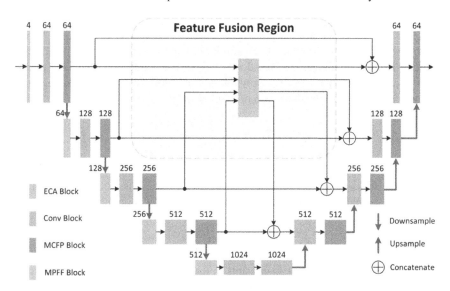

Fig. 3. The proposed 3M-FF network for MRI brain tumor segmentation.

that measure the electromagnetic waves with different physical properties. T1 contrast-enhanced images show the degree of blood saturation, while FLAIR images highlight the cerebrospinal fluid and lesions containing bound water. All images have the size of 240 × 240 × 155, with a voxel spacing of 1 × 1 × 1 mm. The segmentation task involves three regions: the whole tumor area (all areas except for the black background), the tumor core area (including non-enhancing regions, necrotic regions, and edema), and the enhancing tumor area (only including enhancing tumor regions).

Due to the large size of the original images and the varying contrast of different modalities, we preprocessed the data by first applying Z-score standardization to each modality, normalizing the data to have zero mean and unit standard deviation. As brain tumor images contain a high proportion of useless background information compared to useful tumor information, the data is imbalanced. To address this, we performed image cropping to reduce the size of the original images to 160 × 160 pixels.

3.2 Experimental setup

The experimental setup used Ubuntu 18.04 LTS 64-bit as the operating environment and was equipped with an NVIDIA GeForce RTX 2080 Ti GPU and an Intel Xeon E5-2630 v3 CPU. The deep learning framework used for the experiments was PyTorch with CUDA 11.0. During training, the Adam optimizer was used for parameter updates, and an early stopping strategy was employed to prevent overfitting with a parameter set to 20. The model was trained for 200 epochs with a batch size of 16, learning rate of 3e−4, and momentum of 0.9. The loss function used was a weighted combination of BCELoss and sigmoid, which can handle multi-classification problems and improve the accuracy of the model.

3.3 Evaluation Metrics

In brain tumor segmentation tasks, Dice Similarity Coefficient (DSC), Positive Predictive Value (PPV), sensitivity, and Hausdorff distance are commonly used as evaluation metrics to calculate the performance of whole tumor, tumor core, and enhancing tumor separately. Among them, the definition of DSC is as follows:

$$Dice(GT, AT) = \frac{2|GT \cap AT|}{|GT| + |AT|} \tag{1}$$

Here, GT represents the set of pixels in the label that are truly segmented, and AT represents the set of pixels actually segmented. PPV represents the proportion of true positive samples in the predicted positive samples, and PPV is defined as follows:

$$PPV = \frac{TP}{TP + FP} \tag{2}$$

Here, TP represents the true positive results in the predicted positive results, while FP represents the false positive results in the predicted positive results. Sensitivity refers to the proportion of true positive results among all positive results, and is defined as follows:

$$Sensitivity = \frac{TP}{TP + FN} \tag{3}$$

Here, FN represents the results predicted as negative but actually positive. The Hausdorff distance measures the distance between the model prediction and the true segmentation, and is defined as follows:

$$Hausdorff(P, T) = \max \left\{ \sup_{p \in P} \inf_{t \in T} d(p, t), \sup_{t \in T} \inf_{p \in P} d(t, p) \right\} \tag{4}$$

Here sup represents the upper bound, and inf represents the lower bound.

3.4 Results and Analysis

Quantitative Results. In this paper, we evaluated the performance of our proposed network for brain tumor segmentation task. To quantify the accuracy of our approach, we used widely-accepted segmentation metrics, including Dice coefficient, PPV, sensitivity, and Hausdorff distance. The results of our ablation experiments are summarized in Tables 1 and 2, and they demonstrate the significant performance improvement achieved by the addition of the MCFP and MPFF modules.

We found that the MCFP module greatly enhances the performance of our network in terms of the Dice score for the whole tumor and tumor core, while the MPFF module improves the Dice score for the tumor core. Overall, our proposed network performs well in various segmentation tasks, especially in small tumor segmentation, as evidenced by the 5.24% improvement in Dice score for the tumor core.

To further validate the efficacy of our approach, we compare our segmentation results with those obtained using other methods, and summarize the findings in Tables 3 and 4. Compared to the baseline network U-Net, our method improves the Dice score for WT, TC, and ET by 2.13%, 5.24%, and 2.27%, respectively. Additionally, when compared to U-Net++, our method shows an improvement in the Dice score for WT, TC, and ET by 1.6%, 2.3%, and 0.9%, respectively. These results demonstrate the superior performance of our proposed network in accurately segmenting brain tumors.

Table 1. Ablation study on BraTS'2019 training dataset (50 samples)

Method	Dice			PPV			params	FLOPs
	WT	TC	ET	WT	TC	ET		
U-Net	0.8391	0.8204	0.7679	0.8623	0.8469	0.7873	39.40	20.138
+ECA	0.8525	0.8636	0.7897	0.8759	0.8937	0.8095	39.40	20.138
+MCFP	0.8489	0.8532	0.7834	0.8598	0.8882	0.7864	35.43	18.097
+MPFF	0.8480	0.8530	0.7817	0.8827	0.8816	0.8153	41.57	26.117
+ECA+MCFP	0.8538	0.8652	0.7890	0.8742	0.8988	0.8046	35.43	18.098
+ECA+MPFF	0.8489	0.8679	0.7845	0.8781	0.8894	0.8128	41.58	26.118
ours	**0.8551**	**0.8728**	**0.7906**	**0.8722**	**0.9018**	**0.8028**	**37.61**	**24.077**

Table 2. Ablation study on BraTS'2019 training dataset (50 samples).

Method	Specificity			Hausdorff			params	FLOPs
	WT	TC	ET	WT	TC	ET		
U-Net	0.8612	0.9073	0.8167	2.6477	1.7568	2.8415	39.40	20.138
+ECA	0.8722	0.9133	0.8275	2.5625	1.5801	2.7143	39.40	20.138
+MCFP	0.8764	0.9057	0.8359	2.5944	1.6325	2.7650	35.43	18.097
+MPFF	0.8629	0.9147	0.8149	2.6137	1.6401	2.7666	41.57	26.117
+ECA+MCFP	0.8752	0.9115	0.8332	2.5804	1.5824	2.7289	35.43	18.098
+ECA+MPFF	0.8732	0.9248	0.8228	2.5795	1.5840	2.7146	41.58	26.118
ours	**0.8825**	**0.9168**	**0.8413**	**2.5693**	**1.5845**	**2.7284**	**37.61**	**24.077**

Table 3. Compare with other methods on BraTS'2019 training dataset 50 samples.

Method	Dice			PPV		
	WT	TC	ET	WT	TC	ET
U-Net [3]	0.8391	0.8204	0.7679	0.8623	0.8469	0.7873
U-Net++ [6]	0.8475	0.8498	0.7816	0.8734	0.8790	0.8037
HybridResU-Net [3]	0.8402	0.8182	0.7709	0.8894	0.8351	0.8182
DenseU-Net [15]	0.8422	0.8498	0.7756	0.8746	0.8892	0.8018
Deep ResU-Net [16]	0.8472	0.8343	0.7818	0.8879	0.8609	0.8141
ours	**0.8551**	**0.8728**	**0.7906**	**0.8722**	**0.9018**	**0.8028**

Table 4. Compare with other methods on BraTS'2019 training dataset 50 samples.

Method	Specificity			Hausdorff		
	WT	TC	ET	WT	TC	ET
U-Net [3]	0.8612	0.9073	0.8167	2.6477	1.7568	2.8415
U-Net++ [6]	0.8686	0.9132	0.8215	2.6090	1.6546	2.7729
HybridResU-Net [3]	0.8538	0.9176	0.8019	2.6275	1.8041	2.8147
DenseU-Net [15]	0.8588	0.9029	0.8226	2.6250	1.6459	2.7967
Deep ResU-Net [16]	0.8627	0.9113	0.8210	2.5888	1.6977	2.7791
ours	**0.8825**	**0.9168**	**0.8413**	**2.5693**	**1.5845**	**2.7284**

Qualitative Results

In this study, we selected 50 samples from the BraTS 2019 training set as the testing set and visualized the segmentation results in Fig. 4. The first column of the figure shows four different cases. In the segmentation result images, the green color represents the edema region, the red color represents the tumor core, and the yellow color represents the enhancing tumor. By comparing the segmentation results obtained by different methods, it can be seen from the blue boxes that the 3M-FF Net proposed in this paper has significant improvements in tumor segmentation, especially for small areas and small tumors. The visualized results demonstrate the effectiveness of our proposed network in segmenting brain tumors.

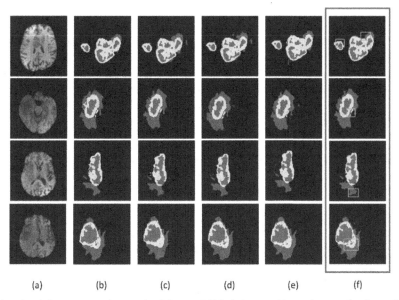

Fig. 4. Visual the segmentation result of the BraTS2019 dataset. (a) raw images (b) Ground Truth (c) U-Net (d) U-Net++ (e) Deep ResU-Net (f) 3M-FF Net

4   Conclusion

In this paper, we propose a feature fusion network with a multi-channel feature pyramid module and a multi-path feature fusion module. The multi-channel feature pyramid module is based on the feature pyramid channels and can extract locally dense features without increasing additional parameters. The multi-path feature fusion module can improve the problem of low information utilization rate, add effective information, and improve the segmentation accuracy of the network. The proposed network can alleviate problems such as insufficient multi-resolution feature fusion, low segmentation accuracy of small targets, and class imbalance, and has significant improvements in the entire tumor, tumor core, and enhanced tumor parts, especially in the tumor core part. The experimental results show significant improvements compared to several other advanced methods, but at the same time, the up-sampling process in the network decoder loses a lot of information, so the network still needs to be improved in the up-sampling part.

References

1. Havaei, M., et al.: Brain tumor segmentation with deep neural networks. Med. Image Anal. **35**, 18–31 (2017)
2. Prasoon, A., Petersen, K., Igel, C., Lauze, F., Dam, E., Nielsen, M.: Deep feature learning for knee cartilage segmentation using a triplanar convolutional neural network. In: Mori, K., Sakuma, I., Sato, Y., Barillot, C., Navab, N. (eds.) MICCAI 2013. LNCS, vol. 8150, pp. 246–253. Springer, Heidelberg (2013). https://doi.org/10.1007/978-3-642-40763-5_31

3. Ronneberger, O., Fischer, P., Brox, T.: U-net: convolutional networks for biomedical image segmentation. In: Navab, N., Hornegger, J., Wells, W.M., Frangi, A.F. (eds.) MICCAI 2015. LNCS, vol. 9351, pp. 234–241. Springer, Cham (2015). https://doi.org/10.1007/978-3-319-24574-4_28

4. Zhang, Z., Zhang, X., Peng, C., Xue, X., Sun, J.: ExFuse: enhancing feature fusion for semantic segmentation. In: Ferrari, V., Hebert, M., Sminchisescu, C., Weiss, Y. (eds.) ECCV 2018. LNCS, vol. 11214, pp. 273–288. Springer, Cham (2018). https://doi.org/10.1007/978-3-030-01249-6_17

5. Oktay, O., et al.: Attention U-net: learning where to look for the pancreas. In: Computer Vision and Pattern Recognition (CVPR) (2018)

6. Zhou, Z., Rahman Siddiquee, M.M., Tajbakhsh, N., Liang, J.: UNet++: a nested U-net architecture for medical image segmentation. In: Stoyanov, D., et al. (eds.) DLMIA/ML-CDS - 2018. LNCS, vol. 11045, pp. 3–11. Springer, Cham (2018). https://doi.org/10.1007/978-3-030-00889-5_1

7. Chen, C., Liu, X., Ding, M., Zheng, J., Li, J.: 3D dilated multi-fiber network for real-time brain tumor segmentation in MRI. In: Shen, D., et al. (eds.) MICCAI 2019. LNCS, vol. 11766, pp. 184–192. Springer, Cham (2019). https://doi.org/10.1007/978-3-030-32248-9_21

8. Chen, X., Liew, J.H., Xiong, W., Chui, C.-K., Ong, S.-H.: Focus, segment and erase: an efficient network for multi-label brain tumor segmentation. In: Ferrari, V., Hebert, M., Sminchisescu, C., Weiss, Y. (eds.) ECCV 2018. LNCS, vol. 11217, pp. 674–689. Springer, Cham (2018). https://doi.org/10.1007/978-3-030-01261-8_40

9. Chen, L.-C., Zhu, Y., Papandreou, G., Schroff, F., Adam, H.: Encoder-decoder with atrous separable convolution for semantic image segmentation. In: Ferrari, V., Hebert, M., Sminchisescu, C., Weiss, Y. (eds.) ECCV 2018. LNCS, vol. 11211, pp. 833–851. Springer, Cham (2018). https://doi.org/10.1007/978-3-030-01234-2_49

10. Chen, L.C., Papandreou, G., Schroff, F., Adam, H.: Rethinking atrous convolution for semantic image segmentation. In: Proceedings of the IEEE International Conference on Computer Vision (ICCV), pp. 2402–2410 (2017)

11. Szegedy, C., Liu, W., Jia, Y., Sermanet, P., Rabinovich, A.: Going deeper with convolutions. In: 2015 IEEE Conference on Computer Vision and Pattern Recognition (CVPR), pp. 1–9 (2015)

12. Szegedy, C., Vanhoucke, V., Ioffe, S., Shlens, J., Wojna, Z.: Rethinking the inception architecture for computer vision. In: 2016 IEEE Conference on Computer Vision and Pattern Recognition (CVPR), pp. 2818–2826 (2016)

13. Wang, P., et al.: Understanding convolution for semantic segmentation. In: 2018 IEEE Winter Conference on Applications of Computer Vision (WACV), pp. 1451–1460 (2018)

14. Wang, Q., Wu, B., Zhu, P., Li, P., Hu, Q.: ECA-net: efficient channel attention for deep convolutional neural networks. In: 2020 IEEE/CVF Conference on Computer Vision and Pattern Recognition (CVPR) (2020)

15. Wu, Y., Wu, J., Jin, S., Cao, L., Jin, G.: Dense-u-net: dense encoder–decoder network for holographic imaging of 3d particle fields. Opt. Commun.Commun **493**, 126970 (2021)

16. Zhang, Z., Liu, Q., Wang, Y.: Road extraction by deep residual u-net. IEEE Geosci. Remote Sens. Lett.Geosci. Remote Sens. Lett. **15**(5), 749–753 (2018)

Near Infrared Video Heart Rate Detection Based on Multi-region Selection and Robust Principal Component Analysis

Ziye Zhang, Chang-hong Fu[(✉)], Li Zhang, and Hong Hong

School of Electronic and Optical Engineering, Nanjing University of Science and Technology, Nanjing, China
enchfu@njust.edu.cn

Abstract. Heart rate (HR) is a crucial indicator of human health, and accurate monitoring of heart rate can effectively prevent the occurrence of diseases, thereby reducing the morbidity rate. In recent years, remote photoplethysmography (rPPG) has gained widespread use in non-contact heart rate measurement. This technology employs a camera to capture subtle changes in the skin surface to obtain the heart rate. However, currently, the technology is primarily limited to stable visible light environments. Therefore, the purpose of this study was to utilize rPPG technology under infrared light to capture heart rate parameters in dark or insufficient light conditions. Nevertheless, skin pulsations in the near-infrared range are much weaker and more susceptible to other noise factors than ambient light. In this study, a region containing high-quality rPPG signals was selected from multiple regions of interest (ROIs), and the single-channel signal was extended to a multi-channel signal. Furthermore, through the use of robust principal component analysis (RPCA), the distortion effects caused by noise were mitigated, thereby improving pulse extraction.

Keywords: Heart rate · rPPG · Infrared video

1 Introduction

In recent years, cardiovascular and cerebrovascular diseases are increasingly threatening human health. Heart rate, being one of the most crucial vital signs of humans, directly reflects their health status. However, at present, in hospitals, the contact heart rate detection equipment is used as a vital signs measurement tool, which is limited in application scenarios and cannot be real-time monitoring. In recent years, a contactless way of monitoring blood volume and pulse using conventional cameras has emerged called remote photoplethysmography (rPPG), which uses subtle changes in the surface of the skin to capture heart rate.

At present, rPPG technology can stably extract heart rate in an environment with stable light [1, 2]. These are done in ambient light, which provides three channels for RGB, but only one channel for infrared light, which is used in dark environments. Generally, single-channel signals are extended to multi-channel signals by utilizing multiple

H. Lu et al. (Eds.): ICIG 2023, LNCS 14359, pp. 37–47, 2023.
https://doi.org/10.1007/978-3-031-46317-4_4

infrared filters or by selecting multiple regions of interest (ROI). Van Gastel et al. proved the feasibility of exercise-robust heart rate detection by simultaneously recording video images from multiple narrow-band wavelengths of near-infrared light [3]. With this extension, some of the heart rate detection algorithms applied to RGB video can also be applied to near-infrared video. Favilla et al. selected three different areas of interest in the forehead and left and right cheeks in the monochrome face video as research objects to obtain corresponding three single-channel signals for independent component analysis [4]. He et al. combined near-infrared camera with Euler video amplification technology to measure human heart rate and respiration rate under dark conditions [5]. Zhang et al. obtained heart rate measurements from near infrared videos under the condition of complex illumination changes through EMD technology, and conducted relevant experiments in the vehicle driving environment [6]. Poh et al. performed blind source separation and applied independent component analysis (ICA) to separate the heart rate signal from the noise [7] in three color channels. The above studies demonstrate the possibility of extracting subjects' heart rates from near-infrared videos.

The near-infrared video signals are relatively weak in the near-infrared spectrum region, making them highly susceptible to noise interference. Traditional methods are significantly impacted by noise when separating the heart rate signal, resulting in considerable deviations in the results. The primary contributions of this paper are as follows: 1) The ROI region with high quality rPPG signal is selected based on rough heart rate estimation, so as to obtain the original signal with better quality. 2) RPCA is used to reduce the interference brought by noise to rPPG signal, so that accurate heart rate value can be extracted.

In the 2 section of this paper, we will provide a comprehensive description of our proposed method flow. Section 3 presents the effectiveness verification and experimental results of this method. Finally, Sect. 4 summarizes the entire work.

2 Proposed Method

In this section, the method flow of extracting heart rate from infrared single-channel video proposed in this paper is described in general. The overall process is shown in Fig. 1. The details of the process are described as follow.

The overall process of this method is:

1) We employed the MediaPipe face mesh method to detect and track the face region and feature points in infrared video. The tracking areas are then averaged in each frame to obtain multiple original single-channel signals.
2) The original signal undergoes pre-processing, which includes standardization processing and band-pass filtering.
3) To obtain signals with the highest quality rPPG signal, we propose a two-step ROI selection method. Firstly, a rough estimated heart rate value is obtained through the aforementioned multiple signals. Secondly, based on the rough heart rate estimation, the three signals with the highest quality rPPG signal are selected.
4) Three candidate heart rate signals are obtained through robust principal component analysis of the three-way signal by RPCA algorithm.

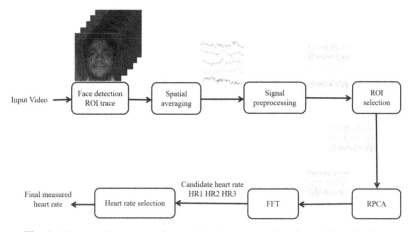

Fig. 1. The overall process of extracting heart rate values from infrared video.

5) The three candidate heart rate signals are obtained by performing fast Fourier transform (FFT), and the frequency values corresponding to the three spectral peaks are taken as candidate heart rate values.
6) The final measured heart rate is obtained by taking the median value of the three candidate heart rate values.

2.1 Signal Pre-processing

The original signal obtained from different regions have varying amplitudes, and is often contaminated with noise across different frequency ranges. These noise frequencies are usually quite different from the normal heart rate distribution range, making it difficult to extract signal with high quality rPPG from the original signal. Therefore, pre-processing methods are necessary to enhance the quality of the signal and isolate the heart rate signal from noise.

This paper employed two pre-processing methods: mean-variance normalization and band-pass filtering. Mean-variance normalization involves scaling the amplitude of the signal to have zero mean and unit variance, as shown in Formula 1:

$$\widetilde{x(t)} = \frac{x(t) - x_{mean}}{\sigma} \tag{1}$$

where, $x(t)$ is the original signal, x_{mean} is the mean value of the signal, σ is the standard deviation of the signal, and $\widetilde{x(t)}$ is the normalized signal. After mean variance normalization, the original signal will be transformed into a signal with zero mean and unit standard deviation.

After the mean-variance normalization, a band-pass filter is utilized to remove noise signals outside the heart rate frequency range. The cutoff range of frequency is [0.75, 4.0] Hz, corresponding to a heart rate range of [49, 240] bpm, which is in line with the human heart rate range.

2.2 Optimal Region Selection

Different from general video under natural light, infrared video only contains one channel, while general video has three RGB channels. In addition, since skin pulsation signals in infrared video are weak, selecting ROI regions with high signal-to-noise ratio (SNR) is very important to ensure accurate heart rate extraction.

In the whole facial region, the area with large exposed skin area includes the forehead, nose, left and right cheeks and chin. Generally, as the exposed area of the skin increases, the pixel value that can be calculated also increases. This increase in pixel value is directly proportional to the amount of heart rate information contained in the area, resulting in improved accuracy. Therefore, selecting regions with larger exposed skin areas can enhance the quality of the signal and improve the accuracy of heart rate measurement. The area mentioned above are commonly used in experimental research, whereas areas such as the eyes and mouth are not considered due to the interference caused by blinking and speaking. Therefore, in face tracking, we select the above five areas for tracking and obtain five original signals.

However, in the face areas, The SNR of signals extracted from different locations is different, and the higher the SNR is, the better rPPG signal quality is [9]. The quality of rPPG signal in each of the five signals above is different, and the less useful information there is, the less accurate the final heart rate measurement will be. If selected arbitrarily, the accuracy of heart rate measurement will be reduced. Therefore, we need to select the signals with the highest quality rPPG signal from the five signals to be selected as the input signals for subsequent processing.

Specific process of ROI selection: First, we add the above five pre-processed signals in each window to get the overall signal. Since each channel has the same rPPG signal but different noises, adding the channels strengthens the heart rate signal and weakens the noise components. Thus the highest frequency component of the summed signal in the frequency domain can be used as a rough estimate of heart rate. Second, calculate the SNR of the five signals based on the rough estimation of heart rate, the specific formula of SNR is given in Formula 2 below. To mimic the three channels of RGB video under normal natural light, the first three signals with the highest SNR are selected as the three signals for subsequent processing, so as to ensure to a large extent that the selected signals contain higher quality rPPG signal in each time window. The specific flow chart of this process is shown in Fig. 2 below.

$$SNR = 10 \, log_{10} \frac{\int_{HR-6\,\mathrm{bpm}}^{HR+6\,\mathrm{bpm}} P}{\int_{HR=49}^{240} P - \int_{HR-6\,\mathrm{bpm}}^{HR+6\,\mathrm{bpm}} P} \qquad (2)$$

where P represents the corresponding power spectrum value of each frequency point after the signal is transferred from the time domain to the frequency domain. HR represents the estimated heart rate for reference.

The signals from the nose and the left and right cheek regions [10] (Fig. 3 (a)), which are commonly used, are compared with the signals after our selection (Fig. 3 (b)), and the reference signals are also shown at the bottom of Fig. 3 (black).

It can be observed that the quality of the selected signals is significantly higher than that of the unselected signals, and the fluctuation of the selected region signals is more

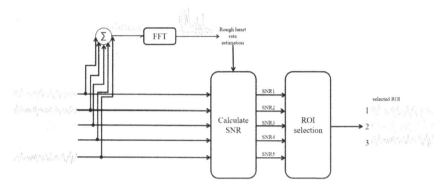

Fig. 2. Specific process of ROI selection.

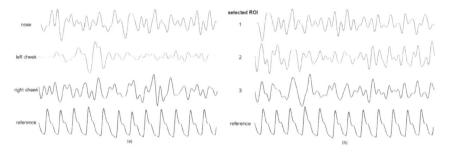

Fig. 3. (a) The areas commonly used. (b) The selected areas.

similar to the reference signal, indicating that they contain higher quality rPPG signal. Therefore, after selecting the regional signals, the highest quality signals can be obtained in each time window, so as to ensure the accuracy of heart rate measurement.

2.3 Robust Principal Component Analysis (RPCA)

The original signals extracted from different facial regions of interest all contain common pulse wave signals, and pulse wave signals are the signals with the strongest correlation between the signals in each region. The target pulse wave signal can be obtained by performing robust principal component analysis (RPCA) on the three selected signals. However, the original heart rate signals also have some noise that are quite different from pulse wave signals. In order to be more intuitive, we show each point of the three signals (The blue dots in Fig. 4). The existence of these noise points will seriously affect the quality and accuracy of subsequent extraction of pulse wave signals.

Robust principal component analysis (RPCA) is a robust extension of principal component analysis (PCA). The robustness of RPCA is reflected in that PCA will be seriously affected when encountering large noises or serious outlier noises. However, RPCA originally assumes that these noise points are sparse, and no matter what the noise intensity is, the results will not be affected by strong noise, so as to ensure the accuracy and stability of the obtained target pulse signal.

Figure 4 shows the difference in result between the two methods, where the blue dot represents the original signal scatter and the red dot represents the signal scatter after RPCA or PCA. It is obvious that RPCA can separate components concentrated in the main components from the three signals, which can greatly reduce the influence of outlier noise points. However, there is a certain gap between the results presented by PCA and the expected target, which is caused by these outlier noise points.

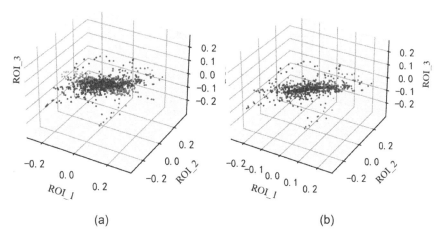

(a)   (b)

Fig. 4. Signal scatter diagram processed by (a) RPCA and (b) PCA. (Color figure online)

The essence of this algorithm is to decompose matrix D, which contains both information and noise, into the sum of low-rank information matrix A and sparse noise matrix E. So the objective function is written as:

$$\min_{AE} rank(A) + \lambda \|E\|_0 \tag{3}$$

where D represents the matrix composed of the three signals after selected, and the current signals contain a lot of noise and common rPPG information. The low rank of the matrix A indicates that the three signals have a common signal component. And among the signals obtained from different facial regions of interest, the most relevant component is the target rPPG signal, so matrix A is the matrix we want to obtain. The matrix E is a collection of isolated points that are quite different from the rPPG data, namely the noise.

2.4   Selection of Final Heart Rate

The signal after the robust principal component analysis is performed by fast Fourier transform (FFT), and the signal is transferred from the time domain to the frequency domain to obtain the power spectral density diagram. From the power spectrum distribution diagram of the signal, the frequencies corresponding to the three power peaks can be obtained respectively as candidate heart rate values (see Formula 4). During the experiment, we found that there would be individual abnormal value among the three candidate heart rates obtained. That's because most of the five original signals from this video window contain low quality rPPG signal. Moreover, when there are inaccurate heart rate measurements among the three candidate heart rates, if the average value is selected as the final heart rate measurement, the result will be inaccurate. Therefore, we selected the median of the three candidate heart rates as the final target heart rate. A more accurate measurement of heart rate can be obtained in this case.

$$HR_{estimate} = mid\,(HR_1, HR_2, HR_3) \qquad (4)$$

3   Experimental Results

3.1   Experimental Setting

The MR-NIRP datasets [8] is used to verify the accuracy of this method. The database contains in-room videos of eight healthy subjects, two female and six male, aged between 20 and 40. The dataset is divided into two cases, namely motion and still. In the still case, the subjects were asked to sit still in nature for video filming. In the motion case, subjects are allowed to move their heads and communicate naturally. The original image was recorded at 30 fps at 640×640 resolution. The IR camera is equipped with a narrow-band 940 nm band-pass filter with a pass-band of 10 nm, and the exposure is fixed for all participants. Two lighting fixtures were installed to ensure a more even illumination of the face area. Each video is about 3 min long. The real PPG waveform was also recorded using a finger pulse oximeter with a resolution of 60 fps.

Set the length of the video window to 300 frames (10 s) and the step size to 10 frames, that is, 10 frames per window come from the new time window. The window length is long enough to ensure the accuracy of heart rate extraction, and short enough to ensure real-time tracking of heart rate changes.

3.2   Evaluation Index

During the experiment, the following evaluation parameters were considered to determine the results. These indicators are common statistical error indicators. They are respectively the proportion of absolute error less than 6 relative to bpm, RMSE, MAE and MER. The corresponding calculation methods of the five evaluation indicators are shown in Table 1 below.

In each indicator formula below, n is the total number of video windows, HR_i is the ith true heart rate, and HRm_i is the ith measured heart rate obtained through video.

3.3   Experimental Results

In order to verify the performance of the method proposed in this paper, we use the near infrared video of MR-NIR database for experimental verification. And through the above evaluation indicators to evaluate the method of this paper. In addition, we also use other commonly used methods to detect heart rate from near infrared video. We then

Table 1. Algorithm result parameter evaluation definition.

Metric	Definition
Accuracy rate (%)	$accuracy\ rate = \frac{\sum_{i=1}^{n} a_i}{n}$ $a_i = \begin{cases} 1\ if\ \lvert HR_i - HRm_i \rvert < 6 \\ 0\ if\ \lvert HR_i - HRm_i \rvert > 6 \end{cases}$
Root mean square error (RMSE) (bpm)	$\text{RMSE} = \sqrt{\frac{\sum_{i=1}^{n} \lvert HR_i - HRm_i \rvert^2}{n}}$
Mean absolute error (MAE) (bpm)	$\text{MAE} = \frac{1}{n}\sum_{i=1}^{n} \lvert HR_i - HRm_i \rvert$
Mean error rate percentage (MER) (%)	$\text{MER} = \frac{1}{n}\sum_{i=1}^{n} \frac{\lvert HR_i - HRm_i \rvert}{HR_i} \times 100\%$

compare our method with the other three to compare the performance of the different methods. We also compare the performance of selected facial signals with those from the nose and left and right cheek areas used in general studies.

This method extracts heart rate results from videos in the still part, and the data of specific evaluation indicators are shown in Table 2.

Table 2. Heart rate detection performance of different methods in still case of MR-NIRP.

Metric	ICA [4]	EMD [6]	PCA	General region	proposed
Accuracy rate (%)	79.2	78.0	74.5	87.4	**92.8**
RMSE (bpm)	9.1	9.8	7.6	5.4	**3.9**
MAE (bpm)	5.0	5.5	4.7	3.0	**2.0**
MER (%)	7.1	8.3	6.7	4.2	**2.7**

As shown in the table, the proposed method outperforms other methods in terms of heart rate accuracy and error indicators. This highlights the importance of selecting signals in ROI regions and the effectiveness of our proposed method. For our method, the accuracy rate is 92.8%, the root mean square error is 3.9 (bpm), the mean error is 2.0 (bpm), and the mean error rate is 2.7 (bpm). The results demonstrate that our method is capable of accurately extracting heart rate information from near infrared video, and has potential applications in various fields such as healthcare.

In order to more intuitively and clearly observe the performance effect of the heart rate measurement results of the method presented in this paper, the window measurement results of each video in the database were counted and compared with the real heart rate value of the reference signal. The measured heart rate and reference heart rate of each window are respectively displayed in scatter plots in Fig. 5. The horizontal coordinate in the figure is the number of each window, and the vertical coordinate is the heart rate value. This visualization provides a more intuitive and comprehensive understanding of the performance of the proposed method.

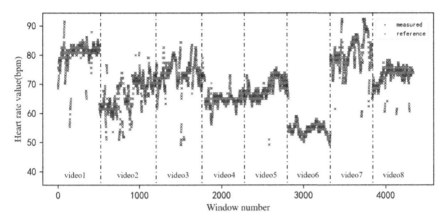

Fig. 5. The method of measuring heart rate and reference heart rate in each window.

As shown in the Fig. 5, reference heart rate and measured heart rate coincide in most cases, indicating that the measured heart rate has a good fit, which can achieve ideal heart rate detection effect, and at the same time, it can verify that the proposed method has a good accuracy. And when the heart rate changes, the measured heart rate also changes, which can prove that the window length can better adapt to the change of heart rate.

In addition to testing the proposed method on still videos, we also evaluated its performance on videos with motion. The results of the evaluation are shown in Table 3, which displays the specific evaluation indicator data.

Table 3. Heart rate detection performance of different methods in motion case of MR-NIRP.

Metric	ICA [4]	EMD [6]	PCA	General region	proposed
Accuracy rate (%)	56.8	53.2	51.3	57.7	**63.5**
RMSE (bpm)	10.9	88	11.6	11.3	**8.5**
MAE (bpm)	7.6	7.4	8.8	7.9	**5.7**
MER (%)	10.2	9.9	11.8	9.8	**7.7**

As shown in Table 3, the proposed method outperforms other methods in terms of heart rate accuracy and error indicators even in the presence of head movement and conversation. The results once again demonstrate the importance of selecting signals in the ROI region and the effectiveness of our proposed method.

It is worth noting that the comparison between Table 2 and Table 3 shows that there are differences in the performance of the proposed methods in videos under different conditions. This indicates that there is room for improvement in the performance of the proposed method in complex shooting environments, such as videos with motion and conversation. Future research can focus on developing more advanced techniques and algorithms to address the challenges posed by complex shooting environments and improve the accuracy and reliability of heart rate extraction under these conditions. Nonetheless, the proposed method still outperforms other existing methods in both static and motion videos, highlighting its effectiveness and potential for practical applications in various fields.

4   Conclusion

In this paper, we propose a method to extract heart rate from single channel infrared video, which can reduce the influence of large outlier noise on the accuracy of heart rate extraction. The signals with more high-quality rPPG signal are selected out from the signals of a large area of skin, so that the single channel of infrared video can be expanded into multiple channels. For the combination of signals with the highest content of heart rate information in each time window proposed in this paper, the accuracy rate of heart rate measurement can reach 92.8%, the root mean square error is 7.41 (bpm), the average error is 2.0 (bpm), and the average error rate is 2.7 (bpm). It shows that this method can detect heart rate in the dark condition by using infrared light which cannot be recognized by human eyes, and obtain high heart rate accuracy.

However, in this study, there were facial movements in part of the videos, which would lead to a low signal-to-noise ratio of the initial signal, thus decreasing the accuracy of heart rate measurement. Further research is needed to improve the motion robustness of infrared video heart rate detection.

References

1. Mcduff, D.J., Estepp, J.R., Piasecki, A.M., Black, E.B.: A survey of remote optical photo-plethysmographic imaging methods. Eng. Med. Biol. Soc. Conf. Proc. IEEE Eng. Med. Biol. Soc., 6398 (2015)
2. Poh, M.-Z., McDuff, D.J., Picard, R.W.: Advancements in noncontact, multiparameter physiological measurements using a webcam. IEEE Trans. Biomed. Eng. **58**(1), 7–11 (2011)
3. Van Gastel, M., Stuijk, S., Haan, G.D.: Motion robust remote-PPG in infrared. IEEE Trans. Biomed. Eng. **62**(5), 1425–1433 (2015)
4. Favilla R., Zuccalà, V.C., Coppini, G.: Heart rate and heart rate variability from single-channel video and ICA integration of multiple signals. IEEE J. Biomed. Health Inf. **23**(6), 2398–2408 (2018)
5. He, X., Goubran, R., Knoefel, F.: IR night vision video-based estimation of heart and respiration rates. In: 2017 IEEE Sensors Applications Symposium (SAS), pp. 1–5 (2017)
6. Zhang, Q., Zhou, Y., Song, S., Liang, G., Ni, H.: Heart rate extraction based on near-infrared camera: towards driver state monitoring. IEEE Access **6**, 33076–33087 (2018)
7. Poh, M.-Z., McDuff, D.J., Picard, R.W.: Non-contact, automated cardiac pulse measurements using video imaging and blind source separation. Opt. Express **18**(10), 1076210774 (2010). 1, 2, 3, 7
8. Nowara, E.M., Marks, T.K., Mansour, H., Veeraraghavan, A.: SparsePPG: towards driver monitoring using camera-based vital signs estimation in nearinfrared. In: Proceedings of the IEEE Conference on Computer Vision and Pattern Recognition Workshops (CVPRW 2018), pp. 1272–1281 (2018)

9. Mayank, K., Ashok, V., Ashutosh, S.: DistancePPG: robust non-contact vital signs monitoring using a camera. Biomed. Opt. Express **6**(5) (2015)
10. Rui, C.: Research on non-contact heart rate measurement method under quasi-static condition. Nanjing University of Posts and Telecommunications (2021). https://doi.org/10.27251/d.cnki. gnjdc.2021.000993

Neural Video: A Novel Framework for Interpreting the Spatiotemporal Activities of the Human Brain

Jingrui Xu[1], Jianpo Su[1], Kai Gao[2], Zhipeng Fan[1], Ming Zhang[1], Dewen Hu[1], and Ling-Li Zeng[1(✉)]

[1] College of Intelligence Science and Technology, National University of Defense Technology, Changsha, Hunan, China
xujingrui_nudt@163.com, fan_00970@163.com, yas-zm@163.com,
{sujianpo10,dwhu,zengphd}@nudt.edu.cn
[2] Brain Science Center, Beijing Institute of Basic Medical Sciences, Beijing, China
gaokai_14@163.com

Abstract. Deep learning has become a powerful tool for brain image analysis. However, high dimensionality hinders the direct application of deep learning models to 4D functional magnetic resonance imaging (fMRI) data of the brain. Previous methods usually simplified fMRI data with Regions-Of-Interest (ROI) based methods, which may lead to information loss. To address this issue, we proposed a novel framework that converts 4D fMRI data into 3D "neural video" based on area-preserving geometry mapping. In detail, 3D cortical surface mesh constructed with FreeSurfer could be converted into 2D planar mesh by using area-preserving geometry mapping, and then each fMRI volume could be aligned to the 2D planar mesh and then converted into a 2D image. Thus, a 4D fMRI scan could be converted into a 3D neural video. We further constructed CNN+Transformer models to process the converted neural video. We evaluated the framework with gender (females vs. males) and brain age (22–25 years vs. 31–35 years) classification tasks using data from the S1200 data release of the Human Connectome Project (HCP). The classification accuracy are 0.8811 ± 0.0254, 0.8612 ± 0.0199 and 0.8996 ± 0.0278 for the left hemisphere, right hemisphere and whole brain in gender classification as well as 0.5996 ± 0.0396, 0.6369 ± 0.0387 and 0.6479 ± 0.0453 in brain age classification. The results suggest that the proposed framework may provide a new avenue for deep learning of 4D spatiotemporal data such as brain fMRI.

Keywords: Functional magnetic resonance imaging · Neural video · Area-preserving geometry mapping · CNN+Transformer

1 Introduction

Functional magnetic resonance imaging (fMRI) is a non-invasive method that can be used to measure and localize brain activities [9]. It reflects the actual neural activities and possesses relatively high spatial and temporal resolution [11].

H. Lu et al. (Eds.): ICIG 2023, LNCS 14359, pp. 48–56, 2023.
https://doi.org/10.1007/978-3-031-46317-4_5

Owing to its ability to delineate functional brain activities, fMRI has been widely applied to diagnostic classification, foci localization and cognitive status assessment, etc.

Benefiting from its powerful feature extraction and representation capabilities, deep learning also attracts lots of attention for brain imaging analysis. However, due to the high dimensionality of the fMRI data, deep learning models for it have many limitations. Most previous deep learning models were designed based on low-dimensional data such as 1D time series, 2D images, 3D videos, etc. Deep learning models that can process 4D data are lacking. Even though a few deep learning models are compatible with 4D data, there are also some problems such as containing too many parameters, being hard to converge, or consuming too many computing resources.

To address this issue, lots of studies tried to reduce the dimensionality and complexity of fMRI data with the Regions-Of-Interest (ROI) based methods [2,4,21,22]. However, these methods may result in information loss. Thus, a framework for the analysis of 4D spatiotemporal data such as brain fMRI that can be compatible with contemporary deep learning models and does not rely on ROI based methods is necessary.

In this study, we proposed a novel framework for interpreting the spatiotemporal activities of the human brain based on fMRI. To be specific, we used the area-preserving geometry mapping to map 3D cortical surface mesh constructed with FreeSurfer into 2D planar mesh, and then each fMRI volume was aligned to the 2D planar mesh and then converted into a 2D image [5,6]. In this way, a 4D fMRI scan could be converted into 2D images arranged in chronological order, which we called "neural video". The neural video is a kind of 3D spatiotemporal data, that reduced the dimension and increased information density compared with 4D fMRI data while preserving its spatiotemporal patterns. In this way, abundant deep learning models designed for 3D spatiotemporal data can be applied to fMRI data directly and the models pretrained on image or video datasets can also be used. On this basis, we further constructed CNN+Transformer models to realize the spatiotemporal feature extraction model of the neural video. And we demonstrated the effectiveness of the proposed framework using gender and brain age classification tasks.

The major contributions of this study are summarized as followed:

(1) A new avenue for deep learning of 4D spatiotemporal data such as brain fMRI by mapping 4D data to 3D data based on area-preserving geometry mapping.
(2) We demonstrated the effectiveness of applying deep learning models designed for 3D spatiotemporal data to the analysis of fMRI data using the proposed framework.

2   Method

2.1   Overview

Area-preserving geometry mapping [15,23] is a kind of geometry mapping approach which can map 3D surface meshes into 2D planar meshes [6]. For brain image analysis, it can map the brain surface meshes into 2D planar meshes [20]. In this study, we applied it to fMRI data so that fMRI data could be converted into neural video.

By converting 4D fMRI data into 3D neural video, abundant deep learning models designed for 3D spatiotemporal data such as video could be introduced into the analysis of fMRI. To demonstrate the effectiveness of the proposed framework, we further constructed CNN+Transformer models and tested them with gender and brain age classification tasks. The architecture of the proposed framework is shown in Fig. 1.

2.2 Datasets

Gender and brain age are two fundamental issues in brain fMRI studies. However, they are still factors worth to be considered for the other fMRI studies [21] so we chose these two classification tasks to demonstrate the effectiveness of the proposed framework.

The datasets for gender and brain age classification were selected from the S1200 data release of the Human Connectome Project (HCP) [16,17]. The fMRI was scanned by a 3.0T Siemens scanner at Washington University. The scanner parameters are followed: resolution= $2 \times 2 \times 2mm^3$, repetition time (TR) = 720 ms, time echo (TE) = 33.1 ms, flip angle (FA) = $52°$, filed of view (FOV) = $208 \times 180mm^2$, slices=72, time points=1200.

For the gender classification, we selected 807 subjects with four runs of the resting-state fMRI (rs-fMRI) including 446 females and 361 males. And for the brain age classification, we selected 457 subjects with four runs of the rs-fMRI too. In particular, we divided the 457 subjects into two groups. The younger group included 174 subjects whose ages from 22 to 25 years old and the older group included 283 subjects whose ages from 31 to 35 years old.

2.3 Neural Video

The pipeline of neural video is shown in Fig. 1a. There were three steps for converting fMRI data into neural video. First, the FreeSurfer preprocessing pipeline [7] was applied to structural MRI (sMRI) data and fMRI data, respectively. And then we could obtain the constructed cortical mesh from the sMRI data and the vertex-wise time series data from the fMRI data. Next, area-preserving geometry mapping was used to convert the constructed 3D cortical mesh into 2D planar mesh. Finally, the vertex-wise fMRI time series data was aligned to the generated 2D planar mesh and then converted into 2D images arranged in chronological order. In this way, fMRI data could be converted into neural video.

In particular, the two hemispheres were mapped into two images, respectively. And the size of the mapped images was set to 224×224 to match the size of regular natural images so that the deep learning models pretrained on natural images could be applied to the neural video.

We also did some other preprocessing to the neural video besides the FreeSurfer preprocessing pipeline and area-preserving geometry mapping including missing value filling, mean-subtraction (time series of each pixel), z-score normalization (images of each time point), 3σ outlier handling and rescaling.

On the other hand, we split the preprocessed neural video into clips to capture its dynamic temporal patterns. And the window size of the clips is critical for the capture of dynamic temporal patterns. In previous studies, it has been found that windows of functional connectivity with sizes too long or too short will cause a negative impact [13]. The window size of 30–60 s could remain a relatively good performance for identifying cognitive states [14]. And the window size of 40 s and size of 30–60 s took the best performance in the previous studies for gender classification and brain maturity prediction [4,13], respectively. Even if the neural video rather than functional connectivity was applied in this study, we still believed that this range of the window size can be helpful to capture the dynamic temporal patterns of the fMRI data. In this way, we split the preprocessed neural video into 20 clips with a window size of 60 time points and the scan time of each clip is 43.2 s (60 TRs).

2.4   CNN+Transformer

The neural video is similar to video data in the spatial and temporal dimensions, as mentioned above, which is represented as 2D images arranged in chronological order. However, the spatiotemporal information contained in the neural video is different from the video data. In detail, each image of the neural video reflects the spatial distribution of brain functional activation at the corresponding time point. And the pixels of it at the same position of different images reflect the temporal dynamics of brain function. To capture the spatiotemporal patterns of the neural video, referring to the ViT model [3] and the ViViT model [1], we constructed CNN+Transformer models and the details of it are shown in Fig. 1c.

In this model, the CNN module was used to extract the spatial features of the neural video. Specifically, we used the ResNet18 [8] that was pretrained on ImageNet as the CNN module. Even if the model was pretrained on the natural image database, it is still helpful to extract spatial features of brain image data [20].

The temporal patterns of neural activities are embedded in relatively long timescales. And the attention mechanism of Transformer [18] can model the long-range dependencies of the input sequence [1] so that it is suitable for the temporal feature extraction of neural video. In this study, we used a two-layer Transformer encoder to encode the temporal activities and each layer contained eight heads of self-attention. Self-attention was calculated as [10,18]:

$$Attention(Q, K, V) = Softmax(\frac{QK^T}{\sqrt{d_k}})V \qquad (1)$$

The Q, K and V represented queries, keys and values matrix that were transformed from the input of self-attention.

Concretely, each image of the neural video was used as the input of the CNN module to obtain the spatial features encoded as a vector. In this way, the neural video was converted into spatial feature vectors that were arranged in chronological order.

The learnable classification token and positional embedding were also added to the spatial feature vectors after the CNN module [3]. Then, we used the spatial feature vectors with classification token and positional embedding as the input of the Transformer module to obtain the spatiotemporal features. Finally, the classification token learned spatiotemporal features of the neural video was fed to a fully connected layer for classification. In particular, we trained two classifiers for the neural video converted from the left and right hemispheres, respectively. And the average score of two classifiers was defined as the combined score of the whole brain for classification.

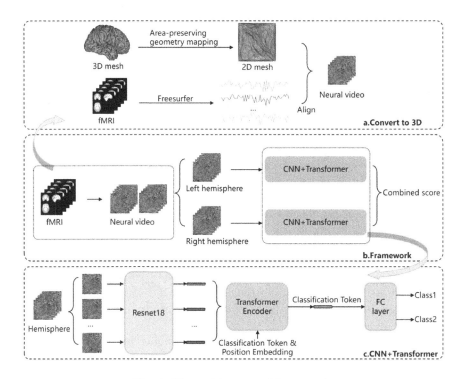

Fig. 1. The architecture of framework.

2.5   Experiments

The CNN+Transformer models were constructed based on Pytorch [12]. In particular, the CNN module was the ResNet18 from Timm (PyTorchImageModels) [19], which was pretrained on ImageNet. This model was trained by Adam optimizer with a batch size of 4. The initial learning rate was set to 0.0001 and the learning rate was multiplied by 0.85 per epoch. The number of epochs for gender and brain age classification were set to 15 and 12, respectively.

A five-fold cross-validation strategy was applied in this study. The fMRI data were randomly divided into five folds and we selected four folds for training and the left one for testing in each experiment. In particular, we used subjects in four folds for training and subjects in the left one fold for testing rather than the clips so that one subject will not appear in the training set and testing set at the same time.

3   Results

The classification results of gender and brain age classification are shown in Table 1. For these two classification tasks, as mentioned above, we trained two classifiers for the left and right hemispheres, respectively. And the combined score of two classifiers was used as the classification score for the whole brain.

Table 1. The results of gender and brain age classification.

Variable	Accuracy	Precision	Recall	AUC
Gender (Left hemisphere)	0.8811 ± 0.0254	0.8782 ± 0.0512	0.9140 ± 0.0424	0.9518 ± 0.0185
Gender (Right hemisphere)	0.8612 ± 0.0199	0.8663 ± 0.0277	0.8892 ± 0.0427	0.9358 ± 0.0144
Gender (Whole brain)	0.8996 ± 0.0278	0.8914 ± 0.0421	0.9349 ± 0.0123	0.9622 ± 0.0133
Brain age (Left hemisphere)	0.5996 ± 0.0396	0.6764 ± 0.0593	0.7028 ± 0.1223	0.6407 ± 0.0583
Brain age (Right hemisphere)	0.6369 ± 0.0387	0.6759 ± 0.0564	0.8028 ± 0.0454	0.6294 ± 0.0518
Brain age (Whole brain)	0.6479 ± 0.0453	0.6909 ± 0.0688	0.7918 ± 0.0631	0.6618 ± 0.0544

In the gender classification, the classification accuracy $\pm$ standard deviation of the left hemisphere, right hemisphere and whole brain were 0.8811 ± 0.0254, 0.8612 ± 0.0199 and 0.8996 ± 0.0278, respectively. The classification accuracy of the whole brain were 1.85% and 3.84% higher than that of the left hemisphere and the right hemisphere, respectively. And in the brain age classification, the classification accuracy $\pm$ standard deviation of the left hemisphere, right hemisphere and whole brain were 0.5996 ± 0.0396, 0.6369 ± 0.0387 and 0.6479 ± 0.0453, respectively. The classification accuracy of the whole brain were 4.83% and 1.1% higher than that of the left hemisphere and the right hemisphere, respectively.

The ROC curves of the gender and brain age classification are shown in Fig. 2, respectively. Figure 2a is the ROC curves of the left hemisphere, right hemisphere and whole brain for the gender classification. And Fig. 2b is the ROC curves of the left hemisphere, right hemisphere and whole brain for the brain age classification. In the gender classification, the AUCs $\pm$ standard deviation of the left hemisphere, right hemisphere and whole brain were 0.9518 ± 0.0185,

0.9358 ± 0.0144 and 0.9622 ± 0.0133, respectively. And in the brain age classification, the AUCs $\pm$ standard deviation of the left hemisphere, right hemisphere and whole brain were 0.6407 ± 0.0583, 0.6294 ± 0.0518 and 0.6618 ± 0.0544, respectively.

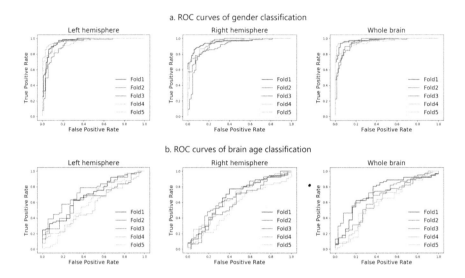

Fig. 2. The ROC curves of the gender and brain age classification.

4   Discussion

In this study, we proposed a novel framework for interpreting the spatiotemporal activities of the human brain. Using the proposed framework, 4D fMRI data could be converted into 3D neural video while preserving its spatiotemporal patterns. On this basis, we further constructed CNN+Transformer models to extract the spatiotemporal features from the converted neural video. To demonstrate the effectiveness of the proposed framework, we tested it with gender and brain age classification tasks using data from the HCP S1200.

fMRI is a powerful tool for brain imaging analysis because it reflects functional brain activities. Meanwhile, thanks to its excellent performance of feature extraction and representation, deep learning has also been widely used in brain imaging analysis. However, the direct application of deep learning models to the fMRI data is hindered by the high dimensionality of fMRI data. Most previous studies tried to simplify fMRI data with ROI based methods. These ROI based methods can effectively simplify fMRI data but may result in information loss. To address this issue, the proposed framework converted 4D fMRI data into 3D neural video using area-preserving geometry mapping, which could reduce the model dimensionality without ROI based methods. In this way, abundant deep learning models designed for 3D spatiotemporal data or pretrained on 2D or 3D datasets could be applied to 4D fMRI data. On the other hand, it could also improve computational efficiency due to the increased information density. On this basis, we further constructed CNN+Transformer models. We used ResNet18 as the CNN module to extract the spatial features of neural video and embed them into vectors. The spatial feature vectors were fed to the Transformer encoder with classification token and positional embedding to obtain the spatiotemporal feature representation of neural video. Finally, the spatiotemporal feature representation extracted from the neural video was used for classification.

There are still some limitations in the current study. First, the performance of the proposed framework for brain age classification was not ideal. The reasons for it may be the age label and the way that the brain age groups were divided. The age label of subjects in the HCP S1200 is an approximate range rather than an exact value, which may affect the performance of the classifier. Influenced by the age distribution of subjects, the age difference between the two selected groups was too small to achieve an ideal performance in the brain age classification. On the other hand, the relatively small size of the brain age classification dataset may also affect the classification performance. Second, in this study, we demonstrated the effectiveness of the proposed framework by constructing CNN+Transformer models. We will further demonstrate that applying deep learning models based on 3D spatiotemporal data to neural video is feasible by testing other compatible models. Third, we tested the ability to capture the spatiotemporal patterns of the proposed framework with gender and brain age classification in this study. In the future study, we will further test the ability of the proposed framework to capture the spatiotemporal patterns with other behavioral measures. Fourth, we will further convert the fMRI data of the cerebellum to neural video to obtain more spatiotemporal information of the human brain.

Acknowledgements. This work was supported by the STI 2030-Major Projects (2022ZD0208903), the National Natural Science Foundation of China (62036013, 61722313, and 62006239), the Fok Ying Tung Education Foundation (161057).

References

1. Arnab, A., Dehghani, M., Heigold, G., Sun, C., Lučić, M., Schmid, C.: ViViT: a video vision transformer. In: Proceedings of the IEEE/CVF International Conference on Computer Vision, pp. 6836–6846 (2021)
2. Arslan, S., Ktena, S.I., Glocker, B., Rueckert, D.: Graph saliency maps through spectral convolutional networks: application to sex classification with brain connectivity. In: Stoyanov, D., et al. (eds.) GRAIL/Beyond MIC -2018. LNCS, vol. 11044, pp. 3–13. Springer, Cham (2018). https://doi.org/10.1007/978-3-030-00689-1_1
3. Dosovitskiy, A., et al.: An image is worth 16x16 words: Transformers for image recognition at scale. arXiv preprint arXiv:2010.11929 (2020)
4. Fan, L., Su, J., Qin, J., Hu, D., Shen, H.: A deep network model on dynamic functional connectivity with applications to gender classification and intelligence prediction. Front. Neurosci. **14**, 881 (2020)
5. Fischl, B.: Freesurfer. Neuroimage **62**(2), 774–781 (2012)

6. Gao, K., et al.: Deep transfer learning for cerebral cortex using area-preserving geometry mapping. Cereb. Cortex **32**(14), 2972–2984 (2022)

7. Glasser, M.F., et al.: The minimal preprocessing pipelines for the human connectome project. Neuroimage **80**, 105–124 (2013)

8. He, K., Zhang, X., Ren, S., Sun, J.: Deep residual learning for image recognition. In: Proceedings of the IEEE Conference on Computer Vision and Pattern Recognition, pp. 770–778 (2016)

9. Heeger, D.J., Ress, D.: What does fMRI tell us about neuronal activity? Nat. Rev. Neurosci. **3**(2), 142–151 (2002)

10. Khan, S., Naseer, M., Hayat, M., Zamir, S.W., Khan, F.S., Shah, M.: Transformers in vision: a survey. ACM computing surveys (CSUR) **54**(10s), 1–41 (2022)

11. Logothetis, N.K.: What we can do and what we cannot do with fMRI. Nature **453**(7197), 869–878 (2008). https://doi.org/10.1038/nature06976

12. Paszke, A., et al.: Automatic differentiation in pytorch (2017)

13. Qin, J., et al.: Predicting individual brain maturity using dynamic functional connectivity. Front. Hum. Neurosci. **9**, 418 (2015)

14. Shirer, W.R., Ryali, S., Rykhlevskaia, E., Menon, V., Greicius, M.D.: Decoding subject-driven cognitive states with whole-brain connectivity patterns. Cereb. Cortex **22**(1), 158–165 (2012)

15. Su, Z., Zeng, W., Shi, R., Wang, Y., Sun, J., Gu, X.: Area preserving brain mapping. In: Proceedings of the IEEE Conference on Computer Vision and Pattern Recognition, pp. 2235–2242 (2013)

16. Van Essen, D.C., et al.: The WU-Minn human connectome project: an overview. Neuroimage **80**, 62–79 (2013)

17. Van Essen, D.C., et al.: The human connectome project: a data acquisition perspective. Neuroimage **62**(4), 2222–2231 (2012)

18. Vaswani, A., et al.: Attention is all you need. In: Advances in Neural Information Processing Systems. vol. 30 (2017)

19. Wightman, R.: Pytorch image models. https://github.com/rwightman/pytorch-image-models (2019). https://doi.org/10.5281/zenodo.4414861

20. Zeng, L.-L., et al.: A deep transfer learning framework for 3D brain imaging based on optimal mass transport. In: Kia, S.M., et al. (eds.) MLCN/RNO-AI -2020. LNCS, vol. 12449, pp. 169–176. Springer, Cham (2020). https://doi.org/10.1007/978-3-030-66843-3_17

21. Zhang, C., Cahill, N.D., Arbabshirani, M.R., White, T., Baum, S.A., Michael, A.M.: Sex and age effects of functional connectivity in early adulthood. Brain Connectivity **6**(9), 700–713 (2016)

22. Zhang, C., Dougherty, C.C., Baum, S.A., White, T., Michael, A.M.: Functional connectivity predicts gender: evidence for gender differences in resting brain connectivity. Hum. Brain Mapp. **39**(4), 1765–1776 (2018)

23. Zhao, X., et al.: Area-preservation mapping using optimal mass transport. IEEE Trans. Visual Comput. Graphics **19**(12), 2838–2847 (2013)

Local Fusion Synthetic CT Network for Improving the Quality of CBCT in Cervical Cancer Radiotherapy

Dong Huang[1], XiaoShuo Hao[1], Hua Yang[2], Yao Zheng[1], YueFei Feng[1], and Yang Liu[1(✉)]

[1] School of Biomedical Engineering, Air Force Medical University, Xi'an 710032, ShaanXi, China
yliu@fmmu.edu.cn
[2] Department of Radiation Oncology, Xijing Hospital of Air Force Medical University, Xi'an 710032, ShaanXi, China

Abstract. Cervical cancer is a prevalent gynecologic malignancy that poses a significant threat to women's health. Radiotherapy is a primary treatment method for cervical cancer, and real-time cone-beam computed tomography (CBCT) images are used for image-guided radiotherapy. However, CBCT images often have poor quality due to the presence of artifacts, making it difficult to monitor a patient's treatment response in real-time. The current approach to addressing this issue is primarily focused on enhancing the overall image quality. However, it must be acknowledged that the significance of radiotherapy target area is frequently overlooked. And the local radiotherapy target area is often the most able to reflect the tumor changes of the patient as the radiotherapy progresses. For this reason, we propose a local fusion synthetic CT method based on generative adversarial network. Specifically, we devise a local fusion module (LFM) to emphasize the local information of the radiotherapy target area, enabling the network to pay more attention to this area. Our proposed method not only improves the overall quality of CBCT, but also focuses on the target area, enabling the synthesized CT images to reflect the tumor changes of the patient. Experimental results show that our method can significantly improve the quality of CBCT in cervical cancer radiotherapy. Specially, compared with existing methods that improve the overall CBCT quality, our method could provide clearer and more realistic images.

Keywords: Cervical Cancer · Cone-Beam Computed Tomography · Image Quality Improvement · Radiotherapy Target Area

1 Introduction

Cervical cancer is a serious illness that poses a significant threat to women's health. Radiation therapy, as an important treatment for cervical cancer, has been widely used in clinical practice [10,11]. With the rapid development of

---

D. Huang and X. Hao—contributed equally to this work.

© The Author(s), under exclusive license to Springer Nature Switzerland AG 2023
H. Lu et al. (Eds.): ICIG 2023, LNCS 14359, pp. 57–67, 2023.
https://doi.org/10.1007/978-3-031-46317-4_6

tumor radiotherapy technology, radiation therapy has entered the era of adaptive radiation therapy. Adaptive radiation therapy means more accurate radiation dose and more precise irradiation range, which can effectively protect normal tissues and have important clinical significance in improving local control rate of tumors and patients' quality of life. However, the imaging quality of CBCT images collected during radiation therapy is generally poor, which cannot provide real-time information reflecting radiotherapy response [7,12].

Currently, researchers have proposed methods to improve the quality of CBCT images [5], mainly by converting CBCT to CT modalities. The existing CBCT-to-CT conversion methods mainly include strong supervised methods and modality transformation methods. Strong supervised methods achieve CBCT-to-CT conversion by training neural networks [2,16], which have high accuracy and stability but are sensitive to pixels and prone to producing anatomical artifacts [1,4]. Modality transformation methods use existing CT data and CBCT data to transform CBCT into CT through generative adversarial networks [17]. Compared to strong supervised methods, the generated images have fewer artifacts, but these methods tend to a style change, and the generated images are prone to losing detailed information [9]. Besides, these two methods are an overall quality improvement and do not pay attention to the target areas that radiotherapy focuses on. For radiotherapy, the generation of the target area (the area of interest) is particularly important. The tumor and organ changes in the target area could accurately reflect the patient's treatment response.

In this paper, we propose a local fusion synthetic CT network that not only enhances the overall quality but also focuses on the image quality of the target area. Specifically, we construct a generative adversarial network consisting of a decoder and an encoder to improve image quality. Secondly, we devise a local fusion module to the generator, which matches the similarity between the local target area and the overall image. This module replaces the several features in overall features with the most relevant local features, to emphasize the improvement of the quality of the target area.

Among the salient contributions of this paper, we can cite:

- We propose a local fusion synthetic CT network that could improve the quality of CBCT in radiotherapy.
- We design a local fusion module that focuses on the information of the target area, and add it to the generator of the adversarial generation network to emphasize the improvement and enhancement of the quality of the target area.
- Extensive experiments are implemented, which shows our method yielded better results in improving CBCT quality, particularly in facilitating better synthetic of the tumor target area. This confirms the efficacy of our proposed method.

2   Related Work

Synthesis CT-like images from cone-beam computed tomography (CBCT) is a challenging task. With the rapid development of deep learning in generating synthetic modalities, many researchers have attempted to address this problem, which can be broadly divided into two aspects.

2.1 Strong Supervised Methods

On the one hand, convolutional neural networks are directly used for the generation. For example, Kida et al. [6] constructed a 39-layer U-Net network to learn the transformation relationship between CBCT and CT images using pre-treatment CBCT and planned CT images. The experimental results showed that the generated pseudo-CT images had significant improvements compared to CBCT images in both overall image performance and quantitative indicators [6]. Xie et al. used the VGG19 network to represent CBCT and planned CT images in the feature domain and minimized the difference between the generated pseudo-CT images and CT images in the feature domain using a content mutual information loss function. Experimental results showed their method effectively removed metal artifacts in CBCT images [15]. These studies supervised the pixel-level generation network by the corresponding relationship between paired CBCT and CT images, learning the transformation method from CBCT to CT images. Although this approach improved the quality of CBCT to some extent, this strong supervision methods may make the loss function sensitive to the pixel-level generation process, resulting in more anatomical artifacts in the generated pseudo-CT images.

2.2 Modality Transformation Methods

On the other hand, to address the issue of anatomical artifacts caused by strong supervised methods training, many researchers have attempted to use generative adversarial networks (GANs) to transform CBCT in terms of style. For example, Rossi et al. [13] tried to use CycleGAN to transform CBCT in terms of style and achieved pseudo-CT images with image quality comparable to planned CT. They also compared the differences between strong supervision and style transfer in results, and experimental results showed that the images generated by their CycleGAN had fewer anatomical artifacts. Sun et al. [14] updated CycleGAN's structure and added a gradient loss function to improve its generation performance. The five-fold experimental results showed that the method generated CT images with higher image quality. Zhao et al. [18] added noise to CycleGAN's training process to make the network more robust in terms of generating performance. In addition, Xiao et al. [8] developed a cycle-consistent GAN and compared it with other unsupervised learning methods, concluding that the performance of the CycleGAN network was superior to other models.

Whether strong supervised or modality transformation methods, both approaches take a global perspective and may lose detailed information. However, during the generation process, it is hoped to better generate images in the target area. Therefore, it is necessary to design a network framework that focuses on improving the quality of the target area images while enhancing the overall quality, with a particular emphasis on improving the quality of the regions of interest.

To address the current issue, we will propose a specific local fusion module. This module is based on matching the semantic similarity between the base image and the local image to obtain a localized representation. We then replace the original local features with the most relevant local features to improve the quality of the generated images in the target regions.

3   Methodology

3.1   Overall Framework

The constructed CBCT to CT image synthetic model framework is shown in Fig. 1. This study builds a model based on the principle of the generative adversarial network (GAN), which includes a generator and a discriminator. The generator contains an encoder, a local fusion module (LFM), and a decoder. The discriminator uses a fully convolutional network. Compared to classical GAN networks, this model can not only generate higher quality images but also focus on the target area, thereby improving the quality of local images. This model adopts a fully supervised method, using paired input and output images to train the model. The trained model synthesizes the target image for the specified task from the input image. First, CBCT and the locally cropped target area from CBCT are input into the generator to synthesize CT. Then, the synthetic CT and real CT scans are fed into the discriminator to distinguish them. The generator and discriminator compete with each other until the generator can synthesize high-quality CT that the discriminator cannot distinguish.

The generator comprises an encoder, a decoder, and a local fusion module. Both the encoder and decoder adopt the classic U-Net network, while the local fusion module is mainly used to improve the generation quality of key areas. For specific structures, please refer to Sect. 3.2

The discriminator does not use the traditional GAN discriminator network, but instead adopts the PatchGAN discriminator principle [3]. The discriminator performs real/fake discrimination on N x N image blocks that are treated as independent. To achieve this, the model divides a given image into several N x N patches, and the discriminator performs real vs. fake judgments on each patch. The final discriminator output is the average result of all patches. The discriminator is constructed using a fully convolutional small network that takes an N x N input. The last layer applies a sigmoid function to each pixel to output its probability of being real, and the BCE loss function determines the final loss. This approach provides significant benefits such as producing high-quality, clear images and lower input dimensions, fewer parameters, and faster operation compared to traditional GAN.

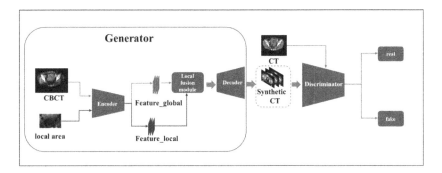

Fig. 1. The proposed local fusion synthetic CT network includes the generator and discriminator, with the addition of the local fusion module in the generator. The discriminator does not use the traditional GAN discriminator network, but instead adopts the PatchGAN discriminator principle.

3.2 Local Fusion Module

As mentioned earlier, there are differences in the positional changes and organ states of patients during CT and CBCT scans, and current registration methods are unable to fully address deformation variations in detail. To address this problem, the model incorporates locally designed generation modules into the generation process to achieve better results in generating regions of interest.

The architecture of the local fusion module is shown in Fig. 2, and the entire fusion process can be divided into three steps: local selection, local matching, and local reconstruction. The CBCT and target area are encoded to generate their respective feature maps. The corresponding position of the target area feature on the CBCT feature is found through similarity judgment. Then weighted coefficients are assigned to each feature map to generate the fused feature map, which is used to replace the corresponding feature at the target area position in the CBCT feature map. In this way, the module could achieve better synthesis results for the region of interest.

Local Selection: After extracting both local and global features, it is necessary to find the corresponding features in the global feature for the specific local features that need to be replaced. This step involves randomly selecting several local features from the global feature . Through this feature selection process, we obtain a set of local features randomly sampled from the global features, which will be used for the subsequent feature matching step.

Local Matching: After selecting the local features of a specific part, calculate the similarity between the target image feature ψ_{local} at the corresponding position and the global feature ϕ_{global}.

$$M = g\left(\phi_{global}, \psi_{local}\right) \tag{1}$$

Obtaining a similarity feature map allows us to identify and merge local features that are most similar to the global image.

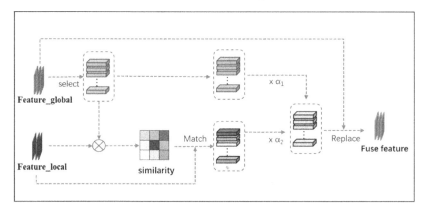

Fig. 2. Local fusion module. First, a subset of features is randomly selected from the entire image. Next, their similarity is calculated with local features. If the calculated similarity satisfies certain criteria, feature fusion is performed. Finally, the corresponding features at the original location of the image are replaced.

Local Reconstruction: Local reconstruction here refers to integrating the local features mentioned above at the image level. Specifically, through the local matching step, we are able to locate the CBCT feature map position that is most similar to the target region feature. Subsequently, we assign weighting coefficients to each feature map, allowing us to blend them together into a new composite feature map. This fused feature map will then be used to replace the corresponding features in the target region of the CBCT feature map.

3.3 Model Learning

In the model, the synthetic network continuously attempts to optimize the following objective function (where G is the generator, D is the discriminator, x is the input and y is the output):

$$\mathcal{L}_{GAN}(G, D) = \mathbb{E}_{x,y}[log D(x, y)] + \mathbb{E}_x[\log(1 - D(x, G(x)))] \qquad (2)$$

To ensure the similarity between the input and output images, an L1 loss is added as a loss function.

$$\mathcal{L}_{L1}(G) = \mathbb{E}_{x,y}[\|y - G(x)\|_1] \qquad (3)$$

4   Datesets and Results

4.1   Datasets Preparation and Metrics

Datasets Preparation. We selected data from 20 cervical cancer patients in ** Hospital. With the patients' consent, each patient underwent one planned

CT and CBCT scan before radiotherapy. The model used a fully supervised approach, requiring paired image inputs for better generation effects. To meet the requirements of the model input and achieve better results, the data needs to be registered layer by layer in data processing. The image resolution of all CT and CBCT images is 1344*800. Non-rigid registration method was used to register the CT and CBCT images of each patient to achieve hierarchical matching. After non-rigid registration, a total of 1362 pairs of CBCT-CT images were formed. We collaborated with medical professionals to define and extract the regions of interest from CBCT images that are of particular significance to doctors. These regions were carefully delineated and cropped, resulting in the generation of a dataset comprising 1362 pairs of CT-CBCT-CBCT target images. Three patients' individual images were used as the test set, and the others were used as the training set.

Evaluation Metrics. To evaluate the image quality of synthesized CT images, we use three metrics - Peak Signal-to-Noise Ratio (PSNR), Structural Similarity Index (SSIM), and Learned Perceptual Image Patch Similarity (LPIPS). PSNR is defined as:

$$PSNR = 10 \bullet \log_{10} \left(\frac{MAX_I^2}{MSE} \right) \tag{4}$$

MAX_I represents the maximum numerical value of the color of image pixels, and MSE is the mean squared error, defined as follows (where m and n denote the dimensions of the image):

$$MSE = \frac{1}{mn} \sum_{i=0}^{m-1} \sum_{j=0}^{n-1} \left[I\left(i,j\right) - k(i,j) \right]^2 \tag{5}$$

SSIM is defined as:

$$SSIM(x,y) = \left[l(x,y) \right]^\alpha \left[c(x,y) \right]^\beta \left[s(x,y) \right]^\gamma \tag{6}$$

In the above equation, l(x,y) is estimated using mean for luminance, c(x,y) using variance for contrast, and s(x,y) using covariance for structural similarity.

$$LPIPS\left(x, x_0\right) = \sum_l \frac{1}{H_l W_l} \sum_{h,w} \| w_l \odot \left(\hat{y}_{hw}^l - \hat{y}_{0hw}^l \right) \|_2^2 \tag{7}$$

The LPIPS metric measures similarity by computing the distance between features. Specifically, $\hat{y}_{hw}^l$ and $\hat{y}_{0hw}^l$ represent the normalized activation results of x and x_0 through their respective feature and network layers. The equation calculates the distance between x and x_0. It extracts feature maps from L layers and performs unit normalization along the channel dimension. It scales the number of activation channels using vector W_l, and finally calculates the L2 distance across spatial dimensions and all layers.

4.2 Experimental Results

The Evaluation of LFM Effectiveness. In order to better evaluate the performance of the model and validate its advantages, we trained and tested the model without LFM. The test results are shown in Table 1. It can be seen that the proposed model with the local fusion module performs well in all indicators for both global and local images.

Table 1. Comparison of the proposed Networks with and without Local Fusion Module (wo-LFM).

		CBCT	wo-LFM	Ours
Local	SSIM(%)	30.21	50.37	70.77
	MSE	1921.78	725.07	529.69
	PSNR(dB)	15.29	19.52	20.89
	LPIPS	0.69	0.33	0.24
Global	SSIM(%)	52.32	73.24	77.89
	MSE	1531.3	534.19	456.59
	PSNR(dB)	16.52	20.85	21.59
	LPIPS	0.39	0.2	0.15

The Comparison with Other Methods. To verify the performance of the model in synthetic CT image tasks, we compared its synthetic images with those produced by other commonly used generative adversarial models. To ensure a fair evaluation of each model's performance, all training and testing data were consistent across all models. The test results are shown in Table 2.

Table 2. Comparison of existing methods.

		CBCT	cycleGAN	wo-LFM	Ours
Local	SSIM(%)	30.21	50.13	50.37	70.77
	MSE	1921.78	864.19	725.07	529.69
	PSNR(dB)	15.29	18.76	19.52	20.89
	LPIPS	0.69	0.46	0.33	0.24
Global	SSIM(%)	52.32	70.67	73.24	77.89
	MSE	1531.3	652.99	534.19	456.59
	PSNR(dB)	16.52	19.98	20.85	21.59
	LPIPS	0.39	0.3	0.2	0.15

Our model equipped with a local fusion module, outperformed both Cycle-GAN and GAN-without local fusion module models in synthesizing images with superior local and global quality. Various examples of image synthesized results by different models were shown in Fig. 3.

CBCT   CT   sCT(cycleGAN)   sCT(wo-LFM)   sCT(propsed method)

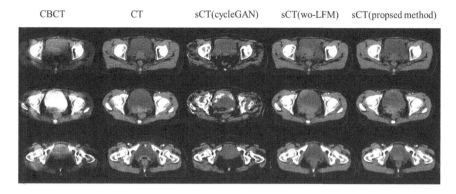

Fig. 3. Comparison of visualization results of several models. A patient image is shown in each row. The first and second columns are the original CBCT image and the CT image obtained by registration, and the other columns are the model synthetic results (sCT).

To better evaluate the quality of synthetic regions, we cropped local regions for comparison. Figure 4 shows the synthetic results of different models on local regions. It can be observed that the model with local fusion modules performs better in terms of tissue contours and image quality.

CBCT   CT   sCT(cycleGAN)sCT(wo-LFM)   sCT(propsed method)

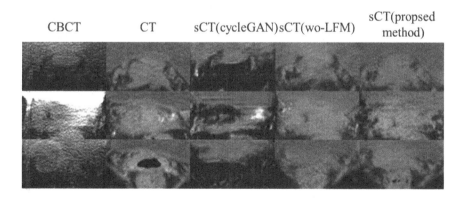

Fig. 4. Comparison of synthetic results of different models on target regions. Each row depicts a patient image, with the first and second columns showing the original CBCT image and the registered CT image, respectively, while the remaining columns show the synthetic results (sCT) of different models.

5   Conclusion

Cervical cancer poses a great threat to women. However, CBCT imaging has poor quality in the treatment of cervical cancer, and existing image quality enhancement models have not well balanced image restoration of the region of interest. To address this problem, we propose an image synthesis model with a local fusion module based on GAN. Extensive experiments show that the proposed model can not only improve the overall image quality, but also perform well in enhancing the quality of the region of interest. The proposed model makes the image structure clearer and assists doctors in adjusting the radiation dose and range in a timely manner, promoting the development of adaptive radiation therapy for cervical cancer.

Acknowledgments. This work was supported by the National Natural Science Foundation of China under grant No. 81871424, the Natural Science Foundation of Shaanxi Province No. 2020JZ-28, No. 2023-JC-QN-0704 and Key Research and development plan of Shaanxi Province No. 2021SF-192.

References

1. Chen, L., Liang, X., Shen, C., Jiang, S., Wang, J.: Synthetic CT generation from CBCT images via deep learning. Med. Phys. **47**(3), 1115–1125 (2020)
2. Choi, K., Lim, J.S., Kim, S.: StatNet: statistical image restoration for low-dose CT using deep learning. IEEE J. Sel. Top. Sig. Process. **14**(6), 1137–1150 (2020)
3. Demir, U., Unal, G.: Patch-based image inpainting with generative adversarial networks. arXiv preprint arXiv:1803.07422 (2018)
4. Gao, L., et al.: Streaking artifact reduction for CBCT-based synthetic CT generation in adaptive radiotherapy. Med. Phys. **50**(2), 879–893 (2023)
5. Higaki, T., Nakamura, Y., Tatsugami, F., Nakaura, T., Awai, K.: Improvement of image quality at CT and MRI using deep learning. Jpn. J. Radiol. **37**, 73–80 (2019)
6. Kida, S., et al.: Cone beam computed tomography image quality improvement using a deep convolutional neural network. Cureus **10**(4), e2548 (2018)
7. Lei, Y., et al.: CBCT-based synthetic MRI generation for CBCT-guided adaptive radiotherapy. In: Nguyen, D., Xing, L., Jiang, S. (eds.) AIRT 2019. LNCS, vol. 11850, pp. 154–161. Springer, Cham (2019). https://doi.org/10.1007/978-3-030-32486-5_19
8. Liang, X., et al.: Generating synthesized computed tomography (CT) from cone-beam computed tomography (CBCT) using cycleGAN for adaptive radiation therapy. Phys. Med. Biol. **64**(12), 125002 (2019)
9. Liu, Y., et al.: CBCT-based synthetic CT generation using deep-attention cycle-GAN for pancreatic adaptive radiotherapy. Med. Phys. **47**(6), 2472–2483 (2020)
10. Ma, X., et al.: Efficacy and safety of adjuvant chemotherapy for locally advanced cervical cancer: a systematic review and meta-analysis. Crit. Rev. Oncol. Hematol. **184**, 103953 (2023)
11. Mundt, A.J., et al.: Intensity-modulated whole pelvic radiotherapy in women with gynecologic malignancies. Int. J. Radiat. Oncol. Biol. Phys. **52**(5), 1330–1337 (2002)

12. Oldham, M., et al.: Cone-beam-CT guided radiation therapy: a model for on-line application. Radiother. Oncol. **75**(3), 271-E1 (2005)
13. Rossi, M., Cerveri, P.: Comparison of supervised and unsupervised approaches for the generation of synthetic CT from cone-beam CT. Diagnostics **11**(8), 1435 (2021)
14. Sun, H., et al.: Imaging study of pseudo-CT synthesized from cone-beam CT based on 3D cycleGAN in radiotherapy. Front. Oncol. **11**, 603844 (2021)
15. Xie, S., Liang, Y., Yang, T., Song, Z.: Contextual loss based artifact removal method on CBCT image. J. Appl. Clin. Med. Phys. **21**(12), 166–177 (2020)
16. Yang, H.K., Liang, K.C., Kang, K.J., Xing, Y.X.: Slice-wise reconstruction for low-dose cone-beam CT using a deep residual convolutional neural network. Nucl. Sci. Tech. **30**(4), 59 (2019)
17. Zhang, Y., et al.: Improving CBCT quality to CT level using deep learning with generative adversarial network. Med. Phys. **48**(6), 2816–2826 (2021)
18. Zhao, J., et al.: MV CBCT-based synthetic CT generation using a deep learning method for rectal cancer adaptive radiotherapy. Front. Oncol. **11**, 655325 (2021)

Causality-Inspired Source-Free Domain Adaptation for Medical Image Classification

Suo Qiu[✉]

School of Electronic Information and Electrical Engineering,
Shanghai Jiao Tong University, Shanghai, China
jiaodaqiusuo@sjtu.edu.cn

Abstract. Domain adaptation can mitigate the domain shift problem of deep learning methods in medical image classification but is restricted in medical applications due to limited access to sensitive medical images and scarce labels caused by strong requirement of expertise in medicine. Source-free domain adaptation (SFDA) only requires unlabeled target domain data and a pre-trained source domain model without access to source domain data but usually suffers from degraded performance. In this paper, we propose a causality-inspired source-free domain adaptation (CSDA) approach for medical image classification to address this problem from a causal view. We achieve causal graph modeling for medical imaging and unify two causal modules with SFDA to alleviate the interference caused by acquisition process and prototypes of the pretrained source model during self-training for adaptation. Specifically, data augmentation and source-prototype based causal interventions are achieved to remove the confounding of irrelevant background and bias of pre-trained source models. Experiments on public dataset like Pulmonary Chest X-Ray Abnormalities show that CSDA outperforms existing domain adaptation approaches and state-of-the-art source-free methods on unlabeled target data for medical image classification.

Keywords: Causality · Source-free domain adaptation · Medical image classification

1 Introduction

Medical image classification is of fundamental interest in clinical treatment and medical research. Recently, deep learning strategies have been widely used in medical image analysis and have achieved promising results by employing sophisticated models like convolutional neural networks (CNNs). However, these models usually suffer from significantly degraded performance when the training and testing data are from different distributions. Such difference in distributions, also known as domain shift [1], can stem from various organs, modalities, acquisition devices, background noise and resolutions for medical imaging. Thus, the deployment of deep learning models is restricted for medical image classification, especially when medical images are with scarce labeling information.

H. Lu et al. (Eds.): ICIG 2023, LNCS 14359, pp. 68–80, 2023.
https://doi.org/10.1007/978-3-031-46317-4_7

Domain adaptation approaches have been widely considered in recent studies [2] to solve the problem of domain shift. Particularly, unsupervised deep domain adaptation has attracted most attention [3] in medical image analysis, due to the fact that medical data in target domain is mostly unlabeled. Deep learning methods usually require full access of the source domain data with corresponding labels. However, in real-world clinical applications, private medical dataset is usually inaccessible due to privacy and security concerns. Recently, source-free domain adaptation (SFDA) methods are developed for tasks of medical image segmentation [4] and classification [5]. It tackles the problem of significantly degraded performance without violating the privacy policies.

Despite their success, a series of problems arise since no source data is available. For example, source knowledge adaptation is hard to realize because pseudo labels generated by the pre-trained source model are noisy [6], and image-level alignment between source and target domains becomes impossible. From causal perspective, these problems are caused by the confounders in acquiring medical images (e.g., imaging modalities, scanning protocols and acquisition devices) and are exaggerated by the bias induced by the source prototype without accessing the source data [7]. To this end, it is promising to incorporate causal intervention on these confounders in data pre-processing and learning strategies to further facilitate SFDA for medical image classification.

In this paper, we propose a causality-inspired source-free domain adaptation (CSDA) approach for medical image classification. Our CSDA model consists of a regularized self-training module, a contrastive feature alignment module, and two causal modules to alleviate different kinds of biases that may degrade model performance. Specifically, the following two modules are included in causal view:

- Data-augmentation-based intervention is applied to learn domain-invariant features and remove the confounding of shifted correlation across relevant region of interest and irrelevant background.
- Source-prototype-based intervention is applied to remove the confounding of pre-trained source prototype' impact on target domain data.

The contributions of this paper are summarized as below.

- We propose a novel causality-inspired domain adaptation approach for medical image classification that incorporates causality-based data augmentation and source prototype adaptation into source free domain adaptation.
- We build a causal graph to model the generation process of medical images and develop data-augmentation-based and source-prototype-based causal modules to alleviate the interference caused by acquisition process and prototypes of the pre-trained source model.
- We design a regularized self-training that unifies the causal modules to remove the confounding of irrelevant background and bias of pre-trained source model for enhanced classification accuracy.

To our best knowledge, CSDA is the first attempt that unifies the causal inference and source-free domain adaptations for medical image classification in practical domain adaptation tasks. CSDA successfully alleviates the interference caused by the lack of labeled source data in SFDA from the causal view. Evaluations on public dataset Pulmonary Chest X-Ray Abnormalities [8,9] demonstrate that CSDA has superior classification ability in domain adaptation tasks.

2   Related Work

2.1   Source-Free Domain Adaptation

Deep domain adaptation methods have been widely used to alleviate the "domain shift" problem [10–13], which is very common in the field of medical image analysis especially in multi-center studies. However, general domain adaptation methods usually require full access to source and target data, which may violate privacy protection or security issues [2]. Source-free domain adaptation has been proposed recently to address this problem. Yang et al. [4] explicitly leverage batch normalization (BN) statistics and generate source-like images via a two-stage coarse-to-fine learning strategy. Tian et al. [14] construct pseudo source samples directly from the provided target samples under the guidance of sample transport rule. Kurmi et al. [15] synthesize images by training a GAN-based generator, instead of using target domain data to approximate the source domain. Qiu et al. [16] generate feature prototypes for source categories leveraging a conditional generator and produce pseudo-labels.

2.2   Causality in Machine Learning

Castro et al. [7] argue that causal inference can be used to alleviate some of the most prominent problems in medical imaging. Causality aware methods can achieve better explanatory capability and model robustness [17]. Wang et al. [18] use a normalizing flow-based causal model to harmonize heterogeneous medical data. In domain adaptation area, learning causalities and mitigating confounding require causal intervention in many situations [19]. By fixing the variable-of-interest in a causal relationship and incorporating other variables, a model will learn causalities from intervened samples. Zhang et al. [20] analyze the domain shifts experienced in clinical deployment from a causal perspective. Ouyang et al. [21] apply a causal analysis in segmentation of medical images under domain shift. They intervene upon the images by data-augmentation such that spurious correlations are removed. Valvano et al. [22] design a method to reuse adversarial mask discriminators to tackle domain shift under a causal lens.

3   Method

3.1   Overview

As illustrated in Fig. 1, we propose a novel framework of CSDA that leverages causality-inspired data augmentation and prototype adaptation to enhance medical image classification tasks under source-free domain adaptation (SFDA) scenarios. Existing SFDA methods [6,21] utilizes pre-trained source model rather

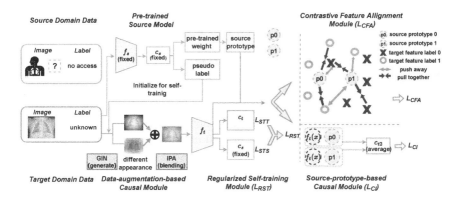

Fig. 1. The overall architecture of the proposed CSDA approach. CSDA consists of source domain part (arrows in blue) with all fixed parameters and trainable target domain part (arrows in purple) associated with four modules. Both images and labels of source domain data are inaccessible. Only the pre-trained source model and unlabeled target domain data is being used for adaptation. (Color figure online)

than source data for adaptation but ignore the interference caused by the domain shift between source and target data and the domain bias induced by the pre-trained model. To this end, we propose a novel causality-inspired domain adaptation (CSDA) approach to remove such interference during SFDA. As elaborated in Sect. 3.2, we first establish a causal graph that models the generation process of medical images by considering the causal effects of both source data and source prototype. Subsequently, we develop two causal modules to remove the confounders in SFDA via causal intervention. The data-augmentation-based causal module eliminates domain-dependent acquisition process, whereas the source-prototype-based causal module cuts off the interference in predicting target data. Furthermore, we develop a regularized self-training module that incorporates causality-based modules into contrastive feature alignment for CSDA, as described in Sect. 3.3.

We commence by presenting an overview of the proposed CSDA approach, comprising four modules. The parameters of these modules are initialized with the pre-trained source model, and a final classifier is trained to maintain robust classification capabilities within the target domain.

Data-Augmentation-Based Causal Module. Data-augmentation-based causal module applies basic augmentation and causal intervention, including global intensity non-linear augmentation (GIN) and interventional pseudo-correlation augmentation (IPA) [21], to generate diverse images. Applying on target data training process, this module ensures consistent predictions and makes our model less affected by domain shift correlations by eliminating related confounding.

Source-Prototype-Based Causal Module. In source-prototype-based causal module, backdoor adjustment is utilized to eliminate the impact of source domain prototypes on target data, as elaborated in Sect. 3.3. The Loss L_{CI} is adopted to train the source-prototype-based module in end-to-end learning.

Constrastive Feature Alignment Module. Contrastive feature alignment module aligns the features of the target data with the source prototypes by pushing apart from features of different categories and pulling together with features of the same category. Since we do not have no access to source domain data, we use weights from the pre-trained source model classifier to represent the source prototype feature. The loss of training the domain feature alignment module is formulated as follows [6].

$$L_{CFA} = -\sum_{i=1}^{n}\sum_{c=1}^{C} \log \frac{\exp(F_{xi}^{t} \cdot X_{p}^{c})}{\sum\limits_{j=1}^{C} \exp(F_{xi}^{t} \cdot X_{p}^{j})} \cdot \beta, \left|co_{xi}^{t} - 0.5\right| \geq \tau - 0.5 \ \& \ p_{xi}^{t} = c, \quad (1)$$

where $co_{xi}^{t} = \sigma\left(c_t\left(f_t\left(x_i\right)\right)\right), p_{xi}^{t} = argmax\left(c_t\left(f_t\left(x_i\right)\right)\right), F_{xi}^{t} = f_t\left(x_i\right)$. The target domain data is denoted by x_i, while the number of target images included in the training process is denoted by n. The feature extractor of the target model is denoted by f_t, whereas the classifier of the target model is denoted by c_t. The prediction confidence of the target model is denoted by co_{xi}^{t}, and the corresponding pseudo label assigned by the target model is denoted by p_{xi}^{t}. The feature of x_i obtained after feature extraction is denoted by F_{xi}^{t}. The source prototypes of category c are represented by normalized weight vectors of pre-trained source model classifier, denoted by X_{p}^{c}. In our framework, there are a total of C categories in the training data, and in our binary classification task, $C = 2$. The coefficient to control the order of L_{CFA} magnitude is denoted by β. The given threshold for the selection of relatively reliable pseudo labels of high confidence is denoted by τ, which is a value between 0.5 and 1.

Regularized Self-training Module. The regularized self-training module generates the loss of pseudo labels L_{RST} under the supervision of the target and source classifiers respectively, which will be further formulated in Sect. 3.3.

Combining the loss functions of source-prototype-based module, contrastive feature alignment module and regularized self-training module, the overall loss of CSDA for an end-to-end training is formulated as:

$$L_{TOTAL} = \alpha \cdot L_{CI} + L_{RST} + \lambda_1 \cdot L_{CFA}. \quad (2)$$

3.2   Causal Representation Learning for Medical Images

In this section, we will introduce our method based on causal inference and propose to alleviate the impact of non-causal factors. We leverage Structural Causal Model (SCM) to analyze the data generation process of medical image and reconstruct the causal graph for source-free domain adaptation. We take two steps to mitigate the interference caused by the two non-causal factors: acquisition process and prototypes obtained in source domain training process. First, the confounder of acquisition process is successfully removed by applying the global intensity non-linear augmentation (GIN) and interventional pseudo-correlation augmentation (IPA) [21] in data-augmentation-based module. Second, backdoor adjustment is used to eliminate the impact of source domain prototypes in source-prototype-based module.

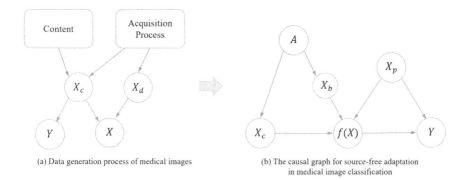

(a) Data generation process of medical images

(b) The causal graph for source-free adaptation in medical image classification

Fig. 2. (a) The data generation process of medical images. (b) The causal graph for source-free domain adaptation based on (a).

Causal Graph Modeling for Medical Images. Figure 2(a) shows the causal graph that describes the data generation process of medical images. The nodes in the graph correspond to the variables and the directed edge means that two variables have causal effects. Intuitively, the medical image X can be decoupled into two parts: content feature X_c and domain feature X_d. Only X_c yeilds the true label Y and this is the real causal relationship that model should learn. Considering the specificity of medical images, the process that X_d is generated by acquisition process A can be reflected in two aspects: (1) In the medical imaging, the most notorious source of domain shift is the differences in image acquisition (i.e. imaging modalities, scanning protocols and device manufacturers). (2) The severity of the disease may vary due to the selection bias in different regions. For example, the Montgomery dataset contains chest X-ray imagery with less severe manifestations of tuberculosis, while the Chinese dataset comprises mostly of chest X-ray imagery with more severe manifestations of tuberculosis. Note that the sampling schedule is different for the two datasets.

Under the guidance of the data generation process for medical image, we adapt this causal graph to source-free domain adaptation situation. As shown in Fig. 2(b), the acquisition process A yeilds X_c and X_b, in which X_c means the region of object-of-interest and X_b is the region of a potentially correlated unlabeled object in the background. Both X_c and X_b can lead to extracted features $f(x)$. In the source-free domain adaptation scenarios, the prototypes X_p obtained by source pre-trained model become another confounder to interfere with the prediction process in target domain. Therefore, to extract the causal feature X_c, the interference of A and X_p should be alleviated completely.

Data-Augmentation-Based Causal Module. To eliminate domain-dependent acquisition process A which controls image appearances, we implement
data-augmentation-based causal module. We first use global intensity non-linear
augmentation (GIN) to transform the target domain images into various intensities and textures. Then we apply interventional pseudo-correlation augmentation
(IPA) to blend two GIN-augmented images generated from the same image in a
spatially variable manner. The blending operation will randomize and add disturbance to eliminate potential correlation [21]. In this way, data augmented by
GIN-IPA process enables our network to be relatively immune to the shifted-
correlation effect. The extracted features $f(x)$ are now less affected by A and
able to generate more accurate and consistent results predictions through a well-
trained classifier. This intervention can be formally formulated as:

$$p\left(Y|do\left(X_c = x_c\right)\right) = \sum_{x_b} p\left(Y|X_c = x_c, X_b = x_b\right) p\left(X_b = x_b\right)$$

$$= \sum_{x_b} \sum_{a} p\left(Y|X_c = x_c, X_b = x_b\right) p\left(x_b|A = a\right) p(A = a), \quad (3)$$

where $p(A = a)$ is a prior of possible acquisition processes. By applying the
intervention $do\left(X_c = x_c\right)$, this operation resamples the appearances of correlated
objects Xb and removes $A \to X_c$ in the causal graph.

Source-Prototype-Based Causal Module. In the source-free domain adaptation, the prototypes generated in source domain training process may effect the
prediction process in target domain. Therefore, we leverage backdoor adjustment
to cut out the causal effects between X_p and $f(x)$ in our source-prototype-based
causal module. We suppose that different prototypes are generated equally and
assume a uniform prototype prior as $P(X_p = x_p) = 1/C$. Following [23], the
backdoor adjustment is formulated as:

$$P(Y|do(f(x))) = \sum_{c=1}^{C} P(Y|f(x), X_p = x_p^c) P(X_p = x_p^c) = \frac{1}{C} \sum_{c=1}^{C} P(Y|f(x), X_p = x_p^c)$$

$$(4)$$

where $P(Y|f(x), X_p = x_p^c)$ is the conditional probability of Y when X_p is set to
x_p^c. In our framework, we represent the conditional probability with the output
of classifiers that take the concatenation of $f_t(x)$ and x_p^c as inputs.

3.3   Regularized Self-Training Module

Initial pseudo labels are generated by pre-trained source model directly applying
on target data. We further elaborate on the overall loss for self-training in (2).
Based on the initial labels, we process the following self-training. The baseline
self-training method for the i-th sample can be formulated as:

$$L_{STT}^i = \begin{cases} L_{CE}\left(co_{xi}^t, p_{xi}^t\right), & |co_{xi}^t - 0.5| \geq \tau - 0.5 \\ 0, & |co_{xi}^t - 0.5| < \tau - 0.5 \end{cases}, \quad (5)$$

where $co_{xi}^t = \sigma\left(c_t\left(f_t\left(x_i\right)\right)\right)$, $p_{xi}^t = argmax\left(c_t\left(f_t\left(x_i\right)\right)\right)$, p_{xi}^t denotes the pseudo label assigned by target model, L_{CE} denotes the cross-entropy loss function, τ is the given threshold range from $(0.5, 1)$ for the selection of relatively reliable pseudo labels of high confidence. The loss $L_{STT} = \sum_{i=1}^{n} L_{STT}^i$.

According to Sect. 3.2, after introducing source-prototype-based causal module, we rewrite the origin L_{STT}^i loss to L_{CI}^i as follows:

$$L_{CI}^i = \begin{cases} \sum_{c=1}^{C} L_{CE}(co_{xi}^{tc}, p_{xi}^{tc}), & |co_{xi}^{tc} - 0.5| \geq \tau - 0.5 \\ 0, & |co_{xi}^{tc} - 0.5| < \tau - 0.5 \end{cases}, \qquad (6)$$

where $co_{xi}^{tc} = \sigma\left(c_t[f_t(x_i), X_p^c]\right)$, $p_{xi}^{tc} = argmax\left(c_t[f_t(x_i), X_p^c]\right)$, X_p^c denotes source prototypes of category c, $[,]$ denotes the concatenation operation of two features. Thus, the loss $L_{CI} = \sum_{i=1}^{n} L_{CI}^i$.

Baseline self-training performs well when there is little noise in those relatively reliable initial pseudo labels that satisfying the given threshold τ. However, due to domain shift, it is common that even the reliable pseudo labels have certain amount of noise among them. The baseline self-training strategy will accumulate the error and lead to self-biasing during the process of training. For binary classification tasks as our dataset, the final accuracy may drop to a nearly 50% random guessing condition. To alleviate this problem, a pseudo label loss function is adopted for regularization. Different from the baseline self-training, the regularized part of self-training is based on source model rather than target model. For the i-th sample, we have

$$L_{STS}^i = \begin{cases} L_{CE}\left(co_{xi}^{st}, p_{xi}^s\right), & |co_{xi}^s - 0.5| \geq \tau - 0.5 \\ 0, & |co_{xi}^s - 0.5| < \tau - 0.5 \end{cases}, \qquad (7)$$

where $co_{xi}^s = \sigma\left(c_s\left(f_s\left(x_i\right)\right)\right)$ $co_{xi}^{st} = \sigma\left(c_s\left(f_t\left(x_i\right)\right)\right)$, $p_{xi}^s = argmax\left(c_s\left(f_s\left(x_i\right)\right)\right)$, f_s denotes the feature extractor of source model, c_s denotes the classifier of source model, co_{xi}^s denotes the prediction confidence of source model, co_{xi}^{st} denotes the output generated by a target feature extractor and a fixed source classifier, p_{xi}^s denotes the pseudo label assigned by source model, other corresponding parameters remain the same. The loss L_{STS} is calculated as $\sum_{i=1}^{n} L_{STS}^i$.

It has been known that during early stage training, the pseudo labels generated by target model is quite noisy. By aligning higher weight to source model loss L_{STS} in the early stage of training and gradually increase the weight of target model loss L_{STT} as the training proceeds is a valid solution of the self-biasing problem [6]. So, we formulate the following loss function to guide the training, α is a coefficient designed to gradually increase from 0 to 1 in the training process:

$$L_{RST} = \begin{cases} \alpha \cdot L_{STT} + (1 - \alpha) \cdot L_{STS}, & \text{w/o causality} \\ (1 - \alpha) \cdot L_{STS}, & \text{w/ causality} \end{cases}. \qquad (8)$$

4   Experiments

4.1   Datasets and Implementation Details

The proposed method CSDA is validated on public dataset Pulmonary Chest X-Ray Abnormalities [8,9] that consists of two separate datasets acquired from the Department of Health and Human Services, Montgomery County, Maryland, USA (*MO* for short) and Shenzhen No. 3 People's Hospital in China (*SZ* for short), respectively. Both datasets contain normal and abnormal chest X-ray images with manifestations of pulmonary tuberculosis (TB). *MO* contains 138 frontal chest X-rays, where 80 are normal cases and 58 are cases with manifestations of TB. *SZ* contains 662 frontal chest X-rays, where 326 are normal cases and 336 are cases with manifestations of TB. Note that there are obvious domain shift between the two datasets since they were captured using different X-ray machines and are of different sizes.

Table 1. Classification results on public dataset Pulmonary Chest X-Ray Abnormalities. From top to bottom, compared methods are deep learning domain adaptation approaches including DAN, DANN, ADDA, MCD and state-of-the-art SFDA methods including SOTA-SFDA and NRC-SFDA.

Methods	$MO \rightarrow SZ$				$SZ \rightarrow MO$			
	ACC (%)	AUC (%)	TPR (%)	TNR (%)	ACC (%)	AUC (%)	TPR (%)	TNR (%)
DAN [10]	55.76	54.23	50.60	57.98	55.27	53.62	53.45	53.75
DANN [11]	66.47	69.81	67.26	65.64	62.32	63.97	22.41	98.84
ADDA [12]	48.04	53.39	44.34	51.84	35.51	43.64	37.93	33.75
MCD [13]	50.76	59.92	50.60	50.92	55.80	56.24	51.72	58.75
SHOT [25]	75.23	78.44	80.65	69.63	70.29	73.83	56.90	80.00
NRC [26]	59.52	60.57	60.41	58.59	61.59	69.12	34.48	81.25
CSDA	**78.10**	**81.07**	**81.55**	**74.54**	**72.46**	**75.65**	44.83	92.56

In our experiment, we adopt ENet [24] as the backbone to pre-train the source domain model. During source domain pre-training, all the images are resized into 512×512 and data augmentation strategies are employed, including random affine, random horizontal flip and random vertical flip. The training process minimizes the cross-entropy loss using Adam optimizer with the learning rate decreased by a ratio of 0.99 for every 10 epochs. The target model is trained using a combined loss of L_{RST}, L_{CFA} and L_{CI} with an extra causality-inspired data augmentation and learning rate is decayed by 0.1 for every 10 epochs.

4.2 Classification Results

We evaluate CSDA and the baselines by alternately taking *MO* and *SZ* as source and target domains. The baselines include deep learning domain adaptation approaches including DAN [10], DANN [11], ADDA [12], MCD [13] and state-of-the-art SFDA methods including SHOT-SFDA [25] and NRC-SFDA [26]. Note that there are few source-free domain adaptation methods specifically for medical image classification. We adopt accuracy (ACC), area under the receiver operating characteristic curve (AUC), true positive rate (TPR) and true negative rate (TNR) as metrics for performance evaluation.

Table 1 shows that CSDA significantly improves the domain adaptation performance across *MO* and *SZ* datasets. It outperforms traditional domain adaptation methods [10–13] even under the source-free setting by well exploring target data. CSDA is also superior to state-of-the-art DA methods through the intervention of causality-related issues that may degrade model performance in previous studies. Fig. 3 provides the t-SNE visualizations for examples from *SZ* (when transferring from *MO* to *SZ*). When using CSDA for adaptation, the features representing normal and abnormal chest X-ray images are better separated on target data domain. We further visualize in Fig. 4 the heatmaps with and without adaptation for two examples from *SZ*. After adaptation, CSDA clearly focuses more on regions of interest rather than the background mark located at the upper right corner. This fact suggests a more reliable classification result yielded by CSDA. These results demonstrate that CSDA evidently improves the source-free domain adaptation for medical image classification by considering causality in data augmentation and source prototype adaptation.

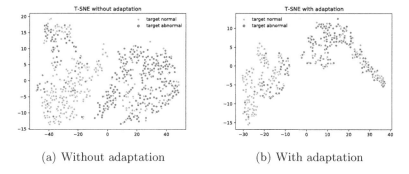

(a) Without adaptation   (b) With adaptation

Fig. 3. The t-SNE visualization of target domain features extracted by our model without and with adaptation under *MO→SZ*.

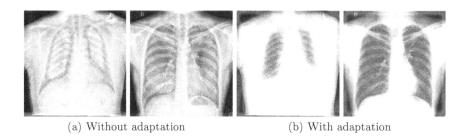

(a) Without adaptation   (b) With adaptation

Fig. 4. The heatmap visualization without and with adaptation for samples from *SZ* (left for normal and right for abnormal in (a) and (b) respectively).

Table 2. Ablation study on each component of the proposed CSDA.

L_{RST}	L_{CFA}	L_{CI}	causalaug	MO→SZ		SZ→MO	
				ACC (%)	AUC (%)	ACC (%)	AUC (%)
✔	✘	✘	✘	69.33	73.59	56.52	53.91
✔	✔	✘	✘	70.54	76.27	65.94	66.46
✔	✔	✔	✘	73.87	75.15	70.29	70.11
✔	✔	✔	✔	78.10	81.07	72.46	75.65

4.3 Ablation Study

Ablation study is performed to further validate the effectiveness of each component of CSDA. As shown in Table 2, based on regularized self-training, domain feature alignment module as well as source-prototype based and data augmentation based causality module all contribute to the performance improvement. Particularly, both causal modules significantly improve the accuracy of classification results on the basis of source-free domain adaptation module, demonstrating the effectiveness of causality interventions for confounding removal.

5   Conclusion

In this paper, we propose a novel causality-inspired domain adaptation framework for medical image classification under source-free setting. By only accessing to pre-trained source model and unlabeled target data, we take privacy protections and security issues into consideration. Our CSDA model unifies two causal modules with SFDA to alleviate the interference caused by acquisition process and prototypes of the pre-trained source model during self-training for adaptation. Specifically, data-augmentation and source-prototype based causal interventions are achieved to remove the confounding of irrelevant background and bias of pre-trained source models. Our model is validated on public dataset Pulmonary Chest X-Ray Abnormalities and outperforms tradition domain adaptation approaches and source-free methods. Results illustrate our model's valid classification ability in domain adaptation tasks for medical images.

References

1. Quinonero-Candela, J., Sugiyama, M., Schwaighofer, A., Lawrence, N.D.: Dataset Shift in Machine Learning. MIT Press, Cambridge (2008)
2. Guan, H., Liu, M.: Domain adaptation for medical image analysis: a survey. IEEE Trans. Biomed. Eng. **69**(3), 1173–1185 (2021)
3. Wilson, G., Cook, D.J.: A survey of unsupervised deep domain adaptation. ACM Trans. Intell. Syst. Technol. (TIST) **11**(5), 1–46 (2020)
4. Yang, C., Guo, X., Chen, Z., Yuan, Y.: Source free domain adaptation for medical image segmentation with Fourier style mining. Med. Image Anal. **79**, 102457 (2022)

5. Zhou, C., Zhang, W., Chen, H., Chen, L.: Domain adaptation for medical image classification without source data. In: 2022 IEEE International Conference on Bioinformatics and Biomedicine (BIBM), pp. 2224–2230. IEEE (2022)

6. Liu, Y., Chen, Y., Dai, W., Gou, M., Huang, C.T., Xiong, H.: Source-free domain adaptation with contrastive domain alignment and self-supervised exploration for face anti-spoofing. In: Avidan, S., Brostow, G., Cissé, M., Farinella, G.M., Hassner, T. (eds.) ECCV 2022, Part XII. LNCS, vol. 13672, pp. 511–528. Springer, Cham (2022). https://doi.org/10.1007/978-3-031-19775-8_30

7. Castro, D.C., Walker, I., Glocker, B.: Causality matters in medical imaging. Nat. Commun. **11**(1), 3673 (2020)

8. Candemir, S., et al.: Lung segmentation in chest radiographs using anatomical atlases with nonrigid registration. IEEE Trans. Med. Imaging **33**(2), 577–590 (2013)

9. Jaeger, S., et al.: Automatic tuberculosis screening using chest radiographs. IEEE Trans. Med. Imaging **33**(2), 233–245 (2013)

10. Long, M., Cao, Y., Wang, J., Jordan, M.: Learning transferable features with deep adaptation networks. In: International Conference on Machine Learning, pp. 97–105. PMLR (2015)

11. Ganin, Y., Lempitsky, V.: Unsupervised domain adaptation by backpropagation. In: International Conference on Machine Learning, pp. 1180–1189. PMLR (2015)

12. Tzeng, E., Hoffman, J., Saenko, K., Darrell, T.: Adversarial discriminative domain adaptation. In: Proceedings of the IEEE Conference on Computer Vision and Pattern Recognition, pp. 7167–7176 (2017)

13. Saito, K., Watanabe, K., Ushiku, Y., Harada, T.: Maximum classifier discrepancy for unsupervised domain adaptation. In: Proceedings of the IEEE Conference on Computer Vision and Pattern Recognition, pp. 3723–3732 (2018)

14. Tian, Q., Ma, C., Zhang, F.Y., Peng, S., Xue, H.: Source-free unsupervised domain adaptation with sample transport learning. J. Comput. Sci. Technol. **36**(3), 606–616 (2021)

15. Kurmi, V.K., Subramanian, V.K., Namboodiri, V.P.: Domain impression: a source data free domain adaptation method. In: Proceedings of the IEEE/CVF Winter Conference on Applications of Computer Vision, pp. 615–625 (2021)

16. Qiu, Z., et al.: Source-free domain adaptation via avatar prototype generation and adaptation. arXiv preprint arXiv:2106.15326 (2021)

17. Yu, K., et al.: Causality-based feature selection: methods and evaluations. ACM Comput. Surv. (CSUR) **53**(5), 1–36 (2020)

18. Wang, R., Chaudhari, P., Davatzikos, C.: Harmonization with flow-based causal inference. In: de Bruijne, M., et al. (eds.) MICCAI 2021, Part III. LNCS, vol. 12903, pp. 181–190. Springer, Cham (2021). https://doi.org/10.1007/978-3-030-87199-4_17

19. Pearl, J.: Causality. Cambridge University Press, New York (2009)

20. Zhang, Y., et al.: Causaladv: adversarial robustness through the lens of causality. arXiv preprint arXiv:2106.06196 (2021)

21. Ouyang, C., et al.: Causality-inspired single-source domain generalization for medical image segmentation. IEEE Trans. Med. Imaging **42**, 1095–1106 (2022)

22. Valvano, G., Leo, A., Tsaftaris, S.A.: Re-using adversarial mask discriminators for test-time training under distribution shifts. arXiv preprint arXiv:2108.11926 (2021)

23. Pearl, J.: Causal inference. Causality: objectives and assessment, pp. 39–58 (2010)

24. Li, J., et al.: Deep learning with convex probe endobronchial ultrasound multi-modal imaging: a validated tool for automated intrathoracic lymph nodes diagnosis. Endosc. Ultrasound **10**(5), 361 (2021)
25. Liang, J., Hu, D., Feng, J.: Do we really need to access the source data? Source hypothesis transfer for unsupervised domain adaptation. In: International Conference on Machine Learning, pp. 6028–6039. PMLR (2020)
26. Yang, S., van de Weijer, J., Herranz, L., Jui, S., et al.: Exploiting the intrinsic neighborhood structure for source-free domain adaptation. Adv. Neural. Inf. Process. Syst. **34**, 29393–29405 (2021)

Pixel-Correlation-Based Scar Screening in Hypertrophic Myocardium

Bin Lu[1], Cailing Pu[2,3], Chengjin Yu[2(✉)], Yuanting Yan[1], Hongjie Hu[3], and Huafeng Liu[2]

[1] College of Computer Science and Technology, Anhui University, Hefei, China
[2] College of Optical Science and Engineering, Zhejiang University, Hangzhou, China
chengjin.yuahu@gmail.com
[3] Department of Radiology, Sir Run Run Shaw Hospital, Hangzhou, China

Abstract. The screening of myocardial scars in patients with hypertrophic cardiomyopathy(HCM) using cine magnetic resonance images(Cine-MRI) is critical in clinical practice. To tackle this task, we propose a locally-attentive pixel-correlation learning model. In such model, we first divide the image into different patches. Then, we employ a multi-layer perceptron to extract the scar features by modelling the correlation between pixels within each patch, as well as the correlation between pixels of different patches. To further enhance representation capability of the learned features, we incorporates an intra-attention mechanism to focus the pixels within the patches, and an inter-attention mechanism to focus the different the patches. After that, these learned deep features are combined with radiomics features and integrated into a linear classifier. The validation on clinical data shows powerful performance of our model, with accuracy, sensitivity, specificity, positive predictive value(PPV), negative predictive value(NPV), f1-score and area under the curve (AUC) values of 82.9%, 98.4%, 50.0%, 82.7%, 85.7%, 89.9% and 0.867, respectively. Our method has yielded promising experimental results, indicating that it can serve as a valuable tool for clinical physicians to screen scars.

Keywords: hypertrophic cardiomyopathy · scar screening · pixel-correlation · deep learning · radiomics

1 Introduce

Accurate screening for myocardial scars in a non-invasive paradigm is crucial in managing patients with hypertrophic cardiomyopathy(HCM). HCM is a genetic heart disease with an incidence rate ranging from 1/500 to 1/200 and up to 50% heritability [1–3]. Myocardial scars, which result from abnormal thickening of the heart muscle, possibly triggering ventricular fibrillation and increasing the risk of myocardial ischemia, are a leading cause of sudden cardiac death(SCD) in HCM patients [4]. Thus, precise screening is essential for preventing complications and improving patient outcomes.

ⓒ The Author(s), under exclusive license to Springer Nature Switzerland AG 2023
H. Lu et al. (Eds.): ICIG 2023, LNCS 14359, pp. 81–92, 2023.
https://doi.org/10.1007/978-3-031-46317-4_8

Late gadolinium enhancement cardiac magnetic resonance (LGE-CMR) imaging is a valuable technique for identifying areas of myocardial scarring in patients with hypertrophic cardiomyopathy (HCM) [5,6]. LGE-CMR has been shown to be superior to other non-invasive imaging techniques in detecting the extent and distribution of myocardial fibrosis [7,8]. However, the use of LGE-CMR has been controversial due to concerns about potential adverse effects of gadolinium-based contrast agents (GBCA), especially their nephrotoxicity, which can limit the use of LGE-CMR in certain patients [9,10]. Studies have found that LGE-CMR diagnosed hypertrophic cardiomyopathy (HCM) in up to 80% of cases, with the risk of sudden cardiac death (SCD) significantly related to both the presence and extent of LGE [11]. Therefore, excessive LGE-CMR may increase the risk of SCD. Using LGE to monitor myocardial scarring in HCM patients is not appropriate in clinical practice. As a result, it is crucial to develop a non-invasive, non-nephrotoxic, and straightforward method for scar screening.

Although Cine-MRI is a safe imaging technique, it cannot directly visualize scars. The development of deep learning models to extract scars from Cine-MRI has garnered significant attention from studies. However, there are still challenges in extracting scars. (1) Clinical studies have shown that the geometric structure and appearance of myocardial scars are unrelated, which means that the learning efficiency of common CNN networks may be limited as they focus more on learning global and local structural information of the targets [12,13]. (2) Additional prior information is required, for example, the work [14] needs to incorporate motion features of the myocardium to extract scars, but extracting motion features itself is a challenging task. (3) Research based on radiomics has achieved promising results, but the accuracy remains suboptimal with insufficient generalization ability [15,16].

In this work, we propose a locally-attentive pixel-correlation learning(LApcl) to learn the intricate local scar textures and deep pixel features of the myocardium [17,18]. Initially, we partition the image into distinct patches. Next, we apply a multi-layer perceptron to extract scar features, which learns the inter-patch pixel correlation and intra-patch pixel correlation through linear mapping between MLPs. To intensify the pixel emphasis within and between patches, we also introduce an attention mechanism, enabling the model to focus on the pixels related to the scars. The advantages of our method include: (1) Providing a non-invasive and non-nephrotoxic screening method for non-gadolinium-enhancing myocardial scar in clinical practice; (2) Introducing a local block correlation learning network based on Cine-MRI, which efficiently learns myocardial scar features [19]; (3) Combining imaging omics features, we achieve high performance in terms of seven metric indices.

2   Method

The workflow of our scar screening method is presented in Fig. 1. Firstly, we apply a fully convolutional network (FCN) model to segment myocardial tissue. Next, We utilized the locally-attentive pixel-correlation learning(LApcl) model to extract local texture information and deep pixel information of the myocardium. Additionally, we utilize radiomics to extract a maximal amount of information from CineMRI images, encompassing first-order, second-order, and higher-order statistical information, to derive texture, shape, and other features. Lastly, we integrate both types of features, and feed them into a linear classifier for scar prediction.

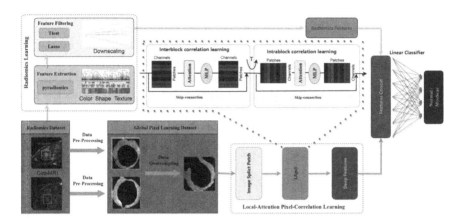

Fig. 1. The images are first processed with myocardial segmentation to obtain the regions of interest. The model is divided into two paths, with the upper path learning radiomics features, and the lower path learning deep features. In the deep network, the data is first oversampled, and then learned through our locally-attentive pixel-correlation learning network, which applies different weights to the block-wise pixels when exploring intra- and inter-block relationships.

2.1 Data Preparation

Data preprocessing is divided into three steps: (1) A fully convolutional network is employed to segment the myocardial structure. (2) Each instance $X^{H \times W \times C}$ is normalized into 12 layers, and croped and resized into $X^{100 \times 100 \times 12}$. (3) Multiply the segmented mask with the original image to obtain myocardial pixel features.

$$\widetilde{X}^{100 \times 100 \times 12} = \text{Cut}(X^{H \times W \times C} \times \gamma(X^{H \times W \times C})) \tag{1}$$

where H, W and C represent the width, height, and channels, respectively. γ represents the segmentation model, and Cut represents the cropping and resizing of the regions of interest.

To address the issue of imbalanced data between scarred and normal instances, we performed data oversampling on the scarred tissue data using the Feature SMOTE sampling technique [21]. This involved encoding the image $X_i^{100 \times 100 \times 12}$ to extract encoded features $I_{i,j}^{+}$, which were then oversampled using

SMOTE oversampling along with the corresponding labels. The oversampled encoded features were then decoded to obtain the oversampled image X_*.

$$I_i = \delta^+(Decoder(X_i^+)) \tag{2}$$

$$I_j = \delta^+(Decoder(X_j^+)) \tag{3}$$

$$I^* = I_i + rand(0,1) \times \mid I^i - I^j \mid \tag{4}$$

$$X^* = \text{Encoder}(\delta^-(I^*)) \tag{5}$$

where X_i^+ and X_j^+ represent the i-th and j-th images in the scar category, respectively. δ^+ represents the reduction of a two-dimensional feature matrix to a one-dimensional feature array, and δ^- represents the expansion of a one-dimensional feature array to a two-dimensional feature matrix. rand(0,1) represents the generation of random numbers between 0 and 1. I^* represents the oversampled synthesized feature array. Decoder represents the encoder, and Encoder represents the decoder. X^* represents the synthesized new image.

2.2   Pxiel-Correlation-Learning

As shown in Fig. 1, the model takes multiple image patch blocks as input. In particular, the model can be divided into two main modules: inter-block attention learning and intra-block attention learning. Both modules are enhanced by attention mechanisms and utilize high-dimensional mappings through linear dense layers to achieve correlation learning inter-block and intra-block, leading to the extraction of complex deep features $\mathbf{T}^d$ of myocardial scars.

The image $\mathbf{X}$ is partitioned into patches using a dedicated convolutional block that serves as a patch slicer, generating a tensor $\mathbf{F}_i, i \in N$, where N is the number of patches. The model architecture involves an attention layer, obtaining pixel weighting and scar block focusing. Next, the structure of the MLP involves layer normalization, followed by linear high-dimensional mapping, passed through the gelu activation function, and then follow a linear dimensionality reduction mapping. Feature fusion between the two is achieved through reference connections to prevent gradient disappearance in the model.

Finally, the extracted features $\mathbf{T}^d$ are fed into a fully connected layer with a softmax layer for output $\mathbf{P}^d$.

$$\mathbf{Z}_i = \widetilde{F}_i + \mathbf{W}_1(Gelu(\mathbf{W}_0 \times \Gamma(\widetilde{F}_i))) \tag{6}$$

$$\mathbf{P}^d = \mu(\mathbf{W}_2 \times (\mathbf{Z}_0, \mathbf{Z}_1, ...) + \mathbf{W}_3(Gelu(\mathbf{W}_4 \times \Gamma(\mathbf{Z}_0, \mathbf{Z}_1, ...)))) \tag{7}$$

where $\mathbf{W}$ represents the weight matrix between dense linear layers. Γ refers to the attention mechanism. μ denotes the softmax activation function.

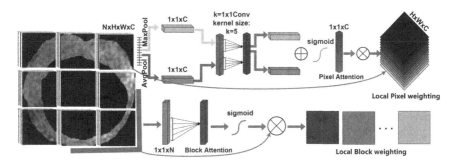

Fig. 2. The upper part of the model is an attention module=within local block. It first focuses on the spatial information of the local block, followed by attention on the channels within the same block, ultimately producing an attention feature. The lower part of the model utilizes an attention mechanism between the local blocks, similar to the channel framework in the upper part. This enables the model to focus on multiple local blocks and obtain the attention feature. These two attention modules are connected in series within the overall architecture of the model.

2.3   Scar Attention Mechanism

The flowchart of the attention module is shown in the Fig. 2. The existence of attention mechanisms allows our models to better understand our local blocks [22,23]. Under the action of attention mechanisms, different parts of the image can be assigned different weights. Our attention mechanisms are mainly divided into two modules.

(1) Attention mechanism module within local block, the intra-block attention mechanism is designed to enable local scar texture focus within each block. The local block F_i is first pooled, generating two tensors that are then combined, convolved, and passed through a sigmoid activation to create the spatial attention feature M_s. By multiplying M_s with the input feature map F, weighted by sparse pixels, the resulting feature tensor $\widetilde{M_s}$ is obtained.

$$\mathbf{M}_s = \mathbf{F}_i \times \mathbf{M}_s = \mathbf{F}_i \times \sigma(\mathrm{Conv}_k^{1\times1}(\mathrm{AvgPool}(\mathbf{F}_i)) + \mathrm{Conv}_k^{1\times1}(\mathrm{MaxPool}(\mathbf{F}_i)))$$

(8)

where σ represents the sigmoid activation function. $\mathrm{Conv}^{1\times1}$ refers to tensor one dimensional convolution, k for convolution kernel size. MaxPool and AvgPool represent max-pooling and average-pooling, respectively.

(2) Attention mechanism module between local blocks, the inter-block attention mechanism is intended to facilitate scar information focus across different blocks. We further process the feature tensor by applying average-pooling, and then input the tensor into a 1×1 convolution. Finally, the sigmoid activation is applied to generate the attention feature M_b between local blocks. Ultimately, the weighted feature of the local blocks is obtained by multiplying M_b with the input local blocks.

$$\widetilde{\mathbf{F}} = \mathbf{F_i} \times \sigma(\mathrm{Conv}^{1\times1}(\mathrm{AvgPool}(\mathbf{F})))$$

(9)

where σ represents the sigmoid activation function. $\mathrm{Conv}^{1\times1}$ refers to tensor one dimensional convolution. AvgPool represent average-pooling.

2.4 Radiomics-Learning

Radiomics can extract relevant features such as first-order statistics, texture analysis, and shape analysis [15]. Cine-MRI contains valuable information that is not visible to the naked eye but can be captured using mathematical methods. Radiomics can accomplish these tasks and focus on texture and shape features that cannot be captured by our DeepMLP.

We meticulously adhered to the workflow of radiomics and utilized the pyradiomics open-source Python software package to extract radiomics features from medical imaging. The software incorporates various filters for feature extraction, encompassing shape, color, and texture. We inputted CineMRI end-systolic images along with the corresponding segmented masks into pyradiomics and derived 1415 valid features. Upon screening these features through Ttest and Lasso, we successfully identified 26 valid features $\mathbf{T}^r$.

Finally, we fed the 26 valid features through the fully connected layer to obtain the grade of myocardial scarring, denoted as $\mathbf{P}^r$.

2.5 Feature Merging

Combining deep learning and radiomics through feature fusion can lead to more precise and reliable image analysis and diagnosis. Our proposed method uses LApcl to learn patterns of myocardial scarring, while radiomics extracts features such as texture, shape, and color to aid in diagnosis and treatment. Feature fusion integrates these features to provide a more comprehensive view of the myocardium and improve the accuracy of scar screening. We merge the features $\mathbf{T}^d$ extracted from the global pixel contrastive learning module with the features $\mathbf{T}^r$ selected by radiomics. The concatenated features $\mathbf{T}$ will then be embedded into a linear classifier to obtain the final prediction scores $\mathbf{P}$ of the model, completing the screening for myocardial scar.

$$\mathbf{P} = \mu(\mathbf{W}_5 \times \mathrm{Gelu}([\mathbf{T}^d, \mathbf{T}^r])) \tag{10}$$

where $\mathbf{W}_5$ is the weight matrix of the linear classifier. μ is the softmax activation function.

3 Results

3.1 Experiment Setting

Our experimental data was collected from Sir Run Run Shaw Hospital. The dataset comprised 273 HCM patients, 214 scar patients, and 59 patients with no scars. The patients provided written consent, which was approved by the institutional review board, allowing their medical information to be used for research

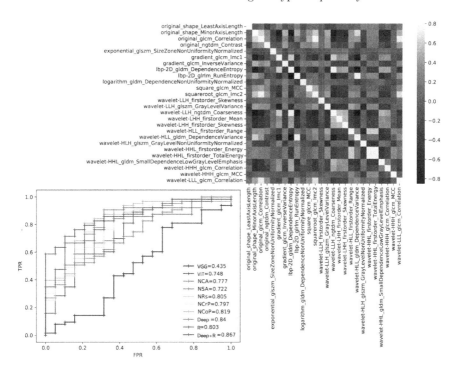

Fig. 3. The upper section of the figure presents the 26 radiomics features selected for scar screening and their corresponding heatmaps depicting the inter-feature correlations. These features were carefully chosen through a rigorous screening process, and the heatmaps provide valuable insights into their relationships and potential interplay. The lower section of the figure shows the ROC curves of all the experiments conducted, providing a comprehensive evaluation of the performance of each model and highlighting the superiority of our proposed model in detecting myocardial scars.

purposes. Data were collected from short-axis images during end-diastole. We trained and tested the model using 5-fold cross-validation, with the data randomly split into subsets. The evaluation metrics included **Accuracy**, **Sensitivity**, **Specificity**, **Positive Predictive Value(PPV)**, **Negative Predictive Value(NPV)**, **F1-Score**, and **Area Under Curve (AUC)**. The reported results are the average of five experiments.

3.2 Results of the Scar Screening

We first employ a FCN model to segment the myocardial region from cine-MRI, capturing all pixel information and reflecting accurate morphology. We designed different cutting windows for various data shapes, retaining only the myocardial contour, while using a FCN model for segmentation. The model achieved excellent results, with MeanIOU and Dice scores of 0.842 and 0.914, respectively. Figure 4 visualizes the efficacy of the FCN model in myocardial segmen-

Table 1. We showcase the performance metrics of our method, comparative experiments, and ablation experiments. The "backbone" refers to the framework used for each model, with the best metric results highlighted in bold within each column.

Method	Accuracy↑	Specificity↑	Sensitivity↑	PPV↑	NPV↑	F1-Score↑	AUC↑	Backbone
Zhou [13]	–	**78.23%**	83.33%	–	–	–	0.840	CNN
Mancio [16]	–	62.0%	91%	–	–	–	0.830	CNN
Fahmy/R [12]	62.0%	36.0%	91.0%	–	–	–	0.750	CNN
Fahmy/DL [12]	64.0%	42.0%	92.0%	–	–	–	0.760	CNN
Fahmy/DL+R [12]	65.0%	40.0%	91.0%	–	–	–	0.810	CNN
VGG16	51.2%	50.8%	52.26%	78.0%	24.4%	61.5%	0.435	CNN
ViT	62.2%	60.3%	68.4%	86.4%	34.2%	71.0%	0.747	Transformer
NCA	57.3%	84.2%	49.2%	91.2%	33.3%	63.9%	0.777	MLP
NSA	76.8%	10.5%	96.8%	78.2%	50.0%	86.5%	0.722	MLP
NRs	81.7%	36.8%	95.2%	83.3%	70.0%	88.9%	0.805	MLP
NCrP	65.8%	63.5%	73.6%	88.9%	37.8%	74.1%	0.797	MLP
NCoP	79.2%	79.3%	78.9%	92.6%	53.5%	85.5%	0.819	MLP
NFCNs	67.7%	58.3%	83.5%	87.7%	49.6%	75.9%	0.752	MLP
Our/DeepMLP	**0.841%**	**57.9%**	92.1%	**87.9%**	68.8%	89.9%	0.840	MLP
Our/Radiomics	79.3%	47.0%	96.8%	80.3%	66.7%	87.8%	0.803	–
Ours	82.9%	50.0%	**98.4%**	82.7%	**85.7%**	**89.9%**	**0.867**	MLP

tation. Our experimental results for scar screening are shown in Table 1. Our LApcl model achieved accuracy, sensitivity, specificity, ppv, npv, f1-socre and area under the curve (AUC) value were 84.1%, 92.1%, 57.9%, 87.9%, 68.8%, 89.9% and 0.840, respectively. The results validated the effectiveness of pixel-correlated learning in the myocardial scar screening for HCM. Our radiomics model achieved accuracy, sensitivity, specificity, ppv, npv, f1-socre and area under the curve (AUC) value were 79.3%, 96.8%, 47.0%, 80.3%, 66.7%, 87.8% and 0.803, respectively. The feasibility of radiomics features was confirmed by the results, which are further supported by the corresponding heatmap showcasing 26 features extracted by the model. Our final model achieved accuracy, sensitivity, specificity, ppv, npv, f1-socre and area under the curve (AUC) value were 82.9%, 98.4%, 50.0%, 82.7%, 85.7%, 89.9% and 0.867, respectively. The ROC curve and the corresponding heatmap of the results is shown in the Fig. 3. The 26 chosen features are visualized using a correlation heatmap, highlighting a significant inclination towards myocardial texture orientation. Our experimental results demonstrate a effectiveness of our LApcl network and radiomics features analysis on scar screening. Moreover, integrating these two approaches significantly enhances the accuracy of scar screening. This indicates that the use of feature merging methods can more comprehensively and accurately depict the characteristics of myocardial scar.

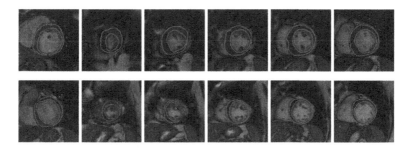

Fig. 4. Visualization of segmentation results of FCN in the Shaw data test set. The red area represents the predicted myocardial contour by the model. The blue area represents the myocardial contour annotated in ground truth. (Color figure online)

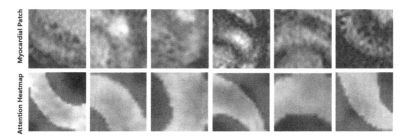

Fig. 5. By utilizing GRAD-CAM to generate feature heatmaps that visualize local spatial attention within blocks, and combining them with LGE images of myocardial patches, it has been demonstrated that the attention mechanism is selectively focused on the scar tissue.

3.3   Comparison Experiments and Ablation Experiments

Results of Comparison Experiments. As shown in Table 1, we compare our method with previous researches on myocardial scar screening. Compared to three existing methods (Zhou, Mancio, Fahmy), our method can achieve higher accuracy, sensitivity and AUC. Then, we also compare our method with VGG16 and ViT models. The VGG16 is established based on the CNN, which may pay more attention to the cardiac geometric morphology, resulting in slightly inferior results. Conversely, the ViT model, which leveraged correlation learning between pixel blocks, exhibited better performance than VGG in scar screening. Different from those compared methods, our approach can fully explore the correlation between pixels and patches, so as achieving the best results in most metric indices. Those comparative analysis underscores the superior performance of our approach.

Figure 6 illustrates the visualization results of T-SNE of features extracted from different models [24]. The figure offers a visual representation of the correlation between features and myocardial scar screening. When features are highly correlated with myocardial scar screening, the two features displayed in the figure

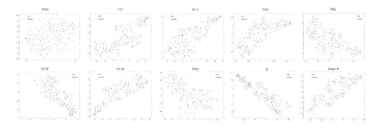

Fig. 6. T-SNE dimensionality reduction visualization was performed on the features extracted from both the comparative and ablation experiments, providing an intuitive representation of the features' ability to screen for scars.

will exhibit robust classification. Notably, the figure highlights the inferiority of the VGG and ViT models' features compared to our model.

Results of Ablation Experiments. To validate the efficacy of each component in our model, we designed five ablation experiments. (1) We removed the inter-block attention mechanism and retained all other structures in the model(NSA). (2) We removed the intra-block attention mechanism and retained all other structures in the model (NCA). (3) We ablated the residual mechanism in the LApcl model, resulting in a shallow model (NRs). (4) We ablated the inter-block-correlation learning and intra-block-correlation learning in LApcl model to verify their effectiveness in feature pattern extraction for scar screening (NCrP and NCoP, respectively). (5) We removed myocardial oversampling from the FCN(NFCNs) to assess the screening's impact on neighboring myocardial pixels. As shown in Fig. 3 presents the results of the ablation experiments. Notably, all ablation experiments produced scores lower than our full model's, underscoring the indispensable role of each block in the scar screening process. The Table 1 reveals that incorporating the FCN module considerably improves scar screening. Moreover, by imposing constraints on the FCN's accuracy, we observed a robust correlation between the FCN's precision and the accuracy of our scar screening method. Moreover, the feature heatmap generated by GRAD-CAM [25], as depicted in Fig. 5, effectively demonstrates the attention mechanism's ability to selectively focus on the scar tissue.

4   Conclusion

In this work, to address the screening task of gadolinium-free contrast agent for hypertrophic myocardial scar, we proposed a local correlation learning network based on Cine-MRI. We devised a morphological-free network model that integrates pixel attention weighting and local pixel-correlation learning for scar screening. Our study findings reveal that our model surpasses existing techniques, underscoring the feasibility of myocardial scar screening without factoring in morphology for detecting scarring in hypertrophic cardiomyopathy. The amalgamation of deep features and radiomics features can additionally elevate the precision of scar screening. This implies that the fusion of deep features and radiomics features can impart a more comprehensive representation of scar information.

References

1. Maron, B.J., Casey, S.A., Poliac, L.C., Gohman, T.E., Almquist, A.K., Aeppli, D.M.: Clinical course of hypertrophic cardiomyopathy in a regional united states cohort. JAMA **281**(7), 650–655 (1999)
2. Semsarian, C., Ingles, J., Maron, M.S., Maron, B.J.: New perspectives on the prevalence of hypertrophic cardiomyopathy. J. Am. Coll. Cardiol. **65**(12), 1249–1254 (2015)
3. Maron, B.J., et al.: Hypertrophic cardiomyopathy in children, adolescents, and young adults associated with low cardiovascular mortality with contemporary management strategies. Circulation **133**(1), 62–73 (2016)
4. Monserrat, L., Elliott, P.M., Gimeno, J.R., Sharma, S., Penas-Lado, M., McKenna, W.J.: Non-sustained ventricular tachycardia in hypertrophic cardiomyopathy: an independent marker of sudden death risk in young patients. J. Am. Coll. Cardiol. **42**(5), 873–879 (2003)
5. Bruder, O., et al.: Myocardial scar visualized by cardiovascular magnetic resonance imaging predicts major adverse events in patients with hypertrophic cardiomyopathy. J. Am. Coll. Cardiol. **56**(11), 875–887 (2010)
6. Kim, R.J., et al.: Relationship of MRI delayed contrast enhancement to irreversible injury, infarct age, and contractile function. Circulation **100**(19), 1992–2002 (1999)
7. Gulati, A., et al.: Association of fibrosis with mortality and sudden cardiac death in patients with nonischemic dilated cardiomyopathy. JAMA **309**(9), 896–908 (2013)
8. Schelbert, E.B., Fonarow, G.C., Bonow, R.O., Butler, J., Gheorghiade, M.: Therapeutic targets in heart failure: refocusing on the myocardial interstitium. J. Am. Coll. Cardiol. **63**(21), 2188–2198 (2014)
9. Kanda, T., et al.: Gadolinium-based contrast agent accumulates in the brain even in subjects without severe renal dysfunction: evaluation of autopsy brain specimens with inductively coupled plasma mass spectroscopy. Radiology **276**(1), 228–232 (2015)
10. Ramalho, J., et al.: High signal intensity in Globus pallidus and dentate nucleus on unenhanced t1-weighted MR images: evaluation of two linear gadolinium-based contrast agents. Radiology **276**(3), 836–844 (2015)
11. Chan, R.H., et al.: Prognostic value of quantitative contrast-enhanced cardiovascular magnetic resonance for the evaluation of sudden death risk in patients with hypertrophic cardiomyopathy. Circulation **130**(6), 484–495 (2014)
12. Fahmy, A.S., Rowin, E.J., Arafati, A., Al-Otaibi, T., Maron, M.S., Nezafat, R.: Radiomics and deep learning for myocardial scar screening in hypertrophic cardiomyopathy. J. Cardiovasc. Magn. Reson. **24**(1), 1–12 (2022)
13. Zhou, H., et al.: Deep learning algorithm to improve hypertrophic cardiomyopathy mutation prediction using cardiac cine images. Eur. Radiol. **31**, 3931–3940 (2021)
14. Xu, C., et al.: Direct delineation of myocardial infarction without contrast agents using a joint motion feature learning architecture. Med. Image Anal. **50**, 82–94 (2018)

15. Lambin, P., et al.: Radiomics: the bridge between medical imaging and personalized medicine. Nat. Rev. Clin. Oncol. **14**(12), 749–762 (2017)
16. Mancio, J., et al.: Machine learning phenotyping of scarred myocardium from cine in hypertrophic cardiomyopathy. Eur. Heart J.-Cardiovasc. Imaging **23**(4), 532–542 (2022)
17. He, K., Zhang, X., Ren, S., Sun, J.: Deep residual learning for image recognition. In: Proceedings of the IEEE Conference on Computer Vision and Pattern Recognition, pp. 770–778 (2016)
18. Touvron, H., et al.: Resmlp: feedforward networks for image classification with data-efficient training. IEEE Trans. Pattern Anal. Mach. Intell. **45**, 5314–5321 (2022)
19. Long, J., Shelhamer, E., Darrell, T.: Fully convolutional networks for semantic segmentation. In: Proceedings of the IEEE Conference on Computer Vision and Pattern Recognition, pp. 3431–3440 (2015)
20. Zhou, L., Zhang, Z., Chen, Y.C., Zhao, Z.Y., Yin, X.D., Jiang, H.B.: A deep learning-based radiomics model for differentiating benign and malignant renal tumors. Transl. Oncol. **12**(2), 292–300 (2019)
21. Zhang, H., Huang, L., Wu, C.Q., Li, Z.: An effective convolutional neural network based on smote and gaussian mixture model for intrusion detection in imbalanced dataset. Comput. Netw. **177**, 107315 (2020)
22. Wang, Q., Wu, B., Zhu, P., Li, P., Zuo, W., Hu, Q.: ECA-Net: efficient channel attention for deep convolutional neural networks. In: Proceedings of the IEEE/CVF Conference on Computer Vision and Pattern Recognition, pp. 11534–11542 (2020)
23. Woo, S., Park, J., Lee, J.Y., Kweon, I.S.: Cbam: Convolutional block attention module. In: Proceedings of the European Conference on Computer Vision (ECCV), pp. 3–19 (2018). shenme
24. Van der Maaten, L., Hinton, G.: Visualizing data using t-SNE. J. Mach. Learn. Res. **9**(11) (2008)
25. Selvaraju, R.R., Cogswell, M., Das, A., Vedantam, R., Parikh, D., Batra, D.: Grad-cam: visual explanations from deep networks via gradient-based localization. In: Proceedings of the IEEE International Conference on Computer Vision (ICCV) (2017)

Dictionary Matching Based 2D Thin Slice Generalized Slice-dithered Enhanced Resolution (gSlider) Variable Flip Angle T_1 Mapping

Yuting Chen📷, Huafeng Liu, and Huihui Ye(✉) 📷

State Key Laboratory of Extreme Photonics and Instrumentation, College of Optical Science and Engineering, Zhejiang University, Hangzhou 310027, China
yehuihui@zju.edu.cn

Abstract. The accurate estimation of the T_1 parameter plays an important role in many fields such as the diagnosis of neurological disorders in clinical practice and dynamic contrast-enhanced studies of tissue perfusion. Many T_1 mapping methods suffer from long scan times and inaccurate estimation. As a rapid T_1 mapping method, 2D variable flip angle (VFA) enables high temporal and in-plane spatial resolution acquisition. However, 2D VFA is sensitive to inhomogeneity of RF transmit field (B_1^+) and RF slice profile imperfection, which introduces excitation flip angle variations both in-plane and slice direction, and leads to T_1 estimation bias. In this paper, we developed a dictionary matching based 2D VFA T_1 mapping method by Bloch equation simulation incorporating B_1^+ correction and slice profile correction to reduce the T_1 estimation bias. To further improve the quality of thin slice T_1 mapping, a slab RF encoding generalized slice-dithered enhanced resolution (gSlider) acquisition was introduced and combined with 2D VFA and dictionary matching. The 1.5 mm thin slice T_1 mappings showed high accuracy as compared with the inverse recovery (IR) gold standard method in phantom experiments, and show similar image quality as 3 mm thick result in in-vivo experiments.

Keywords: T_1 Mapping · Variable Flip Angle · Dictionary Matching · gSlider

1 Introduction

Compared with conventional contrast-weighted MRI, quantitative MRI (qMRI) can extract characteristics from MR images and generate quantitative maps of specific tissue parameters with high repeatability and comparability. The longitudinal relaxation time (T_1) is one of the most frequently mapped parameters in qMRI, which directly reflects the biophysical properties of tissues at a molecular level [1]. Quantitative T_1 mapping can help to non-invasively characterize and discriminate biological tissues and has many clinical applications, particularly in the treatment of some neurological disorders such as multiple sclerosis and Parkinson's disease [2, 3].

Numerous T_1 mapping methods have been developed to calculate the T_1 values. However, the majority of these methods require a long scan time and result in inaccurate

© The Author(s), under exclusive license to Springer Nature Switzerland AG 2023
H. Lu et al. (Eds.): ICIG 2023, LNCS 14359, pp. 93–105, 2023.
https://doi.org/10.1007/978-3-031-46317-4_9

T_1 mapping, making clinical application challenging. Variable flip angle (VFA) is a fast T_1 mapping method, which is widely used in basic and clinical research for its high time efficiency and large spatial coverage [4]. There are two kinds of acquisition modes in VFA: 2D and 3D. 2D VFA permits high temporal resolution for a small number of slices acquisition, while the through-plane resolution is limited by the signal to noise ratio (SNR). In contrast, 3D VFA has the SNR benefit from larger slice coverage while leading to long acquisition time and thus low temporal resolution. Additionally, the 3D acquisition is sensitive to motion, which induces phase error and degrades image quality. Therefore, 3D VFA does not apply to some fields where T_1 changes rapidly such as T_1-based thermometry and dynamic contrast enhanced (DCE) T_1 mapping when rapid dynamic T_1 mapping is needed [5].

The knowledge of the distributions of the flip angles is necessary to accurately calculate T_1 values in 2D VFA method. All measurements will undoubtedly experience radio frequency (RF) transmit field (B_1^+) inhomogeneities, which will change the in-plane excitation flip angles [8–10]. Additionally, the actual slice profile deviates from the ideal rectangular slice profile due to imperfect RF induced slice profile imperfection which can be treated as through-plane B_1^+ variation [6, 7]. To reduce the bias of T_1 estimation in 2D VFA, several methods based on Bloch equation simulation have been studied [8–11]. However, in most of these methods, the computational efficiency is not high and B_1^+ correction needs to be performed in advance. Some methods only consider one of the factors that cause estimation bias of T_1. In Magnetic resonance fingerprinting, dictionary matching is applied to identify signal parameters simultaneously [12], which may be combined with VFA to simultaneously correct the factors that affect the accuracy of T_1 estimate.

Apart from these factors needed to be corrected to provide accurate T_1 mapping, 2D VFA suffers from low SNR when thin slice thickness is used. As a novel slab RF encoding acquisition, generalized slice-dithered enhanced resolution (gSlider) [13] acquires multiple thick slice images to reconstruct high SNR thin slice images, which has been validated to achieve submillimeter isotropic resolution T_2 mappings [14].

In this work, we propose a dictionary matching based 2D VFA T_1 mapping method. Rather than using the conventional nonlinear least square (NLS) method to calculate T_1 values, dictionaries constructed based on Bloch equation simulation which integrates slice profile imperfection and B_1^+ inhomogeneity effects are designed to match signals from 2D VFA. We further extend 2D VFA with gSlider RF encoding and adapt dictionary matching to achieve high SNR thin slice T_1 mapping. Experiments in phantom and in vivo were conducted, which show the accuracy of T_1 estimation and validate the feasibility and utility of the proposed methods.

2   Method

2.1   2D VFA Method

In 2D VFA, T_1 is estimated from a series of gradient recall echo (GRE) image sets acquired over a range of different flip angles with a constant TR [15–17]. Neglecting T_2^* effects, the measured steady-state signal intensity S is a function of the flip angle α, the longitudinal relaxation time T_1, the repetition time TR, and the equilibrium magnetization M_0:

$$S = M_0 \frac{\left[1 - \exp(-\text{TR}/T_1)\right] \sin \alpha}{1 - \exp(-\text{TR}/T_1) \cos \alpha}. \tag{1}$$

Equation (1) can be written in a linear form $y = kx + b$:

$$\frac{S}{\sin \alpha} = \exp(-\text{TR}/T_1) \frac{S}{\tan \alpha} + M_0\left[1 - \exp(-\text{TR}/T_1)\right]. \tag{2}$$

Therefore, T_1 and M_0 can be calculated from the slope $k = \exp(-\text{TR}/T_1)$ and the intercept $b = M_0\left[1 - \exp(-\text{TR}/T_1)\right]$ as:

$$T_1 = -\text{TR}/\ln(k) \tag{3}$$

$$M_0 = b/\left[1 - \exp(-\text{TR}/T_1)\right] \tag{4}$$

As the slope is determined by steady-state signals with at least two flip angles, T_1 estimation is sensitive to flip angles.

2.2   Slice Profile and B_1^+ Correction

Excitation slice profile imperfections caused by truncation and apodization of RF pulses (Fig. 1) and B_1^+ inhomogeneity (Fig. 4(a)) occurring from tissue dielectric effects will result in variations of flip angles [10]. Thus, slice profiles and B_1^+ inhomogeneity correction should be performed in 2D VFA to correct the nominal flip angles, thereby reducing T_1 estimation errors.

Some VFA correction studies have been studied by simplifying the steady-state signal formula and using a correction factor to acquire corrected flip angles [16–18]. But the approximate conditions for formula derivation are strict. To further reduce the bias of T_1 estimation, we propose a method based on Bloch equation to simulate the effect of both slice profile imperfection and B_1^+ inhomogeneity on acquired signals in real acquisition situations.

To simulate the actual excitation slice profiles, the free procession Bloch equation,

$$d\vec{M}/dt = \vec{M} \times \gamma\vec{B}, \tag{5}$$

is used to simulate the response of the magnetization vector $M_x(z)$, $M_y(z)$, and $M_z(z)$ generated by the Hanning windowed sinc RF pulse and slice select gradient simulated according to scan parameters. The actual flip angle distribution is calculated by:

$$\alpha(z) = \tan^{-1}\left(\sqrt{M_x(z)^2 + M_y(z)^2}/M_z(z)\right). \tag{6}$$

Since a flip angle varies across the whole slice width, (1) should be modified to include the phase of transverse magnetization [16]:

$$\Phi(z) = \tan^{-1}\left(M_y(z)/M_x(z)\right) \tag{7}$$

Therefore, the measured single slice signal $\tilde{S}$ is the integral of (1) over slice thickness and can be converted to a discrete summation along the slice position:

$$\tilde{S} = M_0 \sum_{n=1}^{N} \left[\frac{(1 - \exp(-TR/T_1)) \sin(\alpha(n))}{1 - \exp(-TR/T_1) \cos(\alpha(n))} e^{i\Phi(n)} \right] \Delta z \qquad (8)$$

where Δz is the interval between adjacent samples, N is the number of discrete samples and n is the index of discrete samples.

Simulated flip angle distribution

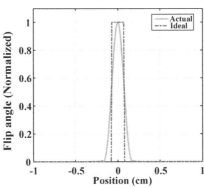

Fig. 1. Normalized actual and ideal flip angles distribution along slice position simulated with a duration time of 2 ms and time bandwidth product (TBWP) of 2.7 RF pulse at $TR = 194$ ms and $T_1 = 1000$ ms.

To simplify the B_1^+ correction, the low resolution B_1^+ maps are premeasured and calculated based on turbo-FLASH B_1^+ mapping method [19] and then interpolated and used voxel-wise. As the correction factor of nominal flip angles, the B_1^+ value at position r is defined as:

$$B_1^+(r) = \alpha_{corr}/\alpha_{norm} = \cos^{-1}(SS \ Pr \ e(r)/PD(r))/\alpha_{norm} \qquad (9)$$

where α_{corr} is the flip angle after B_1^+ correction, α_{norm} is a nominal flip angle, SS- Pre(r) is a slice-selective preconditioning RF pulse image, and PD(r) is a proton density image.

To sum up, the nominal flip angles can be corrected by both slice profile simulations based on Bloch equation according to Eq. (5)–(7) and B_1^+ maps according to Eq. (9). Then the simulated signals are generated to construct dictionaries that are matched with the collected signals, see Sect. 2.3 for details.

2.3 Dictionary Matching

In the conventional 2D VFA method, T_1 mapping is acquired by performing NLS fitting according to Eq. (2), which is linearized by multiplying a weighting factor to signal model as analyzed before. However, the weighting factor is variable for different flip angle sets causing a suboptimal fit to the measured signal. The excitation slice profile imperfections and B_1^+ inhomogeneity can also lead to variations of actually excited flip angles and thus reduce the accuracy of T_1 estimation. Additionally, it is not efficient to calculate T_1 values by NLS.

We proposed a dictionary matching based 2D VFA T_1 mapping method by Bloch equation stimulation to correct slice profile imperfections and B_1^+ inhomogeneity simultaneously. The dictionary simulates signal evolutions according to Eq. (8) with different combinations of T_1 series and flip angles, which is constructed based on the VFA signal model. Specifically, the range of T_1 is set between 100 and 5000 ms (with an increment of 20 ms below a T_1 of 2000 ms, an increment of 100 ms between a T_1 of 2000 ms and 3000 ms, and an increment of 200 ms above). The TR and nominal flip angles are obtained according to the applied sequence parameters. Slice profile correction is then conducted based on Bloch equation simulation to correct the nominal flip angles and acquire the simulated actual flip angles as described in Sect. 2.3. B_1^+ inhomogeneity is also considered during dictionary design to further correct the simulated actual flip angles. According to Eq. (9), a series of dictionaries about different B_1^+ values including the range between 10% and 200% with an increment of 1% are generated as correction coefficients of nominal flip angles to simulate B_1^+ variation in-plane direction. Finally, the simulated actual flip angles after slice profile correction, TR, and T_1 series are used to construct dictionaries about different B_1^+ values by Eq. (8).

After dictionaries are constructed, choose the corresponding dictionary according to the B_1^+ maps acquired by turbo-FLASH based sequence [19]. Compare dictionary entries with acquired signal evolutions about flip angles to perform pattern matching and assign the T_1 value corresponding to the entry of maximum dot product as the measured properties. This process can be performed in parallel by utilizing efficient matrix operations to generate T_1 mappings.

2.4 gSlider Acquisition and Reconstruction

To enhance SNR and through-plane resolution of 2D VFA, we further combine 2D VFA with gSlider and call it 2D thin slice gSlider VFA. As a novel slab RF encoding acquisition, gSlider is already applied in diffusion imaging to achieve fast high SNR and high isotropic resolution diffusion imaging [13, 20–23].

gSlider encodes volumes similar to Hardamard encoding by designing a series of highly independent RF-encoding basis. Slice-phase dithering is used to modulate the thin slice of a slab with a π phase, which efficiently distributes RF energy of each excitation pulse to real and imaginary components [13]. In this work, based on IDEA sequence development platform from Siemens, we implemented four gSlider RF pulses into the conventional GRE sequence. Each gSlider RF pulse is constructed by adding four consecutive sinc RF pulses corresponding to four thin slices. In every gSlider pulse, one of the four sinc pulses is set with a π phase offset as is shown in Fig. 2. Mix signals from four thin slices are generated after the excitation of gSlider pulses. To obtain high resolution thin slice signals from the mixed signals, Tikhonov regularization reconstruction is performed based on a forward model,

$$X = \left(A^T A + \lambda I\right)^{-1} A^T Y \tag{10}$$

where Y is the concatenation of the acquired RF-encoded slab signals in coding order, X is the corresponding high resolution thin slice reconstruction signals, A is the RF-encoding matrix describing the forward model containing slab excitation profiles simulated by Bloch equation, λ is a Tikhonov regularization parameter, and I is the identity matrix. With this reconstruction, thin slice signal is slice profile corrected inherently. However, the 2D thin slice VFA is still sensitive to B_1^+ inhomogeneity that leads to T_1 estimation errors, dictionary matching is performed to improve the accuracy of T_1 mapping. The dictionary matching steps for 2D thin slice gSlider VFA T_1 mapping are as follows:

1. Set T_1 value range and step size as in Sect. 2.3 to generate T_1 series.
2. Get the nominal flip angles and TR according to the applied sequence parameters.
3. Calculate simulated actual flip angles based on the four gSlider RF pulses and Bloch equation to correct the nominal flip angles and perform slice profile correction.
4. Set the value range of B_1^+ as in Sect. 2.3 to further correct the simulated flip angles.
5. Generate simulated mixed signals to construct dictionaries about B_1^+ values by Eq. (8), which include parameters of the T_1 series, TR, and the simulated flip angles of the four gSlider RF pulses.
6. Reconstruct the simulated mixed signals by Tikhonov regularization to construct 2D thin slice dictionaries about different B_1^+ values.
7. Choose the corresponding dictionary according to the B_1^+ maps acquired by turbo-FLASH based sequence.
8. Reconstruct the acquired signals by Tikhonov regularization and match them with the 2D thin slice dictionaries to get T_1 mappings.

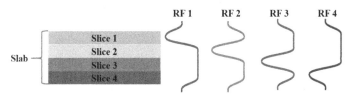

Fig. 2. In gSlider, n (four in this case) RF-encoding pulses with a π phase modulation are designed to excite each slab and modulate one of the slices in each excitation.

3 Experiments and Results

3.1 Phantom Experiments

A homemade tube agar phantom with 12 regions of interest (ROI) was scanned by 2D GRE sequence to evaluate the T_1 mapping accuracy of 2D VFA T_1 mapping. The parameters of 2D GRE sequence were as follows: TR = 194 ms, field of view (FOV) = $174 \times 192 \times 114$ mm^3, in-plane resolution = 1×1 mm^2, slice thickness = 1.5 mm. The RF pulse with a duration time of 2 ms and time bandwidth product (TBWP) of 2.7 was used to excite each slice. We changed the flip angles of the sequence to acquire a series of data with flip angles = [5°, 10°, 30°, 34°, 40°, 50°]. The acquisition time of each slice is about 15 s. The $B_1{}^+$ map was measured using Turbo-FLASH sequence with a resolution of $1.2 \times 1.2 \times 6$ mm^3 and 25% gap. T_1 mappings of 2D VFA were acquired by using the conventional NLS method. The corrected T_1 mappings were obtained by using the dictionary matching method.

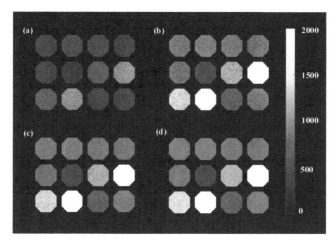

Fig. 3. Comparison of T_1 mappings using (a) 2D VFA method without slice profile correction and $B_1{}^+$ correction at $1 \times 1 \times 1.5$ mm^3, (b) dictionary matching based 2D VFA method at $1 \times 1 \times 1.5$ mm^3, (c) dictionary matching based 2D thin slice gSlider VFA method at $1 \times 1 \times 1.5$ mm^3, and (d) gold standard IR at $1 \times 1 \times 5$ mm^3. Twelve ROIs from the same slice correspond to the 12 tubes presented in the phantom.

To achieve high SNR thin slice T_1 mapping, 2D GRE gSlider sequence with four different RF-encoding pulses (duration time = 4 ms, TBWP = 4) was used to scan the same phantom and excite each slab with the slab thickness of 6 mm. A total of 19 slabs consisting of 19×4 slices were acquired and combined to reconstruct 76 thin slice images with 1.5 mm slice thickness by Tikhonov regularization. The acquisition time of each slice is about 15 s, which is approximately equal to that in 2D GRE sequence. Other parameters and $B_1{}^+$ map in 2D gSlider GRE sequence were set the same as 2D GRE sequence. Dictionaries were constructed according to these sequence parameters and matched with signals after Tikhonov regularization reconstruction to perform 2D thin slice gSlider VFA and acquire T_1 mappings after correction.

For comparison, the gold standard sequence: inverse recovery (IR) was used with TI of 200, 500, 800, 1200, 1700 ms, TR = 5000 ms, in-plane resolution = 1×1 mm^2, FOV = 150×192 mm^2, slice thickness = 5 mm. The acquisition time of a slice was about 507 s, which took more time than using 2D GRE and 2D gSlider GRE sequence. The reference T_1 mappings were obtained by the conventional NLS method based on IR signal model.

All phantom experiments were performed on a 3T Prisma scanner (Siemens Healthcare, Erlangen, Germany) with a 20-channel head-neck coil.

Twelve ROIs of T_1 mappings using different methods are shown in Fig. 3, which correspond to the 12 tubes presented in the phantom. T_1 values calculated by dictionary matching based 2D VFA (Fig. 3(b)) and 2D thin slice VFA (Fig. 3(c)) method are closer to the results of gold standard IR (Fig. 3(d)) than conventional 2D VFA method without slice profile and B_1^+ correction (Fig. 3(a)). Table 1 shows the mean values and standard deviations (STD) of T_1 in 12 ROIs adopting different methods. Using T_1 values obtained by gold standard IR as a reference, the mean error of T_1 estimation in 12 ROIs using dictionary matching based 2D VFA and 2D thin slice gSlider VFA method respectively are ~30 ms and ~32 ms, which are smaller than that using 2D VFA method (~522 ms). The STD of 12 ROIs with the same thickness (1.5 mm) demonstrates SNR enhancement with gSlider acquisition.

3.2   In Vivo Experiments

To validate the proposed method in vivo, whole brain data were acquired from a volunteer with the approval of the Institutional Review Board. The following 2D GRE sequence parameters were used: TR = 194 ms, FOV = $174 \times 192 \times 114$ mm^3, in-plane resolution = 1×1 mm^2. The slice thickness of 2D GRE sequence was set to 3 mm for better SNR. The B_1^+ map was measured using a low-resolution Turbo-FLASH sequence. A series of data with flip angles = $[10°, 20°, 30°, 34°, 40°, 50°]$ were acquired to calculate T_1 by dictionary matching method. 2D GRE gSlider sequence was used to demonstrate the improved quality of thin slice T_1 mapping. Four different RF-encoding pulses with a duration time of 4 ms and TBWP of 4 were used to excite each slab (slab thickness = 6 mm) and total 19 slabs consisting of 19×4 slices were acquired and combined to reconstruct 76 thin slice images with 1.5 mm slice thickness by Tikhonov regularization reconstruction. Except for flip angles = $[10°, 20°, 34°, 50°]$, other sequence parameters including B_1^+ map in 2D GRE gSlider were the same as those in 2D GRE sequence.

All in vivo experiments were performed on a 3T Prisma scanner (Siemens Healthcare, Erlangen, Germany) with a 20-channel head-neck-coil.

Figure 4(a) are B_1^+ maps, which show the B_1^+ inhomogeneity described in Sect. 2.2 and verify the necessity of B_1^+ correction. T_1 mappings by dictionary matching based 2D VFA (Fig. 4(b)) and 2D thin slice gSlider VFA (Fig. 4(c)) demonstrate the utility of the proposed methods in vivo. Table 2 shows the T_1 values of white matter and gray matter labeled by color rectangles in Fig. 4(b) and (c). The results obtained by the proposed dictionary matching method are very close to the gold standard IR method from reference (thickness = 5 mm) [9]. After using gSlider acquisition, the STD of T_1 mappings at the thickness of 1.5 mm are comparable with 2D VFA without gSlider at the thickness of 3 mm. Besides, the whole brain T_1 mappings estimated by dictionary matching based 2D thin slice VFA (Fig. 5(b)) show higher resolution in slice direction than that without gSlider (Fig. 5(a)).

Table 1. The T_1 mean values, standard deviations, and the mean error of twelve ROIs in phantom shown in Fig. 3.

Method	T_1(ms) ROI 1	ROI 2	ROI 3	ROI 4	ROI 5	ROI 6	ROI 7	ROI 8	ROI 9	ROI 10	ROI 11	ROI 12	Mean error
2D VFA	446 ± 35	530 ± 29	516 ± 30	429 ± 40	446 ± 39	319 ± 26	623 ± 38	1006 ± 64	695 ± 47	989 ± 57	404 ± 33	435 ± 40	522
DM based VFA[a]	860 ± 58	893 ± 58	858 ± 53	830 ± 63	824 ± 70	494 ± 41	1155 ± 74	2070 ± 150	1349 ± 98	1910 ± 135	695 ± 52	851 ± 63	30
DM based gSlider VFA[b]	861 ± 20	883 ± 21	853 ± 24	838 ± 23	830 ± 25	482 ± 16	1145 ± 30	2047 ± 30	1348 ± 38	1892 ± 53	700 ± 19	864 ± 23	32
IR	904 ± 16	890 ± 10	866 ± 11	861 ± 16	862 ± 12	471 ± 6	1189 ± 20	2130 ± 73	1401 ± 25	1941 ± 67	702 ± 7	882 ± 12	–

a. Dictionary matching based 2D VFA method
b. Dictionary matching based 2D thin slice gSlider VFA method

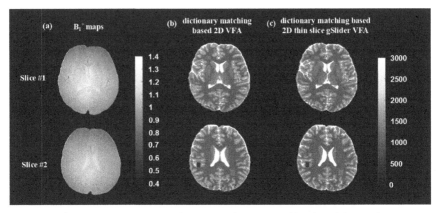

Fig. 4. (a) B_1^+ maps; T1 mappings using (b) dictionary matching based 2D VFA (at $1 \times 1 \times 3$ mm^3), and (c) dictionary matching based 2D thin slice gSlider VFA (at $1 \times 1 \times 1.5$ mm^3).

Table 2. The T_1 Mean values, standard deviations, and the mean SNR of white matter and gray matter corresponding to ROIs in Fig. 4 acquired by different methods and thicknesses.

Method		T_1 (ms)			
	Slice	White matter[c]	Gray matter[d]	Mean error of white matter	Mean error of gray matter
DM based VFA[a]	# 1	967 ± 12	1737 ± 50	72	59
	# 2	998 ± 18	1611 ± 47		
DM based gSlider VFA[b]	# 1	961 ± 17	1608 ± 27	76	23
	# 2	1013 ± 15	1577 ± 41		
IR [9]	–	911 ± 15	1615 ± 149	–	–

a. Dictionary matching based 2D VFA method
b. Dictionary matching based 2D thin slice gSlider VFA method
c. The corresponding regions of white matter in Fig. 4 are green in slice #1 and purple in slice #2
d. The corresponding regions of gray matter in Fig. 4 are blue in slice #1 and black in slice #2.

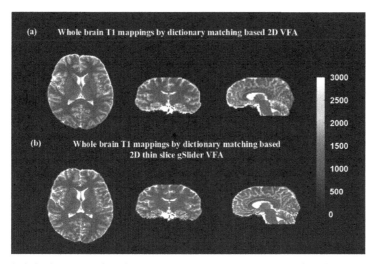

Fig. 5. Whole brain T1 mappings including sagittal and coronal plane using dictionary matching based 2D thin slice gSlider VFA at $1 \times 1 \times 1.5$ mm^3 (b) show higher SNR and resolution in slice direction than using dictionary matching based 2D VFA at $1 \times 1 \times 3$ mm^3 (a).

4 Conclusion

In this work, we developed a dictionary matching method based on Bloch equation simulation to correct slice profile imperfections and B_1^+ inhomogeneity in 2D VFA. Besides, a novel RF-encoding acquisition gSlider was combined with 2D VFA GRE sequence to enhance SNR for thin slice T_1 mapping acquisition, which was demonstrated in in-vivo experiments with 1.5 mm slice thickness. For future work, we will further optimize the flip angle arrays, investigate less than 1 mm thinner slice T1 mapping with acceleration from parallel imaging, simultaneous multi-slice, and compressed sensing, and investigate model-based reconstruction and also the deep learning based reconstruction.

Acknowledgements. This work was supported in part by the National Key Research and Development Program of China (No: 2020AAA0109502), by the National Natural Science Foundation of China (No: U1809204, 61701436), and by the Zhejiang Provincial Natural Science Foundation of China (No: LY22F010007).

Complicance with Ethical Standards. This study was approved by the Ethic Review Board of Zhejiang University College of Biomedical Engineering and Instrument Science (No. 2022-IRB-02). And all the volunteers were given informed approval before scanning.

References

1. Heule, R., Pfeuffer, J., Meyer, C.H., Bieri, O.: Simultaneous B_1 and T_1 mapping using spiral multislice variable flip angle acquisitions for whole-brain coverage in less than one minute. Magn. Reson. Med. **81**, 1876–1889 (2019)

2. Kober, T., et al.: MP2RAGE multiple sclerosis magnetic resonance imaging at 3 T. Invest. Radiol. **47**, 346–352 (2012)
3. Baudrexel, S., et al.: Quantitative mapping of T1 and T2* discloses nigral and brainstem pathology in early Parkinson's disease. Neuroimage **51**, 512–520 (2010)
4. Christensen, K.A., Grant, D.M., Schulman, E.M., Walling, C.: Optimal determination of relaxation times of fourier transform nuclear magnetic resonance. Determination of spin-lattice relaxation times in chemically polarized species. J. Phys. Chem. **78**(19), 1971–1977 (1974)
5. Hey, S., et al.: Simultaneous T1 measurements and proton resonance frequency shift based thermometry using variable flip angles. Magn. Reson. Med. **67**, 457–463 (2012)
6. Hurley, S.A., Yarnykh, V.L., Johnson, K.M., Field, A.S., Alexander, A.L., Samsonov, A.A.: Simultaneous variable flip angle–actual flip angle imaging method for improved accuracy and precision of three-dimensional T1 and B1 measurements. Magn. Reson. Med. **68**, 54–64 (2012)
7. Heule, R., Ganter, C., Bieri, O.: Variable flip angle T1 mapping in the human brain with reduced T2 sensitivity using fast radiofrequency-spoiled gradient echo imaging: VFA T1 Mapping in the Human Brain with Reduced T2 Sensitivity. Magn. Reson. Med. **75**, 1413–1422 (2016)
8. Svedin, B.T., Parker, D.L.: Technical Note: the effect of 2D excitation profile on T1 measurement accuracy using the variable flip angle method with an average flip angle assumption. Med. Phys. **44**, 5930–5937 (2017)
9. Dieringer, M.A., et al.: Rapid parametric mapping of the longitudinal relaxation time T1 using two-dimensional variable flip angle magnetic resonance imaging at 1.5 Tesla, 3 Tesla, and 7 Tesla. PLoS ONE **9**, e91318 (2014)
10. Siversson, C., et al.: Effects of B1 inhomogeneity correction for three-dimensional variable flip angle T1 measurements in hip dGEMRIC at 3 T and 1.5 T. Magn. Reson. Med. **67**, 1776–1781 (2012)
11. Boudreau, M., Tardif, C.L., Stikov, N., Sled, J.G., Lee, W., Pike, G.B.: B1 mapping for bias-correction in quantitative T1 imaging of the brain at 3T using standard pulse sequences. J. Magn. Reson. Imaging **46**, 1673–1682 (2017)
12. Ma, D., et al.: Magnetic resonance fingerprinting. Nature **495**, 187–192 (2013)
13. Setsompop, K., et al.: High-resolution in vivo diffusion imaging of the human brain with generalized slice dithered enhanced resolution: simultaneous multislice (gSlider-SMS): high-Resolution Diffusion Imaging With gSlider-SMS. Magn. Reson. Med. **79**, 141–151 (2018)
14. Cao, X., et al.: Efficient T2 mapping with blip-up/down EPI and gSlider-SMS (T2-BUDA-gSlider). Magn. Reson. Med. **86**, 2064–2075 (2021)
15. Cheng, H.-L.M., Wright, G.A.: Rapid high-resolution T1 mapping by variable flip angles: accurate and precise measurements in the presence of radiofrequency field inhomogeneity. Magn. Reson. Med. **55**, 566–574 (2006)
16. Deoni, S.C.L., Rutt, B.K., Peters, T.M.: Rapid combined T1 and T2 mapping using gradient recalled acquisition in the steady state. Magn. Reson. Med. **49**, 515–526 (2003)
17. Wang, H.Z., Riederer, S.J., Lee, J.N.: Optimizing the precision in T1 relaxation estimation using limited flip angles. Magn. Reson. Med. **5**, 399–416 (1987)
18. Preibisch, C., Deichmann, R.: Influence of RF spoiling on the stability and accuracy of T1 mapping based on spoiled FLASH with varying flip angles. Magn. Reson. Med. **61**, 125–135 (2009)
19. Chung, S., Kim, D., Breton, E., Axel, L.: Rapid B_1^+ mapping using a preconditioning RF pulse with TurboFLASH readout. Magn. Reson. Med. **64**, 439–446 (2010)
20. Liao, C., et al.: High-fidelity, high-isotropic-resolution diffusion imaging through gSlider acquisition with and T_1 corrections and integrated ΔB_0 / Rx shim array. Magn. Reson. Med. **83**, 56–67 (2020)

21. Haldar, J.P., Liu, Y., Liao, C., Fan, Q., Setsompop, K.: Fast submillimeter diffusion MRI using gSlider-SMS and SNR-enhancing joint reconstruction. Magn. Reson. Med. **84**, 762–776 (2020)
22. Liao, C., et al.: Distortion-free, high-isotropic-resolution diffusion MRI with gSlider BUDA-EPI and multicoil dynamic B_0 shimming. Magn. Reson. Med. **86**, 791–803 (2021)
23. Ramos-Llordén, G., et al.: High-fidelity, accelerated whole-brain submillimeter in vivo diffusion MRI using gSlider-spherical ridgelets (gSlider-SR). Magn. Reson. Med. **84**, 1781–1795 (2020)

Deep Low-Rank Multimodal Fusion with Inter-modal Distribution Difference Constraint for ASD Diagnosis

Minhao Xue, Li Wang[✉], Jie Shen, Kangning Wang, Wanning Wu, and Long Fu

Nanjing Tech University, Nanjing 211816, China
wangli@njtech.edu.cn

Abstract. Autism spectrum disorder (ASD) is a neurodevelopmental disorder characterized by complex symptoms, which makes ASD difficult to be identified. Combining different brain imaging modalities to provide complementary information has been extensively used in the diagnosis of brain disorders. However, it is still very difficult to fully integrate different modalities by capturing the complex connections between different modalities. To solve this problem, we propose a deep low-rank multimodal fusion (DLMF) network that takes into account distribution discrepancy between different modalities. This network aims to learn the complex connections between rest-state functional magnetic resonance imaging (rs-fMRI) and structural magnetic resonance imaging (sMRI) in order to effectively perform multimodal identification of Autism Spectrum Disorder (ASD). Firstly, two different networks are used to extract the features that represent complex information in the rs-fMRI and sMRI data. Then, a measurement function is proposed to quantify distribution discrepancy between different modalities. This measurement function is then incorporated into the loss function of our low-rank multimodal fusion network.

Therefore, our method can reduce the distribution discrepancy between different modalities through joint learning from rs-fMRI and sMRI data. The classifier in our approach adopts Support Vector Machines (SVM). The proposed network was trained with the new loss function using an end-to-end training approach. We verify the effectiveness of our method on a publicly available multimodal dataset: ABIDE database. Experimental results show that our methods are superior to several of the most advanced ASD diagnostic methods currently available.

Keywords: Autism Spectrum Disorder · Low-rank Multimodal Fusion · distribution discrepancy

1 Introduction

Autism Spectrum Disorder (ASD) is a progressive disease that leads to deficiencies in social interaction and social communication, as well as limited repetitive patterns of behavior, interests and activities [1]. Moreover, most patients have already missed the optimal treatment window at the time of their diagnosis. Currently, ASD imposes a

H. Lu et al. (Eds.): ICIG 2023, LNCS 14359, pp. 106–115, 2023.
https://doi.org/10.1007/978-3-031-46317-4_10

heavy burden on patients' families and society. An accurate diagnosis is essential for effective ASD treatment. Neuroimaging disease diagnosis methods have been shown to be effective in enhancing our comprehension of the potential pathological mechanisms of various brain diseases [2–6] and have been applied in the early diagnosis of ASD.

Studies have indicated that cognitive deficits and behavioral abnormalities in autism individuals are related to functional connections in the brain [7, 8]. Rs-fMRI can capture changes in brain function, which extensively used for ASD identification [9, 10]. Rs-fMRI data are used to build functional networks and use machine learning methods to predict the ASD classification. However, the brain structure of ASD individuals also exhibits certain morphological changes. SMRI can clearly display the structural morphology of the brain, such as information about white matter, gray matter, and cerebrospinal fluid [11, 12]. Therefore, more and more researchers have attempted to combine rs-fMRI and sMRI data to identify ASD individuals [13].

The key of these methods is the effective fusion of two different modalities: rs-fMRI and sMRI. From the perspective of fusion stages, the existing methods of multimodal fusion can be roughly divided into three categories: pixel-level fusion, feature-level fusion, and decision-level fusion. Pixel-level fusion methods mainly involves the fusion of pixel information from different modalities of original images [14]. Feature-level fusion methods [15] first utilize feature extractors to extract informative features from different modalities, and then combine the extracted features to form a more representative feature representation. Decision-level fusion methods [16] train a separate classifier for each modality, and then combine the output results of multiple classifiers to obtain the final classification result.

As a typical feature-fusion approach, the low-rank multimodal fusion method performs multimodal fusion using low-rank tensors [17]. However, LMF mainly focus on learning the interactions between different modalities while lacking quantitative measurement of inter-modal dynamics information. Moreover, capturing the complex nonlinear relationship between multiple modalities is another challenge for LMF. Recently, deep learning methods have received growing attention in neuroimage based diagnosis of mental disorders due to its ability to learn optimal representations automatically from neuroimaging data. Therefore, we propose a deep low rank multimodal fusion considering the distribution discrepancy between different modalities for ASD identification. The main contributions to this paper are summarized as follows:

1) A novel multimodal fusion method is proposed to perform automated ASD identification using rs-fMRI and sMRI data.
2) By introducing a new measurement function into the loss function of our method, our method can reduce the distribution differences between different modality. More specifically, a measurement function is proposed to quantify the distribution discrepancy between the two different modalities.
3) Two different deep networks are employed to extract the features that represent complex information in the rs-fMRI and sMRI data respectively. The optimal parameters of feature extraction network and classifier are obtained by minimizing the total loss.

The rest of this paper is organized as follows. The related work is presented in Sect. 2. The materials and proposed model is described in detail in Sect. 3. The experimental results and discussion are provided in Sect. 4. Finally, we conclude the paper in Sect. 5.

2 Related Works

Recently, feature-level multimodal fusion has attracted widespread attention in the field of medical imaging analysis. Different modalities that serve the same task must have some common connections. Zhu et al. [18] used a multi-kernel learning method to perform multimodal fusion by projecting two modality data into the reconstructed Hilbert space. Zhou et al. [19] proposed a multimodal deep learning network that can extract relevant information between modalities and project them to public potential space. However, the existing methods only simply map different modal features into the public potential space while ignoring the interaction information between various modalities. Recently, the fusion strategy based on tensor brings possibilities for solving this problem. Fukui et al. [20] developed a two-linear pooling method that took advantage of the various properties of modalities by calculating tensions. Zadeh et al. [21] proposed a tension fusion network that computes the Cartesian product of three different modal feature vectors to model the interactions between different modalities. However, due to the cross product of vectors involved, as the dimension of the input vector increases, the computational complexity of these methods often increases exponentially. Therefore, Liu et al. [17] proposed a new method for multimodal fusion using low rank tensor decomposition to reduce the computational complexity of tensor fusion. The LMF method has been applied successfully to a variety of neuroimaging-based disease studies [22, 23]. However, this method lacks objective measurement of inter-modal information. The DLMF model proposed in this article solves this problem by building a correlation factor on the loss function. Our method is much better than other models in terms of the performance, and the new loss function can better coordinate the optimization of the model to extract the various modal features.

3 Materials and Method

3.1 Database Acquisition

To verify the effectiveness and efficiency of our proposed method, we employ a publicly available multimodal autism dataset, named Autism Brain Imaging Data Exchange (ABIDE) based as our material. It contains two modalities: rs-fMRI and SMRI data. We use 646 subjects processed by the Configurable Pipeline for the Analysis of Connectomes (CPAC) for experiments, including 310 ASD patients and 336 NCs.

3.2 Data Pre-processing

Preprocessing of rs-fMRI Data. In this paper, we use Data Processing Assistant for Resting-State fMRI (DPARSF) software to preprocess rs-fMRI [24]. The rs-fMRI images were segmented into 116 regions of interest (ROIs) based on the automated anatomical labeling (AAL) atlas and the mean time series of 116 ROIs are calculated by determining the average of the intensities of all voxels within an ROI. For each subject, we obtain a 116 × 116 symmetric functional connectivity matrix by computing the Pearson correlation between the mean time series from each pair of ROIs. We remove the upper triangle and

116 diagonal elements (i.e., correlation of an ROI to itself), and transform the remaining triangles into a 6670-dimensional feature vector to represent each subject.

Preprocessing of sMRI Data. The scanners for acquiring SMRI data may be from different manufacturers, which results in varying sizes of SMRI images acquired by different scanners. We performed a unified down-sampling to all sMRI data sample and the size of each SMRI image is standardized to $64 \times 64 \times 64$.

3.3   Deep Low-Rank Multimodal Fusion Network

Framework. The overall structure of the model is shown in Fig. 1. The model consists of three major components: 1) Feature extraction moduleuses DNN and 3DCNN networks to extract the features vectors from the preprocessed rs-fMRI and sMRI data separately. 2) Feature fusion module performs fusion of rs-fMRI and sMRI features vectors using low-rank tensors. 3) Classifier adopts support vector machines (SVM). The distribution difference between different modalities is incorporated into the loss function. The optimal feature extractor and classifier can be acquired through the minimization of the loss function using an end-to-end training approach.

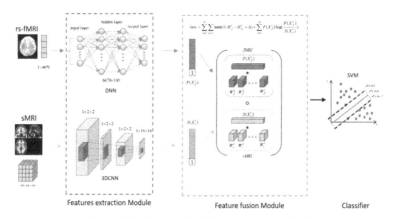

Fig. 1. The framework of our proposed method

Feature Extraction Network. A Deep Neural Network (DNN) is employed as a feature extraction network to extract feature vectors from rs-fMRI data. DNN mainly consists of a full connection layer, a dropout layer, a ReLU activation function layer and two batch normalization layers. One Batch normalization layer is located in front of the full connection layer, and the other is located between the Dropout layer and the ReLU Activation function layer. The number of nodes for each hidden layer were set as 100, respectively. The dimension of the output feature vector is 100. Use the ReLU activation function and batch norm to process hidden layer data and input layer data.

A 3DCNN network is utilized as a feature extraction network to extract feature vectors from SMRI data. 3DCNN comprises two 3D convolutional layers, the kernel size is $1 \times 2 \times 2$, which is then embedded within the Maxpooling layer and categorized in the full-connection layer. The number of nodes for full-connection layer were set as100 respectively.

Low-Rank Multimodal Fusion. The objective of multimodal fusion is to combine the individual unimodal representations into a cohesive and compact multimodal representation, which can be effectively utilized for downstream tasks. Upon the completion of the feature extraction module, two feature vectors of identical dimensions are obtained: $F_s \in R^{d_s}$, $F_f \in R^{d_f}$. Fs is the feature vector from sMRI data and F_f the other from rs-fMRI data. d_s and d_f represent the dimension of sMRI and rs-fMRI modality feature vectors, respectively. We assume that h is the output vector space. The calculation formula for the input tensor Z represented by this method is:

$$Z = z_s \otimes z_f \tag{1}$$

Among them, $\otimes$ represents tensor outer product. z_s and z_f is the vector F_s and F_f of Appendix 1 [21]. Then, the feature fusion expression tensor $Z \in R^{d_s \times d_f}$ is generated through the linear layer to g(.) generate a vector representation:

$$h = g(Z; W) = W \cdot Z, h \in R^{d_y} \tag{2}$$

To reduce the computational complexity of the vector, the weight tensor is decomposed into r modality specific factors, as shown in Eq. (3) below

$$W = \sum_{i=1}^{r} w_s^{(i)} \otimes w_f^{(i)} \tag{3}$$

Among them, $w_s^{(i)}$ and $w_f^{(i)}$ are represented as the i-th low rank weight factors of sMRI and rs-fMRI, respectively, $w_s^{(i)} = [w_{s,1}^{(i)}, w_{s,2}^{(i)}, ..., w_{s,d_h}^{(i)}]$, $w_f^{(i)} = [w_{f,1}^{(i)}, w_{f,2}^{(i)}, ..., w_{f,d_h}^{(i)}]$;

The weight tensor decomposition formula is introduced into the calculation of vectors as shown in Eq. (4):

$$h = (\sum_{i=1}^{r} w_s^{(i)} \otimes w_f^{(i)}) \cdot Z = \sum_{i=1}^{r} (w_s^{(i)} \otimes w_f^{(i)}) \cdot (z_s \otimes z_f) = [\sum_{i=1}^{r} w_s^{(i)} \cdot z_s] \circ [\sum_{i=1}^{r} w_f^{(i)} \cdot z_f] \tag{4}$$

Among them, $\circ$ represented as a product per element.

3.4 Loss Function

The total Loss function of the model consists of classification loss and distribution difference loss between modes. The hinge Loss function [25] L_{Hinge} is selected as the classification loss of the model, and the distribution difference index function L_{DDM} between modes is designed to measure the distribution difference between modes.

Fusion Loss. We take the two parts of the above function summary as total loss functions [26], so that they can be adapted to the current mainstream optimization method. In this paper, we. As a result, the fusion loss function in this paper is a combination of hinge loss functions and *IDD* functions:

$$L = L_{Hinge} + L_{DDM} \tag{5}$$

Hinge Loss. We classify i-th sample after the multimodal fusion of the output vector h, whose label is y_i, h_j represent output predictions as feature vectors of class j, and then the loss function for that outcome is calculated as:

$$L_{Hinge} = \sum_{j=y_i} \max(0, h_j^i - h_{y_i}^i + \Delta) \tag{6}$$

where Δ is the threshold value, default value is 1.

DDM Measure Function. This function takes the amount of information lost between the distributions of two variables f and s as a measure of the distribution between the two modalities. In this paper, we label the i-th sample as y_i, the output forecast as j class and the resulting modality distribution measure is:

$$L_{DDM} = \sum_{i=1}^{n} F_f^i(j) \log(\frac{F_f^i(j)}{F_s^i(j)}) \tag{7}$$

4 Experiment and Discussion

4.1 Experimental Setting

The model was trained on the computer with an CPU Intel Xeon (R) Silver 4210 CPU @ 2.20 GHz 2.19 GHz (2 processors), and a NVIDIA GeForce RTX 3090. The model was based on the Pytorch framework. The network was trained with the fusion loss by the Adam optimizer with an initial learning rate of 0.001. The batch size was set to 64. The maximum number of iterations is set to 150. We perform 5 cross-validation on data to evaluate our method.

4.2 Experiment Results

Comparison with Other Loss Functions. To evaluate the effectiveness of fusion loss of the proposed method, experiments were conducted on the proposed deep low-rank multimodal fusion network with different loss functions. As shown in Table 1, compared with other commonly used loss functions, the proposed fusion loss function L_{fusion} obtains significant performance improvement compared to only L_{Hinge}. Achieving an accuracy increase of 12% and a sensitivity increase of 30.75%. Compared with other loss function, the accuracy and sensitivity are improved to varying degrees. However, there was a slight decrease in specificity.

Comparison with Other Methods. As shown in Table 2, under the condition of fusion loss function, compared to other unimodal and multimodal methods, such as fMRI, sMRI and Concat, Deep Collaborative (DCL), Deep canonical correlation analysis (DCCA). Our method has greatly improved performance in all aspects. Figure 2 is performance of different methods in ASD classification on the ABIDE database.

Convergence Analysis. We verify the convergence of the proposed method through experiments on the ABIDE dataset. The convergence curves of training loss and training

Table 1. Mean Results of Different Loss Functions (%)

Loss function	ACC	SEN	SPE
L_{Hinge}	66.88 ± 7.10	40.74 ± 21.44	91.35 ± 4.83
L_{DDM}	63.28 ± 4.61	24.69 ± 11.63	95.90 ± 4.85
L_{MSE}	66.67 ± 7.16	32.10 ± 26.05	91.88 ± 6.62
$L_{Crossentropy}$	61.46 ± 3.28	18.52 ± 12.39	94.92 ± 4.45
L_{fusion}	**78.88 ± 1.97**	**71.19 ± 6.35**	**84.96 ± 5.60**

Table 2. Effects of Different models (%)

NET	ACC	SEN	SPE
fMRI	70.00 ± 3.20	36.45 ± 11.66	91.35 ± 6.73
sMRI	63.79 ± 1.67	66.42 ± 18.76	63.78 ± 17.30
Concat	53.15 ± 5.53	32.59 ± 10.05	68.73 ± 18.20
DCL [27]	53.28 ± 7.53	32.75 ± 15.53	69.15 ± 10.53
DCCA [28]	58.28 ± 6.35	40.74 ± 11.53	93.15 ± 5.53
LMF [21]	61.46 ± 3.28	18.52 ± 12.39	94.92 ± 4.45
Our Method	**78.88 ± 1.97**	**71.19 ± 6.35**	**84.96 ± 5.60**

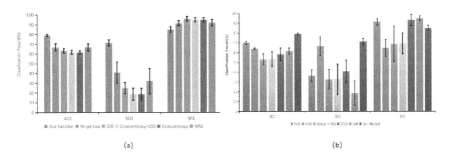

(a)   (b)

Fig. 2. Performance of different methods in ASD classification on the ABIDE database: (a). Effects of different loss functions: Using the model framework in Fig. 1, change the loss function. (b). Effects of different models: Comparison with other single and multimodal models.

accuracy is presented in Fig. 3. From Fig. 3, we can see that the values of the objective function decrease rapidly within thirty iterations and then levels off, which means our algorithm can converge well, especially after 40 iterations. Model training losses converge at 0.892, and training accuracy tends to converge after iterative rounds reach 100.

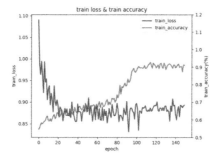

Fig. 3. The training process of our proposed method

4.3 Discussion

Based on the results of the above experiments, we have the following observations. 1) By incorporating the distribution differences between different modalities into the loss function, we observed a significant improvement in the classification accuracy of the deep low-rank multimodal fusion network. This finding provides strong evidence that reducing the distribution differences between modalities contributes to enhancing the fusion effectiveness of multiple modalities. 2) Research has found that in identifying ASD tasks using rs-fMRI and sMRI data. The effect of multimodal fusion may not necessarily be better than that of single modality, which is related to the fusion strategy. 3) Experimental research has found that LMF is indeed effective in fusion compared to other fusion strategies.

5 Conclusion

In this paper, we propose a deep low-rank multimodal fusion network that incorporate distribution discrepancy between different modalities into loss function for ASD classification. The proposed method takes fully advantage of rs-fMRI and sMRI jointly to identify ASD.

Feature fusion technique for the diagnosis of ASD that incorporates rs-fMRI and sMRI data into a feature vector. Enabling the model to better control the differences in distribution between modalities during the training process. Through a succession of experiments employing various fusion strategies and loss functions, we demonstrated the effectiveness of the proposed modal distribution difference indicator DDM. From the experimental results, it can be seen that our proposed method is superior to the unimodal method.

References

1. Wang, J., Zhang, F., Jia, X., et al.: Multi-class ASD classification via label distribution learning with class-shared and class-specific decomposition. Med. Image Anal. **1892**, 68–73 (2022)
2. Pappaianni, E., Siugzdaite, R., Vettori, S., et al.: Three shades of grey: detecting brain abnormalities in children with autism by using source-, voxel- and surface-based morphometry. Eur. J. Neurosci. **47**(Pt 2) (2017)

3. Wang, J., Fu, K., Chen, L., et al.: Increased gray matter volume and resting-state functional connectivity in somatosensory cortex and their relationship with autistic symptoms in young boys with autism spectrum disorder. Frontiers Physiol. **588** (2017)
4. Yttredahl, A.A., Mcrobert, E., Sheler, B., et al.: Abnormal emotional and neural responses to romantic rejection and acceptance in depressed women. J. Affect. Disord. **234**, 231 (2018)
5. McKinnon, M.C., Yucel, K., Nazarov, A., et al.: A meta-analysis examining clinical predictors of hippocampal volume in patients with major depressive disorder. J. Psychiatry Neuro sci. **34**(1), 41–54 (2009)
6. Hajek, T., Kozeny, J., Kopecek, M., et al.: Reduced subgenual cingulate volumes in mood disorders: a meta-analysis. J. Psychiatry Neurosci. **33**(2), 91–99 (2008)
7. Anderson, J.S., Nielsen, J.A., Froehlich, A.L., et al.: Functional connectivity magnetic resonance imaging classification of autism. Brain **134**(12), 3742–3754 (2011)
8. Uddin, L.Q., Supekar, K., Lynch, C.J., et al.: Salience network-based classification and prediction of symptom severity in children with autism. JAMA Psychiat. **70**(8), 1–11 (2013)
9. Hazlett, H.C., Poe, M., Gerig, G., et al.: Magnetic resonance imaging and head circumference study of brain size in autism: birth through age 2 years. Arch Gen Psychiatry **62**(12), 1366–1376 (2005)
10. Redcay, E., Courchesne, E.: When is the brain enlarged in autism? A meta analysis of all brain size reports. Biolog. Psychiatry **58**(1), 1–9 (2005)
11. Dvornek, N.C., Ventola, P., Pelphrey, K.A., et al.: Identifying autism from resting-state fMRI using long short-term memory networks. In: International Workshop on Machine Learning in Medical Imaging, pp. 362–370 (2017)
12. Wang, M.L., Lian, C.F., Yao, D.R., Zhang, D.Q., et al.: Spatial-temporal dependency modeling and network hub detection for functional MRI analysis via convolutional-recurrent network. IEEE Trans. Biomed. Eng., 2241–2252 (2020)
13. Wang, J., Wang, Q., Peng, J., et al.: Multi-task diagnosis for autism spectrum disorders using multi-modality features: a multi-center study. Hum. Brain Mapp. **38**(6), 3081–3097 (2017)
14. Tan, W., Thitn, W., Xiang, P., et al.: Multimodal brain image fusion based on multi-level edge-preserving filtering. Biomed. Signal Process. Control **64**(11), 102280 (2021)
15. Zhang, D., Wang, Y., Zhou, L., et al.: Multimodal classification of Alzheimer's disease and mild cognitive impairment. Neuroimage **55**(3), 856–867 (2011)
16. Dai, Z., Yan, C., Wang, Z., et al.: Discriminative analysis of early Alzheimer's disease using multimodal imaging and multi-level characterization with multi-classifier (M3). Neuroimage **59**(3), 2187–2195 (2012)
17. Liu, Z., Shen, Y., Lakshminarasimhan, V.B., et al.: Efficient low-rank multimodal fusion with modality-specific factors. arXiv preprint arXiv:1806.00064 (2018)
18. Zhu, X., Thung, K.-H., Adeli, E., Zhang, Y., Shen, D.: Maximum mean discrepancy based multiple kernel learning for incomplete multimodality neuroimaging data. In: Descoteaux, M., Maier-Hein, L., Franz, A., Jannin, P., Collins, D.L., Duchesne, S. (eds.) Medical Image Computing and Computer Assisted Intervention – MICCAI 2017, pp. 72–80. Springer, Cham (2017). https://doi.org/10.1007/978-3-319-66179-7_9
19. Zhou, T., Thung, K.H., Zhu, X., et al.: Effective feature learning and fusion of multimodality data using stage-wise deep neural network for dementia diagnosis. Hum. Brain Mapp. **40**(3), 1001–1016 (2018)
20. Fukui, A., Park, D.H., Yang, D., Rohrbach, A., Darrell, T., Rohrbach, M.: Multimodal compact bilinear pooling for visual question answering and visual grounding (2016). arXiv preprint arXiv:1606.01847
21. Zadeh, A., Chen, M., Poria, S., Cambria, E., Morency, L.-P.: Tensor fusion network for multimodal sentiment analysis. In: Empirical Methods in Natural Language Processing, EMNLP (2017)

22. Chen, Z.G., Wan, Y.Q., Wang, Y.L., et al.: Prognosis of bacterial membrane mixture based on heterogeneous low rank multimodal fusion networks. Zhejiang University School J. (Eng. Ed.) **55**(11), 2045–2053 (2021)
23. Cao, Y.L., Deng, Z.H., Hu, S.D., Wang, S.T.: Classification of Alzheimer's disease based on personality features and fusion features [J/OL]. Comput. Sci. Explor., 1–13 (2023). http://kns.cnki.net/kcms/detail/11.5602.TP.20220322.1155.002.html
24. Yan, C.G., Zhang, Y.F.: DPARSF: a MATLAB toolbox for "pipeline" data analysis of resting-state fMRI. Frontiers Syst. Neurosci. **4**, 1662–5137 (2010)
25. Rosasco, L., De Vito, E., Caponnetto, A., et al.: Are loss functions all the same? Neural Comput. **16**(5), 1063–1076 (2004)
26. Li, Y.C., Yeh, C.C.: Some characterizations of convex function. Comput. Math. Appl. **59**, 327–337 (2010)
27. Wu, W.X., Cai, B., Zhang, A.Y., et al.: Deep collaborative learning with application to the study of multimodal brain development. IEEE Trans. Biomed. Eng. **12**(66), 3346–3359 (2019)
28. Andrew, G., Arora, R., Bilmes, J., et al.: Deep canonical correlation analysis. In: International Conference on International Conference on Machine Learning, pp. 1247–1255 (2013)

Cross-domain Tongue Image Segmentation Based on Deep Adversarial Networks and Entropy Minimization

Liang Zhao, Shuai Zhang[✉], and Xiaomeng Zhao

Tianjin MedValley Technology Co. Ltd., Tianjin 300392, China
`ctxqlxs@126.com`

Abstract. The semantic segmentation of tongue image is a key problem in the development of TCM (Traditional Chinese Medicine) modernization, and there are a lot of research dedicated to the development of tongue segmentation. Although the performance improvement in tongue segmentation with the evolution of deep learning, there are major challenges in generalizing it to the diverse testing domain. As we known, the worse the consistency of cross-domain data distribution between source and target domain is, the lower the performance of model in test domain gets. Existing semantic segmentation methods based on supervised learning are difficult to deal with such problems when it is impossible to re-label the tongue image with poor generalization performance in the target domain. To address this problem, we design a adversarial training framework with regularizing entropy on target domain, aiming to enforce high certainty of model's prediction on target domain during the trend of domain alignment. Specifically, we pre-trained the tongue image segmentation model with deep supervised method on the source domain. In addition to segmentation task, the segmentation model need to regularize entropy of output on target domain and maximally confuse the discriminator. The discriminator tries to distinguish whether the output of segmentation model from the source domain or the target domain. In this study, two datasets is constructed, and the five-fold cross-validation experiment is performed on it. Experimental results show that the tongue image segmentation performance in the open environment was improved by 21.5% mIOU (59.2% $\rightarrow$ 80.7%) after domain adaptation. As opposed to the pseudo label learning with different thresholds(0.6, 0.9), the mIOU of proposed method increased by 17%, 16.1%. Moreover, as opposed to MinEnt, the mIOU increased by 6%. The tongue images cross-domain segmentation method proposed in this paper significantly improves the segmentation accuracy in the unlabeled target domain by reducing the influence of the cross-domain discrepancy and enhancing the certainty of model output in target domain.

Keywords: Chinese Medicine Tongue Image · Tongue Segmentation · Domain Adaptation · Adversarial Learning

© The Author(s), under exclusive license to Springer Nature Switzerland AG 2023
H. Lu et al. (Eds.): ICIG 2023, LNCS 14359, pp. 116–128, 2023.
https://doi.org/10.1007/978-3-031-46317-4_11

1 Introduction

As one of the important diagnostic methods in traditional Chinese medicine, tongue diagnosis has significant implications for determining the nature of a disease, the balance between yin and yang and the progression of the disease. Nowadays, the standardization and objectification of tongue diagnosis research is an important component of the construction of a modernized traditional Chinese medicine system, and has an extremely profound impact on the development of traditional Chinese medicine [1].

However, interference factors such as the face, chin, and lips can lead to inaccurate analysis of tongue diagnosis, so it is necessary to segment the tongue area from the digital images collected. In recent years, many scholars and researchers have made efforts in this area, which can be generally divided into traditional image processing methods and deep learning-based methods. Traditional image processing methods mainly include threshold segmentation algorithms and active contour models, such as the maximum inter-class variance method [2–4] and the tongue image segmentation based on the principle of energy minimization of Snakes [5]. However, these traditional image processing methods can not mine the deep semantic information of images and can not be generalized to various testing scenarios, so tongue image segmentation still faces challenges.

Convolutional neural networks, with their powerful feature representation capabilities, have been widely used in computer vision fields such as object detection, object recognition, and semantic segmentation, such as R-CNN [6], Faster R-CNN [7], FCN [8], SegNet [9], ResNet [10], PSPNet [11], YOLO [12], SSD [13], and so on. Inspired by these works, many deep convolutional neural network-based works have emerged in tongue image segmentation. [14] adopts a two-stage structure design, first using Rsnet to realize coarse segmentation of the tongue image, that is, to locate the tongue body, and then using Fsnet to realize semantic segmentation of the tongue body. The experimental results show that deep learning-based tongue image segmentation greatly outperforms traditional segmentation methods in segmentation accuracy. [15] compared the performance of several popular deep convolutional neural networks in tongue image segmentation. [16] applied the high-resolution network HRnet to tongue image segmentation, improving the segmentation accuracy of the tongue body edge in segmentation.

Although there has been so much work on tongue image segmentation, few people have paid attention to the problem of unsupervised domain adaptation (UDA) in tongue image segmentation, that is, obtaining tongue images and pixel-level annotations from the source domain, and obtaining tongue images from the target domain without label information, aiming to learn a semantic segmentation network that can correctly predict pixel-level labels of the target domain tongue images. In fact, this is a very meaningful task because tongue image collection for traditional Chinese medicine diagnosis often occurs in a closed standard environment, and the segmentation network is also trained based on tongue images in a closed environment. However, with the needs of business, the demand for open environment tongue image segmentation has also emerged. At this time, the previously trained segmentation network often performs poorly. There are two solutions, one is to re-label the tongue images in the open environment, but this requires a lot of manpower and material resources. The other solution is based on UDA, which is more popular in the industry because it does not require labeling information, but also presents great challenges due to the lack of labeling information. This paper proposes a deep adversarial domain adaptation-based tongue cross-domain segmentation approach starting from UDA. The paper's contributions can be summarized as follows:

1. We propose a method that combines adversarial learning and entropy minimization for training a tongue segmentation network, which greatly alleviates the problem of performance degradation in the testing environment due to cross-domain discrepancy.
2. The domain adaptation solution for some semantic segmentation or classification tasks is extended to the tongue segmentation task, and performance comparison is conducted on cross-domain tongue segmentation tasks.
3. This is the first time an unsupervised domain adaptation method has been proposed to solve the problem of cross-domain discrepancy in tongue segmentation in real-world scenarios.

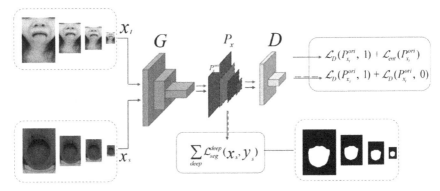

Fig. 1. Approach overview. Firstly, a multi-scale deep supervision training strategy is employed to train the segmentation network G. Then, an adversarial training method is used to reduce the cross-domain gap of the original scale feature map $P_{x_t}^{ori}$. Meanwhile, the entropy minimization is utilized to decrease the uncertainty of the segmentation network's predictions on the target domain tongue images.

2 Related Work

2.1 Adversarial Learning

The biggest challenge in unsupervised domain adaptation tasks is the discrepancy in data distribution between source and target domains [17]. In the field of semantic segmentation, the most commonly used method for unsupervised domain adaptation is adversarial learning. [18] first applied adversarial learning to unsupervised domain adaptation semantic segmentation tasks. [19] used adversarial learning in the output space for domain adaptation, adding a discriminator network to the original segmentation network. The output of the segmentation network was used as input to the discriminator network, whose task was to distinguish whether the output of the segmentation network came from the source or target domain. In addition to the original segmentation task, the segmentation network also needed to confuse the discriminator, making different domains have similar data distributions or making semantic features domain-invariant. ADVENT [20] did not directly use the output of the semantic segmentation network as input to the discriminator, but instead calculated the entropy of the semantic segmentation network's output pixel by pixel as an entropy map, and then input the entropy map to the discriminator, thus making the output semantic segmentation entropy distributions of the target and source domains consistent.

2.2 Generative Learning

Unlike the previous mentioned adversarial learning methods that aim to align high-level semantic features, generative networks work on visual feature consistency. They transform source domain images into ones with the same style as the target domain, thus obtaining data and labels with the target domain style, such as CyCADA [21] and DCAN [22]. As this article focuses on the alignment of deep hierarchical features, there will not be too much introduction on the alignment work at the pixel level.

2.3 Pseudo Label Learning and Entropy Minimization

Unsupervised domain adaptation using pseudo-label learning is a simple yet highly effective method in semi-supervised learning [23]. The main idea is to use labeled data from the source domain to assign approximate labels to unlabeled data in the target domain, and then retrain the model to adapt to the target domain. [24] uses pseudo-label learning in unsupervised domain adaptation for semantic segmentation while introducing class balance and spatial priors, achieving relatively competitive performance. Despite the performance gains that pseudo-labels bring, they can be noisy, so pseudo-labels may give overly confident labels to the wrong categories, causing the network to deviate from our expectations. To address this issue, [18] introduces label normalization and model regularization to output soft pseudo-labels while encouraging the network's outputs to be smoother.

Entropy minimization constrains the model's output to have high confidence and has attracted attention for its successful application in semi-supervised learning [25]. [26] applies it to the domain adaptation problem in the classification task, and ADVENT [20], mentioned earlier, first applies it to the domain adaptation problem in the semantic segmentation task, while explaining the relationship and differences between minimizing entropy and pseudo-label learning.

3 Proposed Methods

We mainly deal with the problem of unsupervised domain adaptation (UDA) in tongue semantic segmentation. The tongue image $X_S \subset \mathbb{R}^{H \times W \times 3}$ of source domain with it's two category pixel-level annotation $Y_S \subset \mathbb{R}^{H \times W \times 1}$, however the tongue image $X_T \subset \mathbb{R}^{H \times W \times 3}$ of target domain have no annotation, the goal of the semantic segmentation network G is predicting the pixel-level label of the tongue image in the target domain. The proposed method consists of two networks, in addition to the basic semantic segmentation network, an additional network (discriminator) is added to achieve domain adaptation. Entropy minimization is only related to the probability corresponding to pixels, ignoring the structural correlation between local semantics [19]. Therefore, we introduce entropy minimization into the semantic output of the target domain while reducing the distribution discrepancy of the source and target domains through adversarial training, in order to improve the confidence of the segmentation network output in the target domain. The whole framework structure is illustrated in Fig. 1. Different from [19], considering that the entropy map of binary classification contains insufficient information, we still directly input the output of the segmentation network into the discriminator, without converting it into an entropy map and then inputting it into the discriminator; we do not directly minimize entropy, but integrates it into the process of adversarial training; we used a light semantic segmentation network structure for faster inference.

3.1 Entropy Minimization

For the target domain, as we do not have the annotations y_t for image samples $x_t \subset X_T$, , we cannot learn the deep features by (1). Some methods use the model's prediction $\widehat{y}_t$ as a proxy for y_t which is used only for pixels where prediction is sufficiently confident. However, these methods are susceptible to the threshold selection of proxy. To address this problem, some researches constrain the segmentation model such that it produces high-confident prediction, such as entropy minimization [19] and Batch Nuclear-norm Maximization(BNM) [20].

We constrict the output uncertainty of semantic segmentation model by minimizing Shannon entropy $\mathcal{L}_{ent}$. For a set of tongue image x_t of target domain, the loss of entropy minimization can be formulated as:

$$\mathcal{L}_{ent} = -\sum_{h,w} P_{x_t}^{(h,w,1)} \log P_{x_t}^{(h,w,1)} \tag{1}$$

3.2 Adversarial Learning

An adversarial learning approach is used to train the network to discover deep semantic features that are domain-invariant. Similar to previous adversarial learning methods, in addition to the segmentation network, a discriminator is trained to distinguish between tongue images from the source and target domains. The network strives to confuse the discriminator so that it cannot distinguish the domain of the tongue image to learn domain-invariant features by minimizing the adversarial loss:

$$\mathcal{L}_{adv}(G, D) = -log(D(G(X_s))) - log(1 - D(G(X_t))) \tag{2}$$

3.3 Proposed Methods

Pre-training. In the first stage, a supervised based approach is used to pre-train the semantic segmentation network G with labeled tongue images from the source domain. Formally, we consider a set $X_S \subset \mathbb{R}^{H \times W \times 3}$ of source examples along with associated ground-truth 2-class segmentation maps, $Y_S \subset \mathbb{R}^{H \times W \times 1}$. The parameters θ_G of G are learned to minimize the segmentation loss:

$$\min_{\theta_G} \frac{1}{|X_s|} \sum_{x_s \in X_s} \mathcal{L}_{seg}(x_s, y_s) \tag{3}$$

As for $\mathcal{L}_{seg}(*, *)$, we use Tversky Loss:

$$TI^{deep} = \frac{\sum\limits_{i=1}^{N} p_{ic} g_{ic} + \in}{\sum\limits_{i=1}^{N} p_{ic} g_{ic} + \alpha \sum\limits_{i=1}^{N} p_{\bar{i}c} g_{ic} + \beta \sum\limits_{i=1}^{N} p_{ic} g_{\bar{i}c} + \in} \tag{4}$$

$$\mathcal{L}_{seg}^{deep}(x_s, y_s) = 1 - TI^{deep}$$

$$\mathcal{L}_{seg}(x_s, y_s) = \sum_{deep} \mathcal{L}_{seg}^{deep}(x_s, y_s)$$

In the above equation, N represents the number of pixels in each image, $deep$ indicates different scales of deep supervision. $p = G(x_s)$, p_{ic} represents the probabilities of pixel i belonging to the class c, $p_{\bar{i}c}$ represents the probabilities of pixel i belonging to the class $\bar{c}$, respectively, while $g_{ic}, g_{\bar{i}c} \in y_s$ denotes the binary ground truth of each pixel. The hyper parameters α, β are used to balance false negatives and false positives, thus improving the recall rate in the case of class imbalance, and ensuring numerical stability during computation.

Collaborative Training of Entropy Minimization and Adversarial Learning. Formulate the multiple scale feature-maps of segmentation model prediction as P_x, we only feed the original scale feature-map P_x^{ori} into discriminator D for adversarial training.. Figure 1 illustrates our adversarial learning procedure. The fully convolution discriminator D with parameters θ_D produces domain classification outputs, i.e., class label 1 (resp.0) for the source (resp. Target) domain. In the training phrase, the discriminator aims to discriminate the outputs of segmentation model coming from source and target image, and at the same time, segmentation model tries to fool the discriminator and decrease the output uncertainty of target domain. In detail, let $\mathcal{L}_D$ be the cross entropy domain loss, the adversarial loss (2) can be optimized in two steps.

Firstly, training the discriminator model D:

$$\min_{\theta_D} \frac{1}{|X_s|} \sum_{x_s} \mathcal{L}_D(P_{x_s}, 1) + \frac{1}{|X_t|} \sum_{x_t} \mathcal{L}_D(P_{x_t}, 0) \tag{5}$$

Secondly, training the segmentation model G:

$$\min_{\theta_G} \frac{1}{|X_t|} \sum_{x_t} \mathcal{L}_D(P_{x_t}, 1) \tag{6}$$

Combining (1) (3) and (6) the final training objective of segmentation model can be derived:

$$\min_{\theta_G} \frac{1}{|X_s|} \sum_{x_s} \mathcal{L}_{seg}(x_s, y_s) + \frac{\lambda_{adv}}{|X_t|} \sum_{x_t} \mathcal{L}_D(P_{x_t}, 1) - \frac{1}{|X_t|} \sum_{x_t} \sum_{h,w} P_{x_t}^{(h,w,1)} log P_{x_t}^{(h,w,1)} \quad (7)$$

with the weighting factor λ_{adv} for the adversarial loss $\mathcal{L}_D$. we train the segmentation model with $\mathcal{L}_{seg}(*, *)$ by deep supervised method which factor of different depths is 1.0.

During training, we alternatively optimize the segmentation model G and the discriminator model D using objective loss functions in (5) and (7).

4 Experiments

In this section, we demonstrate the experimental results. Section 4.1 mainly introduces the datasets, network structure, and some specific experimental details. Section 4.2 mainly presents some ablation experiments, segmentation examples in target domains, and comparison experiments with existing methods.

4.1 Implementation Details

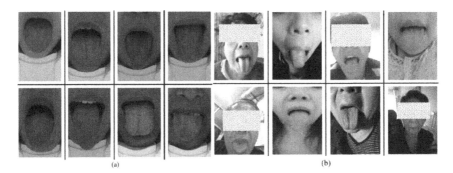

(a)   (b)

Fig. 2. Examples of the datasets, where (a) represents samples collected in a closed environment (source domain), and (b) represents samples collected in an open environment (target domain).

The datasets used in this study consists of Datasets A and Datasets B, which represent tongue images collected in closed and open environments, respectively. Both datasets are self-built, with Datasets A collected using the MT-SX-02 modern standard tongue image collection equipment from Tianjin MedValley Technology Co., Ltd. The pixel-level semantic information was annotated by multiple medical professionals in multiple rounds. Datasets B, on the other hand, was captured using a smartphone by users and the semantic labels were also annotated for the purpose of evaluating the performance of the cross-domain segmentation network.

Datasets A. It was collected in a closed environment using a standard simulated natural light condition box and the same CCD image sensor. It consists of 2934 tongue image samples, as shown in Fig. 2a.

Datasets B. It was collected in an open environment with varying lighting conditions and different resolutions. It includes tongue image samples with lower resolutions, images where the tongue occupies a small area of the entire image, and images with beauty effects applied. The datasets contains 758 tongue image samples captured using different mobile phones, as shown in Fig. 2b.

We focus on the unsupervised domain adaptation task for tongue image segmentation from a closed environment domain to an open environment domain. To validate the effectiveness of the proposed algorithm, the original tongue segmentation network is trained on tongue images with semantic label information in the closed environment and validated in the open environment. For domain adaptation, this paper takes tongue images in the closed environment, i.e., datasets A, as the source domain and tongue images in the open environment, i.e., datasets B, as the target domain.

To validate the reliability of the method, the datasets B is randomly divided into 5 groups, and the five-fold cross-validation method is used for experimentation. Specifically, datasets B is divided into 5 equally sized subsets. In each experiment, 4 of these subsets are chosen for training the model, while the remaining one and it's annotations is used for testing the model's performance. This process is repeated 5 times, using a different subset for testing each time. By analyzing the average of all experimental results, more reliable evaluation results can be obtained. Mean Intersection-over-Union (mIOU), a commonly used evaluation metric for semantic segmentation, is adopted as the evaluation criterion for the segmentation network.

Network Architecture. We use a multi-scale attention UNet [17] as the backbone of tongue semantic segmentation network, and the same deep supervision training strategy is used for training. The specific structure is shown in Fig. 3(a). It can be seen that in addition to the backbone consistent with UNet, an attention gate (AG) unit is added (as shown in Fig. 3(b)). The AG unit multiplies the attention coefficients with the input features, only retaining the activations related to coarse-scale spatial information. Then, the refined activations are concatenated with the original activations after upsampling and passed to the output of the decoding layer, thereby propagating the attention to the output of the decoding layer. Moreover, different scales have richer semantic information, so the image pyramid is used as the input of the network, combined with the deep supervision training strategy to further improve the feature representation ability of the network.

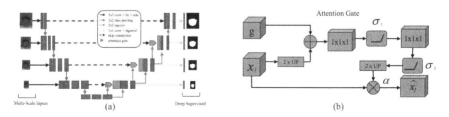

Fig. 3. The Attention U-Net architecture.

The discriminator used in the adversarial network has a similar network structure to the discriminators in DCGAN [18] and ADVENT [19]. It consists of 5 convolution layers with a kernel size of 4x4 and a stride of 2, and the number of filters in each layer is {64,128,256,512,64,1}. Except for the last layer, all convolution layers are followed by a Leaky_ReLU activation layer with a parameter of 0.2. This paper adds a GlobalAveragePooling layer to the last layer for domain classification.

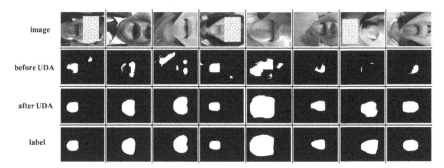

Fig. 4. The results of UDA. The four rows from top to bottom show the RGB input image, the result before domain adaptation (only source domain), the result after domain adaptation, and the actual label.

Details. The implementation details are as follows: TensorFlow deep learning framework is used in this paper. All experiments were implemented on an NVIDIA 2060 GPU with 6GB of video memory. The semantic segmentation network and discriminator were trained using the Adam optimizer with a learning rate of 1e–4. In all experiments, the weight parameter for the adversarial loss is fixed at 0.01, the weights for the source domain segmentation loss are fixed at 0.7 and 0.3, and the smoothing parameter is fixed at 1.0.

Data Augmentation. To improve the network's generalization ability, we employed various data augmentation techniques including random cropping, horizontal and vertical flipping, random 90-degree rotation, random transposition, random affine transformations (translation, flipping, scaling), random adjustment of image brightness and contrast, and random blurring of images with different kernel sizes.

4.2   The Effectiveness of Proposed Method

To validate the effectiveness of the proposed method, a segmentation model G based on the network structure of [17] was trained using deep supervision strategy on datasets A until it was fully fitted. Then, domain adaptation comparison experiments were conducted on datasets B from three aspects: no domain adaptation, UDA-Adv (adversarial learning) and Min-Ent (minimizing entropy). All of these processes were based on unsupervised learning, without using the labels of datasets B. UDA-Adv represents minimizing adversarial loss to reduce domain discrepancy, Min-Ent represents optimizing the segmentation network using entropy minimization in the target domain, thus reducing the uncertainty of the segmentation network output.

Table 1. Lightweight backbone comparison on val set. All experiments utilize the same segmentation model and same experiment settings.

Methods	threshold	mIOU	mIOU↑	Dice	Dice↑
Pseudo label + BCE	> 0.6	0.483 ± 0.0098	-	0.569 ± 0.0109	-
Pseudo label + BCE	> 0.9	0.428 ± 0.0094	-	0.569 ± 0.0104	-
Pseudo label + Tversky	> 0.6	0.629 ± 0.0063	0.037	0.705 ± 0.0109	0.030
Pseudo label + Tversky	> 0.9	0.646 ± 0.0011	0.054	0.730 ± 0.0043	0.055
MinEnt [19]	-	0.747 ± 0.0075	0.155	0.817 ± 0.0059	0.142
AdvEnt [19]	-	0.479 ± 0.0014	-	0.599 ± 0.0187	-
BNM [20]	-	0.377 ± 0.0098	-	0.512 ± 0.0012	-
ours	-	**0.807 ± 0.0124**	**0.215**	**0.862 ± 0.0034**	**0.187**

Experiment 1. In this section, the performance of pseudo-label learning is compared using different thresholds (0.6, 0.9) and different loss functions. MinEnt is set to the same as the original paper. As we deal with binary semantic segmentation tasks, the difference between AdvEnt and the original paper is that the output channel of the segmentation network is reduced to 1, and the activation function of the last layer is changed from softmax to sigmoid. For batch maximum norm (BNM), a similar idea to the original paper is used. First, adversarial loss is used to reduce domain differences, and then BNM optimization is performed on the target domain after domain adaptation. To ensure fair comparison, the basic segmentation network used is multi-scale attention Unet.

From Table 1, it can be seen that when using different loss functions trained on the source domain, the domain adaptation performance actually decreased significantly. However, when using the same loss function, performance improved regardless of the threshold value chosen. MinEnt [19] domain adaptation resulted in a 15.5% increase in mIOU, while AdvEnt [19] actually decreased. This may be due to the fact that the discriminator cannot fully exploit semantic information when fed with a single-channel entropy map. Batch Maximum Norm (BMN) [20] was mainly designed to address the problem of high data density near segmentation boundaries, which may not be well-suited for tongue segmentation scenarios and thus resulted in decreased performance. Finally, it can be observed that the proposed method achieved the highest improvement, with a 21.5% increase in mIOU and 18.7% increase in Dice.

Experiment 2. In this section, we analyze the performance improvement of the entire framework from its components. As shown in Table 2, when only using UDA-Adv or Min-Ent, the segmentation model exhibits similar performance (mIOU), but both are much higher than the performance of only using source domain training without domain adaptation (mIOU). This proves the effectiveness of UDA. When entropy minimization and adversarial learning are trained collaboratively, the mIOU reaches 80.7%. Some specific visual comparison examples of tongue segmentation before and after domain adaptation are shown in Fig. 4.

Table 2. The effectiveness of our proposed method, the * represents the mean value of the five-fold cross-validation.

w/t UDA	UDA-Adv	Min-Ent	mIOU*	Dice*
√			0.592	0.675
	√		0.750	0.825
		√	0.747	0.817
	√	√	**0.807**	**0.862**

5   Conclusions

Considering the significant drop in semantic segmentation performance of tongue image models on cross-domain tongue images, we propose an unsupervised cross-domain tongue segmentation method. Firstly, a multi-scale tongue segmentation network is trained on the source domain. Then, adversarial learning is used to narrow the distribution difference between the source and target domains. Meanwhile, the entropy of the output in the semantic layer of the segmentation network is minimized to reduce the output uncertainty in the target domain. Experimental results on open-set tongue image data demonstrate the effectiveness of the proposed method in aligning the domains. However, the paper mainly focuses on domain alignment and does not consider some unique features of the target domain, such as discrepancy in class distributions between the source and target domains, the future needs to be considered.

References

1. Shu-qiong, H., Yun-long, Z., Jing, Z., et al.: Research progress on the objectification, quantitation and standardization of tongue manifestation in traditional Chinese medicine. China J. Tradit. Chin. Med. Pharm. **32**(4), 1625–1627 (2017)

2. San-Ii, Y., et al.: Maximum entropy image segmentation based on maximum interclass variance. Comput. Eng. Sci. **40**(10), 1874 (2018)
3. Zhan-peng, H., et al.: An automatic tongue segmentation algorithm based on OTSU and region growing. Shizhen Guoyi Guoyao **28**(12), 3062–3064 (2017)
4. Ling, Z., Jian, Q.: Tongue-image segmentation based on gray projection and threshold-adaptive method. Chin. J. Tissue Eng. Res. **14**(9), 1638 1641 (2010)
5. Xuegang, H.U., Xiulan, Q.I.U.: Novel image segmentation algorithm based on Snake model. J. Comput. Appl. **37**(12), 3523–3527 (2017)
6. Girshick, R., et al.: Rich feature hierarchies for accurate object detection and semantic segmentation. In: Proceedings of the IEEE Conference on Computer Vision and Pattern Recognition, pp. 580–587 (2014)
7. Ren, S., et al.: Faster R-CNN: towards real-time object detection with region proposal networks. In: Advances in Neural Information Processing Systems, pp. 91–99 (2015)
8. Long, J., Shelhamer, E., Darrell, T.: Fully convolutional networks for semantic segmentation. In: Proceedings of the IEEE Conference on Computer Vision and Pattern Recognition, pp. 3431–3440 (2015)
9. Badrinarayanan, V., Kendall, A., Cipolla, R.: SegNet: a deep convolutional encoder-decoder architecture for image segmentation. IEEE Trans. Pattern Anal. Mach. Intell. **39**(12), 2481–2495 (2017)
10. He, K., et al.: Deep residual learning for image recognition. In: Proceedings of the IEEE Conference on Computer Vision and Pattern Recognition, pp. 770–778 (2016)
11. Zhao, H., et al.: Pyramid scene parsing network. In: Proceedings of the IEEE Conference on Computer Vision and Pattern Recognition, pp. 2881–2890 (2017)
12. Redmon, J., Divvala, S., Girshick, R., et al.: You only look once: unified, real-time object detection. In: Proceedings of the IEEE Conference on Computer Vision and Pattern Recognition, pp. 779–788 (2016)
13. Liu, W., et al.: SSD: single shot multibox detector. In: Leibe, B., Matas, J., Sebe, N., Welling, M. (eds.) ECCV 2016. LNCS, vol. 9905, pp. 21–37. Springer, Cham (2016). https://doi.org/10.1007/978-3-319-46448-0_2
14. Liran, W., et al.: Two-phase convolutional neural network design for tongue segmentation. **23**(10), 1571–1581 (2018)
15. Lu, Y.-X., et al.: Review on tongue image segmentation technologies for traditional Chinese medicine: methodologies, performances and prospects. Acta Autom. Sinica **47**(05), 1005–1016 (2021)
16. Ma, L., et al.: Research on tongue image segmentation algorithm based on high resolution feature. Comput. Eng. **46**(10), 248–252 (2020)
17. Abraham, N., Khan, N.M.: A novel focal tversky loss function with improved attention U-Net for lesion segmentation. In: 2019 IEEE 16th International Symposium on Biomedical Imaging (ISBI 2019), pp. 683 687. IEEE (2019)
18. Radford, A., Metz, L., Chintala, S.: Unsupervised representation learning with deep convolutional generative adversarial networks. arXiv preprint arXiv:1511.06434 (2015)
19. Vu, T.H., et al.: ADVENT: Adversarial entropy minimization for domain adaptation in semantic segmentation. In: Proceedings of the IEEE Conference on Computer Vision and Pattern Recognition, pp. 2517–2526 (2019)
20. Cui, S., et al.: Towards discriminability and diversity: batch nuclear-norm maximization under label insufficient situations. arXiv preprint arXiv:2003.12237 (2020)
21. Zheng, Z., Yang, Y.: Rectifying Pseudo label learning via uncertainty estimation for domain adaptive semantic segmentation. arXiv preprint arXiv:2003.03773 (2020)
22. Hoffman, J., et al.: CyCADA: cycle-consistent adversarial domain adaptation. In: ICML (2018)

23. Wu, Z., et al.: DCAN: dual channel-wise alignment networks for unsupervised scene adapta-tion. In: Proceedings of the European Conference on Computer Vision (ECCV), pp. 518–534 (2018)
24. Lee, D.H.: Pseudo-Label: the simple and efficient semi-supervised learning method for deep neural networks. In: Workshop on Challenges in Representation Learning, ICML **3,** 2 (2013)
25. Zou, Y., Yu, Z., Vijaya Kumar, B.V.K., et al.: Unsupervised domain adaptation for semantic segmentation via class-balanced self-training. In: Proceedings of the European Conference on Computer Vision (ECCV), pp. 289–305 (2018)
26. Hoffman, J., et al.: FCNs in the wild: pixel-level adversarial and constraint-based adaptation. arXiv preprint arXiv:1612.02649 (2016)
27. Tsai, Y.H., et al.: Learning to adapt structured output space for semantic segmentation. In: Proceedings of the IEEE Conference on Computer Vision and Pattern Recognition, pp. 7472–7481 (2018)
28. Long, M., et al.: Unsupervised domain adaptation with residual transfer networks. In: Advances in Neural Information Processing Systems, pp. 136–144 (2016)
29. Springenberg, J.T.: Unsupervised and semi-supervised learning with categorical generative adversarial networks. arXiv preprint arXiv:1511.06390 (2015)

Residual Inter-slice Feature Learning for 3D Organ Segmentation

Junming Zhang[1,2], Jian Su[1,2], Tao Lei[1,2(✉)] 🆔, Xiaogang Du[1,2] 🆔,
Yong Wan[3] 🆔, Chenxia Li[4] 🆔, Sijia Wen[1,2], and Weiqiang Zhao[5]

[1] Shaanxi Joint Laboratory of Artificial Intelligence, Shaanxi University of Science
and Technology, Xi'an 710021, China
leitaoly@163.com
[2] The School of Electronic Information and Artificial Intelligence, Shaanxi University
of Science and Technology, Xi'an 710021, China
[3] The Department of Geriatric Surgery, The First Affiliated Hospital of Xi'an
Jiaotong University, Xi'an 710061, China
[4] The First Affiliated Hospital of Xi'an Jiaotong University, Xi'an 710061, China
[5] CETC Northwest Group Co., Ltd. Xi'an Branch, Xi'an 710065, China

Abstract. Although a large number of 2D convolutional neural networks have been reported and used for medical image segmentation, most of them still face the following two problems. First, these networks employ 2D convolution to achieve 3D organ segmentation, which ignores the relationship between different slices. Second, these networks depend on U-shape networks that employ skip-connection to fusion low-level and high-level features, which ignores the semantic gap between them. To address these two issues, we propose a residual inter-slices feature learning method employed by a 2D network that can achieve high-efficient 3D organ segmentation. First, we present an image pre-processing approach named residual inter-slice feature enhancement. We use the residual image including 3D information instead of the original medical slices, which is more efficient and effective than using a 3D network. Second, we present a double-focus skip-connection(DFSC) that is used for replacing the vanilla skip-connection in an encoder-decoder network. Because the DFSC is able to narrow the semantic gap between low-level and high-level features, it achieves better feature fusion. Experiments show that the proposed method is useful for improving feature representation ability of networks and achieving higher organ segmentation accuracy with lower cost.

Keywords: Deep learning · Organ segmentation · Skip-connection · Feature enhancement

1 Introduction

Segmentation of organs or lesions from medical images is one of the most important research contents in computer assistant clinic, and it has been widely used in clinical diagnosis, surgical navigation panning, prognostic assessment [1], etc.

H. Lu et al. (Eds.): ICIG 2023, LNCS 14359, pp. 129–139, 2023.
https://doi.org/10.1007/978-3-031-46317-4_12

At present, a large number of medical image segmentation methods have been reported, and these methods can be grouped into traditional methods and deep learning methods [2–7]. As traditional methods suffer from the difficulty of robust feature extraction, they show poor robustness and only provide low segmentation accuracy. In contrast, deep learning methods overcome the drawbacks of feature extraction, they not only provide hierarchical feature representation on images, but also achieve end-to-end image segmentation. Therefore, deep learning has become the most popular method in medical image segmentation.

As medical CT images are usually 3D volume data, it is necessary to consider the 3D volume information for organ segmentation. Most medical image segmentation networks depend on encoder-decoder structure are 2D networks, such as U-Net [8], CE-Net [9], resUnet [10] etc., where the input image is a slice of CT volume data. Clearly, 2D networks miss the correlation between different slices leading to limited organ segmentation accuracy. To address the problem, researchers present 3D networks such as 3D-Unet [11], V-Net [12], C2fNAS [13], etc. A 3D network usually employs 3D convolutional kernels instead of 2D kernels and receives 3D volume data as the input. Therefore, a 3D network is often able to provide higher segmentation accuracy than a 2D network, but the former requires more parameters due to the employment of high-dimensional convolutional kernels. Moreover, it is more difficult to train a 3D network than training a 2D network. To balance the segmentation accuracy and the number of network parameters, some scholars present 2.5D networks such as H-DenseUnet [14], LW-HCN [15], AdaEn-Net [16], etc., these networks combine a 2D network and a 3D network to form a cascade network structure. On the one hand, the 2.5D networks can provide high segmentation accuracy similar to 3D networks. On the other hand, they require less parameters than 3D networks due to the employment of some 2D convolutional kernels.

We have mentioned above that the mainstream medical image segmentation networks depend on the encoder-decoder structure. For these encoder-decoder networks, one of the most important factors leading to success is skip-connection. Skip-connection is first presented by Long et al. in FCN [17]. It can help networks improving feature representation due to recover high-resolution representation from the low-resolution representation. Although the skip-connection is significant for improving network performance, it suffers from a problem of the large semantic gap between low-level and high-level features. To address the problem, Zhou et al. proposed U-Net++ [18] by introducing dense-connection into skip-connection. As image features from different layers in encoder are fused into decoder, richer feature maps lead to strong feature representation ability, and thus achieving better segmentation results. Furthermore, Huang et al. proposed Unet3+ [19] which leverages the full scale skip-connection and deep supervisions to combine high-level and low-level semantics from different scale feature maps, and that not only brings stronger information flow between layers but also reduces network parameters and improves computing efficiency. Different from the previous strategy, Seo et al. proposed mU-Net [20] that adds a convolution layer between encoder and decoder to obtain better feature fusion.

Inspired by those methods mentioned above, in this paper, we propose a novel residual inter-slice learning method for 3D organ segmentation. First, we consider using image pre-processing strategy to solve the problem of missing 3D information in a 2D network. By computing the residual difference image between adjacent slices, a strengthened new image with rich inter-slice information and little useless background information can be feed to the network. Second, we present a double-focus skip-connection that incorporates pooling operation and lossless pooling operation into skip-connection, which is better than other improved skip-connection such as mU-Net [20], U-Net++ [18], and U-Net3+ [19]. In experiments, we demonstrate that the effectiveness and robustness of the two contributions for 3D organ segmentation.

2   Method

In this paper, we propose a high-efficient 2D convolutional neural network for 3D organ segmentation. The network architecture is shown in Fig. 1. For a given 3D volume data, we first divide it into several small 3D volume data, in which each volume data includes some adjacent slices. Then we use the residual difference information between adjacent slices in a small volume data to achieve image enhancement. At the same time, we employ an encoder-decoder network with double-focus skip-connection to achieve 3D organ segmentation.

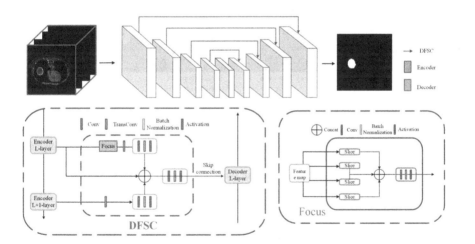

Fig. 1. An overview of Encoder-Decoder network with residual image enhancement and DFSC. The bottom-left box illustrates an double focus skip connection with encoder and decoder block. The bottom-right box presents focus blocks. The top-left box illustrates the residual image input with 5 slices. (Color figure online).

2.1   Residual Image Enhance

A medical volume data usually includes many single slices, these slices have the
temporal properties. Therefore, the prediction results of adjacent slices are only
different at the edges of organs. In view of the above, we can compute a residual
difference image corresponding to an original slice using its adjacent slices. The
residual difference image includes more important and useful information than
the original slice for organ segmentation. In Fig. 2, the first line shows the residual
difference information is clear for feature enhancement, and the second line shows
the residual difference information is also helpful for feature enhancement even
if the residual difference information is unclear. Accordingly, we can incorporate
image 3D inter-slice information into original slices to achieve better feature
learning, which is an efficient strategy for balancing feature representation and
the number of network parameters.

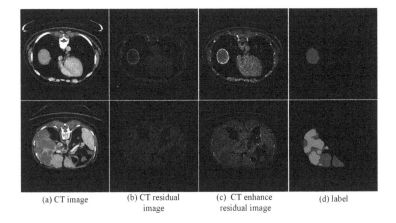

(a) CT image   (b) CT residual   (c) CT enhance   (d) label
image   residual image

Fig. 2. Clear and unclear residual images, where the original images are from LiTS
dataset. The first row is an example of small targets at the marginal layers of the 3D
volume data, and the boundary information is clear. The second row is an example of
middle targets at the middle layers of the 3D volume data. In this region, the size of
the left and right slice is basically similar, so the boundary information is not clear.
However, it can be seen that the contrast between the tumor and the organ is clear.

In order to encode the 3D information, we adopt the sliding window strategy, with a window size as a hyper-parameter, to construct a 3D image block
consisting of continuous medical image slices as the input of residual enhancement module. Use the 3D image block as the input of the residual enhancement
module. Let $X \in R^{N \times H \times W}$ be the consecutive image slices. N is the size of the
sliding window, H and W represent the spatial dimension of 2D medical images.
Particularly, we set $N = 2 * S + 1$, where S is the number of consecutive 2D image
slices stacked on top and bottom of the center slice that is the image slice to
be segmented. First, gather information between 2D slices with sliding windows

strategy in the footprint of N, subtract their pixel values with the center slice, then multiply the results respectively by the initial slice and the center slice, and finally add the results together. Performing the above operation on each slice in the sliding window and concatenating the results, thus obtaining a new matrix with the same size of N. Secondly, since subtracting the pixel values of the center slice from itself is meaningless, we ignore the center node and concatenate the remaining $N-1$ slices as input to the backbone. The pipeline is shown in Fig. 3.

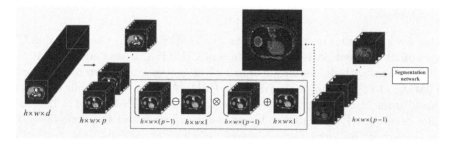

Fig. 3. The pipeline of residual image enhancement. The input is the 3D volume data, and the output is residual image slices.

2.2 Double Focus Skip Connections

The U-Net architecture duplicates low resolution information from encoders into decoders, which may cause smoothing effectiveness of object contours. The something is even serious in medical images due to low contrast of images. The core reason is that pooling operation usually leads to the loss of image detail information. To address the problem, we present the DFSC that employs lossless pooling and convolution operation to improve feature fusion between low-level feature maps from encoders and high-level feature maps from decoders.

Figure 1 shows the specific structure of DFSC. In the DFSC, the up-sampling is implemented by using a deconvolution layer composed by a transposed convolution and an activation function, which is able to filter low-resolution and low-frequency information and thus help the network leaning effective image detail information.

Formally, we formulate the skip pathway as follows: let x^i denote the output of i-th encoder layer X^i, where i indexes the down-sampling layer along the encoder and let y^i denote the input of j-th decoder layer Y^i, where j indexes the down-sampling layer along the encoder. The skip-connection of feature maps is represented by x^i, y^j is computed as:

$$y^j = C(x^i \oplus C(U(F(x^i))) \oplus C(U(x^{i+1}))) + D(y^{i-1}), \qquad (1)$$

where the function $C(\cdot)$ is a convolutional operation followed by an activation function, $U(\cdot)$ denotes the transposed convolution. $F(\cdot)$ is the Focus model, which concatenates the four signal before and after the operation. The four signals are the concatenates of the input feature map x and sample from x, the stride is set to two to yields the output y, then the output propagate with the further convolution layer. $D(\cdot)$ denotes the Decoder up-sampling layer and $\oplus$ denotes the concatenation layer.

3   Experiment

3.1   Dataset

In this work, we use two datasets. One is CHAOS-CT [21] that contains CT images of 40 different patients. Each data of CHAOS [21] set consists of 16 bit DICOM images with the resolution of 512×512, x-y spacing between 0.7–0.8 mm and having 3 to 3.2 mm inter-slice distance (ISD). And the other public dataset is obtained from Liver Tumor Segmentation Challenge (LiTS-ISBI2017) [22] that dataset is acquired from 130 abdomen contrast computed tomography (CT) scans, in which the input size of images is 512×512, and in-plane resolution has a range from $0.98 \times 0.98 \, \text{mm}^2$ to $0.45 \times 0.45 \, \text{mm}^2$. Specifically, data from 90 patients was used for training (total 43,119 slice images) and 10 patient data were used for validation. The other 31 patient data (total 15,388 images) were used for testing.

3.2   Evaluation Metrics

In order to compare quantitatively different methods, we employ universal segmentation metrics, including dice similarity coefficient (DICE), root maximum symmetric surface distance (MSD) and average symmetric surface distance (ASD, in pixel). For ASD and MSD, small values indicate better performance, while DSC vice versa. We evaluate the overlap areas between the delineated organs and the predicted organs by radiologists with DSC, and measure the Euclidean distance of boundaries with ASD.

3.3   Implementation Details

In this paper, we use both Dice and binary cross-entropy (BCE) loss between the ground truth and prediction to train our network. In U-Net [8] architecture, each encoder block contains two convolution layers and one max pooling layer. In the proposed method, we replace it with the pretrained ResNet-34 [23], which retains the first convolution layer and four feature extracting blocks without the average pooling layer and fully connected layer. We use DFSC instead of the original skip-connection. And the SPP is used as the bottleneck layer. All algorithms were implemented based on PyTorch 1.7.1 and trained on eight NVIDIA GTX 3090 GPU (24 GB). We use the Adam optimizer and set an adaptive batch size to train our network with an initial learning rate of 0.0005, which is divided by 10 every 50 epoches.

3.4   Result

Comparison with State-of-the-Arts. To validate the superiority of the proposed method, nine state-of-the-art networks used for liver segmentation are considered as comparative approaches. These networks can be roughly grouped into three categories: 1) 2-D networks; 2) 3-D networks; and 3) 2.5D networks, where 2-D networks include U-Net, U-Net++, U-Net3+, Attention U-Net, DenseU-Net, and CE-Net, 3-D networks include 3-D U-Net and V-Net, 2.5D networks include H-DenseUNet.

Table 1. Quantitative scores of the liver segmentation results. Comparison with different methods on dataset LiTS [22] and CHAOS [21]. The best values are in bold.

Method	LiTS-CT-Liver			CHAOS-CT-Liver		
	DICE(%)	ASD(mm)	MSD(mm)	DICE(%)	ASD(mm)	MSD(mm)
U-Net	93.99 ± 1.03	5.79 ± 0.53	90.25 ± 6.28	94.04 ± 2.32	1.70 ± 0.94	29.52 ± 12.23
V-Net	94.25 ± 1.3	2.48 ± 0.38	38.28 ± 5.05	92.23 ± 3.29	2.48 ± 1.06	34.21 ± 21.06
3D U-Net	94.10 ± 1.06	2.61 ± 0.43	36.43 ± 5.38	91.62 ± 4.02	2.61 ± 1.20	34.43 ± 22.38
U-Net++	94.01 ± 1.18	5.23 ± 0.45	43.25 ± 5.03	93.96 ± 2.03	2.13 ± 0.88	29.88 ± 13.26
AttentionU-Net	94.09 ± 1.43	3.42 ± 0.51	42.24 ± 6.35	94.23 ± 2.12	1.55 ± 0.55	29.42 ± 15.01
Dense U-Net	94.11 ± 1.42	4.26 ± 0.56	$\mathbf{35.65 \pm 6.21}$	94.15 ± 2.07	1.60 ± 0.90	29.12 ± 14.28
H-Dense U-Net	96.10 ± 1.02	7.02 ± 2.00	37.26 ± 3.64	96.35 ± 1.32	8.83 ± 1.33	31.56 ± 37.26
U-Net3+	96.01 ± 1.01	3.96 ± 1.77	39.86 ± 7.12	96.23 ± 2.54	2.32 ± 1.33	31.09 ± 17.32
CE-Net	94.04 ± 1.06	4.11 ± 0.51	51.22 ± 5.82	94.56 ± 1.87	1.50 ± 0.49	28.43 ± 12.13
Ours	$\mathbf{96.61 \pm 1.22}$	$\mathbf{1.52 \pm 0.61}$	41.86 ± 6.30	$\mathbf{97.05 \pm 2.31}$	$\mathbf{1.49 \pm 0.98}$	$\mathbf{28.21 \pm 18.67}$

As shown in Table 1, it can be seen that 3D networks can obtain better segmentation results than 2D networks, because 3D networks can gain more inter-slice information. However, in spite of these advantages, 3D networks generally need more data to train the feature extraction ability for different inter-slice information. For example, in the CHAOS [21] dataset, the performance of 3D networks is much lower than that of 2D networks, and this may be due to insufficient training data and thickness changes. Compared with our proposed strategy that introducing the correlation information directly into 2D network can effectively remedy the defect, so we achieved good results under the CHAOS dataset. 3D convolution operation also brings high computing costs and more parameters, and is limited by the GPU memory, so the gain of 3D networks is limited. The 2.5D network H-denseUnet [14] can balance feature expression and parameter number, take into account the advantages of 2D and 3D networks, and achieve high segmentation accuracy. 2D networks can also be further subdivided into networks that improve residual connections, including U-Net++ [18], U-Net3+ [19], Attention U-Net [24] and DenseU-Net [25]. As is shown in Fig.4, experimental results also confirm the effectiveness of the residual join strategy. However, these networks tend to do less well at the cut-off points where they intersect with organs. Compared with these methods of dense residual connection which have the problems of the redundancy of low-resolution information, the smooth segmentation boundary and the high-frequency detail information lose of the edge contour, the proposed method, which uses lossless pooling to avoid loss of detail, and achieves the best performance in terms of Dice and ASD metrics and more appealing visual results (Fig. 4).

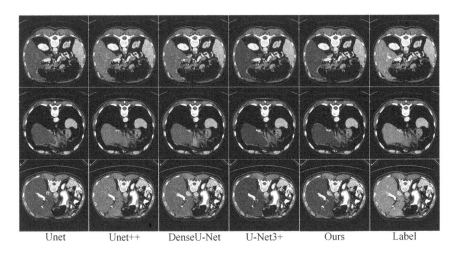

Unet   Unet++   DenseU-Net   U-Net3+   Ours   Label

Fig. 4. The segmentation results produced by different methods and the ground truths of random test subjects. (Color figure online).

Ablation Studies. As shown in Table 2, in order to evaluate the presented two contributions, whether or not there is residual image enhancement and DFSC, we conducted experiments on LiTS liver and CHAOS liver. CE-Net use natural images as pre-training models. Compared with ordinary U-Net and CE-Net, From the experiments results, it can be clearly seen that the input based on residual enhancement has significantly improved the network accuracy. Specifically, for small targets, the residual input can enhance the contour information and as for the middle targets, the residual input can make the interior of the organ evenly distributed, so as to make obviously different from the background. For the residuals different images from different slices, we have also conducted comparative experiments which show that when the number of slices exceeds 5, the accuracy is in a gradually decline, because each residual slices have the same weight. However, for the slices closer to the central slice, it should have a larger weight, thus leaves room for further improvement. In addition, compared with the network with or without DFSC module, we can also observe that DFSC can also effectively capture the high-frequency information of edge contour, and even correct some uncorrected labels.

Table 2. Comparison of ablation study on LiTS and CHAOS test dataset. The best values are in bold. The Res-image slices indicates the number of adjacent slices we use for enhancement therein.

Method	Res-image slices	DFSC	LiTS-CT-Liver DICE(%)	CHAOS-CT-Liver DICE(%)
U-Net			93.99 ± 1.03	94.04 ± 2.32
U-Net	✓(5)		94.44 ± 1.56	95.09 ± 1.93
U-Net	✓(5)	✓	94.64 ± 1.56	95.51 ± 1.80
CE-Net			94.04 ± 1.06	94.56 ± 1.87
CE-Net	✓(5)		95.54 ± 1.39	96.02 ± 2.24
CE-Net		✓	94.70 ± 1.46	95.64 ± 1.99
CE-Net	✓(3)	✓	95.95 ± 1.14	96.52 ± 2.12
CE-Net	✓(5)	✓	$\mathbf{96.61 \pm 1.22}$	$\mathbf{97.05 \pm 2.31}$
CE-Net	✓(7)	✓	96.06 ± 1.28	96.64 ± 2.38
CE-Net	✓(9)	✓	95.78 ± 1.31	96.48 ± 2.72

4 Conclusion

In this work, we proposed a residual inter-slice feature learning method employed by a 2D network that can achieve high-efficient 3D organ segmentation and a double-focus skip-connection that is used for replacing the vanilla skip-connection in an encoder-decoder network. The superior performance we achieved using two public datasets demonstrated the effectiveness of the proposed general medical image enhancement methods. We hope that this work can bring a new perspective on studying 3D feature information by using 2D networks. In the future we plan to further study more applicable methods of inter-slice information.

Acknowledgements. This work was supported in part by Key Research and Development Program of Shaanxi (Program No. 2022GY-436, 2021ZDLGY08-07), in part by Natural Science Basic Research Program of Shaanxi (Program No. 2021JC-47).

References

1. Alom, M.Z., Yakopcic, C., Hasan, M., Taha, T.M., Asari, V.K.: Recurrent residual u-net for medical image segmentation. J. Med. Imaging **6**(1), 014006 (2019)
2. Isensee, F., Jaeger, P.F., Kohl, S.A., Petersen, J., Maier-Hein, K.H.: NNU-net: a self-configuring method for deep learning-based biomedical image segmentation. Nat. Methods **18**(2), 203–211 (2021)
3. Cao, H., et al.: Swin-Unet: Unet-like pure transformer for medical image segmentation. In: Karlinsky, L., Michaeli, T., Nishino, K. (eds.) ECCV 2022, Part III. LNCS, vol. 13803, pp. 205–218. Springer, Cham (2023). https://doi.org/10.1007/978-3-031-25066-8_9

4. Chen, J., et al.: Transunet: transformers make strong encoders for medical image segmentation. arXiv preprint arXiv:2102.04306 (2021)
5. Fu, J., et al.: Dual attention network for scene segmentation. In: Proceedings of the IEEE/CVF Conference on Computer Vision and Pattern Recognition, pp. 3146–3154 (2019)
6. Zhao, H., Shi, J., Qi, X., Wang, X., Jia, J.: Pyramid scene parsing network. In: Proceedings of the IEEE Conference on Computer Vision and Pattern Recognition, pp. 2881–2890 (2017)
7. Wang, X., Girshick, R., Gupta, A., He, K.: Non-local neural networks. In: Proceedings of the IEEE Conference on Computer Vision and Pattern Recognition, pp. 7794–7803 (2018)
8. Ronneberger, O., Fischer, P., Brox, T.: U-Net: convolutional networks for biomedical image segmentation. In: Navab, N., Hornegger, J., Wells, W.M., Frangi, A.F. (eds.) MICCAI 2015. LNCS, vol. 9351, pp. 234–241. Springer, Cham (2015). https://doi.org/10.1007/978-3-319-24574-4_28
9. Gu, Z., et al.: Ce-net: context encoder network for 2D medical image segmentation. IEEE Trans. Med. Imaging **38**(10), 2281–2292 (2019)
10. Ning, M., Bian, C., Yuan, C., Ma, K., Zheng, Y.: Ensembled resunet for anatomical brain barriers segmentation. In: Segmentation, Classification, and Registration of Multi-modality Medical Imaging Data: MICCAI 2020 Challenges, ABCs 2020, L2R 2020, TN-SCUI 2020, Held in Conjunction with MICCAI 2020, Lima, Peru, October 4–8, 2020, Proceedings 23, pp. 27–33. Springer (2021)
11. Çiçek, Ö., Abdulkadir, A., Lienkamp, S.S., Brox, T., Ronneberger, O.: 3D U-Net: learning dense volumetric segmentation from sparse annotation. In: Ourselin, S., Joskowicz, L., Sabuncu, M.R., Unal, G., Wells, W. (eds.) MICCAI 2016. LNCS, vol. 9901, pp. 424–432. Springer, Cham (2016). https://doi.org/10.1007/978-3-319-46723-8_49
12. Milletari, F., Navab, N., Ahmadi, S.A.: V-net: Fully convolutional neural networks for volumetric medical image segmentation. In: 2016 Fourth International Conference on 3D Vision (3DV), pp. 565–571. IEEE (2016)
13. Yu, Q., et al.: C2fnas: coarse-to-fine neural architecture search for 3D medical image segmentation. In: Proceedings of the IEEE/CVF Conference on Computer Vision and Pattern Recognition, pp. 4126–4135 (2020)
14. Li, X., Chen, H., Qi, X., Dou, Q., Fu, C.W., Heng, P.A.: H-denseunet: hybrid densely connected Unet for liver and tumor segmentation from CT volumes. IEEE Trans. Med. Imaging **37**(12), 2663–2674 (2018)
15. Zhang, J., Xie, Y., Zhang, P., Chen, H., Xia, Y., Shen, C.: Light-weight hybrid convolutional network for liver tumor segmentation. In: IJCAI. vol. 19, pp. 4271–4277 (2019)
16. Calisto, M.B., Lai-Yuen, S.K.: Adaen-net: an ensemble of adaptive 2d–3d fully convolutional networks for medical image segmentation. Neural Netw. **126**, 76–94 (2020)
17. Long, J., Shelhamer, E., Darrell, T.: Fully convolutional networks for semantic segmentation. In: Proceedings of the IEEE Conference on Computer Vision and Pattern Recognition, pp. 3431–3440 (2015)
18. Zhou, Z., Siddiquee, M.M.R., Tajbakhsh, N., Liang, J.: Unet++: redesigning skip connections to exploit multiscale features in image segmentation. IEEE Trans. Med. Imaging **39**(6), 1856–1867 (2019)
19. Huang, H., et al.: 3+: A fullscale connected unet for medical image segmentation. ICASSP 2020-2020 IEEE International Conference on Acoustics, Speech and Signal Processing (ICASSP) (2020)

20. Seo, H., Huang, C., Bassenne, M., Xiao, R., Xing, L.: Modified u-net (mu-net) with incorporation of object-dependent high level features for improved liver and liver-tumor segmentation in ct images. IEEE Trans. Med. Imaging **39**(5), 1316–1325 (2019)

21. Kavur, A.E., et al.: Chaos challenge-combined (CT-MR) healthy abdominal organ segmentation. Med. Image Anal. **69**, 101950 (2021)

22. Bilic, P., et al.: The liver tumor segmentation benchmark (lits). Medical Image Analysis p. 102680 (2022)

23. He, K., Zhang, X., Ren, S., Sun, J.: Deep residual learning for image recognition. In: Proceedings of the IEEE Conference on Computer Vision and Pattern Recognition, pp. 770–778 (2016)

24. Oktay, O., et al.: Attention u-net: learning where to look for the pancreas. arXiv preprint arXiv:1804.03999 (2018)

25. Guan, S., Khan, A.A., Sikdar, S., Chitnis, P.V.: Fully dense unet for 2-d sparse photoacoustic tomography artifact removal. IEEE J. Biomed. Health Inform. **24**(2), 568–576 (2019)

Color and Multispectral Processing

A Cross-Paired Wavelet Based Spatiotemporal Fusion Network for Remote Sensing Images

Xingjian Zhang[1], Shaohuai Yu[2], Xinghua Li[1(✉)] (iD), Shuang Li[1] (iD),
and Zhenyu Tan[3] (iD)

[1] School of Remote Sensing and Information Engineering, Wuhan University, Wuhan, China
`lixinghua5540@whu.edu.cn`
[2] CCCC Second Highway Consultants Co., Ltd., Wuhan, China
[3] College of Urban and Environmental Sciences, Northwest University, Xi'an, China

Abstract. Spatiotemporal fusion is an effective way to provide remote sensing images with both high temporal resolution and high spatial resolution for earth observation. Most of the existing methods require at least three images as input, which may increase the difficulty in practical applications. Towards this end, a cross-paired wavelet based spatiotemporal fusion network (CPW-STFN) for remote sensing images is proposed. The wavelet transform decomposes the low and high frequency components of the image into four channels, so that it enables the model to train features of different level separately. The proposed CPW-STFN can extract the detail textures as well as the global information better and easier. In other words, we achieved a spatiotemporal fusion method with only two cross-paired images as inputs which are the fine resolution image at reference date and the coarse resolution image at prediction date. In addition, a compound loss function containing a wavelet loss to promote the spatial detail preservation is proposed. In this paper, the fusion ability of the proposed CPW-STFN was tested by the commonly used datasets CIA and LGC, and compared with other methods including state-of-the-art models STARFM, FSDAF, EDCSTFN, MLFF-GAN and GAN-STFM. CPW-STFN performs better than GAN-STFM which also requires only two input images, and not inferior to the other methods which require at least three inputs, proving its advantage and potential.

Keywords: Convolutional neural network · Remote sensing image · Spatiotemporal fusion · Wavelet transform

1 Introduction

In many remote sensing applications, such as crop monitoring, water quality analysis and land-cover change detection [1], not only the data with high spatial resolution are necessary to capture ground details, but also the data with high temporal resolution are needed to provide change information. However, remote sensing images with both high spatial and temporal resolutions are difficult to capture by a single satellite due to the mutual constraints in spatial and temporal resolutions. The spatiotemporal fusion model is a practical method to break through the limits of current satellite observation

© The Author(s), under exclusive license to Springer Nature Switzerland AG 2023
H. Lu et al. (Eds.): ICIG 2023, LNCS 14359, pp. 143–154, 2023.
https://doi.org/10.1007/978-3-031-46317-4_13

systems. It combines ground details from high spatial resolution images with change information from high temporal resolution images to generate image sequences with both high temporal resolution and high spatial resolution.

Generally, the existing spatiotemporal fusion methods can be divided into five categories: (1) transformation-based methods; (2) reconstruction-based methods; (3) Bayesian-based methods; (4) learning-based methods; (5) hybrid methods [1–3].

Transformation-based methods use advanced mathematical transformations, such as wavelet transform and tassel-cap transform to integrate multi-source information into an abstract space to perform image fusion [3]. Reconstruction-based methods can be further classified into weight function-based methods and unmixing-based methods. The STARFM [4] model is the firstly proposed weight function-based methods, and it is the basis of many fusion methods afterward. Unmixing-based methods predict high spatial resolution image according to the linear theory, such as MMT [7], STDFA [8], etc. Bayesian-based methods transforms the fusion problem into the probability estimation problem, and obtain the fusion result by the maximum posteriori estimation [9, 10]. Learning-based methods show higher accuracy and stability than traditional methods. They learn the complex nonlinear relationship between reference images and prediction images by establishing a model to predict image. Sparse representation or dictionary learning methods are the earliest learning-based methods, such as SPSTFM [11]. Deep-learning-based methods usually adopt CNN network structure. Due to the powerful feature extraction ability of CNN, the accuracy and adaptability of spatiotemporal image fusion can be greatly promoted. Typical CNN-based methods include STFDCNN [12], BiaSTF [13], EDCSTFN [2] and StfNet [14]. In recent years, GAN has also been widely used for its strong information generation ability showing great potential in image fusion, such as GAN-STFM [15], CycleGAN-STF [16] and MLFF-GAN [17]. Hybrid methods combine two or more methods from the above four categories, aiming to improve the performance of spatiotemporal image fusion by combining the advantages of different methods. One representative of hybrid methods is the flexible data fusion model FSDAF [18], which combines two kinds of fusion methods based on unmixing and weight function. As a result, FSDAF is able to generate satisfactory results even in challenging scenarios.

However, most of the current models require three or even five input images, ignoring the fact that proper image pairs are difficult to collect due to bad weather condition or missing data [15]. Thus, how to predict better results with fewer input images is still a major challenge in the field of spatiotemporal fusion. Wavelet transform is a feasible way for this issue. Although wavelet transform has not been used in deep-learning-based spatiotemporal image fusion before, it has been widely used in image super resolution [19–21], proving its superiority. To this end, this paper introduces wavelet transform into spatiotemporal fusion model with only two cross-paired images. A wavelet-based model named CPW-STFN is proposed in this paper, and the comparison experiments with the mainstream spatiotemporal fusion methods verified its effectiveness.

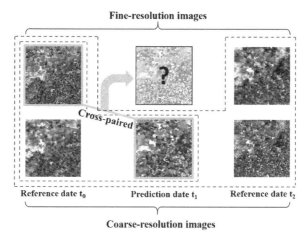

Fig. 1. The basic spatiotemporal fusion schematic. (Color figure online)

2 Proposed Work

Figure 1 demonstrates the basic spatiotemporal fusion schematic. In many cases, spatiotemporal fusion model inputs require at least one coarse-fine resolution image pair at reference date and a coarse resolution image at prediction date in the blue dotted box, or even two coarse-fine resolution image pairs at reference dates and a coarse resolution image at prediction date in the red dotted box. While, CPW-STFN only requires two inputs which are the images with yellow edges. As shown in Fig. 1, the two images are at cross dates, thus they are called the cross-paired inputs.

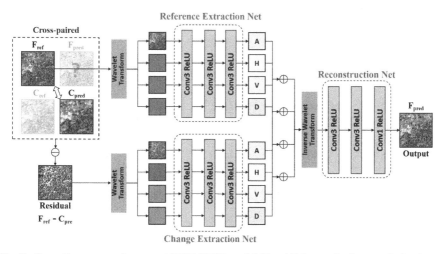

Fig. 2. Overall structure of proposed CPW-STFN model (F and C denote the fine-resolution image and the coarse-resolution image, respectively; The subscripts ref and pred denote the corresponding image is at reference date and prediction date, respectively). (Color figure online)

Figure 2 shows the overall structure of CPW-STFN. The input of our model is a fine-resolution image at reference date and a coarse-resolution image at prediction date. The output is the fine-resolution image at prediction date. Theoretically, the predicted fine-resolution image can be decomposed into the reference information and the change information due to the time span [2]. Based on this theory, our model can be divided into three subnets: the reference extraction net, the change extraction net and the reconstruction net.

For the reference extraction net, four coefficients of the wavelet transform applied on the fine-resolution image at reference date are entered into the network independently, and corresponding features of the four coefficients are obtained. For the change extraction net, the model makes the wavelet transform after the difference between the fine-resolution image at reference date and coarse-resolution image at prediction data. Then the four coefficients are input similarly and independently into the change extraction net to obtain four corresponding changing features. By adding the four corresponding features extracted from the two subnets and performing inverse wavelet transform, features at prediction date can be generated. Finally, for the reconstruction net, features are restored to the pixel space generating the fine-resolution image at prediction time. The process can be formulated as Eq. (1).

$$F_{t*} = f\{IDWT[g(DWT(F_{t_k})) + h(DWT(F_{t_k} - C_{t*}))]\} \tag{1}$$

where F_{t_k} and C_{t*} denote the fine-resolution image at reference date and the coarse-resolution image at prediction date, respectively; F_{t*} denotes the predicted fine-resolution image at prediction date; g and h denote the reference extraction net and the change extraction net, respectively; f denotes the reconstruction net; DWT and $IDWT$ denote the wavelet transform and the inverse wavelet transform, respectively. We use "Haar" kernel throughout our experiments.

2.1 Wavelet Transform

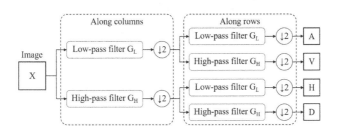

Fig. 3. Process of the wavelet transform.

Figure 3 shows the basic process of wavelet transform [19]. Image X is firstly passed through a low-pass filter GL and a high-pass filter GH, then half downsampled along columns. After that, two paths are both passed to low-pass and high-pass filters respectively, and further half downsampled along rows. Finally, four different coefficients are generated, which comprise average (A), vertical (V), horizontal (H), and diagonal (D) information details from the original image respectively.

Figure. 4 illustrates a wavelet transform example on remote sensing image. As we can see, "A" stores low frequency information, while "V", "H", and "D" focus on high frequency information. Moreover, both the wavelet transform and the inverse wavelet transform are invertible, leading to no information loss. Therefore, with wavelet transform, diverse information will be better preserved by spatiotemporal fusion model because they can be trained separately. Thus, we can achieve better prediction results with fewer input images.

Fig. 4. Wavelet transform example on remote sensing image.

2.2 Loss Function

To enhance the quality of prediction image, a compound loss function instead of single loss function is proposed. It is composed of wavelet loss $L_{wavelet}$, feature loss $L_{feature}$ and vision loss L_{vision}, formulated as Eq. (2).

$$L_{total} = L_{wavelet} + L_{feature} + L_{vision} \qquad (2)$$

To assist the model in generating more detailed textures, we adopt a wavelet loss instead of common RMSE loss or MAE loss in many other spatiotemporal fusion models [22]. The wavelet loss is calculated by the MAE between the coefficients of predicted image and target image, expressed as Eq. (3).

$$L_{wavelet} = \frac{1}{N} \sum_{i=1}^{N} \left| \hat{I}_j - I_j \right| (j = A, V, H, D) \qquad (3)$$

where $\hat{I}_A, \hat{I}_V, \hat{I}_H$, and $\hat{I}_D$ denote the four coefficients of the predicted image, respectively, I_A, I_V, I_H, and I_D denotes the four coefficients of the corresponding ground truth image, respectively.

In our model, feature loss needs to be calculated through a pretrained model [2], as shown in Fig. 5. The encoder extracts the compressed feature from the fine-resolution image to obtain detailed texture information, and the decoder restores the extracted original feature to the original input. With this pretrained model, the function of feature loss is defined in the Eq. (4).

$$L_{feature} = \frac{1}{N} \sum_{i=1}^{N} \left| \hat{FL}_{t_1} - FL_{t_1} \right| \qquad (4)$$

where $\hat{FL}_{t_1}$ and FL_{t_1} denote the features extracted by the pretrained model encoder from the predicted image and the corresponding ground truth image, respectively.

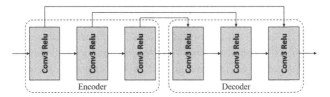

Fig. 5. The pretrained AutoEncoder for feature loss calculation.

Visual loss is designed to improve the overall image quality. Visual loss is calculated by multi-scale structural similarity, which is the average of structural similarity. The larger SSIM is, the better the fusion result will be. Therefore, vision loss is defined in Eq. (5).

$$L_{vision} = -MSSIM = -\frac{1}{N}\sum_{k=1}^{N} SSIM \qquad (5)$$

3 Experiments and Results

3.1 Study Areas and Datasets

In the experiments, two open-source datasets were used to test the proposed model, namely the Coleambally Irrigation Area (CIA) and Lower Gwydir Catchment (LGC) [23]. CIA is a coastal irrigation area with significant phenological changes in crop growing seasons in southern New South Wales, Australia. The dataset is composed of image pairs acquired by Landsat-7 ETM + and MODTRAN4. There are 17 pairs of cloud-less Landsat-MODIS images composed of six spectral bands in CIA, all interpolated to the size of 2040 × 1720. LGC is located in northern New South Wales, Australia. The dataset is composed of Landsat-5 TM and MODIS Terra MOD09GA product. There are 14 pairs of images in LGC, they all have 6 bands with the size of 3200 × 2720. It should be noted that, we clipped the images in both datasets into 1200 × 1200 with major change area to carry out the experiment.

For CIA, the temporal dynamics are mainly related to the seasonal growth of crops, while the surrounding areas vary less. Thus, the CIA dataset is considered as a spatially heterogeneous area. For LGC, significant variation occurs due to the flood event within the time span, making the LGC dataset a temporally dynamic one.

3.2 Experimental Design

To verify the superiority of our proposed CPW-STFN model, the fusion results are analyzed and compared with five state-of-the-art methods including STARFM [4], FSDAF [18], EDCSTFN [2], GANSTFM [15] and MLFF-GAN [17]. Among these comparison methods, only GAN-STFM uses two input images for prediction the same as our method, the other methods all require at least three input images to perform the fusion. To ensure a fair comparison, all these methods adopt the default parameters given by the authors during our experiments.

Four metrics are used to comprehensively evaluate the fusion results quantitatively, including the root mean square error (RMSE), structural similarity index (SSIM) [24], correlation coefficient (CC) and spectral angle mapper (SAM) [25]. Among these metrics, larger SSIM and CC indicate better fusion quality, while RMSE and SAM are the opposite.

3.3 Experimental Results and Analysis

Quantitative comparison. The quantitative evaluations in terms of RMSE, SSIM, CC and SAM for the fusion results of CIA and LGC are presented in Table 1 and Table 2. It can be seen that, among the methods that only require two input images, CPW-STFN performs better than the GAN-STFM in terms of all quantitative metrics. Compared with methods requiring three input images, CPW-STFN has no absolute advantage in terms of quantitative evaluation accuracy, but it can also reach the mainstream accuracy. Therefore, we believe that our proposed method is quite promising in practical applications.

Table 1. Quantitative evaluation results for the CIA dataset.

Model Type	Models	RMSE↓	SSIM↑	CC↑	SAM↓
3 input images	STARFM [4]	454.3621	0.7869	0.7528	0.1058
	FSDAF [18]	263.4145	0.9119	0.8873	0.0840
	EDCSTFN [2]	264.6520	0.9158	0.8981	0.0817
	MLFF-GAN [17]	214.4982	0.9339	0.9165	0.0657
2 input images	GAN-STFM [15]	267.8274	0.9047	0.8754	0.0865
	CPW-STFN	**267.7951**	**0.9119**	**0.8921**	**0.0810**

Qualitative Comparison. Fusion results of different methods are demonstrated in Fig. 6 and Fig. 7. On the whole, we can see that the model can obtain satisfactory results. In order to compare the fusion ability of different models on CIA and LGC datasets, we classified the results to evaluate their application potential. Then we calculated the vegetation index NDVI to further make further analyses and compared the NVDI results with ground truth NDVI to visualize their prediction accuracy.

Figure 8 demonstrates the analyses of fusion results on 2002–03-10 in CIA area. The first column shows the fusion results of different methods and the corresponding observed image. The second column shows the full bands ISODATA classification of the fusion results. The third column displays the zoomed-in details in the yellow box in the first column. And the forth column demonstrates the NDVI results corresponding to the

Table 2. Quantitative evaluation results for the LGC dataset.

Model Type	Models	RMSE↓	SSIM↑	CC↑	SAM↓
3 input images	STARFM [4]	355.4197	0.8219	0.8124	0.0821
	FSDAF [18]	226.3430	0.9190	0.9048	0.0714
	EDCSTFN [2]	236.1960	0.9105	0.8943	0.0811
	MLFF-GAN [17]	181.6687	0.9439	0.9255	0.0591
2 input images	GAN-STFM [15]	252.0493	0.8908	0.8673	0.0840
	CPW-STFN	**224.8918**	**0.9091**	**0.8887**	**0.0769**

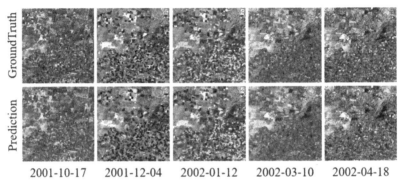

Fig. 6. The fusion results of CIA (All images use NIR-red-green as RGB). (Color figure online)

Fig. 7. The fusion results of LGC (All images use NIR-red-green as RGB). (Color figure online)

third column. The fifth column presents the difference images between NDVI results of different methods in the fourth column and the corresponding ground truth NDVI, and they are stretched to 0–1 for display, 1 represents the largest difference with the actual image, and 0 represents the same. From the original fusion results and the classification maps, it can be seen that, except for the STARFM method which produce obvious noises and poor classification result, other methods can generate satisfactory results. Most

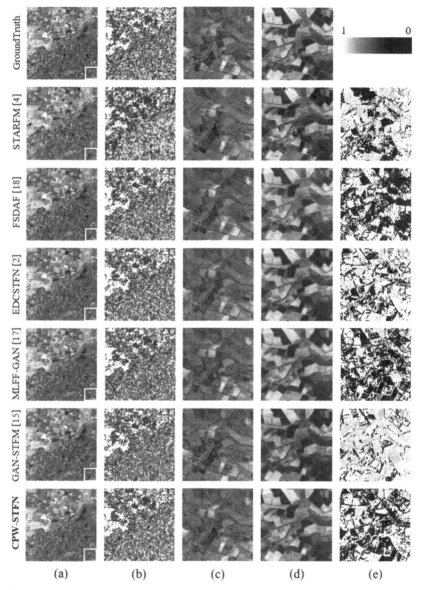

Fig. 8. The fusion results on 2002–03-10 in CIA area. (a) Full view; (b) ISODATA classification; (c) Zoomed details; (d) NDVI; (e) NDVI error maps. (Color figure online)

intuitively, from the difference image of NDVI in the last column, we can conclude that our proposed CPW-STFN is slightly inferior to MLFF-GAN and significantly superior to STARFM, EDCSTFN and GANSTFM.

Figure 9 shows the analysis result of the LGC data on 2005–01-29 using the same method for the CIA data set. Overall, CPW-STFN can compete with other fusion models with less input in terms of quantitative evaluation and visual effects.

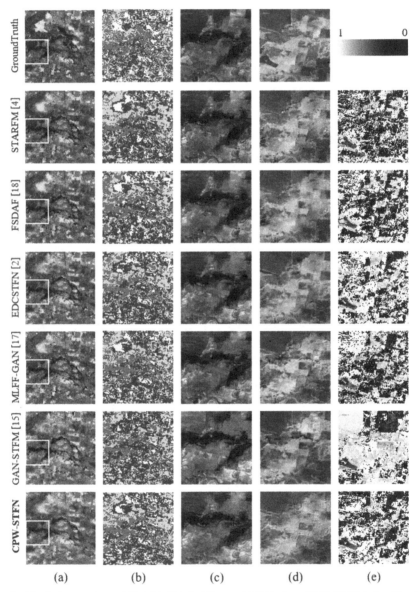

Fig. 9. The fusion results on 2005–01-29 in LGC area. (a) Full view; (b) ISODATA classification; (c) Zoomed details; (d) NDVI; (e) NDVI error maps. (Color figure online)

4 Conclusion

In this paper, a cross-paired wavelet based spatiotemporal fusion network CPW-STFN is proposed, which solves the problem that most of the current fusion methods require at least three input images, improving the practicability of the model in earth observation applications. Experiments were conducted on CIA and LGC datasets which represent spatial heterogeneity and temporal dynamics areas respectively. The fusion results of the proposed CPW-STFN model are compared with those of the existing models, showing that in terms of quantitative accuracy and visual effect of fusion results, CPW-STFN performs better than the only contemporary method requiring two input images, and it is quite competitive with other spatiotemporal fusion methods with less input. Thus, we can conclude that the proposed method has strong applicability and development prospect. In future work, we expect to further improve the fusion quality and accuracy of the model to achieve more satisfactory results with limited inputs.

Acknowledgement. This work was supported by the National Natural Science Foundation of China (NSFC) under Grant no. 42171302 and the Key R&D Program of Hubei Province, China (2021BAA185).

References

1. Li, J., Li, Y., He, L., Chen, J., Plaza, A.: Spatio-temporal fusion for remote sensing data: an overview and new benchmark. Sci. China Inf. Sci. **63**(4), 7–23 (2020)
2. Tan, Z., Di, L., Zhang, M., Guo, L., Gao, M.: An enhanced deep convolutional model for spatiotemporal image fusion. Remote Sensing **11**(24), 2898 (2019)
3. Chen, B., Huang, B., Xu, B.: Comparison of spatiotemporal fusion models: a review. Remote Sensing **7**(2), 1798–1835 (2015)
4. Gao, F., Masek, J., Schwaller, M., Hall, F.: On the blending of the landsat and MODIS surface reflectance: predicting daily Landsat surface reflectance. IEEE Trans. Geosci. Remote Sens.Geosci. Remote Sens. **44**(8), 2207–2218 (2006)
5. Zhu, X., Chen, J., Gao, F., Chen, X., Masek, J.G.: An enhanced spatial and temporal adaptive reflectance fusion model for complex heterogeneous regions. Remote Sens. Environ. **114**(11), 2610–2623 (2010)
6. Hilker, T., Wulder, M.A., Coops, N.C., et al.: A new data fusion model for high spatial- and temporal-resolution mapping of forest disturbance based on Landsat and MODIS. Remote Sens. Environ. **113**(8), 1613–1627 (2009)
7. Zhukov, B., Oertel, D., Lanzl, F., Reinhackel, G.: Unmixing-based multisensor multiresolution image fusion. IEEE Trans. Geosci. Remote Sens.Geosci. Remote Sens. **37**(3), 1212–1226 (1999)
8. Wu, M., Niu, Z., Wang, C., Wu, C., Wang, L.: Use of MODIS and Landsat time series data to generate high-resolution temporal synthetic Landsat data using a spatial and temporal reflectance fusion model. J. Appl. Remote. Sens. **6**(1), 063507 (2012)
9. Xue, J., Leung, Y., Fung, T.: A bayesian data fusion approach to spatio-temporal fusion of remotely sensed images. Remote Sensing **9**(12), 1310 (2017)
10. Shen, H., Meng, X., Zhang, L.: An integrated framework for the spatio-temporal-spectral fusion of remote sensing images. IEEE Trans. Geosci. Remote Sens.Geosci. Remote Sens. **54**(12), 7135–7148 (2016)

11. Huang, B., Song, H.: Spatiotemporal reflectance fusion via sparse representation. IEEE Trans. Geosci. Remote Sens.Geosci. Remote Sens. **50**(10), 3707–3716 (2012)

12. Song, H., Liu, Q., Wang, G., Hang, R., Huang, B.: Spatiotemporal satellite image fusion using deep convolutional neural networks. IEEE J. Selected Topics Appli Earth Observat. Remote Sensing **11**(3), 821–829 (2018)

13. Li, Y., Li, J., He, L., Chen, J., Plaza, A.: A new sensor bias-driven spatio-temporal fusion model based on convolutional neural networks. Sci. China Inf. Sci. **63**(4), 140302 (2020)

14. Liu, X., Deng, C., Chanussot, J., Hong, D., Zhao, B.: StfNet: a two-stream convolutional neural network for spatiotemporal image fusion. IEEE Trans. Geosci. Remote Sens.Geosci. Remote Sens. **57**(9), 6552–6564 (2019)

15. Tan, Z., Gao, M., Li, X., Jiang, L.: A flexible reference-insensitive spatiotemporal fusion model for remote sensing images using conditional generative adversarial network. IEEE Trans. Geosci. Remote Sens. **60**, 1–13 (2021)

16. Chen, J., Wang, L., Feng, R., Liu, P., Han, W., Chen, X.: CycleGAN-STF: spatiotemporal fusion via CycleGAN-based image generation. IEEE Trans. Geosci. Remote Sens.Geosci. Remote Sens. **59**(7), 5851–5865 (2020)

17. Song, B., Liu, P., Li, J., Wang, L., Zhang, L., He, G., et al.: MLFF-GAN: a multilevel feature fusion with GAN for spatiotemporal remote sensing images. IEEE Trans. Geosci. Remote Sens.Geosci. Remote Sens. **60**, 1–16 (2022)

18. Zhu, X., Helmer, E.H., Gao, F., Liu, D., Chen, J., Lefsky, M.A.: A flexible spatiotemporal method for fusing satellite images with different resolutions. Remote Sens. Environ. **172**, 165–177 (2016)

19. Xue, S., Qiu, W., Liu, F., Jin, X.: Wavelet-based residual attention network for image super-resolution. Neurocomputing **382**, 116–126 (2020)

20. Huang, H., He, R., Sun, Z., Tan, T.: Wavelet-srnet: a wavelet-based cnn for multi-scale face super resolution. In: IEEE International Conference on Computer Vision, pp. 1689–1697. IEEE, Venice, Italy (2017)

21. Hsu, W.Y., Jian, P.W.: Detail-enhanced wavelet residual network for single image super-resolution. IEEE Trans. Instrum. Meas.Instrum. Meas. **71**, 1–13 (2022)

22. Zhang, H., Jin, Z., Tan, X., Li, X.: Towards lighter and faster learning wavelets progressively for image super-resolution. In: 28th ACM International Conference on Multimedia, pp. 2113–2121. ACM, Seattle, USA (2020)

23. Emelyanova, I.V., McVicar, T.R., Van Niel, T.G., Li, L.T., Van Dijk, A.I.: Assessing the accuracy of blending Landsat–MODIS surface reflectances in two landscapes with contrasting spatial and temporal dynamics: A framework for algorithm selection. Remote Sens. Environ. **133**, 193–209 (2013)

24. Wang, Z., Bovik, A.C., Sheikh, H.R., Simoncelli, E.P.: Image quality assessment: from error visibility to structural similarity. IEEE Trans. Image Process. **13**(4), 600–612 (2004)

25. Yuhas, R.H., Goetz, A.F., Boardman, J.W.: Descrimination among semi-arid landscape end-members using the spectral angle mapper (SAM) algorithm. In: The Third Annual JPL Airborne Geoscience Workshop, pp. 147–149. AVIRIS Workshop. California, USA (1992)

Coupled Dense Convolutional Neural Networks with Autoencoder for Unsupervised Hyperspectral Super-Resolution

Xin Lin[1], Yuanchao Su[1(✉)], Sheng Li[1], Mengying Jiang[2], Bin Pan[3], Pengfei Li[1], Jinying Bai[4], and Feng Liu[1]

[1] College of Geomatics, Xi'an University of Science and Technology, Xi'an, China
suych3@xust.edu.cn
[2] School of Electronics and Information Engineering, Xi'an Jiaotong University, Xi'an, China
[3] School of Statistics and Data Science, Nankai University, Tianjin, China
[4] Xi'an Piesat Information Technology Co., Ltd., Xi'an, China

Abstract. Hyperspectral Imagery (HSI) contains rich spectral information, but the resolution of hyperspectral imagery is often low sometimes. Recently, hyperspectral super-resolution technology has been developed to meet the needs of engineering applications. The new technology can mitigate many problems due to lower original spatial resolution. Nowadays, the development of deep learning provides many paths to design super-resolution methods and facilitates the development of related technologies. DenseNet, a sophisticated tool used to achieve prediction using deep networks, has found applications in various fields. Our contribution to this field involves the development of a coupled dense convolutional neural network (CoDenNet). It comprises three autoencoders that work together to acquire endmembers and abundances. Two of the three autoencoders have been designed explicitly for learning the parameters of the point spread function (PSF) alongside the spectral response function (SRF). The third autoencoder, on the other hand, fosters connections between different types of imagery: HSI and MSI. Compared with other super-resolution (SR) and fusion methods, We demonstrate the effectiveness and competitiveness of the proposed approach.

Keywords: Super-resolution (SR) · Convolutional neural network · Autoencoder · Dense block

1 Introduction

1.1 A Subsection Sample

Hyperspectral images consist of data cubes that contain hundreds of consecutive narrowband images that cover an extensive wavelength range. Hyperspectral images have been extensively utilized in land cover analysis, target detection, and geological surveys during the past few decades due to their high spectral resolution. The hyperspectral images are acquired by hyperspectral sensors (a.k.a. imaging spectrometers).The sensor

© The Author(s), under exclusive license to Springer Nature Switzerland AG 2023
H. Lu et al. (Eds.): ICIG 2023, LNCS 14359, pp. 155–165, 2023.
https://doi.org/10.1007/978-3-031-46317-4_14

can only permit a minute portion of the radiant energy from each band to pass through to the instrument, resulting in high spectral resolution. However, the resolution of hyperspectral image data tends to be low due to technological hardware limitations, restricting its applications. Conversely, multispectral images have fewer bands but superior resolution. HSI Super-resolution achieves higher resolution by fusing MSI and HSI, generating novel data with superior spatial and spectral resolution [1].

The motivation behind solving image fusion in this study primarily originates from the rich spectral information and an ample number of hybrid pixels present in hyperspectral imagery. Effective mixed pixel decomposition is also a significant research topic in computer vision and remote sensing [2]. In general, mixed pixel decomposition is the recovery of spectral response, i.e., recovery of the underlying pure material spectra (called endmembers) and their relative proportions (called abundances). The results of hyperspectral unmixing can be important information not only in practical applications such as geological exploration or HSI super-resolution problems [3]. This can be attributed to the disparity in the number of bands between multispectral and hyperspectral data coupled with the need to maintain endmembers and abundance within the pixels during up-sampling.

Contribution. In this paper, we propose a novel network model to generate high-resolution hyperspectral images based on hyperspectral and multispectral data features. Our paper's contributions can be summarized in three aspects, as follows:

- This paper introduces CoDenNet, an unsupervised network model used to extract information features. CoDenNet does not require prior knowledge, such as PSF and SRF, making it more effective than other existing models (as discussed in Sect. 2).
- The article innovatively introduces the network structure of DenseNet, which is unprecedented in similar models. The results show that the CoDenNet performs better than six state-of-the-art HSI-MSI fusion methods.
- Generates high-resolution hyperspectral data along with endmembers and abundances, which significantly facilitates the application of hyperspectral data.

2 Related Work

The existing methods for the fusion of hyperspectral and multispectral images can be categorized as: 1) extensions of pansharpening methods; 2) Bayesian-based approaches; 3) matrix decomposition-based methods [4]. This article focuses on the third method: it is usually assumed that the HSI consists of a series of pure spectral vectors, and the HSI can be decomposed into abundances and endmembers. Thus the fusion problem becomes a problem—the estimation of abundances and endmembers. So Kawakami et al. [5] proposed an unmixing method to fuse low-resolution HSI (LrHSI) and high-resolution MSI (LrMSI) images.

Deep learning has been successfully applied to many spectral tasks in recent years. Similarly, it can be applied to the HSI-MSI fusion problem. Li et al. [6] proposed a partial dense connectivity network to fuse MSI and HSI spatial and spectral letters. Many fusion methods assume that the SRF and PSF are known, while this information is actually challenging to obtain [7]. So these methods cannot be widely applied in practice. Zheng's proposed approach solves some of the above problems [8].

The autoencoder is usually an unsupervised network that extracts endmembers and estimates the corresponding abundance. It can learn SRF and PSF adaptively through the unmixing assumptions on hyperspectral data. However, many Autoencoder architectures are developed to solve the linear unmixing problem, ignoring the interactions between different endmembers [9]. DenseNet has been an excellent model for extracting image domain features in recent years. The design of the bottle layer in this model makes it well able to alleviate the gradient disappearance problem and reduce the number of parameters at the same time [10].

Based on the advantages of the DenseNet model, this paper replaces the conventional network in the encoder with a densenet layer. The paper improves the dense layer of the DenseNet model several times to analyze endmembers and abundances better, which makes the unmixing ability of our network improved as well (more details will be explained in Sect. 4). Meanwhile, we set up specific 2D convolutional layers to extract the two key parameters, SRF and PSF, in the image fusion problem to obtain them without the prior information. In the third part of the article, we will detail the basic formulas of HSI and MSI data fusion and describe the three Autoencoders of the proposed approach.

3 Method

This section introduces our proposed coupled network for image fusion. As shown in Fig. 1, which demonstrates the flowchart of the proposed approach, the proposed coupled network has three auto-encoder, i.e., the HrMSI-Autoencoder for the estimated target HrHSI Z, the LrHSI-Autoencoder for the reconstructed images, and the LrMSI-autoencoder for estimated target LrMSI.

HSI Super-resolution (SR) problem requires the estimation of the HSI. Following the linear mixing model, we can assume that each pixel of HSI is the linear combination of a set of pure spectral bases (called endmembers) and the coefficients of each pure spectral basis (call abundances) [11]. Let $Y \equiv [Y_1, Y_2, ..., Y_L]^\top \in \mathbb{R}^{MN \times L}$ be the low spatial resolution HSI data, $X \equiv [X_1, X_2, ..., X_l]^\top \in \mathbb{R}^{MN \times l}$ be the high spatial resolution MSI data, and $Z \in \mathbb{R}^{MN \times L}$ be the high spatial resolution HSI data, respectively.

The relation between target HrHSI $\tilde{Z}$ and endmembers A and E can be described as:

$$Z = AE \tag{1}$$

where the matrix $A \in \mathbb{R}^{mn \times L}$ is formed from the abundances, the matrix $E \in \mathbb{R}^{p \times L}$ is made up of the endmembers, and p is the number of pure spectral bases.

Based on the idea of the aforementioned formula, we can also represent the original input hyperspectral data Z as a linear combination of the same endmembers E:

$$Y = A_h E = S * Z = S * AE \tag{2}$$

where the matrix $A_h \in \mathbb{R}^{mn \times L}$ represents the abundances, the matrix $S \in \mathbb{R}^{mn \times p}$ is the PSF, which describes the spatial degradation function, and $*$ denotes the convolution operator.

In this paper, we establish the spectral correlation relationship between HSI and MSI by utilizing the following equation:

$$X = ZR = AER \tag{3}$$

where the matrix $R \in \mathbb{R}^{L \times l}$ is the SRF, which describes the spectral degradation process.

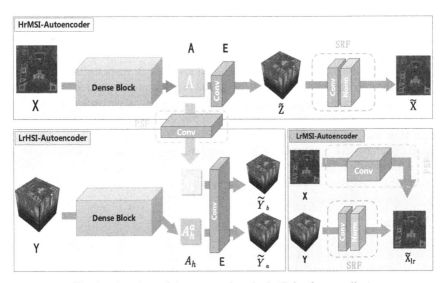

Fig. 1. Flowchart of the proposed method. (Color figure online)

The details of the Dense Block will describe in Fig. 2.

In the model, we use SRF and PSF to respectively describe the spectral and spatial degradation relationships of the input data:

$$X_{lr} = YR = S * X \tag{4}$$

where the matrix $X_{lr} \in \mathbb{R}^{m \times n \times l}$ represents the low spatial resolution multispectral image (LrMSI).

The proposed model in this paper is based on the principle of hyperspectral unmixing and therefore needs to satisfy the following characteristics:

$$\sum a_{ij} = 1 \forall i, j$$

$$a_{ij}0 \geqslant \forall i, j \tag{5}$$

$$1 \geqslant e_{ij} \geqslant 0 \forall i, j$$

where a_{ij} is an unit of abundance A and e_{ij} is an unit of endmember E. Three constraints ensure that the model satisfies the sum-to-one property, non-negativity of abundance, and bounded properties of endmembers.

3.1 LrHSI-Autoencoder

In this Autoencoder, we designed the encoder and decoder: encoder is used for A_h^a and decoder tries to reconstruct the $\tilde{Y}_a$ and $\tilde{Y}_b$. The encoder function can be expressed as:

$$A_h^a = f_{en}(Y) \tag{6}$$

where the f_{en} attempts to learn a non-linear mapping and transforms the input LrHSI to its abundances A_h^a. Considering the superiority of DenseNet in feature extraction, we introduced the dense block to address the traditional self-encoder architecture's shortcomings—neglecting the multiple interactions between different endmembers.

DenseBlock. An important reason for the effectiveness of the model proposed in the article is the addition of the DenseBlock model design to the traditional Autoencoder architecture. DenseNet is an enhanced model inspired by the ResNet network, where each layer has connections to all prior layers, enabling effective utilization of extracted features and minimizing the number of parameters.

To meet the sum-to-one feature of the abundances, the softmax function (shown in blue and labeled "Softmax" in Fig. 2. is added at the end of the Dense block module in CoDenNet. In this article, the structure of the denseblock used is described by the formula:

$$x_i = H_i\left([x_0, x_1, ..., x_{i-1}]\right) \tag{7}$$

where x_i represents the network input of the i-th layer, [] represents all the data from previous i layers. Considering the complexity of hyperspectral images, the structure of $H_i()$ is as follows: we mainly use a 1×1 convolutional layer, LeakRelu, and BatchNorm layer to build. As shown in Fig. 2, Dense Block contains two sets of blocks.

In particular, we found that the DenseBlock module can be used in LrHSI Autoencoder and HrMSI-Autoencoder, which dramatically helps feature extraction of MSI and HSI data. The effectiveness of this approach will be demonstrated in Sect. 4.

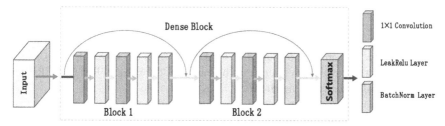

Fig. 2. Details of the Dense block of the proposed method (The blue rectangle in Fig. 1) (Color figure online)

The other part of the decoder in the autoencoder can be represented as follows:

$$\tilde{Y}_a = f_{de}\left(A_h^a\right) \tag{8}$$

where $\tilde{Y}_a$ is the output of this autoencoder, which is the reconstructed input image cube. We design the decoder function f_{de} as a 1×1 convolution layer (shown in orange and labeled "Conv" in Fig. 1). This convolution layer is also used in the HrMSI autoencoder and these two autoencoders share the same parameters.

3.2 HrMSI-Autoencoder

The structure of the HrMSI autoencoder is similar to the LrHSI autoencoder. The encoder function can be expressed as:

$$A = h_{en}(X) \tag{9}$$

where A is the high-resolution abundance, h_{en} is the encoder function and Y is the input HrMSI.

The decoder function is composed of two parts—a shared convolution layer (shown in orange and labeled "Conv" in Fig. 1) and the SRF (pink dotted line in Fig. 2).

$$\tilde{X} = h_{de}(A) = SRF(f_{de}(A)) \tag{10}$$

where $\tilde{Y}$ is the reconstructed HrMSI Y, h_{de} is the decoder function, f_{de} is the shared convolution layer containing the parameters of the endmember matrix E, and SRF() is the spectral resampling operation. The HrHSI is the output of the shared convolution layer:

$$\tilde{Z} = f_{de}(A) \tag{11}$$

where Z is the estimated target image.

A specific structure is employed to learn the parameters of the unknown SRF. This structure includes a convolution layer (shown in orange and labeled "1×1 Conv" in Fig. 1) and a normalization layer(labeled with "Norm" in Fig. 1). The process of SRF can be described as follows:

$$\varphi_i = \frac{\int_{\lambda_i,L}^{\lambda_i,U} R(\lambda)\varepsilon(\lambda)d\lambda}{\int_{\lambda_i,L}^{\lambda_i,U} R(\lambda)d\lambda} \tag{12}$$

where is the spectral radiance of band i of the HrMSI, λ is the wavelength, λ_i, U and λ_i, L together form wavelength bounds of the band i of the HrMSI, R()is the SRF, and $\varepsilon()$ is the spectral radiance of the HrHSI.

The PSF means that a given pixel is a weighted combination of contributions from the pixel and its neighboring pixels. To simulate the effect of the PSF, a convolution layer (labeled "Conv" in Fig. 1) is utilized. The relationship between X and Z can be defined as $Y = PSF(Z)$. Consequently, another A_h^b (low-resolution abundance) can be characterized as:

$$A_h^b = PSF(A) \tag{13}$$

where PSF() is the convolution operation (Orange dotted line in Fig. 2). The PSF serves as a variable bridge between the LrMSI autoencoder and HrMSI autoencoder in our model. Furthermore, the LrHSI $\tilde{Y}_b$ can be reconstructed using A_h^b and E:

$$\tilde{Y}_b = f_{de}\left(A_h^b\right) \tag{14}$$

3.3 LrMSI-Autoencoder

The spatially degraded version of HrMSI is equivalent to the spectral response version of LrHSI. In LrMSI Autoencoder (shown in Fig. 1), we described the relation as:

$$SRF(Y) = \tilde{X}_{lr}^b \approx \tilde{X}_{lr}^a = PSF(X) \tag{15}$$

where $\tilde{Y}_{lr}$ is the estimated LrMSI. Using this autoencoder, a degradation relationship between MSI and HSI is established, enabling effective model training.

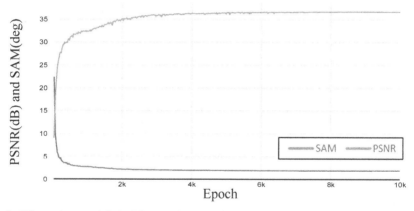

Fig. 3. When σ is set to 0.5, the PSNR and SAM values of the fusion results on Indian Pines data.

4 Experiments

Simulation experiments are conducted in this article to evaluate both the fusion quality and scheme performance. The Pavia University and Indian Pines data were mainly used in the experiments. This image of Pavia University has an area of 610×340 pixels and a ground sampling distance (GSD) of 1.3 m, and the spectral range is 430–840 nm consisting of 115 bands. The main datasets utilized in the experiments were Pavia University and Indian Pines data. The Indian Pines data covers an area of 145×145 pixels with a ground sampling distance (GSD) of 20.0 m. It spans a spectral range of 400–2500 nm, comprising 224 bands.

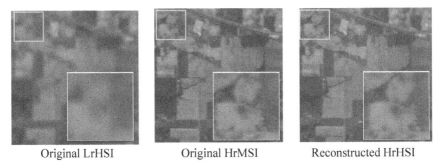

| Original LrHSI | Original HrMSI | Reconstructed HrHSI |

Fig. 4. When σ is set to 0.5, the fusion result of our Coupled Dense Convolutional Neural Networks (CoDenNet) on Indian Pines data.

4.1 Implementation Details

The experiment used a Gaussian filter to obtain LrHSI image data for spatial down-sampling simulation [12]. The width and height of the Gaussian filter were determined based on the ratio between the high-resolution ground sampling distance (GSD) and the low-resolution GSD. Different standard deviations were used in later experiments to evaluate the robustness of the fusion model, and the results are shown in Table 1. To simulate HrMSI, the SRF of Landsat 8 blue to short-wave infrared 2-band was used, and different GSD ratios and the number of bands were used to simulate LrHSI, HrMSI.

The experiment network is built by Pytorch (CPU) with a 2.4-GHz CPU and 8.0-GB RAM. We adapt the Adam optimizer to train the proposed model, and the initial learning rate is set to 5×10^{-3}. The paper shows the complete training results on Indian Pines data when Gaussian filter parameter σ is 0.5 in Fig. 3.

4.2 Evaluation Metrics

To evaluate the performance of our model, we use two quantitative measures to assess the results: mPSNR and mSAM [13]. The mPSNR is the average of the PSNR values of all bands and is an essential metric for evaluating the spatial quality of the fusion results. mSAM is the average of the SAM of all pixels, widely used to assess the HSI consistency.

This paper presents the analysis results on the Indian Pines dataset with a Gaussian filter parameter σ set to 0.5 in Fig. 3 and Fig. 4. The proposed model in this paper reconstructs the High-Resolution Hyperspectral Image (HrHSI) by utilizing the Low-Resolution Hyperspectral Image (LrHSI) and High-Resolution Multispectral Image (HrMSI) data. The two quality training metrics (PSNR and SAM) converge to a more stable range after 10,000 training iterations. Another essential task of our proposed model is to extract the abundance of the HSI data. Figure 5 clearly shows the heatmap of estimated abundances. From the sparse abundance heat map in Fig. 5 (b), we can find that our model works better. However, the abundance results for the three objects estimated by the model are significantly different: The heatmap A_h^b shows that some edge regions do not satisfy the sum-to-one property well. Due to the design of LrHSI and HrMSI, the results of A and A_h^b are much better.

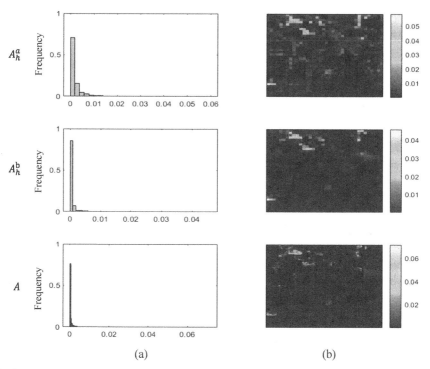

(a)   (b)

Fig. 5. The characters of three abundances (Indian Pines data as an example). (a): Histograms (b): Heatmaps of errors for the sum of estimated abundance.

4.3   Comparsion With the State of the Art

In the experiment, a series of baseline methods were used for comparison, which follows the study of Yokoya [14]. And we used two different quality measures to evaluate the performance of the proposed method (CoDenNet). Table 1 shows the obtained results. Compared with used fusion algorithms, including CNMF [15], GSOMP [11], GSA [16], HySure [17], uSDN [18], and MAPSMM [19], we can observe that the proposed fusion method produces good results for different Simulation data. When σ is set to 2.0, None of the methods, including our proposed method, effectively established the relationship between LrHSI and HSI. Nevertheless, the proposed method shows superior performance when σ is set to 1.0, 2.0. Our method calculates higher PSNR values than most methods and can learn PSF adaptively.

Table 1. Quantitative performance comparison with the different algorithms on the Indian Pines data. The best one is shown in bold

CNMF			GSOMP	GSA	HySure	uSDN	MAPSMM	CoDenNet
$\sigma=0.5$	mSAM	2.42	2.94	2.43	2.42	3.03	2.56	**1.97**
	mPSNR	32.46	32.26	33.59	32.94	32.91	31.14	**35.69**
$\sigma=1.0$	mSAM	2.26	2.81	2.27	2.27	2.93	2.31	**1.84**
	mPSNR	33.46	32.43	34.22	33.67	31.16	33.59	**37.24**
$\sigma=2.0$	mSAM	2.24	2.59	2.22	2.29	2.64	2.24	**1.83**
	mPSNR	33.73	32.82	34.68	33.52	32.11	35.99	**37.43**

5 Conclusion

This paper proposed a novel unsupervised deep learning method that employs the Dense Block to solve the fusion problem of HSI and MSI. Significantly, the method can adaptively learn SRF and PSF from spectral and spatial information. With the use of three autoencoders, the proposed model can readily reconstruct the LrHSI and HrMSI. Moreover, our CoDenNet model can provide a straightforward training strategy through the joint loss function. The experimental results demonstrate the effectiveness of the proposed coupled convolutional neural network. In future work, a multi-scale Dense block will be utilized to decrease the model size and reduce training time.

Funding Information..   This study was supported in part by the National Natural Science Foundation of China under Grant 42001319, in part by the Scientific Research Program of the Education Department of Shaanxi Province under Grant 21JK0762, and in part by the University-Industry Collaborative Education Program of Ministry of Education of China under Grant 220802313200859.

References

1. Su, Y., Xu, X., Li, J., Qi, H., Gamba, P., Plaza, A.: Deep autoencoders with multitask learning for bilinear hyperspectral unmixing. IEEE Trans. Geosci. Remote Sensing. **59**, 8615–8629 (2021)
2. Qian, S.-E.: Hyperspectral satellites, evolution, and development history. IEEE J. Sel. Top. Appl. Earth Observations Remote Sensing. 14, 7032–7056 (2021)
3. Su, Y., Jiang, M., Gao, L., Sun, X., You, X., Li, P.: Graph-Cut-based collaborative node embeddings for hyperspectral images classification. IEEE Geosci. Remote Sens. Lett.Geosci. Remote Sens. Lett.. **19**, 1–5 (2022)
4. Hong, D., Chanussot, J., Yokoya, N., Kang, J., Zhu, X.X.: Learning-shared cross-modality representation using multispectral-lidar and hyperspectral data. IEEE Geosci. Remote Sensing Lett. 17, 1470–1474 (2020)
5. Kawakami, R., Matsushita, Y., Wright, J., Ben-Ezra, M., Tai, Y.-W., Ikeuchi, K.: High-resolution hyperspectral imaging via matrix factorization. In: CVPR 2011, pp. 2329–2336. IEEE, Colorado Springs, CO, USA (2011)

6. Li, J., Zheng, K., Yao, J., Gao, L., Hong, D.: Deep unsupervised blind hyperspectral and multispectral data fusion. IEEE Geosci. Remote Sensing Lett. **19**, 1–5 (2022)
7. Zheng, K., Gao, L., Hong, D., Zhang, B., Chanussot, J.: NonRegSRNet: a nonrigid registration hyperspectral super-resolution network. IEEE Trans. Geosci. Remote Sensing. **60**, 1–16 (2022)
8. Zheng, K., et al.: Coupled convolutional neural network with adaptive response function learning for unsupervised hyperspectral super resolution. IEEE Trans. Geosci. Remote Sensing. **59**, 2487–2502 (2021)
9. Su, Y., Gao, L., Jiang, M., Plaza, A., Sun, X., Zhang, B.: NSCKL: normalized spectral clustering with kernel-based learning for semisupervised hyperspectral image classification. IEEE Trans. Cybern. 1–14 (2022)
10. Huang, G., Liu, Z., Van Der Maaten, L., Weinberger, K.Q.: Densely connected convolutional networks. In: 2017 IEEE Conference on Computer Vision and Pattern Recognition (CVPR), pp. 2261–2269. IEEE, Honolulu, HI (2017)
11. Akhtar, N., Shafait, F., Mian, A.: Sparse spatio-spectral representation for hyperspectral image super-resolution. In: Fleet, D., Pajdla, T., Schiele, B., Tuytelaars, T. (eds.) Computer Vision – ECCV 2014, pp. 63–78. Springer International Publishing, Cham (2014). https://doi.org/10.1007/978-3-319-10584-0_5
12. Yang, X., Chen, J., Wang, C., Chen, Z.: Residual dense autoencoder network for nonlinear hyperspectral unmixing. IEEE J. Sel. Top. Appl. Earth Observations Remote Sens. **15**, 5580–5595 (2022)
13. Arad , B., et al.: NTIRE 2018 challenge on spectral reconstruction from RGB images, In: Proceedings of IEEE/CVF Conference on Computer Vision Pattern Recognition Workshops (CVPR), pp. 929–938 (2018)
14. Yokoya, N., Grohnfeldt, C., Chanussot, J.: Hyperspectral and multispectral data fusion: a comparative review of the recent literature. IEEE Geosci. Remote Sens. Mag. **5**, 29–56 (2017)
15. Yokoya, N., Yairi, T., Iwasaki, A.: Coupled nonnegative matrix factorization unmixing for hyperspectral and multispectral data fusion. IEEE Trans. Geosci. Remote Sens. **50**, 528–537 (2012)
16. Aiazzi, B., Baronti, S., Selva, M.: Improving component substitution pansharpening through multivariate regression of MS + Pan Data. IEEE Trans. Geosci. Remote Sens. **45**, 3230–3239 (2007)
17. Simoes, M., Bioucas-Dias, J., Almeida, L.B., Chanussot, J.: A convex formulation for hyperspectral image superresolution via subspace-based regularization. IEEE Trans. Geosci. Remote Sens. **53**, 3373–3388 (2015)
18. Qu, Y., Qi, H., Kwan, C.: Unsupervised sparse dirichlet-net for hyperspectral image super-resolution. In: 2018 IEEE/CVF Conference on Computer Vision and Pattern Recognition, pp. 2511–2520. IEEE, Salt Lake City, UT (2018)
19. Eismann, M.T., Hardie, R.C.: Hyperspectral resolution enhancement using high-resolution multispectral imagery with arbitrary response functions. IEEE Trans. Geosci. Remote Sens. **43**, 455–465 (2005)

Computational Imaging

Multi-scale Non-local Bidirectional Fusion for Video Super-Resolution

Qinglin Zhou[1,2], Qiong Liu[2], Fen Chen[1(✉)], Ling Wang[1], and Zongju Peng[1]

[1] School of Electrical and Electronic Engineering, Chongqing University of Technology, Chongqing 400054, China
chenfen1@cqut.edu.cn
[2] Huazhong University of Science and Technology, Wuhan 430074, China

Abstract. Long-range dependency is one of the important inscriptions in sequence modeling. For video data, the commonly used convolutional and recurrent operations are a kind of "local coding" for variable-length sequences, which can only capture the local neighborhood information. We introduce the idea of non-local mean to compensate for the shortcomings of repeated convolutional operations, while most of the previous non-local methods used for video super-resolution only focus on positional information or fail to capture temporal information directly. In this study, we propose a non-local bidirectional fusion network (NLBF) for the video super-resolution (VSR) task. This non-local network decouples multidimensional information to reduce computational memory consumption, at the same time capturing long-range dependencies within the temporal-spatial-channel dimension as much as possible. In the multi-scale local and non-local hybrid framework, we further design the bidirectional spatial-temporal fusion module to balance the information obtained from other frames while achieving feature refinement. Experimental results on benchmark datasets show that the proposed NLBF is able to achieve state-of-the-art performance in the VSR task.

Keywords: Non-local · temporal-spatial-channel · bidirectional fusion · video super-resolution

1 Introduction

Super-resolution aims to recover a clear and sharp high-resolution (HR) image from one or more of its corresponding degraded (e.g., blurry, noisy, and distorted) low-resolution (LR) images. It has been successfully applied in medical imaging [1], live streaming [2], medical services [3], and other fields.

In contrast to image super-resolution, video super-resolution (VSR) faces extra challenges. In a video sequence, different frames are strongly correlated in time, which means that the positions of different objects are constantly varying from frame to frame. To overcome this challenge, various approaches have been proposed, and one popular approach is the sliding window-based framework [4, 6–8, 16–18], where each frame in the video sequence is recovered using frames within a local short-time window. However, the approach limits the range of information and requires multiple processing

H. Lu et al. (Eds.): ICIG 2023, LNCS 14359, pp. 169–181, 2023.
https://doi.org/10.1007/978-3-031-46317-4_15

when inferring on each input frame. This is computationally inefficient and can have significant memory consumption. In contrast, the recurrent framework-based methods attempt to keep parameters by reusing the same network to propagate potential features sequentially from one frame to the next [5, 9–14, 32]. However, it limits parallel capabilities for efficient distributed training and inference. Compared to the sliding-window framework it is more difficult to model temporal dependencies over long distances. Some work has also attempted to combine parallel and recurrent framework to build a hybrid framework [15, 19, 20]. However, relying only on the hidden state of long-term information for video reconstruction does not fully exploit their respective advantages.

In this paper, we propose a non-local bidirectional fusion network(NLBF) which is non-optical-flow-based and can capture long-range dependencies to explore the similarity of natural images. Many research methods have confirmed that local and non-local information is crucial for the restoration of low-resolution video sequences. Recently, non-local neural networks have also been applied to video or image super-resolution tasks, showing good feature representation capabilities. However, dimensional conversion by matrix multiplication to achieve feature transformation requires huge computational resources (especially when the input video sequence size is large). Moreover, the above non-local approach involves only the position-attention module, ignoring the interrelationship between temporal, spatial and channel in the video sequence.

Considering the complexity of coding and the fact that video sequences have not only spatial-temporal correlations but also strong correlations among the high-frequency components of their color channels, our non-local attention module is redesigned to fully extract redundant spatial-temporal information as well as rich contextual semantic information between channels, and is combined with the local information attention network to enhance the network's feature representation capability. To further enhance the feature representation capability of the network, we design a novel bidirectional spatial-temporal fusion module to facilitate the exchange of spatial-temporal information between the forward and backward propagation branches.

In summary, the main contributions of this paper can be concluded as follows:

– We propose a non-local attention structure(NLA) which is more suitable for video super-resolution tasks and further designed as a multi-scale local and non-local hybrid attention module (MSNLA), which can effectively capture the long-distance dependencies between spatial-temporal-channels in video frames and enrich high-frequency texture details.
– We design a bidirectional spatial-temporal fusion module (BDSTF) to facilitate the exchange of forward and backward spatial and temporal information and balance the information differences in each frame.

2   Related Work

2.1   Video Super-Resolution

Earlier approaches used conventional optical flow estimation and motion compensation for video super-resolution. However, it is difficult to obtain accurate optical flow estimates in occlusion and large motion scenes. Based on this, Xue et al. [18]

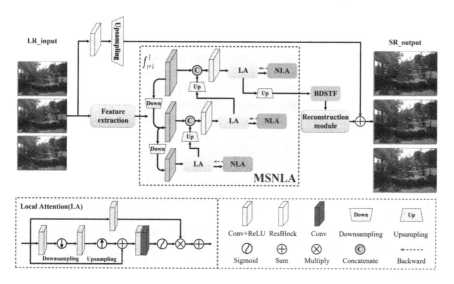

Fig. 1. The architecture of multi-scale non-local bidirectional fusion network(NLBF). Where LA refers to the non-local attention structure, NLA refers to the non-local structure, MSNLA refers to the multi-scale local and non-local hybrid attention module and BDSTF is the bidirectional spatial-temporal fusion network.

reveals that the standard optical flow is not the best motion representation for video restoration. To circumvent this problem, Jo et al. [17] used adaptive upsampling of dynamic filters instead of displaying motion estimation. Li et al. [7] proposed a multi-correspondence aggregation network for video reconstruction using similar patches across frames and self-similarity at different scales within frames. Tian et al. [8] proposed TDAN using deformable convolution for feature alignment. Based on TDAN, Wang et al. [6] extended it to multiple scales, while Chan et al. [10] used optical flow as a guide for offset learning to design a flow-guided deformable alignment network, and Wang et al. [22] based their network design on deformable convolution and non-local networks. Chan et al. [9] grouped the VSR components into four parts: propagation, alignment, aggregation, and upsampling, and used bidirectional propagation to exploit information from the entire input video. To improve the drawback that BasicVSR limits the efficacy of information aggregation, Chan et al. [10] designed a second-order grid propagation.

2.2 Non-local Network

Capturing long-range dependencies is crucial for deep learning-based recovery of low-resolution video sequences. And for video image data, the field of perception is usually expanded by deeply stacking convolutions of different sizes to obtain a larger range of information. However, repeated stacking of multiple convolutions pulls down the overall computational efficiency, making modeling and optimization particularly difficult.

Based on this, Wang et al. [21] proposed a non-local neural network for capturing long-distance dependencies for video classification. Liu et al. [25] proposed a non-local recurrent network for image restoration, integrating non-local operations with recurrent networks for the first time. Zhang et al. [26] proposed a residual non-local attention network for high-quality image restoration. Yi et al. [16] extracted spatial and temporal features using non-local residual blocks instead of motion compensation. Wang et al. [22] proposed a novel deformable non-local network (DNLN) that utilizes a non-local structure to capture the global correlation between reference frames and aligned neighboring frames and simultaneously enhances the desired fine details in aligned frames. Mei et al. [24] proceeded to explore the cross-scale feature correlation of images, proposed the first cross-scale non-local attention module. Li et al. [23] used the non-local module to compute the similarity drive between any two pixels to obtain effective information over long distances. However, most of the above methods only focus on positional information or channel information, and consume a huge amount of memory resources. Some methods try to reduce the computational memory consumption by reducing the number of channels or spatial scales, but they are superficial. In contrast, we start from the design structure level and focus on position, channel, and temporal information while reducing the computational memory consumption.

3   Methodology

NLBF consists of four components, which are feature extraction module, multi-scale local and non-local hybrid attention module, bidirectional spatial-temporal fusion module, and residual reconstruction module. As shown in Fig. 1, given a sequence of 2N+1 consecutive low-resolution videos $\{I_{t-N}^{LR}, \ldots, I_t^{LR}, \ldots, I_{t+N}^{LR}\}$. The size of the input LR video frame is $H \times W$, where H and W refer to the height and width, respectively. Then input to our network and reconstruct as a high resolution video sequence $\{I_{t-N}^{SR}, \ldots, I_t^{SR}, \ldots, I_{t+N}^{SR}\}$ by the residual reconstruction module. Where the HR output size is $rH \times rW$ and the spatial scaling factor is r.

3.1   Multi-scale Local and Non-Local Hybrid Attention Module

Inspired by [16,21], we design a multi-scale hybrid local and non-local attention network (MSNLA), which is more suitable for video super-resolution tasks. The hybrid local and non-local attention (The temporal-spatial-channel non-local module is showed in Fig. 2) effectively captures long-range dependencies while extracting hierarchical features and expanding the field of reception.

As shown in Fig. 2, we first perform shallow feature extraction by 3×3 convolutional layers and complete the depth network construction by residual convolution, and the obtained feature maps of different depths are used as hierarchical features. In order to expand the receptive field and grasp the information with larger distribution breadth, we choose to use large span (stride$\geq$2) convolution to remove redundant information instead of using ensemble layers in the local attention module. Mathematically, the local feature processing operation can be expressed as:

$$y = \sum Sigmoid\left(m(s(s_{t+i}))\right) * f_{t+i} + f_{t+i}, i \in [-N; +N] \qquad (1)$$

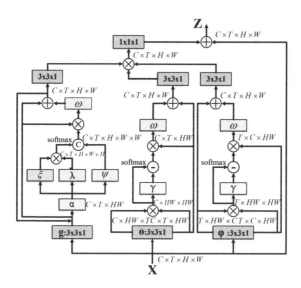

Fig. 2. Architecture of non-local attention module(NLA). We propose a spatial-temporal-channel non-local module to capture long-range dependencies. The feature maps are shown by their dimensions, e.g. $C \times T \times H \times W$.

where f_{t+i} denotes the input of the local operation, y denotes the output of the same size as f_{t+i}. i denotes the input i-th frame. The pairwise function $s(\cdot)$ scales the input, while the $m(\cdot)$ computes the feature representation of the feature space.

The above local attention processes limited information, and one convolution operation only works on the local neighborhood. To solve this problem and better determine the importance of feature nodes, we propose a temporal-spatial-channel non-local attention structure to better perceive the feature information at the global scale. While effectively capturing the long-range dependencies, the respective global relationships of each feature node are fully explored in the decision process thereby learning more robust attention features. The temporal-spatial-channel non-local operation can be defined as:

$$z_j = Sigmoid\left(h\left(\sum_{\forall k} \alpha(y_j, y_k)g(y_k) * \sum_{\forall k} \beta(y_j, y_k)g(y_k) * \sum_{\forall k} \gamma(y_j, y_k)g(y_k)\right) + y_j\right) \quad (2)$$

where y denotes the input of the non-local operation, z denotes the output of the same size as y. j is the output position index, and k is the index of all possible positions. The three functions $\alpha(\cdot)$, $\beta(\cdot)$, $\gamma(\cdot)$ represent the computation of the relationship between y_j and y_k in the C, T, and $H \times W$ dimensions, respectively. $h(\cdot)$ performs the fusion of the above temporal-spatial-channel non-local operations. The function of $g(\cdot)$ computes the representation of the input at position k.

We use an embedded Gaussian function to evaluate the pairwise relationship:

$$\xi\left(y_j, y_k\right) = e^{\theta(y_j)^T \phi(y_k)} = e^{(W_\theta y_j)^T W_\phi y_k} \quad (3)$$

where $\theta(y_j)$ and $\phi(y_k)$ are the two embeddings. The function $\xi(y_j, y_k)$ refers to $\alpha(\cdot)$, $\beta(\cdot)$, $\gamma(\cdot)$, and W_θ and W_ϕ are the weight matrices, with different dimensions and different weights, and different ways to obtain the weights. And then the non-local obtained features are subjected to local operation, and the final output of the obtained local and non-local hybrid attention can be calculated as:

$$F_{t+i} = \sum Sigmoid\left(f(s(z_j))\right) * f_{t+i} + f_{t+i} \tag{4}$$

where F_{t+i} is the output feature of the non-local operation.

In convolutional neural networks, the high-level network has a large receptive field and strong representation of semantic information, but the feature maps have low resolution and lack of spatial geometric feature details. The lower layer network has a smaller perceptual field, strong geometric detail information representation, and usually higher resolution but lacks semantic information representation capability. The video data has objects of different sizes in one video frame, and different objects have different features. For this reason, we design a feature pyramid structure to extract deep and shallow layer features, and stimulate the semantic and contextual information of the objects through multi-scale perceptual fields. Specifically, to generate the features f_{t+i}^l at the L-th layer, we use a hierarchical convolution filter to downsample the features at the (L-1)-th layer with a scale factor r of 2 to obtain the multi-layer pyramid features.

$$F_{t+i}^l = \omega\left(\left(F_{t+i}^{l+1}\right)^{\uparrow r}, f_{t+i}^l\right), l \in [0, 2) \tag{5}$$

where $\uparrow r$ refers to upscaling by a factor r and $w(\cdot)$ is the general function of the multi-layer convolutional composition.

3.2 Bidirectional Spatial-Temporal Fusion Module

Video sequences add extra information in the temporal dimension, while most previous fusion methods extract features in the spatial domain and compensate for motion in the temporal domain, intra- and inter-frame spatial-temporal information is not fully exploited, and the consistency of super-resolution video sequences is repeatedly weakened. Although 3D convolution can model appearance and motion, the extra dimensions increase the number of parameters and are focused on model capacity, ignoring valuable temporal priors and failing to effectively model large motions. To overcome it, we use two-dimensional convolution combined with scale transformation to expand the receptive field while effectively extracting multi-level features and refining spatio-temporal information. In the experiment process, we find that unidirectional propagation have the problem of inconsistent information obtained from different frames. Inspired by BasicVSR [9], we try to compensate the information discrepancy by bidirectional propagation. Different from BasicVSR, we sort the input data in forward and backward order without utilizing the optical flow information. And according to the reference frame selection strategy, each input frame will obtain richer and more balanced information. Experiments show that bidirectional propagation can effectively balance the information of different frames and improve the feature refinement. Specifically, we design a bidirectional spatial-temporal fusion module (BDSTF) in which features are

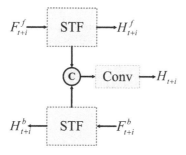

Fig. 3. The architecture of bidirectional spatial-temporal fusion module(BDSTF).

propagated forward and backward independently in time and space. The process can be represented as follows:

$$H_{t+i}^f = O_f(F_{t+i}^f, F_{t+\sigma_f}^f) \tag{6}$$

$$H_{t+i}^b = O_b(F_{t+i}^b, F_{t+\sigma_b}^b) \tag{7}$$

$$H_{t+i} = fusion(H_{t+i}^f, H_{t+i}^b) \tag{8}$$

where $fusion(\cdot)$ performs forward and backward feature fusion. The function $O(\cdot)$ denotes the spatial-temporal fusion function, which can be calculated as:

$$O_f = sigmoid\left(\mu(F_{t+i}^f)^T * \vartheta\left(F_{t+\sigma_f}^f\right)\right) \odot \chi\left(s(F_{t+i}^f), s\left(F_{t+\sigma_f}^f\right)\right) \tag{9}$$

$$O_b = sigmoid\left(\mu(F_{t+i}^b)^T * \vartheta\left(F_{t+\sigma_b}^b\right)\right) \odot \chi\left(s(F_{t+i}^b), s\left(F_{t+\sigma_b}^b\right)\right) \tag{10}$$

$$\sigma_f = \begin{cases} i+1, i < N \\ i-1, i = N \end{cases} , \sigma_b = \begin{cases} i-1, i < N \\ i+1, i = N \end{cases} \tag{11}$$

where f and b denote the forward and backward directions, respectively, H_{t+i}^f and H_{t+i}^b denote the forward spatial-temporal fusion feature output and the backward spatial-temporal fusion feature output, respectively. $\mu(F_{t+i}^{f/b})$ and $\vartheta(F_{t+i}^{f/b})$ are two embeddings, and $\chi(\cdot)$ refers to the spatial feature refinement function. $\odot$ denotes the element-wise multiplication.

4 Experiments

4.1 Training Settings

Datasets. In order to obtain a VSR network with better performance, sufficient data is required as training support, for this reason we choose the widely used dataset Vimeo-90K [18] as our training dataset, which contains 91,701 video sequences, each containing 7 consecutive frames with a resolution of 448×256, where the training and test parts contain 64,612 and 7,824 sequences, respectively. Vimeo-90k-T (test set of Vimeo-90k) with Vid4 [30] was used for evaluation.

Table 1. Quantitative comparison (PSNR/SSIM). All results are calculated on Y-channel except REDS4(RGB-channel). Red and blue colors indicate the best and the second-best performance, respectively. A $4\times$ upsampling is performed following previous studies. Blanked entries correspond to results not reported in previous works.

Methods	Training frames	REDS4 [28] (RGB)	Vimeo-90k-T [18] (Y)	Vid4 [30] (Y)
Bicubic	–	26.14/0.7292	31.32/0.8694	23.78/0.6347
VESPCN [4]	3	–	–	25.35/0.7557
SPMC [31]	3	–	–	25.88/0.7752
ToFlow [18]	7	27.98/0.7990	33.08/0.9054	25.89/0.7651
DUF [17]	7	28.63/0.8251	–	27.33/0.8319
RBPN [32]	7	30.09/0.8590	37.07/0.9435	27.12/0.8180
EDVR-L [6]	7	31.09/0.8800	37.61/0.9489	27.35/0.8264
DNLN [22]	7	–	37.38/0.9473	27.29/0.8247
PFNL [16]	7	29.63/0.8502	36.14/0.9363	27.40/0.8384
MuCAN [7]	7	30.88/0.8750	37.32/0.9465	27.26/0.8215
BasicVSR [9]	14	31.42/0.8909	37.18/0.9450	27.29/0.8267
IconVSR [9]	14	31.67/0.8948	37.47/0.9476	27.39/0.8279
NLBF (Ours)	7	31.37/0.9142	37.72/0.9725	27.51/0.8426

Training Details. In our network, we input 7 consecutive low-resolution video images at a time, and use 5 residual blocks for feature extraction and 20 residual blocks for feature reconstruction. Our convolutional layer has 128 filters to learn more and capture as many potential features as possible. In exploring the best model, we trained our model with the Adam optimizer, setting $\beta 1 = 0.9$ and $\beta 2 = 0.999$, and a scaling factor of 4, which is a challenging scaling factor for video SR. The learning rate is initialized to 4×10^{-4} and the minibatch size is set to 6.

4.2 Comparing with Different Methods

To verify the effectiveness of our model in VSR, we compare the subjective and objective performance with several other super-resolution models of the moment: SPMC [31], VESPCN [4], ToFlow [18], DUF [17], RBPN [32], EDVR [6], DNLN [22], PFNL [16], MuCAN [7], BasicVSR [9] and IconVSR [9]. Most of the video super-resolution methods use different training datasets, downsampling kernels and input frame sizes, we only compare them with the results they provide. In addition, most of the recent methods are based on Transformer [13], while our method is based on CNN. So, we never compare it with them. The evaluation metrics of SR we choose the PSNR and SSIM of the Y channel in the converted YCbCr space i.e., PSNR-Y and SSIM-Y. Table 1 summarizes the quantitative results, and our models in Vid4, Vimeo-90k-T and REDS4 datasets outperforms other non-local methods, which proves the effectiveness of our method.

The qualitative results for Vid4 are shown in Fig. 4, and for a more visual comparison, we mark the locations where there are clear differences in the different VSR methods. In the "Calendar" dataset, most VSR methods recover images that are blurred or have local textures that are so smooth that much detail is lost, while our method achieves better results and is more effective in recovering texture details. In the "city" dataset, most methods do not recover the building surface texture very well or may even fail to recover it due to the finer and richer information it contains, while our method has a better grasp of the edge information. Again, this is well demonstrated in the "walk" dataset. It can be seen in Table 1 that our method outperforms other methods on various datasets, including REDS4, Vid4, and Vimeo-90k-T. NLBF obtains a significant improvement of 0.28 dB on REDS4, and performs competitively on Vimeo-90k-T and Vid4.

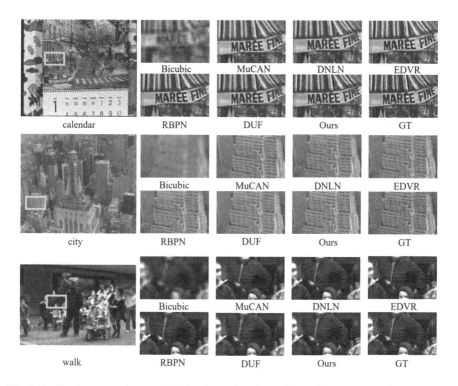

Fig. 4. Qualitative comparison on Vid4 for $4\times$ scaling factor (Zoom in to see better visualization).

REDS4 has a higher resolution compared to Vid4. Figure 5 demonstrates the subjective results of our network over REDS4. Although EDVR and MuCAN can reconstruct some of the HR features, it is clear that our NLBF yields richer details and sharper edges.

4.3 Ablation Study

Multi-scale Local and Non-local Hybrid Attention Module (MSNLA). As shown in Table 2, our baseline model uses only the feature extraction and reconstruction modules. Model 2 uses the multi-scale local and non-local hybrid attention module for multiple dimensions of the features (temporal- spatial-channel) and introduces a multi-scale structure to better extract deep and shallow features, which achieves a gain of 0.69 dB. This effectively demonstrates the effectiveness of MSNLA.

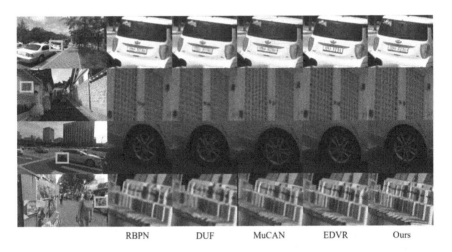

RBPN   DUF   MuCAN   EDVR   Ours

Fig. 5. Qualitative comparison on REDS4 for $4\times$ scaling factor (Zoom in to see better visualization).

Bidirectional Spatial-Temporal Fusion Module (BDSTF). In Model 3, we adopt a novel reference frame selection strategy in order to balance the information captured by each frame, and further design a bidirectional spatial-temporal fusion network (see Fig. 3) to achieve feature refinement. The results show that our BSTF brings a gain of 0.26 dB.

Table 2. Ablation experiments of the proposed network on REDS4 for 4x (Experiments here adopted a smaller model and the number of channels is set to 64).

Model	Model1	Model2	Model3
MSNLA	✗	✔	✔
BDSTF	✗	✗	✔
PSNR	30.16	30.75	31.01

5   Conclusion

In this paper, we propose an end-to-end multi-scale non-local bidirectional fusion framework (NLBF) which is based on non-optical flow. Specifically, we propose a spatial-temporal-channel non-local attention module, which works in conjunction with the local attention module to improve the robustness of the algorithm while recovering more detailed features of the texture. To balance the information obtained from each frame, we design a bidirectional spatial-temporal fusion network. Experimental results show that NLBF can effectively recover high-frequency information from low-resolution video sequences with a gain of 0.28 dB over the optimal method on the REDS4 dataset, and is also competitive in Vid4 and Vimeo-90k-T.

Acknowledgments. This work was supported by the Natural Science Foundation of Chongqing under Grant cstc2021jcyj-msxmX0411 and Grant CSTB2022NSCQ-MSX0873, the Science and Technology Research Program of Chongqing Municipal Education Commission under Grant KJZDK202001105, and the Scientific Research Foundation of Chongqing University of Technology under Grant 2020zdz029 and Grant 2020zdz030.

References

1. Codron, P., et al.: STochastic Optical Reconstruction Microscopy (STORM) reveals the nanoscale organization of pathological aggregates in human brain. Neuropathol. Appl. Neurobiol. **47**, 127–142 (2021)
2. Zhang, Y., et al.: Improving quality of experience by adaptive video streaming with super-resolution. In: IEEE INFOCOM 2020-IEEE Conference on Computer Communications, pp. 1957–1966. IEEE (2020)
3. Koester, E., Sahin, C.S.: A comparison of super-resolution and nearest neighbors interpolation applied to object detection on satellite data. arXiv preprint arXiv:1907.05283 (2019)
4. Caballero, J., et al.: Real-time video super-resolution with spatio-temporal networks and motion compensation. In: Proceedings of the IEEE Conference on Computer Vision and Pattern Recognition, pp. 4778–4787 (2017)
5. Huang, Y., Wang, W., Wang, L.: Video super-resolution via bidirectional recurrent convolutional networks. IEEE Trans. Pattern Anal. Mach. Intell. **40**, 1015–1028 (2017)
6. Wang, X., Chan, K.C., Yu, K., Dong, C., Change Loy, C.: EDVR: video restoration with enhanced deformable convolutional networks. In: Proceedings of the IEEE/CVF Conference on Computer Vision and Pattern Recognition Workshops, pp. 0–0 (2019)
7. Li, W., Tao, X., Guo, T., Qi, L., Lu, J., Jia, J.: MuCAN: multi-correspondence aggregation network for video super-resolution. In: Vedaldi, A., Bischof, H., Brox, T., Frahm, J.-M. (eds.) ECCV 2020. LNCS, vol. 12355, pp. 335–351. Springer, Cham (2020). https://doi.org/10.1007/978-3-030-58607-2_20
8. Tian, Y., Zhang, Y., Fu, Y., Xu, C.: TDAN: temporally-deformable alignment network for video super-resolution. In: Proceedings of the IEEE/CVF Conference on Computer Vision and Pattern Recognition, pp. 3360–3369 (2020)
9. Chan, K.C., Wang, X., Yu, K., Dong, C., Loy, C.C.: BasicVSR: the search for essential components in video super-resolution and beyond. In: Proceedings of the IEEE/CVF Conference on Computer Vision and Pattern Recognition, pp. 4947–4956 (2021)

10. Chan, K.C., Zhou, S., Xu, X., Loy, C.C.: BasicVSR++: improving video super-resolution with enhanced propagation and alignment. In: Proceedings of the IEEE/CVF Conference on Computer Vision and Pattern Recognition, pp. 5972–5981 (2022)

11. Isobe, T., Jia, X., Gu, S., Li, S., Wang, S., Tian, Q.: Video super-resolution with recurrent structure-detail network. In: Vedaldi, A., Bischof, H., Brox, T., Frahm, J.-M. (eds.) ECCV 2020. LNCS, vol. 12357, pp. 645–660. Springer, Cham (2020). https://doi.org/10.1007/978-3-030-58610-2_38

12. Lin, J., Huang, Y., Wang, L.: FDAN: Flow-guided deformable alignment network for video super-resolution. arXiv preprint arXiv:2105.05640 (2021)

13. Liang, J., et al.: Recurrent video restoration transformer with guided deformable attention. arXiv preprint arXiv:2206.02146 (2022)

14. Zhong, Z., Gao, Y., Zheng, Y., Zheng, B.: Efficient spatio-temporal recurrent neural network for video deblurring. In: Vedaldi, A., Bischof, H., Brox, T., Frahm, J.-M. (eds.) ECCV 2020. LNCS, vol. 12351, pp. 191–207. Springer, Cham (2020). https://doi.org/10.1007/978-3-030-58539-6_12

15. Fuoli, D., Gu, S., Timofte, R.: Efficient video super-resolution through recurrent latent space propagation. In: 2019 IEEE/CVF International Conference on Computer Vision Workshop (ICCVW), pp. 3476–3485. IEEE (2019)

16. Yi, P., Wang, Z., Jiang, K., Jiang, J., Ma, J.: Progressive fusion video super-resolution network via exploiting non-local spatio-temporal correlations. In: Proceedings of the IEEE/CVF International Conference on Computer Vision, pp. 3106–3115 (2019)

17. Jo, Y., Oh, S.W., Kang, J., Kim, S.J.: Deep video super-resolution network using dynamic upsampling filters without explicit motion compensation. In: Proceedings of the IEEE Conference on Computer Vision and Pattern Recognition, pp. 3224–3232 (2018)

18. Xue, T., Chen, B., Wu, J., Wei, D., Freeman, W.T.: Video enhancement with task-oriented flow. Int. J. Comput. Vision **127**, 1106–1125 (2019)

19. Yan, B., Lin, C., Tan, W.: Frame and feature-context video super-resolution. In: Proceedings of the AAAI Conference on Artificial Intelligence, pp. 5597–5604 (2019)

20. Jiang, L., Wang, N., Dang, Q., Liu, R., Lai, B.: PP-MSVSR: multi-stage video super-resolution. arXiv preprint arXiv:2112.02828 (2021)

21. Wang, X., Girshick, R., Gupta, A., He, K.: Non-local neural networks. In: Proceedings of the IEEE Conference on Computer Vision and Pattern Recognition, pp. 7794–7803. (2018)

22. Wang, H., Su, D., Liu, C., Jin, L., Sun, X., Peng, X.: Deformable non-local network for video super-resolution. IEEE Access **7**, 177734–177744 (2019)

23. Li, Y., Zhu, H., Hou, Q., Wang, J., Wu, W.: Video super-resolution using multi-scale and non-local feature fusion. Electronics **11**, 1499 (2022)

24. Mei, Y., Fan, Y., Zhou, Y., Huang, L., Huang, T.S., Shi, H.: Image super-resolution with cross-scale non-local attention and exhaustive self-exemplars mining. In: Proceedings of the IEEE/CVF Conference on Computer Vision and Pattern Recognition, pp. 5690–5699 (2020)

25. Liu, D., Wen, B., Fan, Y., Loy, C.C., Huang, T.S.: Non-local Recurrent Network for Image Restoration. In: Advances in Neural Information Processing Systems, vol. 31 (2018)

26. Zhang, Y., Li, K., Li, K., Zhong, B., Fu, Y.: Residual non-local attention networks for image restoration. arXiv preprint arXiv:1903.10082 (2019)

27. Zhang, Z., Cui, P., Zhu, W.: Deep learning on graphs: a survey. IEEE Trans. Knowl. Data Eng. **34**, 249–270 (2020)

28. Nah, S., et al.: Ntire 2019 challenge on video deblurring and super-resolution: dataset and study. In: Proceedings of the IEEE/CVF Conference on Computer Vision and Pattern Recognition Workshops, pp. 0–0 (2019)

29. Schultz, R.R., Stevenson, R.L.: Extraction of high-resolution frames from video sequences. IEEE Trans. Image Process. **5**, 996–1011 (1996)

30. Liu, C., Sun, D.: On Bayesian adaptive video super resolution. IEEE Trans. Pattern Anal. Mach. Intell. **36**, 346–360 (2013)
31. Tao, X., Gao, H., Liao, R., Wang, J., Jia, J.: Detail-revealing deep video super-resolution. In: Proceedings of the IEEE International Conference on Computer Vision, pp. 4472–44802017)
32. Haris, M., Shakhnarovich, G., Ukita, N.: Recurrent back-projection network for video super-resolution. In: Proceedings of the IEEE/CVF Conference on Computer Vision and Pattern Recognition, pp. 3897–3906 (2019)

Multi-view and Stereoscopic Processing

Learning a Deep Fourier Attention Generative Adversarial Network for Light Field Image Super-Resolution

Zhipeng Li[1], Jian Ma[1,2]([✉]) [ID], Dong Liang[1]([✉]), Guoming Xu[1], Xiaoyin Zhang[1], and Junbo Wang[1]

[1] School of Internet, Anhui University, Hefei 230039, China
jian_ma@fudan.edu.cn, dliang@ahu.edu.cn
[2] School of Computer Science, Fudan University, Shanghai 200433, China

Abstract. Human eyes can see the three-dimensional (3D) world because they receive the light emitted by objects, and the light field (LF) is a complete representation of the set of light in the 3D world. Light field image super resolution (LFISR) aims at reconstructing high-resolution LF images from their low-resolution counterparts which captured by the LF camera. In recent years, although convolutional neural networks (CNNs) can bring good performance to LFISR tasks, they cannot recover more real finer texture details. Therefore, it is a difficult challenge to generate realistic images of LF that can satisfy human perception. To address these problems, we propose a novel LFISR model by learning a deep Fourier attention generative adversarial network (GAN). Specifically, the generator network and loss function of the traditional single image super-resolution reconstruction (SISR) GAN model are improved for LFISR reconstruction. Furthermore, we design an attention module based on deep Fourier channel, which leverages the frequency content difference across distinct features to learn precise hierarchical representations of high-frequency information of diverse structures. Extensive experiments are performed on the mainstream LF datasets, leading to the state-of-the-art results of our method.

Keywords: Light Field · Image Super-Resolution · Generative Adversarial Networks · Deep Fourier Channel Attention

1 Introduction

By adding microlens arrays between the main lens and the image sensor, light field (LF) cameras can capture angular information and spatial information at

This work was supported in part by the National Natural Science Foundation of China under Grants 61906118, 62273001, China Postdoctoral Science Foundation under Grants 2022M710745, AnHui Natural Science Foundation under Grants 2108085MF230 and Anhui Province Outstanding Scientific Research and Innovation team Grants 2022AH010005.
Z. Li and J. Ma—Co-first authors.

H. Lu et al. (Eds.): ICIG 2023, LNCS 14359, pp. 185–197, 2023.
https://doi.org/10.1007/978-3-031-46317-4_16

the same time, which is widely used in 3D reconstruction and virtual reality applications, such as foreground de-occlusion [1], depth sensing [2], saliency detection [3] and post-capture refocusing [4]. However, due to the limitations of sensor resolution, light field cameras have to sacrifice spatial resolution for angular resolution. Therefore, limited spatial resolution brings many difficulties to the development of related applications and becomes the main bottleneck of light field cameras. Because of the demand of high-resolution (HR) LF images in many applications, the realization of super resolution (SR) reconstruction of LF image has aroused a wide range of research upsurg in the academic community.

In earlier research, convolutional neural networks (CNN) have been widely used in various LF image processing tasks. For instance, Yoon et al. [5]proposed a CNN based SR algorithm for LF images. However, the complex reality of the scene poses a huge challenge to CNN. In order to solve the complex information interleaving problem, the works of [6–8] combine CNN with epipolar geometry in light field structures. Although a well-designed CNN network can obtain very good SR results, the method using CNN still has two limitations. Specifically, First, we cannot recover finer texture details when we do SR with a large scale factor. Secondly, the SR algorithm based on CNN usually minimizes the mean square error (MSE) between the restored LF and HR images and the real value, and then maximizes the peak signal-to-noise ratio (PSNR), which does not accord with the visual perception of human eyes.

Recently, generative adversarial network (GAN) has achieved good performance in image applications such as texture information processing [9], target detection [10], style migration [11], and image restoration [12]. Inspired by these works, in this paper, we propose a novel LFISR model by learning a deep Fourier attention GAN. Specifically, our generator is based on a residual structure established by the Deep Fourier Channel Attention Module [13] obtain high-frequency information of different structures. Furthermore, we design a fused loss function, which includes content loss, pixel loss and adversarial loss. This allows our discriminator to sense the difference between the generated SR image and the original image to encourage the generator to generate light field images with better texture effects. The contributions of this paper can be summarized as: 1) A novel GAN with a fused loss function is introduced into LFISR recostruction, which can extract more details and recover real texture information. 2) We design an attention module based on a deep Fourier channel, which uses the frequency content differences between different features to learn the precise hierarchical representation of high-frequency information of different structures. 3) Experimental results demonstrate that the proposed LFISR method outperformed current reported top LFISR algorithms on five benchmark LF datasets, and show better consistency with the human perception.

The remainder of this article is organized as follows: an overview of related work is given in Sect. 2. Section 3 introduced the proposed LFISR model. Experimental results are drawn in Sect. 4, followed by a conclusion in Sect. 5.

2   Related Works

2.1   LF Image SR

LF image SR also termed as LF spatial SR which aims at generating high-resolution(HR) LF images from their low-resolution(LR) inputs. In the early years traditional methods [14,15] we re used , then we based on deep CNNs [5–8,16–18] and more recently the Transformer method [19] became popular.

Traditional Methods. Tom et al. [14] proposed a groundbreaking methodology for the restoration of HR images from LF data captured from a LF camera. The 3D depth of the scene is first recovered by matching antialiased LF views, and then deconvolution is performed. Mitra et al. [15] proposed a Gaussian mixture model to encode LF structure for LF spatial SR. Traditional methods can encode LF structures, but these are handcrafted image priors. Therefore, the ability is poor and the performance is limited. In recent years, CNN-based LFSR is superior to traditional methods.

Deep CNNs with Two-Stage. Yoon et al. [5] proposed the first method based on a deep neural network, called LFCNN, to enhance the spatial and angular resolution of LF. In their method, an end-to-end trainable architecture was used to cascade spatial and angular SR networks. Jin et al. [8] proposed an all to one framework that used all remaining views to overlay each view, and designed a structure perception loss to preserve the parallax structure of LF images. Yuan et al. [6] conducted independent SR on each SAI and developed an EPI enhancement network to optimize SR images. Since these two-stage methods take a long training time and cannot be done in one step, some one-stage methods are also proposed.

Deep CNNs with One-Stage. Yeung et al. [16] proposed LFSSR to alternately wash LF features between SAI and macro pixel(MacPI) modes for convolution. Zhang et al. [7] proposed a multi branch residual network that combined the geometric priors of the multidirectional poles of LFSR. Wang et al. [17] proposed that spatial and angular features can be extracted from LF images respectively, and then repeatedly interact to gradually fuse spatial and angular information. Wang et al. [18] proposed a universal disentangling mechanism for light field, which disentangled the light field into different subspaces of spatial, angulaR and epipolar feature for fuller learning of structural features, and experiments showed that their method could bring competitive results for spatial SR, angular SR, and depth estimation.

Transformer. Recently, Transformer have become popular in image processing. Compared with CNN, it can fully and effectively fuse complex information in the LF. Liang et al. [19] proposed a transformer-based structure, and designed a spatial transformer and angular transformer, which captured the local and remote information of sub-aperture images more fully, and experiments proved that its effect reached the leading level.

2.2   GANs for SISR

GAN plays an important role in the field of computer vision, which enables two networks to confront each other and progress towards each other in the form of games. Therefore, the GANs in image SR have important significance in the real world. In recent years, GANs have been initially applied in the field of SISR [20–23], which achieves SR tasks by learning the distribution of training data and generating realistic high-resolution images.

SRGAN. Ledig et al. [20] proposed SRGAN, which introduces a perceptual loss function and utilizes adversarial training to make the generated images more realistic.

ESRGAN. Wang et al. [21] proposed an improved version of SRGAN, which improves the generation effect by introducing residual blocks and a new attention mechanism, while using progressive training methods to make network training more stable.

Real-ESRGAN. In their subsequent work, ESRGAN was upgraded to Real-ESRGAN [22], which uses a higher-order degradation modeling process to better simulate complex real-world degradation. The author made it into an actual recovery application.

IRE. Zhu et al. [23] proposed an improved model based on Real-ESRGAN. They removed the first-order degradation modeling of HDM to mitigate the degree of visual deterioration, and added an attention mechanism to generate an image which more closer to the original image. Then PatchGAN was used as the discriminator structure. Experiments had shown that it improved texture detail and had faster convergence.

3   Method

FCGSR, an acronym for Fourier Channel Attention-based Conditional Generative Adversarial Network (cGAN), utilizes two key models. The first model, G, focuses on learning data distribution and undertaking image conversion. The second model, D, serves as a discriminator, distinguishing between images derived from training data and those generated by the G generator. The G network comprises three stages: initial feature extraction, a residual module employing Fourier channel attention, and upsampling. Ultimately, our generator produces a high-resolution SAI array. To transform input images into the YCbCr color space, we adopt the approach outlined in [7] and [8]. Our focus lies in the super-resolution of the Y channel, while the Cb and Cr channel images are upscaled using bicubic interpolation. In this study, we introduce a unique perceptual loss, denoted as l^{LFSR}, which combines various loss components to restore specific ideal features of LFSR images. For a more comprehensive understanding of the loss functions, please refer to Sect. 3.3. The discriminator, denoted as D, is responsible for evaluating both the generated and real images, and assigns a score reflecting the probability of an image being real. Based on a conventional CNN architecture, our D model comprises 14 convolutional layers.

Fig. 1. Images of different resolutions and their power spectrum.

3.1 Fourier Channel Attention

Popular super-resolution networks on the market focus on spatial structural differences. As shown in Fig. 1, We visualized the picture in dataset INRIA, with the first row being the high-resolution(HR) picture and its power spectrum, and the second row being the low-resolution(LR) picture and its power spectrum. It turned out that, the structural differences between LR images and HR images in the spatial domain are not significant. However, we follow [13] that the MS-SSIM between the paired LR-HR images retain a high score of 0.95 and 0.76. In the Fourier domain, the power spectrum of LR images is limited to the specified cutoff frequency. After down-sampling, the high-frequency information outside the white dashed box is filtered out, so it can be boldly inferred that the structural differences between HR images and LR images are more prominent in the power spectrum covered. This allows the network to extract more meaningful features for high-frequency reconstruction. Thus, we use the deep Fourier channel attention mechanism, which calculates the contribution of frequency components in the corresponding feature map of high-frequency information and weights the rescaling factor with each feature map. Details are mentioned in the next subsection.

3.2 Generator Network Architecture

An overview of our Generator is shown in Fig. 2(a). Given an LR SAI array $\mathcal{I}_{SAIs}^{\mathcal{LR}} \in \mathbb{R}^{AH \times AW}$, we first convert it into an LR MacPI $\mathcal{I}_{MacPI}^{\mathcal{LR}} \in \mathbb{R}^{AH \times AW}$. Then we follow most existing network usage 3×3 convolutions to achieve relatively small model sizes. A convolution with a kernel size of 3×3, a stride of 1 and a dilation of A is used to isolate information from different views on MacPI for preliminary extraction of spatial features. And performs zero padding to ensure

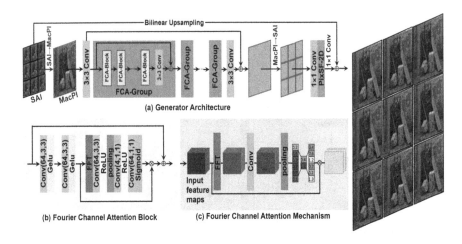

Fig. 2. Framework of the proposed FCGSR method.

that the output and input MacPI have the same space size. The convolution is followed by five identical residual groups(RGs). Each RG consists of ten Fourier Channel Attention Blocks (FCABs), a convolution with a kernel size of 3×3 and a skip connection. The operation of RG is recorded as:

$$RG(x) = x + Conv(FCAB^{(10)}(x)) \tag{1}$$

where:

$$FCAB^{(n)}(x) = Conv(\underbrace{FCAB(FCAB(\cdots FCAB(x))))}_{n \times FCAB} \tag{2}$$

x denotes the input feature maps of the RG. The structure of FCAB is illustrated in Extended Data Fig. 2(b). In each FCAB, feature maps are rescaled in a channelwise manner as follows:

$$FCAB(x) = x + y \times f(W_U \delta(W_D \varphi(y))) \tag{3}$$

where:

$$y = GELU[Conv\{GELU[Conv\{x\}]\}] \tag{4}$$

$$\varphi(y) = Pooling_{global}(ReLU[Conv\{abs(FFT(y))^\gamma\}]) \tag{5}$$

In the provided equation, FFT(·) denotes the utilization of fast Fourier transform. We introduce a parameter γ to amplify the influence of high-frequency components. To obtain representative values for each feature map, a global average pooling layer, referred to as $Pooling_{global}$, is employed on the components of $\varphi(y)$. The downscaling weight, W_D, and the upscaling weight, W_U, are acquired through 1×1 convolutional layers. The sigmoid activation function is denoted as $f(·)$, while $\delta(·)$ represents the rectified linear unit (ReLU) activation function. These components collectively form a gating mechanism, which enables the adaptive calculation of the final rescaling factors.

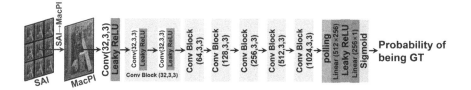

Fig. 3. An overview of our discriminator network.

In each residual block, the FCA mechanism Fig. 2(c) Enables the network to adaptively rescale each characteristic graph based on the combined contribution of all frequency components included in its power spectrum.

Finally, the results are concatenated and fused with spatial convolution, which can well utilize Fast Fourier Transform to guide the extraction of spatial information. To facilitate local residual learning, the fused feature is combined with the input feature. In order to enhance the spatial resolution of the LF features, we initially reshape the feature derived from the cascaded FCA-Groups. This transformation converts the feature from the MacPI pattern to the SAI pattern. Subsequently, a 1×1 convolution is employed to increase the depth of the feature to $\alpha^2 C$, with α representing the upscaling factor. To achieve upsampling to the target resolution of $\alpha AH \times \alpha AW$, a 2D pixel shuffling layer is used. Finally, a 1×1 convolution is applied to compress the number of channels to 1, resulting in the generation of super-resolved SAIs.

3.3   Discriminator Network Architecture

To distinguish between real HR images and generated SR samples, we trained a discriminator network. The architecture is shown in Fig. 3 The output layer of each convolution is the leakage coefficient of the activation function activated by LeakyReLU $\alpha = 0.1$, which can be written as:

$$LeakyReLU(x, \alpha) = max(0, x) - \alpha max(0, -x) \tag{6}$$

The 1024 feature maps obtained are followed by two dense layers and a final sigmoid activation function to obtain the probability of sample classification.

3.4   Loss Function

The definition of our perceptual loss function, denoted as l^{LFSR}, plays a crucial role in enhancing the performance of our generator network. Following the approach described in [20], we have designed a loss function that evaluates a solution based on perceptually relevant attributes. Our loss function encompasses image loss, perceptual loss, and adversarial loss, which are combined using a weighted sum. The formula for the loss function is as follows:

$$l^{LFSR} = \underbrace{l^{LFSR}_{MSE}}_{image\ loss} + \underbrace{6 \times 10^{-3} l^{LFSR}_{VGG}}_{perception\ loss} + \underbrace{10^{-3} l^{LFSR}_{Gen}}_{adversarial\ loss} \tag{7}$$

The pixel-wise MSE loss is calculated as:

$$l_{MSE}^{LFSR} = \frac{1}{r^2 WH} \sum_{x=1}^{rW} \sum_{y=1}^{rH} (I_{x,y}^{LFHR} - G(I^{LFLR})_{x,y})^2 \tag{8}$$

This is the most widely used optimization target for image SR. We use the real images and images generated by the generator as formula input.

The VGG loss function utilizes a pre-trained 19-layer VGG network. We denote the feature map obtained by the j-th convolution (after activation) before the i-th maxpooling layer within the VGG19 network as $\phi_{i,j}$, which is considered as a given. The VGG loss is defined as the Euclidean distance between the feature representations of a generated image $G(I^{LFLR})$ and the original image I^{LFHR}:

$$l_{VGG/i,j}^{LFSR} = \frac{1}{W_{i,j} H_{i,j}} \sum_{x=1}^{W_{i,j}} \sum_{y=1}^{H_{i,j}} (\phi_{i,j}(I^{LFHR})_{x,y} \\ - \phi_{i,j}(G(I^{LFLR}))_{x,y})^2 \tag{9}$$

Here $W_{i,j}$ and $H_{i,j}$ describe the dimensions of the respective feature maps within the VGG network.

In addition, we incorporate the generative component of our GAN into the loss function to promote the preference for solutions that adhere to the manifold of natural images. This is achieved by attempting to deceive the discriminator network. The generative loss, denoted as l_{Gen}^{LFSR}, is defined by taking into account the probabilities assigned by the discriminator $D(G(I^{LFLR}))$ to all training samples:

$$l_{Gen}^{LFSR} = \frac{1}{N} \sum_{n=1}^{N} (1 - D(G(I^{LFLR}))) \tag{10}$$

Here, $D(G(I^{LFLR}))$ is the probability that the reconstructed image $G(I^{LFLR})$ is a natural HR image.

We further define a loss function for discriminator network as:

$$l_{Dis}^{LFSR} = 1 - D(I^{LFHR}) + D(G(I^{LFLR})) \tag{11}$$

We optimize the defined loss function in an alternating manner with G to address the adversarial min-max problem.

4   Experiments

4.1   Datasets and Implementation Details

As listed in Table 1, we use 5 public LF datasets (i.e., EPFL [24], HCInew [25], HCIold [26], INRIA [27], STFgantry [28]). The division of training and test set is set in Table 1. We adopt the approach described in [18], where all light fields (LFs) in the datasets have an angular resolution of 9×9. During the training

Table 1. Datasets used in our experiments.

	EPFL [24]	HCInew [25]	HCIold [26]	INRIA [27]	STFgantry [28]
Training	70	20	10	35	9
Test	10	4	2	5	2

phase, we crop each sub-aperture image (SAI) into patches using a stride of 32. LF patches of size 32×32 are generated by applying bicubic downsampling. To augment the training data, we employ random horizontal flipping, vertical flipping, and 90-degree rotation, resulting in an 8-fold increase in data. It is important to note that when flipping or rotating, both the spatial and angular dimensions are manipulated together to preserve the LF structures.

Our network is optimized using the Adam method [29] and a batch size of 4. Our FCGSR is implemented in PyTorch on a PC with a NVidia RTX4090 GPU. The learning rate of generator is initially set to 1×10^{-4} and the learning rate of discriminator is 2×10^{-5}. The factors for decreasing both the PSNR and SSIM metrics are set at 0.5 after every 15 epochs, while the training process is halted once it reaches 100 epochs. In evaluating the performance, quantitative metrics such as PSNR and SSIM are employed, specifically calculated on the Y channel images. It is important to note that when computing metric scores for a dataset consisting of M test scenes, where each scene has an angular resolution of A×A, we first calculate the metric scores individually on the A×A SAIs for each scene. Subsequently, the score for each scene is determined by averaging its A^2 scores, and finally, the overall score for the dataset is obtained by averaging the scores of all M scenes.

4.2   Comparison to State-of-the-Art Methods

We compare our FCGSR to several state-of-the-art methods, including 6 single image SR methods (i.e., VDSR [30], EDSR [31], RCAN [32], SAN [33], SRGAN [20], ESRGAN [21] and 4 LF image SR methods (i.e., LFBM5D [34], GB [35], reslf [7], LFSSR [16]). To provide a fair comparison, we incorporate bicubic interpolation as a baseline method. It is important to note that all deep learning-based super resolution (SR) methods have been trained anew using the same datasets as our method. For brevity, we present the results specifically for 2× and 4× SR on 5×5 light fields (LFs).

Quantitative Results: Quantitative results in Table 2 demonstrate the state-of-the-art performance of our FCGSR on all the 4 test datasets. Moreover, our FCGSR can achieve a comparable PSNR and SSIM scores as compared to the recent LF image SR method LFSSR [16]. As can be seen from the table, our FCGSR is very effective in improving both the 2×and 4×SR in EPFL, INRIA and STFgantry. It has a higher PSNR than the previous method.

Table 2. PSNR/SSIM values achieved by different methods for 2×and 4×SR.

Method	Scale	EPFL	HCInew	HCIold	INRIA	STFgantry
Bicubic	2×	29.50/0.935	31.69/0.934	37.46/0.978	31.10/0.956	30.82/0.947
VDSR	2×	32.01/0.959	34.37/0.956	40.34/0.985	33.80/0.972	35.80/0.980
EDSR	2×	32.86/0.965	35.02/0.961	41.11/0.988	34.61/0.977	37.08/0.985
RCAN	2×	33.46/0.967	35.56/0.963	41.59/0.989	35.18/0.978	38.18/0.988
SAN	2×	33.36/0.967	35.51/0.963	41.47/0.989	35.15/0.978	37.98/0.987
LFBM5D	2×	31.15/0.955	33.72/0.955	39.62/0.985	32.85/0.969	33.55/0.972
GB	2×	31.22/0.959	35.25/0.969	40.21/0.988	32.76/0.972	35.44/0.983
resLF	2×	33.22/0.969	35.79/0.969	42.30/0.991	34.86/0.979	36.28/0.985
LFSSR	2×	33.69/0.975	**36.86/0.975**	**43.75/0.994**	35.27/0.983	38.07/0.990
FCGSR	2×	**34.30/0.976**	36.76/0.974	43.19/0.993	**36.01/0.983**	**38.32/0.991**
Bicubic	4×	25.14/0.831	27.61/0.851	32.42/0.934	26.82/0.886	25.93/0.843
VDSR	4×	26.82/0.869	29.12/0.876	34.01/0.943	28.87/0.914	28.31/0.893
EDSR	4×	27.82/0.892	29.94/0.893	35.53/0.957	29.86/0.931	29.43/0.921
RCAN	4×	28.31/0.899	30.25/0.896	35.89/0.959	30.36/0.936	30.25/0.934
SAN	4×	28.30/0.899	30.25/0.898	35.88/0.960	30.29/0.936	30.30/0.933
SRGAN	4×	26.85/0.870	28.95/0.873	34.03/0.942	28.85/0.916	28.19/0.898
ESRGAN	4×	25.59/0.836	26.96/0.819	33.53/0.933	27.54/0.880	28.00/0.905
LFBM5D	4×	26.61/0.869	29.13/0.882	34.23/0.951	28.49/0.914	28.30/0.900
GB	4×	26.02/0.863	28.92/0.884	33.74/0.950	27.73/0.909	28.11/0.901
resLF	4×	27.86/0.899	30.37/0.907	36.12/0.966	29.72/0.936	29.64/0.927
LFSSR	4×	28.27/0.908	**30.72/0.912**	**36.70/0.969**	30.31/**0.945**	30.15/0.939
FCGSR	4×	**28.55/0.910**	30.64/0.908	36.11/0.962	**30.42**/0.943	**30.49/0.941**

STFgantry_Cards

Fig. 4. Visual comparisons for 4×SR on STFgantry.

Qualitative Results: Qualitative Results: Let's take 4×SR as an example. Figure 4 and Fig. 5 show the qualitative results achieved by different methods. Our FCGSR can well preserve the textures and details in the SR images and achieves competitive visual performance. Although our FCGSR does not have PSNR as good as LFSSR on HCInew, our visuals are superior to the former. This further proves that the results of the GANs are more in line with human perception.

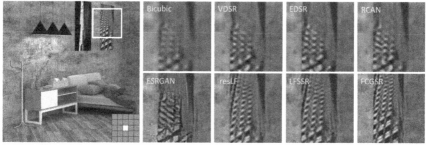

HCInew_Bedroom

Fig. 5. Visual comparisons for 4×SR on HCInew.

5 Conclusion

In this article, we will generate a generative adversarial network for LF image SR. By using the Fourier channel attention mechanism, we obtain frequency content differences between different features to learn high-frequency information from different structures. Experimental results show that our FCGSR performance is superior to general CNN based SR methods. In the future, we will add complementary angle information and subjective evaluation of light fields to the network to further advance the experiment.

References

1. Wang, Y., Wu, T., Yang, J., Wang, L., An, W., Guo, Y.: Deoccnet: learning to see through foreground occlusions in light fields. In: 2020 IEEE Winter Conference on Applications of Computer Vision (WACV), pp. 118–127 (2020)
2. Wang, T.-C., Efros, A.A., Ramamoorthi, R.: Depth estimation with occlusion modeling using light-field cameras. IEEE Trans. Pattern Anal. Mach. Intell. **38**(11), 2170–2181 (2016)
3. Wang, A.: Three-stream cross-modal feature aggregation network for light field salient object detection. IEEE Signal Process. Lett. **28**, 46–50 (2021)
4. Wang, Y., Yang, J., Guo, Y., Xiao, C., An, W.: Selective light field refocusing for camera arrays using bokeh rendering and superresolution. IEEE Signal Process. Lett. **26**(1), 204–208 (2019)
5. Yoon, Y., Jeon, H.-G., Yoo, D., Lee, J.-Y., Kweon, I.S.: Light-field image super-resolution using convolutional neural network. IEEE Signal Process. Lett. **24**(6), 848–852 (2017)
6. Yuan, Y., Cao, Z., Lijuan, S.: Light-field image superresolution using a combined deep cnn based on epi. IEEE Signal Process. Lett. **25**(9), 1359–1363 (2018)
7. Zhang, S., Lin, Y., Sheng, H.: Residual networks for light field image super-resolution. In: 2019 IEEE/CVF Conference on Computer Vision and Pattern Recognition (CVPR), pp. 11038–11047 (2019)
8. Jin, J., Hou, J., Chen, J., Kwong, S.: Light field spatial super-resolution via deep combinatorial geometry embedding and structural consistency regularization. In: 2020 IEEE/CVF Conference on Computer Vision and Pattern Recognition (CVPR), pp. 2257–2266 (2020)

9. Karras, T., Laine, S., Aila, T.: A style-based generator architecture for generative adversarial networks. IEEE Trans. Pattern Anal. Mach. Intell. **43**(12), 4217–4228 (2021)
10. Ehsani, K., Mottaghi, R., Farhadi, A.: Segan: segmenting and generating the invisible. In: 2018 IEEE/CVF Conference on Computer Vision and Pattern Recognition, pp. 6144–6153 (2018)
11. Zhu, J.-Y., Park, T., Isola, P., Efros, A.A.: Unpaired image-to-image translation using cycle-consistent adversarial networks. In: 2017 IEEE International Conference on Computer Vision (ICCV), pp. 2242–2251 (2017)
12. Demir.U., Unal, G.: Patch-Based Image Inpainting with Generative Adversarial Networks. arXiv e-prints, page arXiv:1803.07422 (March 2018)
13. Qiao, C., et al.: Evaluation and development of deep neural networks for image super-resolution in optical microscopy. Nat. Methods **18**(2), 194–202 (2021)
14. Bishop, T.E., Favaro, P.: The light field camera: extended depth of field, aliasing, and superresolution. IEEE Trans. Pattern Anal. Mach. Intell. **34**(5), 972–986 (2012)
15. Kaushik Mitra and Ashok Veeraraghavan. Light field denoising, light field superresolution and stereo camera based refocussing using a gmm light field patch prior. In 2012 IEEE Computer Society Conference on Computer Vision and Pattern Recognition Workshops, pages 22–28, 2012
16. Yeung, H.W.F., Hou, J., Chen, X., Chen, J., Chen, Z., Chung, Y.Y.: Light field spatial super-resolution using deep efficient spatial-angular separable convolution. IEEE Trans. Image Process. **28**(5), 2319–2330 (2019)
17. Wang, Y., Wang, L., Yang, J., An, W., Yu, J., Guo, Y.: Spatial-angular interaction for light field image super-resolution. In: Vedaldi, A., Bischof, H., Brox, T., Frahm, J.-M. (eds.) ECCV 2020. LNCS, vol. 12368, pp. 290–308. Springer, Cham (2020). https://doi.org/10.1007/978-3-030-58592-1_18
18. Wang, Y., Wang, L., Gaochang, W., Yang, J., An, W., Jingyi, Yu., Guo, Y.: Disentangling light fields for super-resolution and disparity estimation. IEEE Trans. Pattern Anal. Mach. Intell. **45**(1), 425–443 (2023)
19. Liang, Z., Wang, Y., Wang, L., Yang, J., Zhou, S.: Light field image super-resolution with transformers. IEEE Signal Process. Lett. **29**, 563–567 (2022)
20. Ledig, C.: Photo-realistic single image super-resolution using a generative adversarial network. In: 2017 IEEE Conference on Computer Vision and Pattern Recognition (CVPR), pp. 105–114 (2017)
21. Wang, X.: ESRGAN: enhanced super-resolution generative adversarial networks. In: Leal-Taixé, L., Roth, S. (eds.) ECCV 2018. LNCS, vol. 11133, pp. 63–79. Springer, Cham (2019). https://doi.org/10.1007/978-3-030-11021-5_5
22. Wang, X., Xie, L., Dong, C., Shan, Y.: Real-esrgan: training real-world blind super-resolution with pure synthetic data. In: 2021 IEEE/CVF International Conference on Computer Vision Workshops (ICCVW), pp. 1905–1914 (2021)
23. Zhu, Z., Lei, Y., Qin, Y., Zhu, C., Zhu, Y.: Ire: improved image super-resolution based on real-esrgan. IEEE Access, 1–1 (2023)
24. Rerábek, M., Ebrahimi, T.: New light field image dataset. In: International Workshop on Quality of Multimedia Experience (2016)
25. Honauer, K., Johannsen, O., Kondermann, D., Goldluecke, B.: A Dataset and Evaluation Methodology for Depth Estimation on 4D Light Fields. In: Lai, S.-H., Lepetit, V., Nishino, K., Sato, Y. (eds.) ACCV 2016. LNCS, vol. 10113, pp. 19–34. Springer, Cham (2017). https://doi.org/10.1007/978-3-319-54187-7_2

26. Wanner, S., Meister, S., Goldlücke, B.: Datasets and benchmarks for densely sampled 4d light fields. In: International Symposium on Vision, Modeling, and Visualization (2013)
27. Le Pendu, M., Jiang, X., Guillemot, C.: Light field inpainting propagation via low rank matrix completion. IEEE Trans. Image Process. **27**(4), 1981–1993 (2018)
28. Vaish, V., Adams, A.: The (new) stanford light field archive. Computer Graphics Laboratory, Stanford University, vol. 6(7) (2008)
29. Kingma, D., Ba, J.: Adam: a method for stochastic optimization. Comput. Sci. (2014)
30. Kim, J., Lee, J.K., Lee, K.M.: Accurate image super-resolution using very deep convolutional networks. In: 2016 IEEE Conference on Computer Vision and Pattern Recognition (CVPR), pp. 1646–1654 (2016)
31. Lim, B., Son, S., Kim, H., Nah, S., Lee, K.M.: Enhanced deep residual networks for single image super-resolution. In: 2017 IEEE Conference on Computer Vision and Pattern Recognition Workshops (CVPRW), pp. 1132–1140 (2017)
32. Zhang, Y., et al.: Image super-resolution using very deep residual channel attention networks. In: Ferrari, V., Hebert, M., Sminchisescu, C., Weiss, Y. (eds.) ECCV 2018. LNCS, vol. 11211, pp. 294–310. Springer, Cham (2018). https://doi.org/10.1007/978-3-030-01234-2_18
33. Dai, T., Cai, J., Zhang, Y., Xia, S.-T., Zhang, L.: Second-order attention network for single image super-resolution. In: 2019 IEEE/CVF Conference on Computer Vision and Pattern Recognition (CVPR), pp. 11057–11066 (2019)
34. Alain, M., Smolic, A.: Light field super-resolution via lfbm5d sparse coding. In: 2018 25th IEEE International Conference on Image Processing (ICIP), pp. 2501–2505 (2018)
35. Rossi, M., Frossard, P.: Geometry-consistent light field super-resolution via graph-based regularization. IEEE Trans. Image Process. **27**(9), 4207–4218 (2018)

Synthesizing a Large Scene with Multiple NeRFs

Shenglong Ye, Feifei Li, and Rui Huang$^{(\boxtimes)}$

The Chinese University of Hong Kong, Shenzhen, China
{shenglongye,feifeili1}@link.cuhk.edu.cn, ruihuang@cuhk.edu.cn

Abstract. Last several years, NeRF achieved great success in view synthesis since it can render high-quality images in a complex scene. However, we find that its ability to rebuild a large scene is low because images that are far apart and do not overlap with each other will affect each other in the training process. In order to solve this problem, we propose Cluster-based NeRF, which splits the original input images into several clusters and then train a NeRF for each cluster. We also design an algorithm to improve the rendering quality in the overlapping areas. In the experiments, we show that our method outperforms the traditional NeRF on both the blender and real world dataset.

Keywords: View synthesis · Image-based rendering · Volume rendering

1 Introduction

View synthesis is a long-standing problem in the field of computer vision. Its object is to render some images from novel views given lots of input images and corresponding poses. Recently, various works [11,15,20] have tried to solve the problem. Although they can acquire the image given a novel view, they all failed to produce high-quality images. Last several years, NeRF: Representing Scenes as Neural Radiance Fields for View Synthesis [14] uses an MLP to map 3-D spatial location to the color and the volume density in the scene, which achieves great success in view synthesis. It can synthesize a high-quality image in a complex scene, which outperforms those prior works.

However, there is a shortcoming for the NeRF that the quality of the image will be lower when it constructs a large scene. If we utilize NeRF to do the view synthesis in a large scene, lots of unrelated inputs will affect each other in the training process, which will lead to lower-quality rendering images. Therefore, for a large scene, we assume that we can split the inputs into some clusters first and then train a NeRF for each cluster.

In this work, we propose Cluster-based Neural Radiance Fields for View Synthesis to synthesize novel view in a large scene. In summary, our key contributions are:

H. Lu et al. (Eds.): ICIG 2023, LNCS 14359, pp. 198–209, 2023.
https://doi.org/10.1007/978-3-031-46317-4_17

1. In the Cluster-based NeRF, we define the distance between two camera poses, which present the relationship between the poses. With the distance, we can describe how close are. We also define the center pose of the poses to describe the relationship between the clusters.

2. In order to help the edge cases in the training process, we propose an overlapping algorithm in our methods. With the overlapping algorithm, we can improve the quality of the images in edge cases and get a better overall performance.

2   Related Work

2.1   3-D Shape Representation and View Synthesis

Recently, many works [3,7] have managed to use deep neural network to implicitly represent the 3-D scene by mapping spatial location to some information in the scene, but none of these methods can work well without the ground truth of 3-D geometry. Since it is difficult to get the ground truth of the 3-D geometry in the real world, a lot of subsequent works [16,20] try to do some relaxation. Although these methods can get a better-quality images in the scene with only 2-D ground truth images supervised, they are poor at synthesizing the images in a complex scene.

When it comes to the view synthesis, some early effort [2,4] has been paid to solve it, but they are very sensitive to the sampling density. There are two popular approaches to solve the problem. One of these approaches is the mesh-based representation of the scenes [1,21], but the optimization of these differentiable methods during the rendering process is difficult, which is likely to converge to a sub-optimal solution. The other approach is to utilize volumetric representations [10,19], but they are time consuming and space consuming. They need to sample points in all space, which means that higher resolution they need to acquire, denser points they will sample.

2.2   NeRF

In order to get the high-quality images from a complex scene with only 2-D images supervised, NeRF was proposed in last several years.

For a specific scene, the author would like to train a MLP network $F \in \mathbf{R}^5 \rightarrow \mathbf{R}^4$. The input of the network is composed of the 3-D location (x, y, z) in the space and the 2-D direction (θ, ϕ). The output of the network is composed of the color (r, g, b) and the volume density σ. More specifically, they use (x, y, z, θ, ϕ) to predict the color (r, g, b) and use (x, y, z) to predict the volume density σ. With the pretrained network, they can get the color and the volume density of any point in the scene from any direction.

With a pretrained network f and the pose π of the camera, they can render the image of the camera. They follow the traditional volume rendering algorithm [8] to produce the image. For each pixel in the image, they consider the ray r from the camera to the pixel. The ray can be expressed as $r(t) = \mathbf{o} + t\mathbf{d}$.

The color of the pixel $C(\mathbf{r})$ of the ray $r(t) = \mathbf{o} + t\mathbf{d}$ with the near bounds t_n and the far bound t_f can be presented as:

$$C(\mathbf{r}) = \int_{t_n}^{t_f} T(t)\sigma(\mathbf{o} + t\mathbf{d})c(\mathbf{o} + t\mathbf{d}, \mathbf{d})dt \tag{1}$$

$$T(t) = exp[-\int_{t_n}^{t} \sigma(\mathbf{o} + s\mathbf{d})ds] \tag{2}$$

where $T(t)$ is the accumulated transmittance along the ray.

Practically, they choose to follow the Direct Volume Rendering Method [13] to render the image. Since an MLP is used to approximate the $\sigma(\mathbf{o} + t\mathbf{d})$ and $c(\mathbf{o} + t\mathbf{d}, \mathbf{d})$, they can only sample some discrete $t \in [t_n, t_f]$.

$$t_i \sim \mathcal{U}[t_n + \frac{i-1}{N}(t_f - t_n), t_n + \frac{i}{N}(t_f - t_n)] \tag{3}$$

where N is the sample number and $\mathcal{U}$ denotes the uniform distribution.

The method above is not sufficient to achieve the state-of-the-art performance, so the authors also propose two strategies to optimize the network, positional encoding and Hierarchical volume sampling.

Although a neural network can approximate nearly any function [6], they find that it is difficult to directly approximate the function from (x, y, z, θ, ϕ) to (r, g, b, σ). Therefore, they adopt a recent work [18] that shows neural networks are more efficient with higher frequency inputs. Based on the theory, they propose a unlearned function $\gamma(\mathbf{p}) \in \mathbf{R}^3 \rightarrow \mathbf{R}^{6L}$.

$$\gamma(\mathbf{p}) = [sin(2^0\mathbf{p}), cos(2^0\mathbf{p}), sin(2^1\mathbf{p}), ..., sin(2^{L-1}\mathbf{p}), cos(2^{L-1}\mathbf{p})] \tag{4}$$

With $\gamma(\mathbf{p})$, they replace the $\mathbf{o} + t\mathbf{d}$ and $\mathbf{d}$ in Eq. 1 and Eq. 2 with $\gamma(\mathbf{o} + t\mathbf{d})$ and $\gamma(\mathbf{d})$. In practice, they set $L = 10$ when calculating $\gamma(\mathbf{o} + t\mathbf{d})$ and $L = 4$ when calculating $\gamma(\mathbf{d})$.

Instead of training one MLP network, the authors train a coarse network and a fine network. For a single ray, they first sample N_c points from the ray and optimize the coarse network. With the output of the coarse network, they can use a new strategy to sample the points. Rewrite the Eq. 1

$$\hat{C}(r) = \sum_{i=1}^{N} w_i c(\mathbf{o} + t_i\mathbf{d}, \mathbf{d}) \tag{5}$$

$$w_i = T_i\{1 - exp[-\sigma(\mathbf{o} + t_i\mathbf{d})\delta_i]\} \tag{6}$$

If we normalize the weights w_i to $\hat{w}_i = w_i / \sum_j w_j$, it will be a piecewise constant PDF along the ray. Given the $\hat{w}_i$, they sample N_f points from this distribution by inverse transform sampling to train the fine network. With these operation, the model can sample more points from the important position which is likely to effect the result of the image. At the rendering process, the authors will use both N_c and N_f points to render the ray with Eq. 1 and 2.

The final loss of the network is,

$$\mathcal{L} = \sum_{\mathbf{r} \in R} [||C_c(\mathbf{r}) - C(\mathbf{r})||^2 + ||C_f(\mathbf{r}) - C(\mathbf{r})||^2] \tag{7}$$

where $\boldsymbol{R}$ denotes the dataset, C_c denotes the coarse network, C_f denotes the fine network and C denotes the ground truth.

NeRF trains the network with all of the inputs, which will lead to a problem. If the scene is too large, there will exist lots of unrelated images in the training process so that they will affect each other. Our method can successfully solve the problem.

3   Method

3.1   Preliminary

Given a set of images $\boldsymbol{\mathcal{I}} = \{\mathcal{I}_1, \mathcal{I}_2, ..., \mathcal{I}_N\}$ and corresponding camera poses $\boldsymbol{\mathcal{II}} = \{\pi_1, \pi_2, ..., \pi_N\}$ including both intrinsics matrixes $\boldsymbol{K}$ and extrinsics matrixes $\boldsymbol{T}_w$, our object is to build a system $G(\theta)$ which can render any image with a certain camera pose.

Based on the traditional NeRF, we propose our Cluster-based NeRF, which is a two-step algorithm.

In the training process, the first step is to split the original dataset into some clusters, the second step is to train a NeRF network for each cluster of the input images and corresponding poses. We will keep the center pose of the cluster and the parameters of the NeRF network.

In the evaluation process, for each input camera pose π, we will first find the nearest center pose from all the cluster. Then we will use the corresponding NeRF network to synthesize the image.

Since the training and the rendering process is the same as the traditional NeRF, we will carefully explain the clustering algorithm below.

3.2   Distance Definition

It is reasonable that we put 'near' inputs in the same cluster and 'far' inputs in different clusters. In order to split the inputs into different clusters, we need to define how near are two inputs $(\mathcal{I}_A, \pi_A)$ and $(\mathcal{I}_B, \pi_B)$. Since we have no information about the scene from a single image without its pose, we claim that the distance L between two inputs is determined by their poses completely, which means $L(\mathcal{I}_A, \pi_A, \mathcal{I}_B, \pi_B) = L(\pi_A, \pi_B)$

The more complex the scene is, the more difficult it is for the neural network to approximate the function. Since we claim the distance is only related to the poses, we will not be informed of the color and the density in the scene. Therefore we assume that the probability distribution of the color and the density is the same in all space, which means the complexity of a scene is directly proportional to the space of the scene. Our purpose is to make the neural network approximate the function easier, which is to make the space of the scene smaller. So we can define the distance as:

$$L(\pi_A, \pi_B) \propto \mathbb{E}_{\mathbf{p}_1, \mathbf{p}_2 \in V_A \cup V_B} ||\mathbf{p}_1 - \mathbf{p}_2||^2$$
$$= \mathbb{E}_{\mathbf{p}_A \in V_A, \mathbf{p}_B \in V_B} ||\mathbf{p}_A - \mathbf{p}_B||^2 + \mathbb{E}_{\mathbf{p}_1, \mathbf{p}_2 \in V_A} ||\mathbf{p}_1 - \mathbf{p}_2||^2 + \mathbb{E}_{\mathbf{p}_1, \mathbf{p}_2 \in V_B} ||\mathbf{p}_1 - \mathbf{p}_2||^2 \tag{8}$$

V denotes the visual view of the camera and $\mathbf{p}$ denotes the coordinate in the space. We find that $\mathbb{E}_{\mathbf{p}_1, \mathbf{p}_2 \in V} ||\mathbf{p}_1 - \mathbf{p}_2||^2$ is only related to one camera, which is the same for all the inputs. With the last two terms omitted, we can get

$$L(\pi_A, \pi_B) \propto \mathbb{E}_{\mathbf{p}_A \in V_A, \mathbf{p}_B \in V_B} ||\mathbf{p}_A - \mathbf{p}_B||^2 \tag{9}$$

It means that we would like to put the inputs which are physically near in the same cluster. Practically, we will sample the points with the same sampling strategy of the coarse network processing in the NeRF, so we can get,

$$L(\pi_A, \pi_B) = k \sum_{\mathbf{p}_A \in P_A, \mathbf{p}_B \in P_B} ||\mathbf{p}_A - \mathbf{p}_B||^2 \tag{10}$$

P is the set of the sampled points from the visual field and k is a constant.

3.3 Center Pose Definition

With the definition between two inputs $L(\pi_A, \pi_B)$, we can split the dataset into some clusters.

In practice, we choose to utilize the K-means clustering algorithm to do the clustering to the original inputs. After performing the clusters, we need to get the center pose of each cluster to do the evaluation, so we need to define the corresponding center pose. Given $\mathcal{II} = \{\pi_1, \pi_2, ..., \pi_N\}$, we will define a center pose π_0 as

$$\pi_0 = \arg\min \sum_{i=1}^{N} L(\pi_0, \pi_i) \tag{11}$$

It will take lots of computational resources to strictly solve the Problem 11, so we can do some approximation. Practically, since the intrinsics matrix of the camera is all the same, we assume that $K(\pi_0) = K(\pi_i)$ and focus on the extrinsics matrix. The extrinsic matrix $T_w(\pi_0)$ is composed of rotation matrix R_0 and translation matrix T_0. For the translation matrix T_0, it is reasonable to define $T_0 = \frac{1}{N} \sum_{i=1}^{N} T_i$. When it comes to the rotation matrix, we cannot do the similar operation since the rotation matrix comes from a more complex space. We adopt the algorithm mentioned in a paper [5] to find the average rotation matrix.

Algorithm 1. Average rotation matrix

Require:
    The set of some rotation matrix $\{R_1, R_2, ..., R_n\}$;
Ensure:
    Average rotation matrix R

Set $R \leftarrow R_1$ and $\epsilon > 0$
Compute $r = \frac{1}{n} \sum_{i=1}^{n} \log(R^T R_i)$
while $||r|| > \epsilon$ **do**
    $R \leftarrow R \exp(r)$
    Compute $r = \frac{1}{n} \sum_{i=1}^{n} \log(R^T R_i)$
end while
return R

By the definition of the center pose $T_w(\pi_0)$ and the definition of the distance $L(\pi_a, \pi_b)$, we can perform our clustering algorithm to the original inputs to split them into some subsets.

3.4 Overlap in Clusters

We can use the clustering algorithm above to improve the quality of the images, but the performance will be extremely low in the edge of each cluster. The reason is that those images lack sufficient information in the training step because some images, which are able to provide information in training step, are in other clusters. In order to increase the quality of the images in the edge, we propose an algorithm in the training process to help train these images. Specifically, for each cluster and corresponding NeRF network, we add some images which were not in the cluster into the training dataset to improve the performance in the edge.

Since we aim to help the case in the edge, we would like to know how much one input can help train the other. For a specific camera pose π_a, we need to define how much another camera pose π_b can help to train the network which is able to render a higher-quality image in the pose π_a. We propose that the helpfulness of camera pose π_b to the π_a is:

$$H(\pi_a, \pi_b) = \frac{V_{ab}}{V_a + V_b + V_{ab}} \qquad (12)$$

V_{ab} is the volume of the intersection of the visual view of camera a and camera b. V_a and V_b are the independent visual view of camera a and camera b respectively.

Adding some inputs $(\mathcal{I}, \pi)$ to the cluster will be sure to be helpful to the edge of the cluster, but it will include some unrelated rays to affect the training process. Therefore we assume that the input $(\mathcal{I}, \pi)$ we add to the cluster D should satisfy,

$$\max_{\pi' \in D} H(\pi', \pi) \geq \alpha \qquad (13)$$

where α is a constant.

With all of the methods we mentioned above. we can present our clustering algorithm as Algorithm 2.

Algorithm 2. Clustering Algorithm

Require:
    The set of poses, $\boldsymbol{II} = \{\pi_1, \pi_2, ..., \pi_N\}$;
    The number of the cluster M.
Ensure:
    M center poses $\{\pi_1^0, \pi_2^0, ..., \pi_M^0\}$ of the cluster;
    M sets of poses $\{D_1, D_2, ..., D_M\}$;

    Do k-means algorithm and get $\{D_1, D_2, ..., D_M\}$;
    Calculate π_i^0 from the D_i with the method we mentioned above;
    for $i = 1, 2, ..., M$ **do**
      set $D_i' = \emptyset$
      for $ii = 1, 2, ..., N$ **do**
        if $\pi_{ii} \notin D_i$ && $\min_{\pi \in D_i} H(\pi_{ii}, \pi) \geq \alpha$ **then**
          $D_i' \leftarrow D_i' + \{\pi_{ii}\}$
        end if
      end for
      $D_i \leftarrow D_i + D_i'$
    end for
    Return $\{\pi_1^0, \pi_2^0, ..., \pi_M^0\}$ and $\{D_1, D_2, ..., D_M\}$

3.5 Time Complexity and Space Complexity

Obviously, since we will use multiple NeRFs to rebuild a large scene. The time complexity and the space complexity may be changed. We will make some analysis in this part.

We denote W as the width of the MLP network, D as the depth of the MLP network N as the number of the training images. We can get that the training time complexity of the NeRF is $O(NDW^2)$, the evaluation time complexity of each image is $O(DW^2)$, and the space complexity to restore the model is $O(DW^2)$.

When it comes to our Cluster-based NeRF, we denote M as the number of the clusters we would like to split the dataset into and α as the overlapping proportion. The time complexity of the C-NeRF is $O((1+\alpha)NDW^2)$, the evaluation time complexity of each image is $O(DW^2)$ and the space complexity to restore the model is $O(MDW^2)$

If we would like to keep the size of the NeRF model equal to the C-NeRF, the time to train the model will be at least M times longer while C-NeRF is only α times longer, which is about 0.5 in our experiment. Also, the time complexity to render a image of the C-NeRF is nearly the same as that of the NeRF. Since NeRF concerns much more about the time to render a image and train the network than the space extent of the model, our method will not make troubles.

4   Experiment

In this section, we will present how our method outperforms the NeRF in the blender dataset and the real world dataset. In the blender dataset, the baseline is NeRF and in the real world dataset, the baseline is NeRF-W [12].

For the clustering algorithm, we choose to split the dataset into two clusters and the iteration is set 20 in the k-means algorithm to ensure the convergence.

For the NeRF training the blender dataset, we choose the 256 hidden layers and 8 depths in the MLP network. We sample 256 points in the coarse sampling process and 512 points in the finement process. The learning rate is set 5×10^{-5}. The total training epoch is 20 and the batch size is 4096. For the real world dataset, we use a code [17] on github and take the default parameters in their setting. We will train a NeRF-W instead for each cluster in our method.

In order to evaluate the quality of the rendering images, we adopt three widely used metrics: Peak Signal-to-Noise Ratio (PSNR), Structural Similarity Index Measure (SSIM) [23] and Learned Perceptual Image Patch Similarity (LPIPS) [22].

4.1   Experiment in Blender Dataset

In the first experiment, the dataset, which is a castle, comes from the sketchfab. We select 3 large scenes from it to build the dataset. There are 100 images in training dataset and 100 images in testing dataset for each scene. Each picture contains 540×360 pixels. Each scene is complex and large enough so that there exists some totally unrelated images in the dataset. The quantitative result can be seen in Table 1 and the qualitative result is shown in Fig. 1.

Table 1. The quantitative result of the experiment on the blender dataset.

Case / Method metrics	Scene 1			Scene 2			Case / Method metrics	Scene 3			Mean		
	PSNR↑	SSIM↑	LPIPS↓	PSNR↑	SSIM↑	LPIPS↓		PSNR↑	SSIM↑	LPIPS↓	PSNR↑	SSIM↑	LPIPS↓
NeRF	36.534	0.9693	0.1393	27.988	0.8929	0.2325	NeRF	28.076	0.9113	0.2265	30.866	0.9245	0.1994
C-NeRF	37.388	0.9733	0.1156	28.367	0.9012	0.2123	C-NeRF	29.990	0.9286	0.1844	31.882	0.9344	0.1708

Since each scene is large enough, our method outperforms the traditional NeRF in all cases. In the first scene, the wall near the leg contain less noise. In the second scene, the pattern of the carpet is more clear in the C-NeRF. In the third scene, the floor and the carpet are even not correctly rendered in the traditional NeRF while C-NeRF can rebuild the scene accurately. We find that the NeRF will fail to render the pixels in the marginal area of the image. We think that these parts are not learned well in the training process because there are too many unrelated images.

(a) NeRF   (b) C-NeRF   (c) GT

Fig. 1. The qualitative result on blender dataset. We can see some failure rendering part in the NeRF.

Table 2. The quantitative result of the experiment in the real world dataset.

Method \ Case	Gate		
metrics	PSNR↑	SSIM↑	LPIPS↓
NeRF	21.351	0.7424	0.6192
C-NeRF	**21.523**	**0.7496**	**0.6171**

4.2   Experiment in the Real World Dataset

In the second experiment, the dataset comes from the Kings in Cambridge Landmarks [9]. The extrinsics matrixes are given in the dataset and we calculate the intrinsics matrixes by Structure from Motion. We select 100 images for the training dataset and 100 images in testing dataset. Each picture is from 'seq4' folder and contains 540×270 pixels. The quantitative result can be seen in Table 2 and the qualitative result is shown in Fig. 2.

(a) NeRF   (b) C-NeRF   (c) GT

Fig. 2. The qualitative result in the real world dataset. Some buildings around the gate are not rebuilt correctly.

The C-NeRF also outperforms the NeRF-W in the real world dataset. In Fig. 2, we find that the top of the building in the left part of the images is blurred in the NeRF-W. We think the reason is that too many images in the dataset focus on the gate, which affects the training of the other buildings.

We also visualize the clustering result of the training dataset in the Fig. 3. We can see that most of the cameras in the cluster 1 concentrate on the left while the cameras in the cluster 2 concentrate on the front. We think that two NeRFs can focus on the front and the left respectively instead of performing the balance with one NeRF.

4.3 Ablation Study

In order to show the effectiveness of the overlapping algorithm, we conduct the ablation study in the first scene in blender dataset. We split the test dataset into the edge case and the other case so that we can see the difference. The quantitative result can be seen in Table 3.

Table 3. The ablation study of the first scene in blender dataset.

Metrics Method	PSNR		
Case	Edge	Other	Total
NeRF	32.040	37.782	36.534
C-NeRF without overlapping	28.550	**38.727**	36.691
C-NeRF	**33.174**	38.441	**37.388**

We can find that without the overlapping algorithm, the PNSR of the images in the edge will drop dramatically while our algorithm can help these cases. Although the other case will be affected with the overlapping, the total result can be improved.

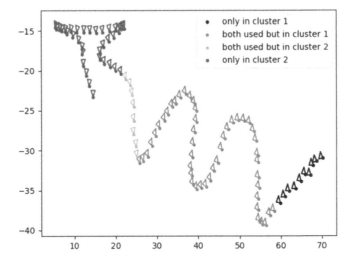

Fig. 3. The clustering result in the real world dataset. The cameras are split into two clusters.

5   Conclusion

In this work, we discover a shortcoming of the NeRF, which its poor performance in a large scene. In order to improve the rendering qualities in the large scene, we propose C-NeRF, which is to split the original dataset first and then train one NeRF for each cluster. We also propose an overlapping algorithm to help train the edge case. In the experiment part, our method outperforms NeRF in big scenes. We find that using multiple NeRFs in relatively independent position of the scene can help improve the quality of rendering, especially for the places that exist in fewer images of the training sets.

References

1. Buehler, C., Bosse, M., McMillan, L., Gortler, S., Cohen, M.: Unstructured Lumigraph rendering. In: Proceedings of the 28th Annual Conference on Computer Graphics and Interactive Techniques, pp. 425–432 (2001)
2. Garrity, M.P.: Raytracing irregular volume data. In: Proceedings of the 1990 Workshop on Volume Visualization, pp. 35–40 (1990)
3. Genova, K., Cole, F., Sud, A., Sarna, A., Funkhouser, T.: Local deep implicit functions for 3D shape. In: Proceedings of the IEEE/CVF Conference on Computer Vision and Pattern Recognition, pp. 4857–4866 (2020)
4. Gortler, S.J., Grzeszczuk, R., Szeliski, R., Cohen, M.F.: The Lumigraph. In: Proceedings of the 23rd Annual Conference on Computer Graphics and Interactive Techniques, pp. 43–54 (1996)
5. Hartley, R., Trumpf, J., Dai, Y., Li, H.: Rotation averaging. Int. J. Comput. Vis. **103**(3), 267–305 (2013)

6. Hornik, K.M., Stinchcomb, M., White, H.: Multilayer feedforward networks are universal approximator. Neural Netw. **2**(5), 359–366 (1989)
7. Jiang, C., Sud, A., Makadia, A., Huang, J., Nießner, M., Funkhouser, T., et al.: Local implicit grid representations for 3D scenes. In: Proceedings of the IEEE/CVF Conference on Computer Vision and Pattern Recognition, pp. 6001–6010 (2020)
8. Kajiya, J.T., Von Herzen, B.P.: Ray tracing volume densities. ACM SIGGRAPH Comput. Graph. **18**(3), 165–174 (1984)
9. Kendall, A., Grimes, M., Cipolla, R.: PoseNet: convolutional networks for real-time 6-DOF camera relocalization. CoRR abs/1505.07427 (2015). arXiv preprint arxiv:1505.07427 (2015)
10. Kutulakos, K.N., Seitz, S.M.: A theory of shape by space carving. Int. J. Comput. Vis. **38**(3), 199–218 (2000)
11. Lombardi, S., Simon, T., Saragih, J., Schwartz, G., Lehrmann, A., Sheikh, Y.: Neural volumes: learning dynamic renderable volumes from images. arXiv preprint arXiv:1906.07751 (2019)
12. Martin-Brualla, R., Radwan, N., Sajjadi, M.S., Barron, J.T., Dosovitskiy, A., Duckworth, D.: NeRF in the wild: neural radiance fields for unconstrained photo collections. In: Proceedings of the IEEE/CVF Conference on Computer Vision and Pattern Recognition, pp. 7210–7219 (2021)
13. Max, N.: Optical models for direct volume rendering. IEEE TVCG **1**(2), 99–108 (1995)
14. Mildenhall, B., Srinivasan, P.P., Tancik, M., Barron, J.T., Ramamoorthi, R., Ng, R.: NeRF: representing scenes as neural radiance fields for view synthesis. In: Vedaldi, A., Bischof, H., Brox, T., Frahm, J.-M. (eds.) ECCV 2020. LNCS, vol. 12346, pp. 405–421. Springer, Cham (2020). https://doi.org/10.1007/978-3-030-58452-8_24
15. Mildenhall, B., et al.: Local light field fusion: practical view synthesis with prescriptive sampling guidelines. ACM Trans. Graph. (TOG) **38**(4), 1–14 (2019)
16. Niemeyer, M., Mescheder, L., Oechsle, M., Geiger, A.: Differentiable volumetric rendering: learning implicit 3D representations without 3D supervision. In: Proceedings of the IEEE/CVF Conference on Computer Vision and Pattern Recognition, pp. 3504–3515 (2020)
17. Quei-An, C.: nerf_pl: a pytorch-lightning implementation of NeRF (2020). https://github.com/kwea123/nerf_pl/
18. Rahaman, N., Arpit, D., Baratin, A., Draxler, F., Courville, A.: On the spectral bias of deep neural networks (2018)
19. Seitz, S.M., Dyer, C.R.: Photorealistic scene reconstruction by voxel coloring. Int. J. Comput. Vis. **35**(2), 151–173 (1999)
20. Sitzmann, V., Zollhöfer, M., Wetzstein, G.: Scene representation networks: continuous 3D-structure-aware neural scene representations. In: Advances in Neural Information Processing Systems, vol. 32 (2019)
21. Waechter, M., Moehrle, N., Goesele, M.: Let there be color! Large-scale texturing of 3D reconstructions. In: Fleet, D., Pajdla, T., Schiele, B., Tuytelaars, T. (eds.) ECCV 2014. LNCS, vol. 8693, pp. 836–850. Springer, Cham (2014). https://doi.org/10.1007/978-3-319-10602-1_54
22. Zhang, R., Isola, P., Efros, A.A., Shechtman, E., Wang, O.: The unreasonable effectiveness of deep features as a perceptual metric. In: Proceedings of the IEEE Conference on Computer Vision and Pattern Recognition, pp. 586–595 (2018)
23. Zhou, W.: Image quality assessment: from error measurement to structural similarity. IEEE Trans. Image Process. **13**, 600–613 (2004)

Neural Implicit 3D Shapes from Single Images with Spatial Patterns

Yixin Zhuang[1(✉)], Yujie Wang[2,3], Yunzhe Liu[3], and Baoquan Chen[3(✉)]

[1] Fuzhou University, Fuzhou, China
`yixin.zhuang@gmail.com`
[2] Shandong University, Jinan, China
[3] Peking University, Beijing, China
`baoquan.chen@gmail.com`

Abstract. Neural implicit representations are highly effective for single-view 3D reconstruction (SVR). It represents 3D shapes as neural fields and conditions shape prediction on input image features. Image features can be less effective when significant variations of occlusions, views, and appearances exist from the image. To learn more robust features, we design a new feature encoding scheme that works in both image and shape space. Specifically, we present a geometry-aware 2D convolutional kernel to learn image appearance and view information along with geometric relations. The convolutional kernel operates at the 2D projections of a point-based 3D geometric structure, called *spatial pattern*. Furthermore, to enable the network to discover adaptive spatial patterns that capture non-local contexts, the kernel is devised to be deformable and exploited by a spatial pattern generator. Experimental results on both synthetic and real datasets demonstrate the superiority of the proposed method.

Keywords: Single Image 3D Reconstruction · Deformable Convolution · Implicit Neural Representation

1 Introduction

3D shape reconstruction from a single image has been one of the central problems in computer vision. Empowering the machines with the ability to perceive the imagery and infer the underlying 3D shapes can benefit various downstream tasks, such as augmented reality, robot navigation, etc. However, the problem is overly ambiguous and ill-posed and thus remains highly challenging due to information loss and occlusion.

In recent years, many deep learning methods have been proposed to infer 3D shapes from single images. These methods rely on learning shape priors from many shape collections and can reason the underlying shape of unseen images. To this end, various learning frameworks have been proposed that exploit different 3D shape representations, including point sets [1,7], voxels [36,37], polygonal

---

Y. Zhuang and Y. Wang—Contributed equally to this work.
The source code can be found at https://github.com/yixin26/SVR-SP.

© The Author(s), under exclusive license to Springer Nature Switzerland AG 2023
H. Lu et al. (Eds.): ICIG 2023, LNCS 14359, pp. 210–227, 2023.
https://doi.org/10.1007/978-3-031-46317-4_18

meshes [10,33], and implicit fields [4,21,24]. In particular, implicit field-based models have shown impressive performance compared to the others.

Implicit field-based networks take a set of 3D samplings as input and predict corresponding values under varying representations (e.g., occupancy, signed distance, etc.). Once fitted, 3D shapes are identified as the zero level of the predicted scalar fields using meshing methods such as Marching Cubes [19]. By conditioning the 3D shape generation on the extracted global feature of input image [4,21], the implicit networks are well-suited to reconstruct 3D shapes from single images. However, this trivial combination often fails to reconstruct fine geometric details and produces overly smoothed surfaces.

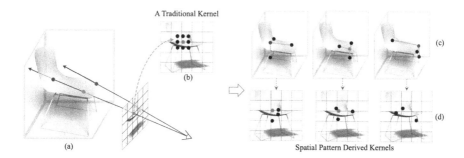

Fig. 1. Illustration of the pipeline of spatial pattern guided kernel. (a) shows that each 3D point sampling (colored differently) of the depicted shape is aligned to a 2D pixel by the given camera pose. Compared with a 2D convolution kernel (b) that only considers neighbors located within a 2D regular local patch, the kernels in (d) derived from the proposed spatial patterns (c) explicitly exploit the underlying geometric relations for each pixel. As a result, the kernels in (d) encode the local image features that capture both image appearance and point relations.

Toward pixel-level accurate reconstruction, DISN [40] proposes a pixel-aligned implicit surface network where individual point sampling is conditioned on a learned local image feature obtained by projecting the point to the image plane according to the camera pose. With local image features, the network predicts a residual field for refinement. Compared to those only acquiring global image features, local features enable the restoration of much finer-level geometry details. However, the strategy of associating 3D samplings with learned local image features would not have intuitive meaning when samples are occluded from the observation view. Hence, to improve the local image feature, Ladybird [41] utilizes the feature extracted from the 2D projection of its symmetric point obtained from the self-reflective symmetry position of the object. The reconstruction is significantly improved upon DISN. Nevertheless, the strategy used in Ladybird is not sufficiently generic as the feature probably would have no intuitive meaning in the situation where the symmetric points are non-visible or the symmetry assumption does not hold. Meanwhile, D^{2}IM-Net [14] samples training points based on the scale of geometry feature and includes image laplacian for loss computation, both targets at sharp surface regions. D^2IM-Net significantly improves the visual quality but can still fail when the quality of image laplacian is low or dramatic self-occlusion happens. Therefore further exploration of local image features is needed in tackling those challenges.

In this paper, we introduce a new image feature encoding scheme, supported by spatial pattern, to achieve further exploitation of local image features. The spatial pattern may include geometric relationships, e.g., symmetric, co-planar, or other structures that are less intuitive. With the spatial pattern, a 2D kernel operating in image space is derived to encode local image features of 3D point samplings. Specifically, the pattern is formed by a fixed number of affinities around a 3D sampling, for which the corresponding 2D projections are utilized as the operation positions of the kernel. Although a traditional 2D convolution is possible to encode contextual information for the central point, it ignores the underlying geometric relations in the original 3D space between pixels and encounters the limitations brought by the regular local area. A 2D deformable kernel [6] is able to operate in irregular neighborhoods, but it is still not able to explicitly consider the underlying 3D geometric relations, which are important in 3D reconstruction tasks.

Figure 1 shows the pipeline of the 3D spatial pattern guided 2D kernel. As shown in Fig. 1(c–d), the kernels operate on points determined by spatial patterns for different point samplings. Specifically, the proposed kernel finds kernel points adaptively for each pixel, which considers its geometric-related positions (e.g., symmetry locations) in the underlying 3D space, rather than only relying upon the appearance information. Furthermore, the spatial pattern is devised to be deformable to enable the network to discover more adaptive geometric relations for point samplings. In the experiments section, we will explore the learned 3D spatial pattern with visualization and statistics.

To demonstrate the effectiveness of spatial pattern guided kernel, we integrate it into a network based on a deep implicit network [40], and extensively evaluate our model on the large collection of 3D shapes – the ShapeNet Core dataset [3] and Pix3D dataset [28]. The experiments show that our method can produce state-of-the-art 3D shape reconstruction results from single images compared to previous works. Ablation experiments and analyses are conducted to show the performance of different spatial pattern variants and the importance of individual points within the spatial pattern.

In this work, we make the following contributions.

- We present spatial patterns to provide the network with more flexibility to discover meaningful image features that explicitly consider the geometric relationships.
- We extend 2D deformable convolutional kernels with a 3D spatial pattern generator to learn meaningful geometric structures that are crucial for 3D shape reasoning.
- We perform extensive experiments on a real and a synthetic dataset to validate the effectiveness of learned spatial patterns. Our method consistently

outperforms STOA methods on several metrics and shows better visual qualities.

2   Related Work

2.1   Deep Neural Networks for SVR

There has been a lot of research on single image reconstruction tasks. Recent works involve 3D representation learning, including points [7,15,20], voxels [5, 37,39], meshes [8,10,33,34] and primitives [23,30,38]. Those representation can also be learned with differentiable rendering that do not require the ground truth 3D shapes [11,13,15,16,18,42].

In this line of research, AtlasNet [10] represents 3D shapes as the union of several surface elements that are generated from the learned multilayer perceptrons (MLPs). Pixel2Mesh [33] generates genus-zero shapes as the deformations of ellipsoid template meshes. The mesh is progressively refined with higher resolutions using a graph convolutional neural network conditioned on the multi-scale image features. 3DN [34] also deforms a template mesh to the target, trained with a differentiable mesh sampling operator pushing sampled points to the target position.

2.2   Implicit Neural Representation for SVR

The explicit 3D representations are usually limited by fixed shape resolution or topology. Recently, implicit functions for 3D objects have shown the advantages at representing complicated geometry [2,4,9,12,14,17,22,26,27,29,40,41]. ImNet [4] uses an MLP-based neural network to approximate the signed distance field (SDF) of 3D shapes and shows improved results in contrast to the explicit surface representations. OccNet [21] generates an implicit volumetric shape by inferring the probability of each grid cell being occupied or not. The shape resolution is refined by repeatedly subdividing the interest cells. While those methods can capture the global shape structure, the geometric details are usually missing. In addition to the holistic shape description, DISN [40] adds a local image feature for each 3D point computed by aligning the image to the 3D shape using an estimated camera pose. With global and local features, DISN recovers much better geometric details and outperforms state-of-the-art methods. The local image feature of each 3D point sampling can be further enriched with its self-symmetry point, as shown in Ladybird [41]. Compared to Ladybird, we investigate a more general point structure, the spatial pattern, along with a deformable 2D kernel derived from the pattern, to encode geometric relationships for local image features.

2.3   Deformable Convolutional Networks

Deformable convolution predicts a dynamic convolutional filter for each feature position [6]. Compared to locally connected convolutions, deformable convolution enables the exploration of non-local contextual information. The idea was

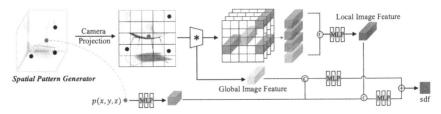

Fig. 2. The overview of our method. Given an image, our network predicts the signed distance field (SDF) for the underlying 3D object. To predict the SDF value for each point p, besides utilizing the global feature encoded from the image and the point feature directly inferred from p, local image features are fully exploited. Particularly, the local feature of a 3D point is encoded with a kernel in the image space whose kernel points are derived from a spatial pattern. $*$, ⓒ and ⊕ denote convolution, concatenation, and sum operations respectively.

originally proposed for image processing and then extended for learning features from natural language [31], 3D point cloud [32,35] and depth images [25]. In contrast to existing deformable kernels that generate kernel points within a 'single' domain, the proposed 2D deformable kernel is manipulated by a 3D spatial pattern generator, interacting between the 3D space and the 2D image plane.

3   Method

3.1   Overview

Given an RGB image of an object, our goal is to reconstruct the complete 3D shape of the object with high-quality geometric details. We use signed distance fields (SDF) to represent the 3D objects and approximate the SDFs with a neural network. Our network takes 3D points $p = (x, y, z) \in \mathbb{R}^3$ and an image I as input and outputs the signed distance s at each input location. With an SDF, the surface of an object can be extracted as the isosurface of $SDF(\cdot) = 0$ through the Marching Cubes algorithm. In general, our network consists of a fully convolutional image encoder m and a continuous implicit function f represented as multi-layer perceptrons (MLPs), from which the SDF is generated as

$$f(p, F_l(a), F_g) = s, s \in \mathbb{R}, \tag{1}$$

where $a = \pi(p)$ is the 2D projection for p, $F_l(a) = m(I(a))$ is the local feature at image location a, and F_g represents the global image feature. Feature $F_l(a)$ integrates the multi-scale local image features from the feature maps of m, from which the local image features are localized by aligning the 3D points to the image pixels via camera c.

By integrating with a spatial pattern at each 3D point sampling, the feature $F_l(a)$ of the sampling is modified by the local image features of the pattern points. We devise a feature encoding kernel h attaching to the image encoder m

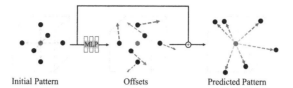

Fig. 3. Illustration of spatial pattern generator. For an input point sampling, a pattern is initialized with n points around it, and the offsets of the surrounding points are predicted by an MLP network. The final pattern is created as the sum of initial points and the corresponding offsets.

to encode a new local image feature from the features extracted from the image feature map. Then our model is reformulated as

$$f(p, h(F_l(a), F_l(a_1), ..., F_l(a_n)), F_g) = s, \qquad (2)$$

where pixels $a_1, ... a_n$ are the 2D projections of the 3D points $p_1, ..., p_n$ belonging to the spatial pattern of the point sampling p. The encoding kernel h is an MLP network that fuses the local image features. n is the number of the pattern points. Points $p_1, ..., p_n$ are generated by a spatial pattern generator which is addressed in the following subsection.

In general, our pipeline is designed to achieve better exploitation of contextual information from local image features extracted according to the predicted 3D spatial patterns, resulting in geometry-sensitive image feature descriptions for 3D point samplings, ultimately improving the 3D reconstruction from single-view images. A schematic illustration of the proposed model is given in Fig. 2.

3.2   Spatial Pattern Generator

Our spatial pattern generator takes as input a 3D point sampling p, and outputs n 3D coordinates, i.e., $p_1, ..., p_n$. Like previous 2D or 3D deformable convolution networks [6,32], the position of a pattern point is computed as the sum of the initial location and a predicted offset. A schematic illustration of the spatial pattern generator is shown in Fig. 3.

Initialization. With proper initialization, the pattern can be learned efficiently and is highly effective for geometric reasoning. We consider two different sampling methods for spatial pattern initialization, i.e., uniform and non-uniform 3D point samplings, as shown in Fig. 4. For simplicity, the input shapes are normalized to a unified cube centered at the origin. To generate uniform patterns, we uniformly sample n points along input point $p = (x, y, z)$. For example, we place a cube centered at p with the edge length of l, where each pattern point lies at the center of one of its side faces. We set $n = 6$ and $l = 0.2$, then each pattern points p_i can be written as the combinations of $p_i = (x \pm 0.1, y \pm 0.1, z \pm 0.1)$.

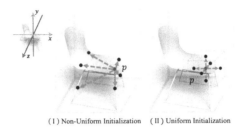

(I) Non-Uniform Initialization   (II) Uniform Initialization

Fig. 4. Examples of spatial pattern initialization obtained by non-uniform sampling (I) and uniform sampling (II) strategies. In (I), a non-uniform pattern is formed by 3D points (in black) that are symmetry to input point p along x, y, z axis, and xy, yz, xz planes; and in (II), a uniform pattern is created by 3D points ling at centers of the side faces of a cube centered at point p.

Unlike the uniform sampling method, the non-uniform sampling method does not have commonly used strategies, except for random sampling. Randomly sampled points always do not have intuitive geometric meaning and are hardly appeared in any kernel point selection methods. As to capture non-local geometric relations, the non-uniform pattern points of p are created at the xy, yz, xz planes

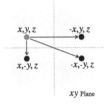

that pass through p. For instance, at xy plane, the non-uniform pattern expands at locations $(-x, y, z), (x, -y, z)$ and $(-x, -y, z)$, as shown in the figure. More pattern points are created in the same way in yz, xz planes. Thus the pattern points p_i can be drawn from the combinations of $p_i = (\pm x, \pm y, \pm z)$.

After initialization, the pattern points, along with input sampling, are passed to an MLP network to generate the offsets and the final pattern is the sum of the initial positions and the predicted offsets. By projecting the 3D spatial pattern to the 2D image plane, we obtain a set of 2D pixels as their corresponding 2D pattern, which is the 2D kernel point. These image features derived from such a 2D kernel imply geometry relations.

3.3   Optimization

Given a collection of 3D shapes and the generated implicit fields from images $\mathcal{I}$, the loss is defined with L_1 distance:

$$L_{SDF} = \sum_{I \in \mathcal{I}} \sum_{p} \omega |f(p, F_l^I, F_g^I) - SDF^I(p)|, \tag{3}$$

where SDF^I denotes the ground truth SDF value corresponding to image I and $f(\cdot)$ is the predicted field. ω is set to ω_1, if $SDF^I(p) < \delta$, and ω_2, otherwise. In practice, the parameters are set to $\omega_1 = 4, \omega_2 = 1$, and $\delta = 0.01$.

4   Experiments

In this section, we show qualitative and quantitative results on single-view 3D reconstruction from our method and comparisons with state-of-the-art methods. We also conduct a study on the variants of spatial patterns to understand the effect of initialization and the number of points. We further investigate the effectiveness of individual points in the spatial pattern with visualization and statistics results.

4.1   Experimental Details

Network Structure. The full network structure is shown in Fig. 2. We use DISN [40] as our backbone network, which consists of a VGG-style fully convolutional neural network m as the image encoder. m has six convolutional layers with the dimension of $\{64, 128, 256, 512, 512, 512\}$. The spatial pattern generator is a MLPs, six layers with $\{64, 256, 512, 512, 256, 3\}$ channels, ReLU activation and Tanh on output. Implicit function is also a MLPs, six layers with $\{64, 256, 512, 512, 256, 1\}$ channels, ReLU activation. The feature aggregation module is a one-layer MLP directly mapping multiple local features to the output.

Dataset and Training Details. We use the ShapeNet Core dataset [3] and Pix3D dataset [28] for evaluation. The ShapeNet Core dataset [3] includes 13 object categories, and for each object, 24 views are rendered with resolution of 137×137 as in [5]. Pix3D Dataset [28] contains 9 object categories with real-world images and the exact mask images. The number of views and the image resolution varies from different shapes. We process all the shapes and images in the same format for the two datasets. Specifically, all shapes are normalized to the range of $[-1, 1]$ and all images are scaled to the resolution of 137×137.

In testing, for the ShapeNet dataset, the camera parameters are estimated from the input images, and we use the trained camera model from DISN [40] for fair comparisons. For the Pix3D dataset, ground truth camera parameters and image masks are used.

3D Point Sampling. For each shape, 2048 points are sampled for training. We first normalize the shapes to a unified cube with their centers of mass at the origin. Then we uniformly sample 256^3 grid points from the cube and compute the sign distance field (SDF) values for all the grid samples. Following the sampling process of Ladybird [41], the 256^3 points are downsampled with two stages. In the first stage, 32,768 points are randomly sampled from the four SDF ranges $[-0.10, -0.03]$, $[-0.03, 0.00]$, $[0.00, 0.03]$, and $[0.03, 0.10]$, with the same probabilities. In the second stage, 2048 points are uniformly sampled from the 32,768 points using the farthest points sampling strategy.

In testing, 65^3 grid points are sampled are fed to the network, and output the SDF values. The object mesh is extracted as the zero iso-surface of the generated SDF using the Marching Cube algorithm.

3D-to-2D Camera Projection. Projecting 3D point sampling p to a pixel a is unfolded into two stages. Firstly, the point is converted from the world coordinate system to the local camera coordinate system c based on the rigid transformation matrix A^c, such that $p^c = A^c p$. Then in the camera space, point $p^c = (x^c, y^c, z^c)$ is projected to the 2D canvas via perspective transformation, i.e., $\pi(p^c) = (\frac{x^c}{z^c}, \frac{y^c}{z^c})$. The projected pixel whose coordinate lies out of an image will reset to 0 or 136 (the input image resolution is fixed as 137×137 in our experiment).

Training Policy. We implement our method based on the framework of Pytorch. For training on the ShapeNet dataset, we use the Adam optimizer with a learning rate of 1e−4, a decay rate of 0.9, and a decay step size of 5 epochs. The network is trained for 30 epochs with a batch size of 20. For training on the Pix3D dataset, we use the Adam optimizer with a constant learning rate 1e−4 and a smaller batch size of 5. For the ShapeNet dataset, at each epoch, we randomly sample a subset of images from each category. Specifically, a maximum number of 36000 images are sampled for each category. The total number of images in an epoch is 411,384 resulting in 20,570 iterations. Our model is trained across all categories.

Evaluation Metrics. The quantitative results are obtained by computing the similarity between generated surfaces and ground truth surfaces. We use the standard metrics including Chamfer Distance (CD), Earth Mover's Distance (EMD), and Intersection over Union (IoU).

Table 1. Quantitative results on the ShapeNet Core dataset for various methods.

Metrics	Methods	plane	bench	cabinet	car	chair	display	lamp	speaker	rifle	sofa	table	phone	watercraft	mean
CD↓	Pixel2Mesh	6.10	6.20	12.11	13.45	11.13	**6.39**	31.41	14.52	4.51	**6.54**	15.61	6.04	12.66	11.28
	OccNet	7.70	6.43	9.36	5.26	7.67	7.54	26.46	17.30	4.86	6.72	10.57	7.17	9.09	9.70
	DISN	9.96	8.98	10.19	5.39	7.71	10.23	25.76	17.90	5.58	9.16	13.59	6.40	11.91	10.98
	Ladybird	5.85	6.12	9.10	5.13	7.08	8.23	21.46	14.75	5.53	6.78	9.97	**5.06**	6.71	8.60
	Ours$_{cam}$	**5.40**	**5.59**	8.43	**5.01**	**6.17**	8.54	14.96	**14.07**	3.82	6.70	**8.97**	5.42	**6.19**	**7.64**
	Ours	3.27	3.38	6.88	3.93	4.40	5.40	6.77	8.48	1.58	4.38	6.49	4.02	4.01	4.85
EMD↓	Pixel2Mesh	2.98	2.58	3.44	3.43	3.52	2.92	5.15	3.56	3.04	2.70	3.52	2.66	3.94	3.34
	OccNet	2.75	2.43	3.05	2.56	2.70	2.58	3.96	3.46	2.27	**2.35**	2.83	2.27	2.57	2.75
	DISN	2.67	2.48	3.04	2.67	2.67	2.73	4.38	3.47	2.30	2.62	3.11	2.06	2.77	2.84
	Ladybird	2.48	2.29	3.03	2.65	2.60	2.61	4.20	3.32	2.22	2.42	2.82	2.06	2.46	2.71
	Ours$_{cam}$	**2.35**	**2.15**	**2.90**	2.66	**2.49**	**2.49**	3.59	3.20	2.04	2.40	**2.70**	**2.05**	**2.40**	**2.57**
	Ours	1.91	1.90	2.58	2.36	2.17	2.08	2.66	2.75	1.52	2.11	2.36	1.77	1.99	2.17
IoU↑	Pixel2Mesh	51.5	40.7	43.4	50.1	40.2	55.9	29.1	52.3	50.9	60.0	31.2	69.4	40.1	47.3
	OccNet	54.7	45.2	**73.2**	73.1	50.2	47.9	37.0	**65.3**	45.8	67.1	**50.6**	70.9	52.1	56.4
	DISN	57.5	52.9	52.3	74.3	54.3	56.4	34.7	54.9	59.2	65.9	47.9	72.9	55.9	57.0
	Ladybird	60.0	53.4	50.8	74.5	55.3	57.8	36.2	55.6	61.0	68.5	48.6	73.6	**61.3**	58.2
	Ours$_{cam}$	**60.6**	**54.4**	52.9	74.7	**56.0**	**59.2**	**38.3**	56.1	**62.9**	**68.8**	49.3	**74.7**	60.6	**59.1**
	Ours	68.2	63.1	61.4	80.7	66.8	67.9	55.9	65.0	75.0	75.2	62.6	81.0	68.9	68.6

4.2   Quantitative and Qualitative Comparisons

We compare our method with the state-of-the-art methods on the single-image 3D reconstruction task. All the methods, including Pixel2Mesh [33], OccNet [21], DISN [40], Ladybird [41], are trained across all 13 categories. The method of Ours uses ground truth cameras while $Ours_{cam}$ denotes the version of Ours using estimated camera poses.

Table 2. Quantitative results on Pix3D dataset.

Categories	CD (x1000)↓		EMD (x100)↓		IoU (%)↑	
	Ladybird	Ours	Ladybird	Ours	Ladybird	Ours
bed	9.84	**8.76**	2.80	**2.70**	70.7	**73.2**
bookcase	**10.94**	14.70	**2.91**	3.32	**44.3**	41.8
chair	14.05	**9.81**	2.82	**2.72**	57.3	57.3
desk	18.87	**15.38**	3.18	**2.91**	51.2	**60.7**
misc	36.77	**30.94**	4.45	**4.00**	29.8	**44.0**
sofa	4.56	**3.77**	2.02	**1.92**	86.7	**87.6**
table	21.66	**14.04**	2.96	**2.78**	56.9	**58.8**
tool	**7.78**	16.24	3.70	**3.57**	**41.3**	38.2
wardrobe	**4.80**	5.60	**1.92**	2.01	**87.5**	87.5
mean	14.36	**13.25**	2.97	**2.88**	58.4	**61.0**

A quantitative evaluation of the ShapeNet dataset is reported in Table 1 in terms of CD, EMD, and IoU. CD and EMD are evaluated on the sampling points from the generated triangulated mesh. IoU is computed on the solid voxelization of the mesh. In general, our method outperforms other methods. In particular, among DISN, Ladybird, and Ours, which share a similar backbone network, Ours achieves much better performance.

In Fig. 9, we show qualitative results generated by Mesh R-CNN [8], Occ-Net [21], DISN [40] and Ladybird [41]. We use the pre-trained models from the Mesh R-CNN, OccNet, and DISN. For Ladybird, we re-implement their network and carry out training according to the specifications in their paper. All the methods can capture the general structure of the shapes. Shapes generated from DISN, Ladybird, and Ours are more aligned with the ground truth shapes. Specifically, our method is visually better at the non-visible regions and fine-scale geometry features.

The quantitative evaluation of the Pix3D dataset is provided in Table 2. Ours and Ladybird are both trained and evaluated on the same train/test split, during which ground truth camera poses and masks are used. Specifically, 80% of the images are randomly sampled from the dataset for training while the rest images are used for testing. In general, our method outperforms Ladybird on the used

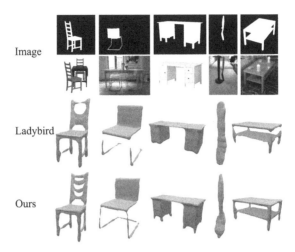

Image

Ladybird

Ours

Fig. 5. Qualitative Results on the Pix3D dataset. Ground truth image masks and camera parameters are used.

metrics. Note that Ladybird already outperforms the other methods shown in Table 1, we only give the results of Ladybird and Ours.

In addition to the quantitative results, we also show the reconstructed shapes in Fig. 5. Compared to the synthetic images from the ShapeNet dataset, the real images are more diverse in terms of camera viewpoints, object sizes, and appearances. Our reconstructed shapes are visually more plausible compared to Ladybird.

4.3 Impact of Spatial Patterns

To figure out the influence of different spatial patterns, we designed several variants of the pattern. Specifically, two factors are considered, including the initialization and the capacity, i.e., the pattern point sampling strategy and the number of points in a pattern. As described before, we consider non-uniform and uniform sampling methods for pattern initialization and set the number of points to three and six. The variants derived from the combinations of those two factors are denoted as

- $\text{Ours}_{uniform-6p}$, in which six points are uniformly sampled on a cube centered at point sampling, such that $p_1 = (x, y, z + 0.1)$, $p_2 = (x + 0.1, y, z)$, $p_3 = (x, y + 0.1, z)$, $p_4 = (x, y, z - 0.1)$, $p_5 = (x - 0.1, y, z)$, and $p_6 = (x, y - 0.1, z)$.
- $\text{Ours}_{non-uni-6p}$, in which six points are non-uniformly sampled at the symmetry locations in the shape space along xy, yz and xz planes and x, y and z axes, such that $p_1 = (x, y, -z)$, $p_2 = (-x, y, z)$, $p_3 = (x, -y, z)$, $p_4 = (-x, -y, z)$, $p_5 = (x, -y, -z)$, and $p_6 = (-x, y, -z)$.
- $\text{Ours}_{non-uni-3p}$, in which three points are non-uniformly sampled at the symmetry locations in the shape space along xy, yz and xz planes, such that $p_1 = (x, y, -z)$, $p_2 = (-x, y, z)$, and $p_3 = (x, -y, z)$.

Table 3. Quantitative results of the variants of our method using different configurations of spatial pattern. Metrics include CD (multiply by 1000, the smaller the better), EMD (multiply by 100, the smaller the better), and IoU (%, the larger the better). CD and EMD are computed on 2048 points.

Metrics	Methods	plane	bench	cabinet	car	chair	display	lamp	speaker	rifle	sofa	table	phone	watercraft	mean
CD↓	$Ours_{uniform-6p}$	3.72	3.73	7.09	3.93	4.59	4.78	7.77	9.19	2.02	4.64	6.71	3.62	4.17	5.07
	$Ours_{non-uni-6p}$	3.27	3.38	6.88	3.93	4.40	5.40	6.77	8.48	1.58	4.38	6.49	4.02	4.01	**4.85**
	$Ours_{non-uni-3p}$	3.33	3.51	6.88	3.87	4.38	4.58	7.22	8.76	3.00	4.45	6.66	3.63	4.11	4.95
EMD↓	$Ours_{uniform-6p}$	2.07	2.02	2.60	2.38	2.19	2.11	2.86	2.85	1.55	2.16	2.41	1.78	2.01	2.23
	$Ours_{non-uni-6p}$	1.91	1.90	2.58	2.36	2.17	2.08	2.66	2.75	1.52	2.11	2.36	1.77	1.99	**2.17**
	$Ours_{non-uni-3p}$	1.96	1.94	2.58	2.35	2.16	2.07	2.81	2.81	1.58	2.13	2.39	1.78	2.00	2.20
IoU↑	$Ours_{uniform-6p}$	66.1	59.5	59.6	80.0	65.8	66.7	53.8	63.7	74.7	74.1	60.8	79.6	68.0	67.1
	$Ours_{non-uni-6p}$	68.2	63.1	61.4	80.7	66.8	67.9	55.9	65.0	75.0	75.2	62.6	81.0	68.9	**68.6**
	$Ours_{non-uni-3p}$	67.4	62.0	60.5	80.5	66.8	67.5	54.1	64.2	73.6	75.1	61.8	80.2	68.7	67.9

In Table 3, we report the numerical results of the methods using ground truth camera pose. In general, $Ours_{non-uni-6p}$ achieves best performance. By reducing the capacity to the number of three points, the performance decreases, as shown by $Ours_{non-uni-3p}$. It indicates that some critical points in $Ours_{non-uni-6p}$ that have high responses to the query point do not appear in $Ours_{non-uni-3p}$. Notably, the sampling strategy is more important. Both $Ours_{non-uni-6p}$ and $Ours_{non-uni-3p}$ outperforms $Ours_{uniform-6p}$ with large margins. Thus, initialization with non-uniform sampling makes the learning of effective spatial patterns easier. It implies that optimizing the pattern position in the continuous 3D space is challenging, and with proper initialization, spatial patterns can be learned more efficiently. To better understand the learned spatial pattern and which pattern points are preferred by the network, we provide analysis with visualization and statistics in the next section. Before that, we evaluate the performance of our method by comparing it with several state-of-the-art methods. Specifically, we use $Ours_{non-uni-6p}$ as our final method.

4.4 Analysis of Learned Spatial Patterns

We have demonstrated the effectiveness of the proposed spatial pattern via achieving better performance than other alternatives, and the experiments on different variants of the spatial pattern show the influence of initialization and capacity. To better understand the importance of individual pattern points, we visualize several learned patterns in Fig. 6 and 7 and calculate the mean offsets of the predicted pattern points visualized in Fig. 8.

In Fig. 6, we show learned spatial patterns in the 2D image plane. In each row, a spatial pattern is shown in six different images with different views. It implies an explicit constraint on view consistency of image encoding.

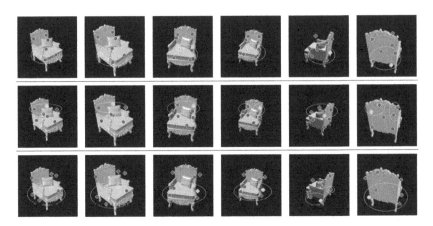

Fig. 6. Visualization of learned spatial patterns in image plane. (Color figure online)

Pattern points (colored in red) that have intuitive geometric relationships (e.g., symmetric and co-planar) with the query points (colored in green) are highlighted by cyan circles in Fig. 6. Figure 7 provides a better visualization in 3D frame, from which we can see that some learned pattern points from the non-uniform initialization are almost stationary, e.g., points p_1, p_2 and p_6 that are highlighted by dash circles. Also, as shown in Fig. 8, the mean offsets of points p_1, p_2 and p_6 are close to zero. To figure out the importance of these stationary pattern points, we train the network using the points p_1, p_2, and p_6 as a spatial pattern and keep their positions fixed during training. As shown in Table 4, the

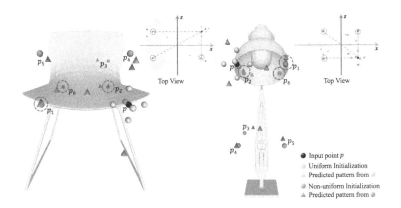

Fig. 7. Visualization of spatial pattern points with different shapes and colors. From the examples in (I) and (II), the learned pattern points (i.e., pink cones) from the non-uniform initialization (i.e., pink balls) are relative stationery, while points (i.e., blue cones) learned from uniform initialization (i.e., blue balls) have much larger deviations from their original positions. Some stationary points p_1, p_2 and p_6 are highlighted in dash circles. (Zoom in for better visualization). (Color figure online)

performance of the selected rigid pattern is better than $\text{Ours}_{non-uni-3p}$ and $\text{Ours}_{uniform-6p}$ and slightly lower than $\text{Ours}_{non-uni-6p}$. This reveals that the pattern points discovered by the network are useful, which finally leads to a better reconstruction of the underlying geometry.

Even though consuming more time and memory, utilizing the auxiliary contextual information brought by other points p_3, p_4, and p_5 only achieve a slight improvement in the performance. The analysis shows that naive selection of more neighboring points is not as effective as the strategy that considers the underlying geometric relationships. Although there is no explicit constraint to guarantee the geometric relations exactly, statistically we found that the network tends to shift the pattern points towards the locations that have geometric relations with the query point, as shown in Fig. 7 and 8. It further proves that encoding geometric relationships with the 2D kernel derived from the proposed spatial pattern are effective for the single-image 3D reconstruction task.

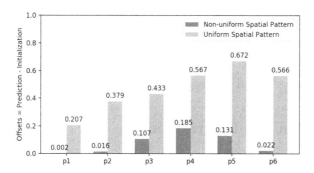

Fig. 8. Statistics on the offsets of spatial pattern points. The offset of individual pattern points is computed as the mean distance between the initial and predicted position. Among all points, p_1, p_2 and p_6 have the smallest learned offsets from the non-uniform initialization (i.e., pink bars), while for uniform initialization (i.e., blue bars), all the predicted points have much larger deviations from their original locations. (Color figure online)

Table 4. Quantitative results of a rigid spatial pattern formed by three pattern points selected from the stationary points of the learned spatial pattern.

	plane	bench	cabinet	car	chair	display	lamp	speaker	rifle	sofa	table	phone	watercraft	mean
CD (x1000)	3.38	3.44	7.06	3.87	4.50	4.57	7.30	8.98	1.66	4.53	6.61	3.45	4.17	4.89
EMD (x100)	1.97	1.92	2.58	2.37	2.16	2.07	2.77	2.82	1.52	2.12	2.35	1.80	2.01	2.19
IoU (%)	67.4	62.8	60.5	80.5	66.6	67.4	54.9	64.5	74.9	75.0	62.5	80.1	68.5	68.1

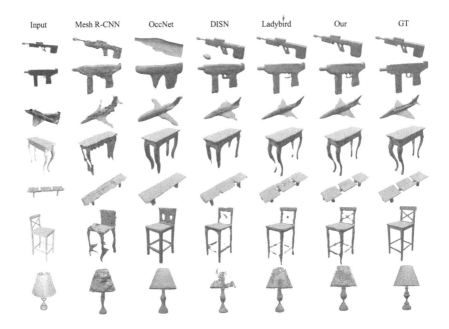

Fig. 9. Qualitative comparison results for various methods.

5   Conclusion and Future Work

In this paper, we propose a new neural network that integrates a new feature encoding scheme to the deep implicit surface network for 3D shape reconstruction from single images. We present spatial patterns to allow the 2D kernel to encode local image features with geometric relations. Using spatial pattern enables the 2D kernel point selection explicitly to consider the underlying 3D geometry relations, which are essential in the 3D reconstruction task, while traditional 2D kernels mainly consider the appearance information. To better understand the spatial pattern, we study several variants of spatial pattern designs regarding the pattern capacity and the way of initialization, and we analyze the importance of individual pattern points. Results on large synthetic and real datasets show the superiority of the proposed method on widely used metrics.

A key limitation is that the model is sensitive to camera parameters. As shown in Table 1, when using ground truth camera parameters, the performance is significantly improved. One possible direction to investigate is to incorporate the camera estimation process in the loop of the 3D reconstruction pipeline, such as jointly optimizing the camera pose and the implicit field within a framework with multiple objectives. Another interesting direction is to learn geometric relations with explicit geometric constraints. Restricting the optimization to an optimized subspace could potentially promote performance and interpretation of learned patterns.

Acknowledgements. We would like to thank the anonymous reviewers for their valuable feedback and suggestions.

References

1. Achlioptas, P., Diamanti, O., Mitliagkas, I., Guibas, L.: Learning representations and generative models for 3D point clouds. In: International Conference on Machine Learning, pp. 40–49. PMLR (2018)
2. Atzmon, M., Lipman, Y.: SAL: sign agnostic learning of shapes from raw data. In: CVPR, pp. 2562–2571. Computer Vision Foundation/IEEE (2020)
3. Chang, A.X., et al.: ShapeNet: an information-rich 3D model repository. arXiv:1512.03012 [cs.GR] (2015)
4. Chen, Z., Zhang, H.: Learning implicit fields for generative shape modeling. In: Proceedings of IEEE Conference on Computer Vision and Pattern Recognition (CVPR) (2019)
5. Choy, C.B., Xu, D., Gwak, J.Y., Chen, K., Savarese, S.: 3D-R2N2: a unified approach for single and multi-view 3D object reconstruction. In: Leibe, B., Matas, J., Sebe, N., Welling, M. (eds.) ECCV 2016. LNCS, vol. 9912, pp. 628–644. Springer, Cham (2016). https://doi.org/10.1007/978-3-319-46484-8_38
6. Dai, J., et al.: Deformable convolutional networks. In: Proceedings of the IEEE International Conference on Computer Vision, pp. 764–773 (2017)
7. Fan, H., Su, H., Guibas, L.J.: A point set generation network for 3d object reconstruction from a single image. In: Proceedings of the IEEE Conference on Computer Vision and Pattern Recognition, pp. 605–613 (2017)
8. Gkioxari, G., Malik, J., Johnson, J.: Mesh R-CNN. In: Proceedings of the IEEE/CVF International Conference on Computer Vision, pp. 9785–9795 (2019)
9. Gropp, A., Yariv, L., Haim, N., Atzmon, M., Lipman, Y.: Implicit geometric regularization for learning shapes. In: ICML. Proceedings of Machine Learning Research, vol. 119, pp. 3789–3799. PMLR (2020)
10. Groueix, T., Fisher, M., Kim, V.G., Russell, B.C., Aubry, M.: A papier-mâché approach to learning 3D surface generation. In: Proceedings of the CVPR, pp. 216–224 (2018)
11. Insafutdinov, E., Dosovitskiy, A.: Unsupervised learning of shape and pose with differentiable point clouds. In: Proceedings of the 32nd International Conference on Neural Information Processing Systems, pp. 2807–2817 (2018)
12. Jiang, Y., Ji, D., Han, Z., Zwicker, M.: SDFDiff: differentiable rendering of signed distance fields for 3D shape optimization. In: Proceedings of the IEEE/CVF Conference on Computer Vision and Pattern Recognition, pp. 1251–1261 (2020)
13. Kato, H., Ushiku, Y., Harada, T.: Neural 3D mesh renderer. In: Proceedings of the IEEE Conference on Computer Vision and Pattern Recognition, pp. 3907–3916 (2018)
14. Li, M., Zhang, H.: D^{2}IM-Net: learning detail disentangled implicit fields from single images. arXiv preprint arXiv:2012.06650 (2020)
15. Lin, C.H., Kong, C., Lucey, S.: Learning efficient point cloud generation for dense 3D object reconstruction. In: Proceedings of the AAAI Conference on Artificial Intelligence, vol. 32 (2018)
16. Liu, L., Gu, J., Zaw Lin, K., Chua, T.S., Theobalt, C.: Neural sparse voxel fields. In: Advances in Neural Information Processing Systems, vol. 33 (2020)

17. Liu, S., Zhang, Y., Peng, S., Shi, B., Pollefeys, M., Cui, Z.: DIST: rendering deep implicit signed distance function with differentiable sphere tracing. In: Proceedings of the IEEE/CVF Conference on Computer Vision and Pattern Recognition, pp. 2019–2028 (2020)

18. Liu, S., Chen, W., Li, T., Li, H.: Soft rasterizer: differentiable rendering for unsupervised single-view mesh reconstruction. arXiv preprint arXiv:1901.05567 (2019)

19. Lorensen, W.E., Cline, H.E.: Marching cubes: a high resolution 3D surface construction algorithm. ACM Siggraph Comput. Graph. **21**(4), 163–169 (1987)

20. Mandikal, P., Navaneet, K., Agarwal, M., Babu, R.V.: 3D-LMNet: latent embedding matching for accurate and diverse 3D point cloud reconstruction from a single image. arXiv preprint arXiv:1807.07796 (2018)

21. Mescheder, L., Oechsle, M., Niemeyer, M., Nowozin, S., Geiger, A.: Occupancy networks: learning 3D reconstruction in function space. In: Proceedings of the CVPR (2019)

22. Niemeyer, M., Mescheder, L., Oechsle, M., Geiger, A.: Differentiable volumetric rendering: learning implicit 3D representations without 3D supervision. In: Proceedings of the IEEE/CVF Conference on Computer Vision and Pattern Recognition, pp. 3504–3515 (2020)

23. Niu, C., Li, J., Xu, K.: Im2Struct: recovering 3D shape structure from a single RGB image. In: Proceedings of the IEEE Conference on Computer Vision and Pattern Recognition, pp. 4521–4529 (2018)

24. Park, J.J., Florence, P., Straub, J., Newcombe, R., Lovegrove, S.: DeepSDF: learning continuous signed distance functions for shape representation. In: CVPR (2019)

25. Park, J., Joo, K., Hu, Z., Liu, C.-K., So Kweon, I.: Non-local spatial propagation network for depth completion. In: Vedaldi, A., Bischof, H., Brox, T., Frahm, J.-M. (eds.) ECCV 2020. LNCS, vol. 12358, pp. 120–136. Springer, Cham (2020). https://doi.org/10.1007/978-3-030-58601-0_8

26. Saito, S., Huang, Z., Natsume, R., Morishima, S., Kanazawa, A., Li, H.: PIFu: pixel-aligned implicit function for high-resolution clothed human digitization. In: Proceedings of the IEEE/CVF International Conference on Computer Vision, pp. 2304–2314 (2019)

27. Sitzmann, V., Zollhöfer, M., Wetzstein, G.: Scene representation networks: Continuous 3D-structure-aware neural scene representations. In: NeurIPS, pp. 1119–1130 (2019)

28. Sun, X., et al.: Pix3D: dataset and methods for single-image 3D shape modeling. In: IEEE Conference on Computer Vision and Pattern Recognition (CVPR) (2018)

29. Tancik, M., et al.: Fourier features let networks learn high frequency functions in low dimensional domains. In: NeurIPS (2020)

30. Tang, J., Han, X., Pan, J., Jia, K., Tong, X.: A skeleton-bridged deep learning approach for generating meshes of complex topologies from single RGB images. In: Proceedings of the IEEE/CVF Conference on Computer Vision and Pattern Recognition, pp. 4541–4550 (2019)

31. Thomas, H., Qi, C.R., Deschaud, J., Marcotegui, B., Goulette, F., Guibas, L.J.: KPConv: flexible and deformable convolution for point clouds. In: ICCV, pp. 6410–6419. IEEE (2019)

32. Thomas, H., Qi, C.R., Deschaud, J.E., Marcotegui, B., Goulette, F., Guibas, L.J.: KPConv: flexible and deformable convolution for point clouds. In: Proceedings of the IEEE International Conference on Computer Vision (2019)

33. Wang, N., Zhang, Y., Li, Z., Fu, Y., Liu, W., Jiang, Y.-G.: Pixel2Mesh: generating 3D mesh models from single RGB images. In: Ferrari, V., Hebert, M., Sminchisescu,

C., Weiss, Y. (eds.) ECCV 2018. LNCS, vol. 11215, pp. 55–71. Springer, Cham (2018). https://doi.org/10.1007/978-3-030-01252-6_4

34. Wang, W., Ceylan, D., Mech, R., Neumann, U.: 3DN: 3D deformation network. In: Proceedings of the IEEE/CVF Conference on Computer Vision and Pattern Recognition, pp. 1038–1046 (2019)

35. Wu, F., Fan, A., Baevski, A., Dauphin, Y.N., Auli, M.: Pay less attention with lightweight and dynamic convolutions. In: ICLR. OpenReview.net (2019)

36. Wu, J., Zhang, C., Xue, T., Freeman, B., Tenenbaum, J.: Learning a probabilistic latent space of object shapes via 3D generative-adversarial modeling. In: Advances in Neural Information Processing Systems, pp. 82–90 (2016)

37. Wu, J., Zhang, C., Zhang, X., Zhang, Z., Freeman, W.T., Tenenbaum, J.B.: Learning shape priors for single-view 3D completion and reconstruction. In: Ferrari, V., Hebert, M., Sminchisescu, C., Weiss, Y. (eds.) ECCV 2018. LNCS, vol. 11215, pp. 673–691. Springer, Cham (2018). https://doi.org/10.1007/978-3-030-01252-6_40

38. Wu, R., Zhuang, Y., Xu, K., Zhang, H., Chen, B.: PQ-NET: a generative part Seq2Seq network for 3D shapes. In: Proceedings of the IEEE/CVF Conference on Computer Vision and Pattern Recognition, pp. 829–838 (2020)

39. Xie, H., Yao, H., Sun, X., Zhou, S., Zhang, S.: Pix2Vox: context-aware 3D reconstruction from single and multi-view images. In: Proceedings of the IEEE/CVF International Conference on Computer Vision, pp. 2690–2698 (2019)

40. Xu, Q., Wang, W., Ceylan, D., Mech, R., Neumann, U.: DISN: deep implicit surface network for high-quality single-view 3D reconstruction. arXiv preprint arXiv:1905.10711 (2019)

41. Xu, Y., Fan, T., Yuan, Y., Singh, G.: Ladybird: quasi-Monte Carlo sampling for deep implicit field based 3D reconstruction with symmetry. In: Vedaldi, A., Bischof, H., Brox, T., Frahm, J.-M. (eds.) ECCV 2020. LNCS, vol. 12346, pp. 248–263. Springer, Cham (2020). https://doi.org/10.1007/978-3-030-58452-8_15

42. Yan, X., Yang, J., Yumer, E., Guo, Y., Lee, H.: Perspective transformer nets: learning single-view 3D object reconstruction without 3D supervision. In: Proceedings of the 30th International Conference on Neural Information Processing Systems, pp. 1704–1712 (2016)

Multimedia Security

Dense Visible Watermark Removal with Progressive Feature Propagation

Chunchi Ren[1], Jiangfeng Zhao[1], Hongjie He[1(✉)], and Fan Chen[2]

[1] School of Information Science and Technology, Southwest Jiaotong University, Chengdu 611756, People's Republic of China
hjhe@swjtu.edu.cn
[2] School of Computing and Artificial Intelligence, Southwest Jiaotong University, Chengdu 611756, People's Republic of China

Abstract. Visible watermark removal is an important task to ensure the robustness of visible watermarks. However, existing techniques are unable to efficiently remove dense visible watermarks in stock content market images. To address this issue, we propose a novel solution called the Progressive Visible Watermark Removal Network (PVWRNet) that achieves efficient and effective dense visible watermark removal. Our approach utilizes a cross-combination structure in the backbone module to balance dense visible watermark spatial and contextual features. Furthermore, progressive modules are incorporated to multi-fuse shallow features of the backbone module, leading to significant improvement in image restoration metric scores and visual quality. To enhance local features of the backbone module, Reinforced Dual Attention Modules (RDAM) are introduced, which reweight the local features. Experimental results demonstrate that our proposed PVWRNet outperforms state-of-the-art approaches in the dense visible watermark dataset, especially in high definition images. In conclusion, the proposed method provides a potent and efficient solution for removing dense visible watermarks in stock content market images, and the use of cross-combination structure, progressive modules, and reinforced dual attention modules enables PVWRNet to outperform existing techniques in solving the challenging dense visible watermark removal problem. The code is available at: https://github.com/HyuuHyuuNeko/PVWRNet.

1 Introduction

Digital imagery is a ubiquitous form of digital media on the internet. As a result, visible watermarks are commonly employed to protect image copyrights on social platforms and stock content marketplaces [17]. With the growth of the internet and social media, the number of digital images being infringed upon is increasing rapidly [25]. In order to safeguard the copyright of digital images, developing

---

This work was supported in part by the National Natural Science Foundation of China (NSFC) under Grant U1936113 and 61872303, and Technology Department of Sichuan Province under Grant 2021004.

H. Lu et al. (Eds.): ICIG 2023, LNCS 14359, pp. 231–242, 2023.
https://doi.org/10.1007/978-3-031-46317-4_19

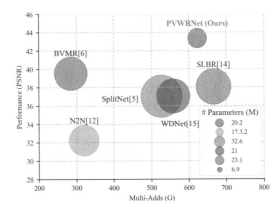

Fig. 1. The removal performance of dense visible watermarks (measured by PSNR on the y-axis) is evaluated on our proposed dataset. The x-axis represents different Multi-adds, while bubble size indicates parameter capacities. In comparison to state-of-the-art methods, PVWRNet exhibits superior performance.

a watermarking system has become an urgent issue. One crucial aspect of this system is visible watermark removal, which is vital to assessing the robustness of the visible watermark. Hence, numerous research works have been investigating various methods of watermark removal.

The removal of visible watermarks presents a complex and daunting challenge [9]. Existing research primarily focuses on removing single visual motif watermarks. However, many commercial HD images employ dense visible watermarks with high motif density and low opacity to safeguard copyright, such as Shutterstock, Depositphotos, 123rf, and iStockphoto. These watermarks extensively cover the texture and smooth areas of the host image, rendering their spatial features intricate and difficult to remove without ample prior knowledge.

In this article, we address the issue of dense visible watermark removal by presenting a novel and compact network called PVWRNet. Our contributions can be summarized as follows:

1. We present a novel approach to address the dense visible watermark removal problem by introducing a highly efficient model, named PVWRNet, which contains fewer parameters as depicted in Fig. 1.
2. In PVWRNet, we have devised progressive modules to propagate shallow features, which can significantly improve quality of watermark removal.
3. In the backbone module, we introduce a novel reinforced dual attention module (RDAM) that effectively refines local features while leveraging the full information of the watermarked image and propagating it to deeper layers.
4. Experiments conducted on the dense watermark dataset showcase the superior performance of our proposed approach. Our method surpasses various state-of-the-art methods under the same experimental conditions.

2   Related Work

While the direct removal of dense watermarks has not been addressed in the literature, there exist related works that address visible watermark removal by Generative Adversarial Networks (GANs) and Convolutional Neural Networks (CNNs).

Visible Watermark Remove by GANs. Wu et al. [23] proposed an effective De-mark GAN for the MeshFace verification problem with dense visible watermarks. Sharma et al. [19] trained a CycleGAN to transform the visible watermark removal of text into an image translation task. Li et al. [13] introduced a multistage framework for photo-realistic visible watermark removal. Cao et al. [2] proposed a GANs model for visible watermark removal (VWGAN), which solved the problem of random visible watermark removal. Liu et al. [15] proposed a new watermark removal method named WDNet, which utilizes the process of watermark decomposition. Nevertheless, the targeted assumption in the method proposed by [19,23] weakens their potential in real-world applications. The above methods [2,13,15] are still struggling to achieve high performance in restoring watermark-free images.

Visible Watermark Remove by CNNs. Cheng et al. [4] introduced a deep learning framework for large-scale visible watermark processing tasks, however, the visual quality was deemed unsatisfactory. Lehtinen et al. [12] proposed a Noise2Noise (N2N) training method that achieved visible watermark removal with consistent color, direction, and coverage area. Hertz et al. [6] presented a technique for identifying and removing visual motifs embedded in images, successfully removing them from the images. Cun et al. [5] built upon Hertz et al.'s work and employed attention-guided ResUNets to replicate the detection, removal, and refinement process. Liang et al. [14] developed a multitask network with innovative MBE, SMR, and CCF modules that can simultaneously localize the watermark and restore the image. The CNN model, when compared to the GANs model, is more adept at producing high-quality image restorations.

3   Progressive Visible Watermark Removal Network

3.1   Main Components of the Network

Numerous low-level vision models rely on single-stage approaches, which excel in extracting comprehensive contextual features but prove unreliable in preserving spatial details [28]. Consequently, researchers have begun to design multi-stage architectures to balance contextual features and spatial details, including both parallel [3] and serial [20] designs. While a single-scale pipeline model [26] can provide spatially accurate outputs, its semantic reliability is often lacking. On the other hand, Encoder-Decoder models typically extract features through scale mapping. The fundamental design of PVWRNet capitalizes on the strengths of the aforementioned methods, with its functions classified into Cropping Modules, Encoder-Decoder Models, and Enhanced Refinement Modules.

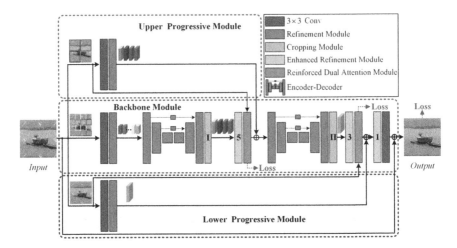

Fig. 2. The architecture of progressive visible watermark removal network (PVWR-Net). The number "5, 3, 1" indicates the number of block stacks. Additionally, the character "I, II" indicates the cropping stage.

Cropping Module. The cropping module in PVWRNet is responsible for splitting the input image into multiple patches. "Cropping module I" merges the input features from 16 equally-sized patches into 4 equal patches, while "Cropping module II" merges the input features from 4 equal patches into the original input image size. This process, as depicted in Fig. 3(a), enables the network to concentrate on different local features in each stage, thus accelerating the convergence of the global network and improving the extraction of deep features.

Refinement Module. We have adopted the U-Net [18] architecture with skip links to connect encoder and decoder features. To ensure a balance between network parameters and feature extraction efficiency, we have introduced refinement modules (RM) as a basic convolution module (refer to Fig. 2(b)). The default U-Net skip connection does not propagate deep features [21], hence we replace the original concatenation with RM modules in our encoder-decoder module. Moreover, we use bilinear upsampling instead of transposed convolution [16] to reduce checkerboard artifacts in the output image and speed up network convergence.

Enhanced Refinement Module. The encoder-decoder architecture primarily relies on structural transformations of up-down sampling to obtain semantic features. However, single-scale pipelines extract spatially-detailed features by stacking modules. In order to fuse fine details from the cropping module, we have proposed an enhanced refinement module based on RM (refer to Fig. 3(c)), which eschews any downsampling operation and generates high-resolution features that are spatially-enriched by stacking itself. This is illustrated in Fig. 3(b) and (c). The difference between the two modules is as follows: (1) The activation function used after the first convolution. Swish provides better smoothness than PReLu. (2) The identity mapping within the modules is different. RM employs a 1×1

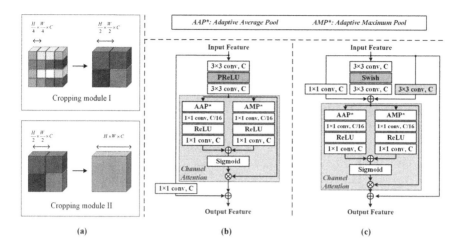

Fig. 3. (a) Cropping module. (b) Refinement module. (c) Enhanced refinement module.

convolution for identity mapping, whereas EnRM uses a 3×3 convolution and a 1×1 convolution for identity mapping.

3.2 Reinforced Dual Attention Module

At the intersection of the progressive and backbone modules, we have integrated a reinforced dual attention module (RDAM), as depicted in Fig. 4. This module improves feature propagation by incorporating two attention mechanisms: a lightweight attention mechanism and a mechanism for supervising weak features.

The pale orange region on the left-hand side of Fig. 4 corresponds to the lightweight attention mechanism. To obtain attention features $F_{Att}^{H \times W \times C}$, we apply the Coordinate Attention module [7]. This attention module combines the best of both Squeeze-and-Excitation (SE) attention [8] and Channel Attention (CA), monitoring inter-channel connections while simultaneously capturing long-range dependencies with accurate spatial information. On the right side in Fig. 4, the light blue area represents the weak feature supervision mechanism. Here, the watermark image $I_{In}^{H \times W \times 3}$ is utilized to establish supervision of the preceding layer of features $F_{Pre}^{H \times W \times C}$, and adaptive enhancement of local feature weights is realized.

The RDMA merges the feature information from both the input image and the previous layer of feature information, utilizing a lightweight attention mechanism and weak supervision to jointly constrain the extracted feature information and thereby enhance feature detail extraction performance.

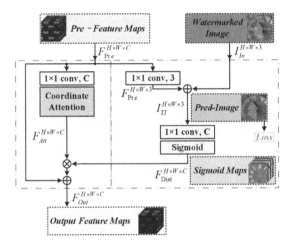

Fig. 4. Reinforced dual attention module. (Color figure online)

3.3 Loss Function

As shown by the red arrows in Fig. 2, PVWRNet comprises of three sub-loss points. The total loss is the sum of the Charbonnier loss L_{Char} [11] and Laplace loss L_{Lapla} of each loss. Specifically, the total loss is defined as follows:

$$L = \sum_{k=1}^{3} \left(\lambda L^{k}_{Char} + (1 - \lambda) L^{k}_{Lapla} \right) \tag{1}$$

In Fig. 2, the marked position of the "Loss" is denoted by k. It is well-known that L2 loss exhibits a weak correlation with the human visual system's perceived image quality in image end-to-end processing tasks [27]. Hence, this study adopts the enhanced Charbonnier loss of L1 loss as the primary loss function. The definition of the improved Charbonnier loss is as follows:

$$L_{Char} = \sqrt{\left\| \hat{X} - X \right\|^2 + \varepsilon^2} \tag{2}$$

The constraint loss is linked to gradient information, which exhibits superior smoothness in images [24]. Therefore, this paper adopts the Laplace loss L_{Lapla} to alleviate artifacts, defined as:

$$L_{Lapla} = \sqrt{\left\| \nabla^2 \left(\hat{X} \right) - \nabla^2 \left(X \right) \right\|^2 + \varepsilon^2} \tag{3}$$

Wherein Eq. (2) and Eq. (3), the constant ε has been set to 10^{-3} and the parameter λ in Eq. (1) has been set to 0.95.

4   Experiments

4.1   Datasets

To ensure a fair evaluation of the control group models on dense visible water-mark removal, we generated five types of grayscale watermarks from 123rf, DepositPhotos, iStock, Shutterstock, and Stock Photo, with pixels set to 255. The transparency of the watermark is randomly chosen from 40% to 60%. The scaling factors of the watermark are {0.9, 1, 1.1, 1.2, 1.3, 1.5}. There are 5400 synthetic images in train set in total. Simultaneously, we use the same water-marks in test set. However, the pixel of the watermark images is randomly chosen from 230 to 250. The scaling factors of the watermark are {0.8, 0.9, 1, 1.1, 1.2, 1.3, 1.4, 1.5, 1.6, 1.7}. There are 1000 synthetic images in the test set. In order to prevent image distortion and blurring caused by using resize. The background images are all selected by cropping large-size images in COCO2017 to 512×512.

4.2   Implementation Details

Environment. All experiments were conducted on a computational system equipped with two NVIDIA GeForce GTX 1080 Ti GPUs, each with 11 GB of memory, and two Intel Xeon Silver 4110 CPUs. The system was deployed on the PyTorch V1.6 framework running on Windows 10, with PyThon V3.7 and CUDA V11.2 environments.

Training Details. For data augmentation, we randomly applied area scaling, watermark scaling, cropping, rotations, and flip to each training image. To expe-dite convergence, we employed 256×256 patches randomly selected from the watermarked image for training, while testing on non-patches 512×512 images. We utilized the Adam optimizer [10] with an initial learning rate of 0.0005, batch size of 6, and momentum parameters of $\beta_1 = 0.9$ and $\beta_2 = 0.999$.

Experimental Group. To the best of our knowledge, there are 5 deep learn-ing methods specifically designed for watermark removal, including Noise2Noise method (N2N) [12], blind visual motif removal method (BVMR) [6], watermark-decomposition network (WDNet) [15], split and refine network (SplitNet) [5] and self-calibrated localization and background refinement method (SLBR) [14]. All codes use official open source code in the control group. All experiments set a random seed with "12345" to improve credibility.

4.3   Experimental Results

As illustrated in Table 1, our PVWRNet method outperforms other state-of-the-art methods in all metrics, including PSNR, SSIM, RMSE, and LPIPS [22]. We conducted multiple training sessions for SplitNet and SLBR and observed that these models consume significant memory resources when trained on high definition images (512×512).

As image quality evaluation metrics are still not strongly correlated with human visual evaluation [1], this paper also provides a qualitative analysis of visible watermark removal samples to complement the quantitative results.

Table 1. Comparisons between the proposed method and other methods. The suffix w denotes the watermark region, while no suffix indicates the whole image region.

Method	PSNR↑	SSIM↑	RMSE↓	LPIPS↓	PSNRw↑	SSIMw↑	RMSEw↓	LPIPSw↓
Test set	26.57	0.9331	2.58	0.1114	14.85	0.7996	9.68	0.3137
N2N [12]	32.22	0.9684	2.30	0.0838	24.40	0.8897	6.97	0.1096
BVMR [6]	39.52	0.9872	2.90	0.0318	28.78	0.9253	6.14	0.0556
WDNet [15]	37.06	0.9772	2.07	0.0648	25.55	0.8917	7.50	0.0938
SplitNet [5]	37.03	0.9762	2.09	0.0607	24.43	0.8903	7.55	0.0934
SLBR [14]	38.08	0.9797	2.08	0.0472	26.94	0.9181	6.98	0.0907
Proposal	**43.36**	**0.9913**	**1.36**	**0.0192**	**31.66**	**0.9319**	**5.12**	**0.0431**

We conducted a series of tests to evaluate the effectiveness of our proposed method in removing watermarks from images with color gradients and striped backgrounds. As depicted in Fig. 5, the first row displays the gradient image, the second row shows the striped image, and the third row displays an image with alternating smooth and textured areas.

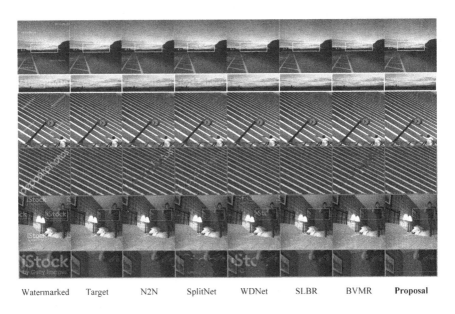

Watermarked   Target   N2N   SplitNet   WDNet   SLBR   BVMR   **Proposal**

Fig. 5. Visible watermark removal for color gradients and striped background areas.

Notably, the N2N and SplitNet methods show poor performance on all three images, while the WDNet's removal performance remains unstable, especially in the second image. The BVMR method exhibits noticeable artifacts in the striped image. However, the SLBR method demonstrates relatively stable performance in all three images, with very few artifacts remaining. Our proposed method stands out with superior visual quality compared to the other methods.

4.4   Image Stock Watermark Removal

In order to substantiate the effectiveness of our proposed method on Internet stock images, we have handpicked a number of preview images from popular online platforms such as Shutterstock and Depositphotos for testing purposes. Given that these preview images come with watermarks that cannot be removed, this section is entirely dedicated to qualitative analysis.

Fig. 6. Visible watermark removal for image stock. (Color figure online)

In Sect. 4.3, we have observed that in terms of image quality metrics and visual evaluation, SLBR and BVMR networks have outperformed other methods. In this section, we provide a comparative analysis of the performance of SLBR, BVMR, and our proposed PVWRNet in removing visible watermarks from stock images, as illustrated in Fig. 6. The results clearly demonstrate that our method excels in completing real-world imagery patterns. However, due to the limited diversity of visible watermarks in the training set, all methods struggle to remove the gray square watermark of Shutterstock, as indicated by the red box in Fig. 6. In summary, the proposed method has shown promising results in visible watermark removal in real-world scenarios.

4.5   Ablation Studies

In this section, we conduct ablation studies to examine the efficacy of each component in our network. Table 2 illustrates our evaluation of the indispensability of each module in our framework by removing it. As each module has only a few parameters, we commence with the backbone module illustrated in Fig. 2 and gradually construct the full model by incorporating the progressive modules (PM), cropping modules (CM), channel attention modules (CA), and reinforced dual attention modules (RDAM).

Table 2. Ablation analysis of the network modules. The suffix w denotes the watermark region, while no suffix indicates the whole image region.

Method	PSNR$^\uparrow$	SSIM$^\uparrow$	RMSE$^\downarrow$	LPIPS$^\downarrow$	Parms(M)
BL (Baseline)	36.15	0.9781	2.03	0.0554	6.550
BL+PM	41.15	0.9879	1.57	0.0278	6.710
BL+PM+CM	42.32	0.9891	1.40	0.0233	6.722
BL+PM+CM+CA	42.87	0.9904	1.35	0.0205	6.803
BL+PM+CM+CA+RDAM (PVWRNet)	**43.36**	**0.9913**	**1.36**	**0.0192**	**6.804**

Table 2 summarizes the quantitative results of our ablation studies. The remarkable performance of our baseline can be attributed to the alternating fusion of the encoder-decoder modules and the refined modules, surpassing the conventional U-Net architecture. Moreover, the progressive strategy employed in the upper and lower progressive modules significantly enhances the baseline's efficiency. Our analysis indicates that the proposed modules have a significant positive impact on the performance improvement of the baseline.

5   Conclusion

In this paper, we present a novel and efficient model called PVWRNet for removing dense watermarks from images. Our method is the first to address the challenge of removing dense watermarks without relying on a watermark mask, transparency feature image, or any additional information. Instead, it establishes a direct end-to-end visible watermark removal network from watermarked images to clean images, effectively reducing the presence of artifacts. Our results demonstrate that PVWRNet outperforms state-of-the-art approaches in the challenging task of dense watermark removal. Furthermore, our model achieves superior performance with a compact architecture, making it a practical and efficient solution for real-world applications. In conclusion, our proposed PVWRNet model presents an innovative approach to the problem of dense watermark removal.

References

1. Blau, Y., Mechrez, R., Timofte, R., Michaeli, T., Zelnik-Manor, L.: The 2018 PIRM challenge on perceptual image super-resolution. In: Leal-Taixé, L., Roth, S. (eds.) ECCV 2018. LNCS, vol. 11133, pp. 334–355. Springer, Cham (2019). https://doi.org/10.1007/978-3-030-11021-5_21
2. Cao, Z., Niu, S., Zhang, J., Wang, X.: Generative adversarial networks model for visible watermark removal. IET Image Proc. **13**(10), 1783–1789 (2019)
3. Chen, L., Lu, X., Zhang, J., Chu, X., Chen, C.: HINet: half instance normalization network for image restoration. In: Proceedings of the IEEE/CVF Conference on Computer Vision and Pattern Recognition (CVPR) Workshops, June 2021, pp. 182–192 (2021)
4. Cheng, D., et al.: Large-scale visible watermark detection and removal with deep convolutional networks. In: Lai, J.-H., et al. (eds.) PRCV 2018. LNCS, vol. 11258, pp. 27–40. Springer, Cham (2018). https://doi.org/10.1007/978-3-030-03338-5_3
5. Cun, X., Pun, C.M.: Split then refine: stacked attention-guided ResUNets for blind single image visible watermark removal. In: Proceedings of the AAAI Conference on Artificial Intelligence, vol. 35, pp. 1184–1192 (2021)
6. Hertz, A., Fogel, S., Hanocka, R., Giryes, R., Cohen-Or, D.: Blind visual motif removal from a single image. In: Proceedings of the IEEE/CVF Conference on Computer Vision and Pattern Recognition (CVPR), June 2019, pp. 6858–6867 (2019)
7. Hou, Q., Zhou, D., Feng, J.: Coordinate attention for efficient mobile network design. In: Proceedings of the IEEE/CVF Conference on Computer Vision and Pattern Recognition (CVPR), June 2021, pp. 13713–13722 (2021)
8. Hu, J., Shen, L., Sun, G.: Squeeze-and-excitation networks. In: Proceedings of the IEEE Conference on Computer Vision and Pattern Recognition (CVPR), June 2018, pp. 7132–7141 (2018)
9. Huang, C.H., Wu, J.L.: Attacking visible watermarking schemes. IEEE Trans. Multimedia **6**(1), 16–30 (2004)
10. Kingma, D.P., Ba, J.: Adam: a method for stochastic optimization. arXiv preprint arXiv:1412.6980 (2014)
11. Lai, W.S., Huang, J.B., Ahuja, N., Yang, M.H.: Fast and accurate image super-resolution with deep Laplacian pyramid networks. IEEE Trans. Pattern Anal. Mach. Intell. **41**(11), 2599–2613 (2019)
12. Lehtinen, J., et al.: Noise2Nois: learning image restoration without clean data. In: International Conference on Machine Learning, pp. 4620–4631. PMLR (2018)
13. Li, X., et al.: Towards photo-realistic visible watermark removal with conditional generative adversarial networks. In: Zhao, Y., Barnes, N., Chen, B., Westermann, R., Kong, X., Lin, C. (eds.) ICIG 2019. LNCS, vol. 11901, pp. 345–356. Springer, Cham (2019). https://doi.org/10.1007/978-3-030-34120-6_28
14. Liang, J., Niu, L., Guo, F., Long, T., Zhang, L.: Visible watermark removal via self-calibrated localization and background refinement. In: Proceedings of the 29th ACM International Conference on Multimedia, October 2021, pp. 4426–4434 (2021)

15. Liu, Y., Zhu, Z., Bai, X.: WDNet: watermark-decomposition network for visible watermark removal. In: Proceedings of the IEEE/CVF Winter Conference on Applications of Computer Vision (WACV), January 2021, pp. 3685–3693 (2021)
16. Odena, A., Dumoulin, V., Olah, C.: Deconvolution and checkerboard artifacts. Distill 1(10), e3 (2016)
17. Qi, W., Liu, Y., Guo, S., Wang, X., Guo, Z.: An adaptive visible watermark embedding method based on region selection. Secur. Commun. Netw. 2021, 1–11 (2021)
18. Ronneberger, O., Fischer, P., Brox, T.: U-Net: convolutional networks for biomedical image segmentation. In: Navab, N., Hornegger, J., Wells, W.M., Frangi, A.F. (eds.) MICCAI 2015. LNCS, vol. 9351, pp. 234–241. Springer, Cham (2015). https://doi.org/10.1007/978-3-319-24574-4_28
19. Sharma, M., Verma, A., Vig, L.: Learning to clean: a GAN perspective. In: Carneiro, G., You, S. (eds.) ACCV 2018. LNCS, vol. 11367, pp. 174–185. Springer, Cham (2019). https://doi.org/10.1007/978-3-030-21074-8_14
20. Tao, X., Gao, H., Shen, X., Wang, J., Jia, J.: Scale-recurrent network for deep image deblurring. In: Proceedings of the IEEE Conference on Computer Vision and Pattern Recognition (CVPR), June 2018, pp. 8174–8182 (2018)
21. Wang, H., Cao, P., Wang, J., Zaiane, O.R.: UCTransNet: rethinking the skip connections in u-net from a channel-wise perspective with transformer (2021)
22. Wang, X., Yu, K., Wu, S., Gu, J., Liu, Y., Dong, C., Qiao, Yu., Loy, C.C.: ESRGAN: enhanced super-resolution generative adversarial networks. In: Leal-Taixé, L., Roth, S. (eds.) ECCV 2018. LNCS, vol. 11133, pp. 63–79. Springer, Cham (2019). https://doi.org/10.1007/978-3-030-11021-5_5
23. Wu, J., Shi, H., Zhang, S., Lei, Z., Yang, Y., Li, S.Z.: De-mark GAN: removing dense watermark with generative adversarial network. In: 2018 International Conference on Biometrics (ICB), pp. 69–74 (2018)
24. Xue, W., Zhang, L., Mou, X., Bovik, A.C.: Gradient magnitude similarity deviation: a highly efficient perceptual image quality index. IEEE Trans. Image Process. 23(2), 684–695 (2014)
25. Ye, G., Pan, C., Dong, Y., Jiao, K., Huang, X.: A novel multi-image visually meaningful encryption algorithm based on compressive sensing and Schur decomposition. Trans. Emerg. Telecommun. Technol. 32(2), e4071 (2021)
26. Zhang, Y., Tian, Y., Kong, Y., Zhong, B., Fu, Y.: Residual dense network for image restoration. IEEE Trans. Pattern Anal. Mach. Intell. 43(7), 2480–2495 (2021)
27. Zhao, H., Gallo, O., Frosio, I., Kautz, J.: Loss functions for image restoration with neural networks. IEEE Trans. Computat. Imaging 3(1), 47–57 (2017)
28. Zhao, M., Zhong, S., Fu, X., Tang, B., Pecht, M.: Deep residual shrinkage networks for fault diagnosis. IEEE Trans. Industr. Inf. 16(7), 4681–4690 (2020)

When Diffusion Model Meets with Adversarial Attack: Generating Transferable Adversarial Examples on Face Recognition

Yuanbo Li, Cong Hu$^{(\boxtimes)}$, Tianyang Xu, and Xiaojun Wu

School of Artificial Intelligence and Computer Science, Jiangnan University, Wuxi, China
conghu@jiangnan.edu.cn

Abstract. Face recognition has witnessed continuous development along with advanced deep convolutional neural networks (DCNNs). However, DCNNs are vulnerable to adversarial examples, resulting in potential security risks to face recognition applications. While the adversarial examples generated by the gradient-based approaches are overfitting into the substitute model, sacrificing transferability. Therefore, this paper proposes a novel transfer-based black-box adversarial attack formulation with the diffusion model (DiffAttack). In particular, DiffAttack employs the dynamic noise from the diffusion process to increase the adversarial perturbation diversity. Besides, DiffAttack obtains ensemble-like effects by re-sampling tactics during the proceeding of diffusion. Accordingly, DiffAttack effectively prevents the overfitting issue, delivering more powerful model capacity. Extensive experiments are conducted on two benchmarking datasets, LFW and CelebA-HQ. The results demonstrate the effectiveness of DiffAttack, which achieves a higher attack success rate than the state-of-the-art, with comparable image quality to that of other transfer-based methods. Codes will be available on the project homepage: https://github.com/LiYuanBoJNU/DiffAttack.

Keywords: Face recognition · Adversarial attack · Transferable adversarial examples · Diffusion model

1 Introduction

Deep convolutional neural networks (DCNNs) have successfully been applied to a wide range of computer vision tasks with remarkable performance, especially in face recognition (FR). As one of the essential computer vision tasks, the performance of advanced FR approaches has exceeded human beings [2,14]. Despite the excellent performance, existing FR systems are vulnerable to adversarial examples [22], which have attracted increasing attention in the FR security field in recent years.

In general, adversarial examples are the data generated by adding well-designed and indistinguishable perturbations to normal data, inducing DCNNs into making wrong predictions that are different from the true labels [6]. The

H. Lu et al. (Eds.): ICIG 2023, LNCS 14359, pp. 243–255, 2023.
https://doi.org/10.1007/978-3-031-46317-4_20

process of generating adversarial examples is called the adversarial attack, which can be divided into the white-box attack and the black-box attack. In the white-box setting, the attacker thoroughly knows the information of the target model, including the parameters, structures and other details [5]. While in the black-box setting, the attacker cannot access any attribute about the target model [7].

Specifically, the black-box attack can generally be divided into query-based and transfer-based methods. Query-based methods [4] require a large number of output queries to obtain effective adversarial examples. However, it is not practical to perform massive queries for the FR model, as such abnormal queries can be easily detected by most real-world FR systems. By contrast, transfer-based methods can generate transferable adversarial examples without query. Several advanced methods have been proposed to train a generative model to generate transferable adversarial examples for FR models, such as Adv-makeup [22]. Nevertheless, the above approaches require massive computational resources to train an excellent generative model. While transfer-based gradient attack methods optimize the gradient to generate transferable adversarial examples, which are high-efficiency. Consequently, many approaches have been studied, such as DIM [20], Admix [18], LIM [11], *etc.* However, the adversarial examples generated by these methods are easily overfitting into the substitute model, which leads to limited transferability.

Recently, diffusion models [9] have presented powerful capacity, enabling high-quality image generation. The essential idea of the diffusion model is to systematically perturb the structure in a data distribution through a forward process and then restore the structure by learning a reverse process, resulting in a highly tractable and flexible path. After studying its nature, the diffusion models are well suited for adversarial attacks. The dynamic noise processing technique and the intermediate images are directly available for adversarial analysis.

In this paper, we are committed to studying the transfer-based adversarial attack on deep FR models. To enhance the transferability of adversarial examples, we propose a novel transfer-based adversarial attack method called DiffAttack. DiffAttack explores the potential of diffusion models in the adversarial attack field. Given access to intermediate images, DiffAttack obtains and integrates samples from them, reflecting comprehensive aggregation. Therefore, the adversarial examples generated by DiffAttack are robust against potential overfit to the substitute model. We provide concrete experimental evidence that the diffusion model helps increase adversarial perturbation diversity by dynamic noise and ensemble effects. A large number of experiments on two benchmarking datasets demonstrate that DiffAttack achieves a higher attack success rate than the state-of-the-art transfer-based approaches.

2   Related Work

Transfer-Based Adversarial Attacks. Transfer-based adversarial attacks can be easily migrated from the image recognition task to the face recognition task due to its flexibility and convenience, especially the gradient-based methods.

Dong *et al.* [3] introduce momentum into the basic iterative method to reduce the variation in update direction and avoid local minima. Jiang *et al.* [11] update adversarial perturbations with the accumulated gradient obtained by looking ahead. These methods improve the transferability of adversarial examples by optimizing the gradient. Several approaches also enhance the transferability of adversarial examples through input transformation. Xie *et al.* [20] apply random resizing and random padding to the inputs for the sake of the transferability of adversarial examples. Wang *et al.* [18] consider mixing the input image and a set of randomly sampled images from other categories to enhance the transferability of adversarial examples.

Adversarial Attacks on Face Recognition. With the improvement of accuracy, face recognition systems have been applied in various fields. Several previous studies have revealed the vulnerability of face recognition systems to adversarial examples. Wei *et al.* [19] design meaningful adversarial stickers to perform physical attacks, which proves that the attacks on face recognition can be applied in the physical world. Dong *et al.* [4] propose an evolutionary attack method for the decision-based adversarial attack in black-box settings, which achieves commendable results on impersonation and dodging attacks. Yang *et al.* [21] try to fit the privacy-preserving scenario by adding a new penalty function to the transfer-based method. Yin *et al.* [22] design a powerful GAN to enhance the transferability of the adversarial makeup faces.

Diffusion Models. Diffusion models [9] have been proposed as a latent variable generative model inspired by non-equilibrium thermodynamics. The diffusion model consists of two processes: (1) A forward process that converts data to noise by gradually injecting noise into the input data. (2) A reverse process that generates data by denoising one step at a time. Several studies have investigated diffusion models due to their excellent performance. Song *et al.* [15] improve the sampling efficiency of diffusion models. Several researchers also adopt stochastic differential equation (SDE) [16] to generalize the diffusion model. Moreover, diffusion models have been developed for various downstream visual tasks. Meng *et al.* [13] introduce a new image synthesis and editing method based on a diffusion model.

3   Methodology

This section introduces our method of generating adversarial examples with the diffusion model on the FR model. Section 3.1 introduces the attack setting. Section 3.2 elaborates the process and algorithm of DiffAttack.

3.1   Attack Setting

Suppose the deep FR model f encodes a face image x into a feature vector $f(x) \in \mathbb{R}^d$, where d indicates the feature dimension. Given a pair of face images

$\{x_1, x_2\}$, the distance between normalized representation vector $f(x_1)$ and $f(x_2)$ can be calculated as follows:

$$\mathcal{D}_f(x_1, x_2) = ||f(x_1) - f(x_2)||_2^2. \tag{1}$$

In this paper, we focus on dodging attacks for face identification. Face identification compares the similarity between a face image and a face image gallery set and recognizes the input image as the identity whose representation is most similar to its. The attacker generates an adversarial face image such that it is recognized as an identity different from the benign face image. Therefore, the objective is to maximize the feature vector distance of adversarial example x^{adv} and benign example x. The objective function can be formulated as:

$$\max_{x^{adv}} \mathcal{L}(x^{adv}, x) = \mathcal{D}_f(x^{adv}, x), \text{ s.t. } ||x^{adv} - x||_\infty \leq \epsilon, \tag{2}$$

where ϵ denotes the maximum perturbation limitation.

3.2 Method

Adversarial Attack with Diffusion Model. Unlike other generative models that only have an output image, the diffusion model can obtain intermediate images because the whole process of diffusion model is carried out in the image domain [13,15]. These images are easy to exploit when performing the attack. Moreover, the noise is gradually removed and the noise carried by each image is different during the proceeding of diffusion model, which generates dynamic noise. The available intermediate images and dynamic noise are the vital elements for combining diffusion model with adversarial attack.

The diffusion model consists of the forward and reverse process. The reverse process is generally performed from noise to image when the pre-trained diffusion model is used to generate images. But the images generated from random noise are unpredictable, which is inconformity with the pattern of adversarial attack. Therefore, in this paper, the amount of noise added in the forward process is reduced, making the image with added noise not a complete noise. The denoised images can remain as the data structure of the input image during the reverse process. As shown in Fig. 1, firstly, several images are sampled to compose an image set X during the proceeding of the diffusion model. These images include: (1) The current input image. It ensures the update direction of the adversarial perturbation. (2) The image with adding noise. It can make adversarial perturbation diverse similar to the effect of image enhancement. (3) Some of the denoised images were obtained by reverse processing. Since the reverse process is performed gradually, the intermediate denoised images contain sufficient dynamic noise and the information of adversarial perturbation from the current input image. To take full advantage of dynamic noise and diversify the adversarial perturbation, some intermediate images are sampled and fed into X. Secondly, the images in X are sent into the FR model and then their gradients are calculated to store in the gradient set G. Finally, the average gradient is

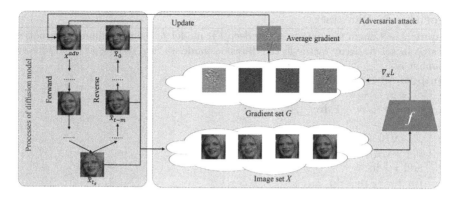

Fig. 1. Illustration of DiffAttack. Firstly, several images are sampled from the process of diffusion model and sent into the image set X. Then these images are fed into the substitute FR model f and the gradient set G is obtained according to the objective function. Finally, the average gradient is computed to update the adversarial example.

computed for updating the adversarial example. On the one hand, the obtained average gradient carries abundant information of dynamic noise and adversarial perturbation, making it diverse to escape the local optimal to prevent from overfitting the substitute model. On the other hand, the operation of multiple re-sampling and averaging the gradients achieves ensemble-like effects, which further prevents the overfitting problem, delivering more powerful adversarial perturbation. Therefore, the final adversarial perturbation is highly aggressive, giving the adversarial examples significant transferability.

Algorithm of DiffAttack. The forward process is a Markov process that adds noise to a clean image gradually. The process from clean data x_0 to x_T is defined as:

$$q(x_{1:T}|x_0) = \prod_{t=1}^{T} q(x_t|x_{t-1}),\ q(x_t|x_{t-1}) = \mathcal{N}(x_t; \sqrt{1-\beta_t}x_{t-1}, \beta_t I), \quad (3)$$

where $\{\beta_t \in (0,1)\}_{t=1}^{T}$ are variance coefficient. According to [9], there is a closed form expression for $q(x_t|x_0)$. By define constants $\alpha_t = 1 - \beta_t$, $\bar{\alpha}_t = \prod_{s=1}^{t}\alpha_s$, the $q(x_t|x_0) = \mathcal{N}(x_t; \sqrt{\bar{\alpha}_t}x_0, (1-\bar{\alpha}_t)I)$. Therefore, $\bar{\alpha}_t$ tends to 0 and $q(x_t|x_0)$ is close to the latent distribution when T is large enough. Note that x_t can be directly sampled through the following equation:

$$x_t = \sqrt{\bar{\alpha}_t}x_0 + \sqrt{1-\bar{\alpha}_t}p, \quad (4)$$

where p is a standard Gaussian noise.

The reverse process predicts and removes the noise added in the forward process, which is a Markov process. The reverse process from latent variable x_t

---

Algorithm 1. DiffAttack

Input: The benign face image x, the deep FR model f, the maximum perturbation ϵ, step factor α, decay factor μ, the diffusion model ϵ_θ, the timestep t_s and interval number m

Output: Adversarial example x^{adv}

1: $x_0^{adv} = x$, $g_0 = 0$
2: **for** $n = 0$ to $N - 1$ **do:**
3:     $X = \bar{x}_0 = x_n^{adv}$
4:     $p \sim \mathcal{N}(0, I)$
5:     $\bar{x}_{t_s} = \sqrt{\bar{\alpha}_{t_s}}\bar{x}_0 + \sqrt{1 - \bar{\alpha}_{t_s}}p$
6:     add $\bar{x}_{t_s}$ in X
7:     **for** $t = t_s$ to 1 **do:**
8:         $z \sim \mathcal{N}(0, I)$
9:         $\bar{x}_{t-1} = \frac{1}{\sqrt{\alpha_t}}\left(\bar{x}_t - \frac{1-\alpha_t}{\sqrt{1-\bar{\alpha}_t}}\epsilon_\theta(\bar{x}_t, t)\right) + \sigma_t z$
10:        add $\bar{x}_{t-1}$ in X if $(t-1)\%m == 0$
11:    **end for**
12:    Compute the gradient $\bar{g}_{n+1}$ by Eq. 8.
13:    $g_{n+1} = \mu \cdot g_n + \frac{\bar{g}_{n+1}}{||\bar{g}_{n+1}||_1}$
14:    Update $x_{n+1}^{adv} = Clip_x^\epsilon\{x_n^{adv} + \alpha \cdot sign(g_{n+1})\}$
15: **end for**
16: return x_N^{adv}

---

to clean data x_0 is defined as:

$$p_\theta(x_{0:T}) = p(x_T)\sum_{t=1}^{T} p_\theta(x_{t-1}|x_t),$$

$$p_\theta(x_{t-1}|x_t) = \mathcal{N}(x_{t-1}; \mu_\theta(x_t, t), \Sigma_\theta(x_t, t)). \tag{5}$$

The mean $\mu_\theta(x_t, t)$ is a neural network parameterized by θ, the variance $\Sigma_\theta(x_t, t)$ is time dependent constants, which is set as $\sigma_t^2 I$. Since x_t is available as input to the model, $\mu_\theta(x_t, t)$ can be parameterization:

$$\mu_\theta(x_t, t) = \frac{1}{\sqrt{\alpha_t}}\left(x_t - \frac{1-\alpha_t}{\sqrt{1-\bar{\alpha}_t}}\epsilon_\theta(x_t, t)\right). \tag{6}$$

To sample $x_{t-1} \sim p_\theta(x_{t-1}|x_t)$ is to compute as follows:

$$x_{t-1} = \frac{1}{\sqrt{\alpha_t}}\left(x_t - \frac{1-\alpha_t}{\sqrt{1-\bar{\alpha}_t}}\epsilon_\theta(x_t, t)\right) + \sigma_t z, \tag{7}$$

where ϵ_θ is the diffusion model to predict noise from x_t, $z \sim \mathcal{N}(0, I)$, σ_t is continuous-time noise scale.

Given an input image x, first, the adversarial example x^{adv} is initialized as x. The image set X and the input image of the diffusion model $\bar{x}_0$ are initialized in the loop instead of acquiring them at the beginning. For the process of diffusion model, the $\bar{x}_0$ is diffused by the forwarding process from $t = 0$ to $t = t_s$ by

Eq. 4. t_s controls the amplitude of the noise. The image $\bar{x}_{t_s}$ is denoised through the reverse process by Eq. 7. Note that the diffusion model ϵ_θ is a pre-trained model. A batch of images are sampled to X from the images generated during the process. Among them, a denoised image is sampled at an interval of m during the reverse process for the selection of the denoised images. After obtaining the image set X, the gradient of each image is calculated and then the average gradient is computed by the following formula:

$$\bar{g} = \frac{1}{K} \sum_{i=1}^{K} \nabla_{x_i} \mathcal{L}(x_i, x), \tag{8}$$

where K is the number of images, x_i is the image in X. Then, the momentum is applied to stabilize the gradient direction. Finally, the adversarial example is updated by the gradient. We summarize the algorithm of DiffAttack in Algorithm 1.

4 Experiments

In this section, we conduct extensive experiments to demonstrate the superiority of the proposed DiffAttack. Section 4.1 introduces the experimental setting. Section 4.2 verifies the effectiveness of DiffAttack. Section 4.3 compares DiffAttack with different transfer-based methods on two benchmark datasets. Section 4.4 analyzes the influence of the parameters. Section 4.5 evaluates the quality of the adversarial examples.

4.1 Experimental Settings

We conduct experiments on LFW [10] and CelebA-HQ [12] datasets. For each dataset, we select 1,000 face images with different identities for performing attack. All the face images are resized to 112×112. We select several FR models with various backbones and training losses to demonstrate the ability to attack performance fully, which are shown in Table 1. For the diffusion model, we select SDEdit model [13], which is mainly used for image synthesis and editing tasks. It is better suited to adversarial attack than the generation task due to its image-to-image mode. Five competitive methods are adopted to compete with DiffAttack, including MIM [3], DIM [20], LIM [11] and Admix [18]. We set the maximum perturbation $\epsilon = 10$, the number of iterations $N = 50$, the step size $\alpha = 8/255$, the timestep $t_s = 100$ and the interval number $m = 50$. All the experiments are conducted on one RTX 3090.

4.2 Effectiveness of DiffAttack

To demonstrate that the dynamic noise of diffusion model is sufficient to make the adversarial perturbation diverse. We try to only add images with random noise (RN) to X in the forward process and adopt the strategy of sampling

Table 1. The FR models with various settings, including different architectures and training objectives.

Model	Backbone	Loss
ArcFace [2]	IR-SE50	Arcface
MobileFace [1]	MobileFaceNet	Softmax
IR50-Softmax [8]	IR50	Softmax
IR50-Arcface [8]	IR50	Arcface
FaceNet [14]	InceptionResNetV1	Triplet
CosFace [17]	Sphere20	LMCL

Table 2. The black-box ASRs (%) of RN and DiffAttack on LFW dataset.

	MobileFace	IR50-Softmax	IR50-Arcface	CosFace	FaceNet
RN	79.2	65.2	75.1	41.7	29.5
DiffAttack	**92.6**	**81.5**	**93.3**	**74.7**	**48.6**

images every m times. The adversarial examples are generated by the Arc-Face model on LFW dataset. As shown in Table 2, compared with RN, DiffAttack achieves higher attack success rates (ASRs) on all black-box models, which shows that DiffAttack can generate more diverse adversarial perturbation than RN to enhance the transferability of adversarial examples. Moreover, re-sampling multiple images to achieve ensemble-like effects also helps improve DiffAttack performance because it can take full advantage of dynamic noise and plentiful adversarial perturbation. The experiments indicate that the diffusion model helps increase the adversarial perturbation diversity by dynamic noise and ensemble-like effects to enhance the transferability of adversarial examples, which shows the potential of the diffusion model in the adversarial attack.

4.3   Comparison Study

To evaluate the performance of DiffAttack, we compare DiffAttack with different transfer-based attack methods on LFW and CelebA-HQ datasets and test the transferability of the adversarial examples. The experimental results are listed in Table 3. Compared with the other transfer-based attack methods, DiffAttack can effectively enhance the transferability of adversarial examples, improving the average black-box ASR by 5.5% on LFW dataset and 3.9% on CelebA-HQ dataset. It can be found that the adversarial examples show significant transferability in the same network structures. DiffAttack performs slightly worse on the IR50-Arcface model because of a similar training loss or network structure as the substitute model. This suggests that the substitute model is a crucial factor when attacking a completely unknown FR model.

To further improve the transferability of adversarial examples, we integrate three substitute models (including ArcFace, MobileFace, IR50-Softmax) to per-

Table 3. The ASRs (%) on different FR models by various attacks and DiffAttack on LFW and CelebA-HQ datasets. The adversarial examples are crafted on ArcFace, MobileFace and IR50-Softmax, respectively. * indicates the white-box model.

		Method	ArcFace	MobileFace	IR50-Softmax	IR50-Arcface	FaceNet	CosFace	Average
LFW	ArcFace	MIM	99.8*	54.2	47.5	56.7	17.4	20.7	39.3
		DIM	99.9*	78.4	66.8	81.7	23.5	39.5	58.0
		LIM	99.8*	79.0	71.3	82.8	35.0	39.9	61.6
		Admix	100*	90.3	72.5	87.2	41.1	73.5	72.9
		DiffAttack	**100***	**92.6**	**81.5**	**93.3**	**48.6**	**74.7**	**78.1**
	MobileFace	MIM	14.4	99.8*	46.1	43.8	11.4	5.5	24.2
		DIM	27.6	99.8*	66.6	71.3	15.1	11.7	38.5
		LIM	47.6	100*	77.1	82.8	30.4	25.9	52.8
		Admix	55.5	100*	83.2	88.6	32.4	27.7	57.5
		DiffAttack	**58.3**	**100***	**87.4**	**92.7**	**40.0**	**34.9**	**62.7**
	IR50-Softmax	MIM	32.5	68.2	100*	81.6	12.2	18.0	42.5
		DIM	38.9	78.3	100*	91.4	18.1	23.4	50.0
		LIM	66.6	90.8	100*	98.0	34.1	44.7	66.8
		Admix	68.3	93.4	100*	97.8	41.6	49.1	70.0
		DiffAttack	**71.9**	**95.1**	**100***	**99.3**	**58.1**	**56.1**	**76.1**
CelebA-HQ	ArcFace	MIM	99.7*	44.3	65.3	67.1	31.2	3.1	42.2
		DIM	99.9*	69.9	87.4	87.7	49.6	13.2	61.6
		LIM	99.8*	63.2	83.9	84.9	49.7	8.4	58.0
		Admix	**100***	67.7	85.2	**88.9**	55.6	13.7	62.2
		DiffAttack	99.9*	**73.3**	**88.8**	88.3	**66.9**	**16.6**	**66.8**
	MobileFace	MIM	10.0	99.9*	65	58.1	18.3	0.9	30.5
		DIM	20.8	99.7*	76.5	76.2	21.8	1.7	39.4
		LIM	34.0	99.9*	88.3	82.8	40.6	3.8	49.9
		Admix	37.1	100*	89.5	87.8	44.2	5.3	52.8
		DiffAttack	**46.0**	**100***	**90.1**	**89.0**	**49.9**	**6.9**	**56.4**
	IR50-Softmax	MIM	12.3	45.5	100*	72.1	17.6	1.3	29.8
		DIM	19.6	65.4	100*	86.8	16.8	0.8	37.9
		LIM	38.6	75.6	100*	**94.3**	33.8	4.8	49.4
		Admix	37.4	70	100*	90.9	32.7	5.0	47.2
		DiffAttack	**43.9**	**76.2**	**100***	92.8	**44.5**	**7.8**	**53.0**

form ensemble attacks. As shown in Table 4, DiffAttack further improves the transferability of the adversarial examples, increasing the average black-box ASR by 6.9%. Moreover, DiffAttack achieves almost 100% ASR on IR50-Softmax model and the ASR of DiffAttack on the FaceNet model increases by 15.3%.

4.4 Parameters Analysis

Since the timestep t_s controls the noise intensity, the value of t_s is vital. If t_s is small, the added noise is unable to make adversarial perturbation diverse. Hence, the adversarial examples overfit into the substitute model, resulting in inadequate transferability. If t_s is large, the denoised image is cluttered or converted to another image. Moreover, redundant noise overlays the adversarial perturbation, weakening the effect of the adversarial perturbation. The update direction of adversarial perturbation thus goes to the wrong place, which generates adversarial examples with poor transferability. Therefore, we try to pick an

Table 4. The ASRs (%) on black-box FR models by ensemble attacks on LFW dataset.

Method	IR50-Arcface	FaceNet	CosFace	Average
E-MIM	93.1	29.0	28.8	50.3
E-DIM	97.6	36.2	36.4	56.7
E-LIM	99.5	58.3	59.1	72.3
E-Admix	99.8	62.5	61.4	74.6
E-DiffAttack	99.9	77.8	66.9	81.5

Table 5. Quantitative evaluations of image quality.

Method	SSIM (↑)	MSE (↓)	PSNR (↑)
MIM	0.74	0.00145	28.39
DIM	0.81	0.00094	30.23
Admix	0.75	0.00148	28.27
LIM	0.73	0.00149	28.25
Diffattack	0.76	0.00141	28.51

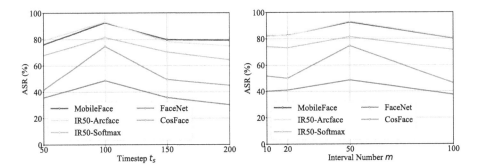

Fig. 2. The black-box ASRs (%) of DiffAttack on LFW dataset when varying the parameters t_s and m.

appropriate t_s for DiifAttack. The left half of Fig. 2 shows the results. It can be found that the ASR is higher when $t_s = 100$ than when t_s takes other values.

Moreover, we explore the influence of interval number m for the transferability of adversarial examples. The results are shown in the right half of Fig. 2. When m increases gradually, the ASR increases first and then decreases. It indicates that the denoised images also need to be selected appropriately. Superabundant denoised images carry masses of noise, which reduces the influence of adversarial perturbation and causes instability of update direction. Thus the transferability of adversarial examples is inadequate. Too few denoised images cannot give full play to the advantage of dynamic noise of diffusion model to increase adversarial perturbation diversity. Hence, there is potential overfitting issue for adversarial examples, leading to insufficient transferability of adversarial examples. Therefore, a proper number of denoised images can help improve the performance of DiffAttack.

4.5   Image Quality

To evaluate the quality of the adversarial examples generated by DiffAttack, we analyze the image quality qualitatively and quantitatively. Figure 3 shows the adversarial examples generated by different methods. There is little difference

Fig. 3. Adversarial examples crafted by MIM, TIM, DIM, LIM, Admix, Diffattack on LFW and CelebA-HQ datasets

between the adversarial examples generated by these methods visually. Table 5 shows the quality of the adversarial examples quantitatively. It can be seen that the quality of the adversarial examples generated by DiffAttack is comparable with that of other transfer-based adversarial attack methods.

5   Conclusion

Deep FR has been widely applied in various real-world application scenarios. Ensuring the security of deep FR has become increasingly essential to study adversarial robustness of the recognition system. In this paper, we study transfer-based adversarial attacks for FR. We propose a novel transfer-based black-box adversarial attack method named DiffAttack, which combines diffusion model with adversarial attack and enhances the transferability of adversarial examples. Extensive experiments on two benchmark datasets demonstrate that DiffAttack can generate adversarial examples with significant transferability and achieve higher attack success rates than the state-of-the-art transfer-based methods. Besides, the image quality of the adversarial examples generated by DiffAttack is comparable with that of these methods. DiffAttack shows the capacity and potential of diffusion models in the field of adversarial attack.

Acknowledgements. This work was supported in part by the National Natural Science Foundation of China (Grant No. 62006097, U1836218), in part by the Natural Science Foundation of Jiangsu Province (Grant No. BK20200593), in part by the China Postdoctoral Science Foundation (Grant No. 2021M701456) and in part by Postgraduate Research & Practice Innovation Program of Jiangsu Province (No. KYCX23_2562).

References

1. Chen, S., Liu, Y., Gao, X., Han, Z.: MobileFaceNets: efficient CNNs for accurate real-time face verification on mobile devices. In: Zhou, J., et al. (eds.) CCBR 2018. LNCS, vol. 10996, pp. 428–438. Springer, Cham (2018). https://doi.org/10.1007/978-3-319-97909-0_46

2. Deng, J., Guo, J., Yang, J., Xue, N., Kotsia, I., Zafeiriou, S.: ArcFace: additive angular margin loss for deep face recognition. IEEE Trans. Pattern Anal. Mach. Intell. **44**(10), 5962–5979 (2022)
3. Dong, Y., et al.: Boosting adversarial attacks with momentum. In: Proceedings of the IEEE/CVF Conference on Computer Vision and Pattern Recognition, pp. 9185–9193 (2018)
4. Dong, Y., et al.: Efficient decision-based black-box adversarial attacks on face recognition. In: Proceedings of the IEEE/CVF Conference on Computer Vision and Pattern Recognition, pp. 7714–7722 (2019)
5. Duan, R., Chen, Y., Niu, D., Yang, Y., Qin, A.K., He, Y.: AdvDrop: adversarial attack to DNNs by dropping information. In: Proceedings of the IEEE/CVF International Conference on Computer Vision, pp. 7506–7515 (2021)
6. Goodfellow, I., Shlens, J., Szegedy, C.: Explaining and harnessing adversarial examples. In: International Conference on Learning Representations (ICLR) (2015)
7. Guo, X., Jia, F., An, J., Han, Y.: Adversarial attack with KD-tree searching on training set. In: Peng, Y., Hu, S.-M., Gabbouj, M., Zhou, K., Elad, M., Xu, K. (eds.) ICIG 2021. LNCS, vol. 12889, pp. 132–142. Springer, Cham (2021). https://doi.org/10.1007/978-3-030-87358-5_11
8. He, K., Zhang, X., Ren, S., Sun, J.: Deep residual learning for image recognition. In: Proceedings of the IEEE/CVF Conference on Computer Vision and Pattern Recognition, pp. 770–778 (2016)
9. Ho, J., Jain, A., Abbeel, P.: Denoising diffusion probabilistic models. Adv. Neural. Inf. Process. Syst. **33**, 6840–6851 (2020)
10. Huang, G.B., Mattar, M., Berg, T., Learned-Miller, E.: Labeled faces in the wild: a database for studying face recognition in unconstrained environments. In: Workshop on Faces in 'Real-Life' Images: Detection, Alignment, and Recognition (2008)
11. Jang, D., Son, S., Kim, D.S.: Strengthening the transferability of adversarial examples using advanced looking ahead and self-CutMix. In: Proceedings of the IEEE/CVF Conference on Computer Vision and Pattern Recognition Workshops, pp. 148–155 (2022)
12. Karras, T., Aila, T., Laine, S., Lehtinen, J.: Progressive growing of GANs for improved quality, stability, and variation. arXiv preprint arXiv:1710.10196 (2017)
13. Meng, C., et al.: SDEdit: guided image synthesis and editing with stochastic differential equations. In: International Conference on Learning Representations (ICLR) (2022)
14. Schroff, F., Kalenichenko, D., Philbin, J.: FaceNet: a unified embedding for face recognition and clustering. In: Proceedings of the IEEE/CVF Conference on Computer Vision and Pattern Recognition, pp. 815–823 (2015)
15. Song, J., Meng, C., Ermon, S.: Denoising diffusion implicit models. In: International Conference on Learning Representations (ICLR) (2021)
16. Song, Y., Sohl-Dickstein, J., Kingma, D.P., Kumar, A., Ermon, S., Poole, B.: Score-based generative modeling through stochastic differential equations. In: International Conference on Learning Representations (ICLR) (2021)
17. Wang, H., et al.: CosFace: large margin cosine loss for deep face recognition. In: Proceedings of the IEEE/CVF Conference on Computer Vision and Pattern Recognition, pp. 5265–5274 (2018)
18. Wang, X., He, X., Wang, J., He, K.: Admix: enhancing the transferability of adversarial attacks. In: Proceedings of the IEEE/CVF International Conference on Computer Vision, pp. 16158–16167 (2021)
19. Wei, X., Guo, Y., Yu, J.: Adversarial sticker: a stealthy attack method in the physical world. IEEE Trans. Pattern Anal. Mach. Intell. **45**(3), 2711–2725 (2023)

20. Xie, C., et al.: Improving transferability of adversarial examples with input diversity. In: Proceedings of the IEEE/CVF Conference on Computer Vision and Pattern Recognition, pp. 2730–2739 (2019)
21. Yang, X., et al.: Towards face encryption by generating adversarial identity masks. In: Proceedings of the IEEE/CVF International Conference on Computer Vision, pp. 3897–3907 (2021)
22. Yin, B., et al.: Adv-Makeup: a new imperceptible and transferable attack on face recognition. In: Proceedings of the Thirtieth International Joint Conference on Artificial Intelligence (IJCAI), pp. 1252–1258 (2021)

TPM: Two-Stage Prediction Mechanism for Universal Adversarial Patch Defense

Huaize Dong, Yifan Jiao$^{(\boxtimes)}$, and Bing-Kun Bao

School of Telecommunications and Information Engineering,
Nanjing University of Posts and Telecommunications, Nanjing, China
`yifanjiao1227@gmail.com`

Abstract. Deep neural networks can be deceived by universal adversarial patches, which introduce adversarial noise within a local region. Universal adversarial patches can be effectively used in diverse conditions, which leads to exposing the vulnerability of computer vision systems and raise a significant safety concern. To solve this problem, we propose a Two-stage Prediction Mechanism (TPM) for universal adversarial patch defense, which consists of two main operations: (1) The Region Treatment locates the most highlighted region via a global adaptive threshold and substitutes it with a mask, thus yielding a masked image that can effectively eliminate the potential universal adversarial patch. (2) The Category Prediction first synthesizes alternative contents from the masked pixels by image inpainting, thus yielding an inpainted image. Based on the above, the final output category is predicted via the weighted combination of the output logits between the masked and inpainted images. Extensive experiments on two datasets demonstrate the effectiveness of the proposed TPM in defending against universal adversarial patches and further show superior performance on multishape attacks, adaptive and multi-target attacks.

Keywords: Adversarial defense · Universal adversarial patch attack · Image classification

1 Introduction

With the advances in Deep Neural Networks (DNN), DNN-based models have achieved remarkable success on all kinds of tasks in recent years. However, the emergence of adversarial attacks, which crafts the inputs with adversarial perturbations to drastically change the predicted results, seriously reduces the performance of the model in practical applications. Unlike other attacks, universal adversarial patch attacks [1,20] are usually placed on arbitrary input images and at arbitrary image locations to achieve a robust attack. Thus it improves the rate of effective attacks, making it one of the most effective and threatening ways to attack real-world computer vision systems [6,19].

To counter the threat, various methods have been proposed for adversarial patch defense [3–5,9,11,13,16–18,20,21]. For example, Naseer *et al.* [13] propose

Local Gradients Smoothing (LGS) that utilizes a fixed threshold to detect the potential adversarial features and smoothes them to eliminate their effect. Hayes *et al.* [9] propose Digital Watermark that uses fixed thresholds to scan the potential adversarial areas and mask them. Chou *et al.* [5] propose SentiNet which leverages the potential adversarial patch and benign samples to discriminate whether the input is an adversarial image. However, most existing methods are still relatively poor in locating or processing universal adversarial patches. Due to poor localization or process of potential universal adversarial patch areas, it is difficult to effectively suppress the aggressiveness of the universal adversarial patches and achieve better prediction performance.

(a)   (b)   (c)   (d)

Fig. 1. (a) is the benign image. (c) is the adversarial image. (b) and (d) illustrate the highlighted areas that can determine the final result of (a) and (c), respectively.

As described in [11], we can use the characteristics of universal adversarial patches to distinguish them from clean images and achieve effective localization. As shown in Fig. 1(a) and (b), the benign image is successfully predicted based on multiple highlighted areas contributing together, *i.e.,* areas such as the head and tail of the bird are important for the prediction. Multiple highlighted areas are relatively distributed in different parts and have different semantics, which together determines the final prediction result. As shown in Fig. 1(c) and (d), the adversarial image utilizes the most highlighted region to achieve attack target prediction. Because the universal adversarial patch is usually constrained in the local contiguous area where all pixels are utilized to suppress other areas' features and make itself the most highlighted region to determine the final attack target category. Based on this, we consider covering the most highlighted region of the input image with a mask [17] to eliminate the effect caused by the potential universal adversarial patch. Even if the input image is benign, removing a small number of clean image pixels does not affect the model prediction [16]. In order to further eliminate the loss of semantics from the masked region due to the pixel erasing, inpainting [22] is applied to synthesize the missing contents. Considering the complexity of the image content, image inpainting can recover some of the correct pixels. However, it can also be influenced by different areas of the image and introduce partially interfering pixel values, which are relatively some additional noise [4]. Therefore, we consider reducing the impact of noise in the context of using semantics. The fusion of masked and inpainted images can preserve the original semantics of the unmasked area. While the fusion of the masked area and the image inpainted area not only preserves part of the semantics restored but also makes the noise greatly reduced.

By considering the above issue, we propose a Two-stage Prediction Mechanism (TPM) for white-box universal adversarial patch defense. TPM is composed of two main operations, *i.e.*, Region Treatment and Category Prediction, to realize the prediction function. Given an input image, the Region Treatment is first designed to locate its most highlighted region according to a global adaptive threshold. Then, the selected region is substituted with a pre-defined mask to achieve effective suppression of potentially universal adversarial patches. Once obtaining the masked image, the Category Prediction uses image inpainting to synthesize the missing contents in the images. The goal is to restore the missing semantic contents of the pixels that are masked and attempt to reconstruct the "benign" image. After, the final predicted category can be obtained via the weighted combination of the output logits between the masked and inpainted images.

The main contributions of this paper can be summarized as follows:

(1) We propose a Two-stage Prediction Mechanism to eliminate the effect of white-box universal adversarial patches.
(2) We demonstrate that locating the most highlighted region via a global adaptive threshold and using the weighted combination of the output logits between the masked and inpainted images can achieve effective prediction.
(3) Extensive experiments on two datasets validate the plausibility of the proposed approach on universal adversarial patches and further show superior performance on multi-shape patches, adaptive and multi-target attacks.

2   Related Work

Most existing methods for adversarial patch defense can be roughly divided into pre-processing and in-processing, according to the stage at which they eliminate the impact of the adversarial patch.

Pre-processing Defense. [4,5,9,11,13,17,18] are pre-processing defenses that perform data pre-processing to suppress the impact of adversarial patches before it is fed into the DNN models. For example, Naseer *et al.* [13] propose LGS that performs a gradient normalization and a thresholding step to choose the potential adversarial features, while it chooses to smooth them. The defense performance of LGS will decrease when facing adversarial patches with stronger attack performance.

In-processing Defense. [3,16,20,21] are in-processing defenses that process the DNN model to improve the robustness against the adversarial patch. For instance, Xiang *et al.* [16] propose PatchGuard which requires a specially designed neural network with a small receptive field and uses the mask to remove the adversarial feature which means that it can't directly use the off-the-shelf convolutional neural network (CNN) models.

Our method is a pre-processing method. Unlike [9,13] which relies on a fixed threshold to detect adversarial features, [4] relies on average filtering to detect adversarial patches. Our method utilizes a global adaptive threshold and a sliding square to achieve effective locating. Besides, we achieve better performance by combining the masked and inpainted images than by predicting only on the masked image [13,16,17] which loses some pixels, or the inpainted image [4] which imports some additional noise.

3   Method

In this section, we briefly introduce the adversarial patch and detail the mechanisms of TPM for defending the white-box universal adversarial patch. Figure 2 is the overview of TPM, which consists of two main operations. The detail of each section is described in the following.

3.1   Formulation

Adversarial patch defense aims to design a robust mechanism for correctly classifying both benign and adversarial image datasets. Formally, the benign dataset is defined as $\mathcal{D}_b = \{(x_i^b, y_i^b)\}_{i=1}^{N_b}$, where x_i^b and y_i^b denote the i-th benign image and its corresponding category, respectively. The adversarial dataset is defined as $\mathcal{D}_a = \{(x_j^a, y_j^a)\}_{j=1}^{N_a}$, where x_j^a and y_j^a denote the j-th adversarial image and its corresponding benign category, respectively. Specifically, if x_j^a is generated by attaching an universal adversarial patch x_k^p from patch dataset $\mathcal{D}_p = \{x_k^p\}_{k=1}^{N_p}$ to x_i^b, x_j^a and x_i^b have the same benign category. Therefore, the adversarial image x_j^a can be formulated as follows:

$$x_j^a = (\mathbb{1} - M) \odot x_i^b + M \odot x_k^p, \tag{1}$$

where M is a mask whose region values are zero used to replace the original pixels with the adversarial patch, $\odot$ is element-wise multiplication.

For the universal adversarial patch x_k^p generation process [1], we assume a white-box attacker which can make the patch achieve successful attacks on arbitary images and locations to cause target misclassification.

Since the universal adversarial patch suppresses the feature of the benign image and leads to misprediction as described in the Sect. 1, the critical problem of adversarial patch defense is how to eliminate the effect caused by the adversarial patch. In this work, Region Treatment is applied to locate the most highlighted region via a global adaptive threshold and sliding square. Then the region is substituted with a pre-defined mask. Category Prediction is designed to predict the benign category of the input image. The proposed pipeline is detailed in Fig. 2. The defense overall algorithm is shown in Algorithm 1.

In what follows, we give a detailed description of the Region Treatment and Category Prediction.

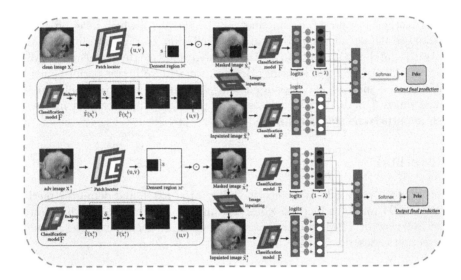

Fig. 2. The overview of our proposed TPM. In the Region Treatment, the patch locator is used to find the densest region of the image for the final prediction via a global adaptive threshold and sliding square. Based on the previous step, we use a pre-defined mask to remove the potential adversarial patch. In the Category Prediction, we use image inpainting to get the inpainted image. The final predicted category can be obtained via the weighted combination of the output logits between the masked and inpainted images. Different color circles in logits represent different categories.

3.2   Region Treatment

Given an input image x (benign image x_i^b or adversarial image x_j^a), we first use the classification model $F(\cdot)$ trained on benign dataset $\mathcal{D}_b$. The patch locator is used to locate the densest region and has several components that work together to achieve it. In the patch locator, the pixel attribution map $\hat{F}(x)$ [14] can be obtained by calculating the gradient information in Eq. (2).

$$\hat{F}(x) = \frac{1}{n} \sum_{1}^{n} \frac{\partial F\left(x + \mathcal{N}\left(0, \sigma^2\right)\right)}{\partial x}, \tag{2}$$

where n is the number of Gaussian noise $\mathcal{N}\left(0, \sigma^2\right)$ with standard deviation $\sigma = 0.1$. Specifically, multiple sets of Gaussian noise can smooth the gradient.

Once obtaining the pixel attribution map $\hat{F}(x)$, we use the global average pooling to generate an adaptive threshold δ as follows,

$$\delta = \frac{\sum_i^H \sum_j^W \hat{F}(x)_{ij}}{H \times W}, \tag{3}$$

where H and W are the height and width of input image x, respectively. According to threshold δ, $\hat{F}(x)$ is updated to $\tilde{F}(x)$ by Eq. (4) to generate a candidate coordinate set $Q = \{(i,j)|\tilde{F}(x)_{ij} > 0\}$.

$$\tilde{F}(x)_{ij} = \begin{cases} \hat{F}(x)_{ij}, \hat{F}(x)_{ij} \geq \delta \\ 0 \quad\quad, \hat{F}(x)_{ij} < \delta \end{cases}. \tag{4}$$

Algorithm 1. The TPM against the white-box universal adversarial patch

---

Input: x: test image; L: sliding square side length; S: mask side length; λ: the weight of combination; F: classification model
Output: c: the final predicted category
1: **function** REGION TREATMENT(x, L, F, S)
2:     $\hat{F}(x)$ = PixelAttributionMap(F(x))   // Eq. 2
3:     δ = AdaptiveThreshold($\hat{F}(x)$)   // Eq. 3
4:     $\tilde{F}(x)$ = CandidateRegion($\hat{F}(x), \delta$)   // Eq. 4
5:     //get the candidate region coordinate set
6:     $Q = \left\{(i,j) \mid \tilde{F}(x)_{ij} > 0\right\}$
7:     //locate the densest region
8:     (u,v) = DensestRegionLoc($Q, L, \hat{F}(x)$) // Eq. 5
9:     $\hat{x}$ = Mask($x, S, (u,v)$) // get the masked image
10: **end function**
11: **function** CATEGORY PREDICTION($\hat{x}$, S, F, (u,v), λ)
12:     $\tilde{x}$ = ImageInpainting($\hat{x}, S, (u,v)$) // get the inpainted image
13:     // predict the final category
14:     c = LogitsWeightedCombin($F(\hat{x}), F(\tilde{x}), \lambda$) // Eq. 7
15:     return c
16: **end function**

After that, we search for the densest region with a sliding square whose center coordinate and side length are $(i,j) \in Q$ and hyperparameter L, respectively. Then, the center coordinate (u,v) of the densest region can be obtained by Eq. (5).

$$(u,v) = \underset{(u,v)\in Q}{\arg\max} \frac{\sum_{i=-\frac{L}{2}}^{\frac{L}{2}} \sum_{j=-\frac{L}{2}}^{\frac{L}{2}} \hat{F}(x)_{u+i\ v+j}}{L \times L}, \tag{5}$$

where $\hat{F}(x)_{u+i\ v+j} = 0$ when $u+i < 0$ or $u+i > H$ or $v+j < 0$ or $v+j > W$.

According to the obtained coordinate (u,v) along with a mask side length S, the most highlighted region of the input image is substituted by a mask $\mathbf{M}'$ to generate the masked image $\hat{x} = \mathbf{M}' \odot x$ for eliminating the effect of the potential adversarial patch.

$$\mathbf{M}'_{ij} = \begin{cases} 0, (i,j) \in \{(i,j)|u - \frac{S}{2} \leq i \leq u + \frac{S}{2}, v - \frac{S}{2} \leq j \leq v + \frac{S}{2}\} \\ 1, otherwise \end{cases}. \tag{6}$$

3.3   Category Prediction

In order to further eliminate the loss of semantics from the masked region due to the pixel erasing, image inpainting [22] is applied to synthesize the missing contents from $\hat{x}$ to generate inpainted image $\tilde{x}$. Since only a part of the pixel value is lost, most of the pixels remain in the image and these pixels can be used to try to reconstruct a "benign" image.

   Considering that inpainting maybe introduce additional noise, we only use part semantics of the inpainted region and the full of the other regions. It can be regarded as the weighted combination of the output logits between the inpainted image $\tilde{x}$ and masked image $\hat{x}$. Therefore, the final predicted category c can be formulated in Eq. (7).

$$c = \lambda \cdot F(\tilde{x}) + (1 - \lambda) \cdot F(\hat{x}), \tag{7}$$

where λ is the weight coefficient which will be discussed in Sect. 4.3 in detail.

4   Experiment

In this section, we evaluate the performance of TPM in defending against the white-box universal adversarial patch. First, TPM is tested in ImageNet and ImageNette datasets and compared with several baseline defense methods. Then, we further conduct the ablation study to evaluate its performance. The experiment results are shown below.

4.1   Experimental Setup

Datasets. We conduct our experiments on ImageNet and ImageNette. ImageNet [7] is a 1000 classes dataset and its validation set has 50,000 images. We randomly choose 10,000 images from its validation set for evaluation. ImageNette is a 10-class subset of ImageNet with 9469 training images and 3925 validation images. All the images are resized to 224 × 224.

Model. On the ImageNet and ImageNette, we adopt ResNet50-v2 [10] as the backbone of the classification model. We initialize the classification model with weights pre-trained on the ImageNet. For the ImageNette, we use a strategy of [8] to retrain weight. We combine [14] and [10] as the main component of the patch locator.

Adversarial Patches. For the adversarial patch generation process, we consider generating 4%–8% size square patches that have achieved high attack success rates and allowed for universal attacks [1]. We also generate rectangle patches and different target patches for experiments.

Defense. We set the sliding square side length L as 50 and mask side length S as 60. We set λ as 0.2 for the ImageNet and 0.1 for the ImageNette. We evaluate the prediction about benign and adversarial images with benign accuracy and robust accuracy, respectively [18]. The above accuracies are equivalent to the top1 accuracy. We use 2 NVIDIA Tesla V100 GPUs and NVIDIA TITAN V GPUs to support the running of the code.

Baseline Defense. We compare with LGS [13], Jujutsu [4], PatchCleanser [17] and PatchGuard [16]. We empirically evaluate the robustness under the same attack settings.

Table 1. Benign and robust accuracy (%) on the ImageNette and ImageNet datasets. 4%–8% denotes the universal adversarial patch size.

Dataset	ImageNette							ImageNet						
Accuracy	clean	4%	5%	6%	7%	8%	Avg.	clean	4%	5%	6%	7%	8%	Avg.
Undefended	99.64	32.89	20.15	14.55	12.46	12.02	18.41	80.34	5.34	0.78	0.59	0.28	0.19	1.44
PatchCleanser [17]	**98.73**	96.33	95.80	95.03	94.62	93.45	95.05	79.13	61.18	58.64	57.36	55.97	54.24	57.48
PatchGuard [16]	91.92	91.46	91.18	90.80	90.52	89.96	90.78	42.78	36.26	35.12	34.27	32.69	31.92	34.05
Jujutsu [4]	96.05	94.39	94.44	94.14	94.37	94.29	94.33	**79.76**	75.11	77.04	76.31	76.57	76.89	76.38
LGS [13]	98.65	**96.64**	96.43	95.72	93.43	92.23	94.89	75.87	77.31	76.81	76.21	75.67	74.99	76.20
TPM	97.88	95.75	**97.17**	**98.65**	**98.27**	**98.14**	**97.60**	73.84	**78.30**	**79.11**	**77.92**	**77.88**	**77.78**	**78.20**

4.2 Defense Performance

To validate our performance, we compare the defense effect of TPM with several existing methods on two datasets, *i.e.,* ImageNet and ImageNette. Table 1 summarizes the comparisons between the TPM and several existing methods under the 4%–8% size square patches. From Table 1, the undefended represents that the universal adversarial patch can seriously affect the normal performance of the vanilla model. For the maximum variation in robust accuracy between 4% and 8% patches on the ImageNet dataset, PatchCleanser, PatchGuard, Jujutsu, and LGS vary by about 7.0%, 4.0%, 2.0%, and 2.5%, respectively. TPM has a variety of less than 1.5%. On the small dataset of ImageNette, PatchCleanser, PatchGuard, Jujutsu, and LGS vary by about 3.0%, 1.5%, 0.5%, and 4.5%, respectively. TPM has about a 3.0% accuracy variation. TPM achieves well stability on the two datasets. The advantage will be more obvious as the size of the adversarial patch increases. The L and S are useful for the different patch sizes. However, since the performance of adversarial patches differs at different sizes and the randomness of placement in the image position, the defense effects of the different patch sizes are slightly different. Due to PatchGuard need to specifically design the neural network, we directly use the ResNet50 designed by the authors. For Jujutsu on the ImageNette dataset, the classification model provided by the author can achieve better performance in the two-stage defense. So we use the model provided by the author, while our method still performs better using the same model.

As shown in Table 1, it also shows that TPM achieves an overall better performance and a better statistical average performance on both datasets. An acceptable benign accuracy is also achieved for benign images. The above experiments demonstrate that our method can effectively defend against universal adversarial patch attacks and outperforms current methods.

4.3   Ablation Study

Table 2. Robust accuracy (%) for different classification models about the output logits weighted combination on the ImageNet.

	Accuracy	4%	5%	6%	7%	8%	Avg.
ResNet50-v2	$\hat{x}$	78.19	79.01	77.80	77.86	77.69	78.11
	$\tilde{x}$	77.24	78.15	76.53	76.44	76.38	76.95
	$\tilde{x} + \hat{x}$	**78.30**	**79.11**	**77.92**	**77.88**	**77.78**	**78.20**
ResNet50	$\hat{x}$	66.53	66.60	65.91	65.50	64.39	65.79
	$\tilde{x}$	69.22	69.55	68.57	68.47	67.66	68.69
	$\tilde{x} + \hat{x}$	**69.61**	**69.93**	**68.95**	**68.84**	**68.04**	**69.07**
InceptionV3	$\hat{x}$	53.87	54.42	56.02	55.71	55.67	55.14
	$\tilde{x}$	57.64	58.34	59.27	59.13	59.02	58.68
	$\tilde{x} + \hat{x}$	**58.12**	**59.05**	**60.00**	**59.92**	**59.86**	**59.39**

Table 3. Robust accuracy (%) for different patch shapes and targets on the ImageNet. -1 and -3 represent target numbers.

	4%	5%	6%	7%	8%	Avg.
square-1	76.60	77.74	77.70	77.57	77.33	77.39
square-3	77.03	78.75	78.78	78.47	78.09	78.22
rectangle-1	74.95	77.10	75.80	75.15	74.45	75.49
rectangle-3	76.23	77.13	76.48	74.67	73.82	75.67

Combination of the Masked and Inpainted Images. We first verify the effectiveness of the weighted combination of the output logits between the masked and inpainted images. Besides, we extend it to other classification models to further verify the generality of the method. We choose 4%–8% square patches on the ImageNet dataset for evaluation. We choose three classification models with different performances to test their robust accuracy for the masked image $\hat{x}$, the inpainted image $\tilde{x}$, and the weighted combined images $\hat{x} + \tilde{x}$. We set λ as 0.8 on the ResNet50 and InceptionV3. Besides, we set L as 70 and S as 70. As shown in Table 2, the performance of the masked and inpainted images is inconsistent for different classification models. However, the weighted combination of the output logits between the masked and inpainted images can yield a better result than the performance of the masked or inpainted image. Since the purpose of combining the two images is to preserve the partially restored semantics while reducing the impact of the noise introduced by the image inpainting. The performance of the three classification models also shows that the method is generalized and can be applied to other classification models. Performance can be further improved with more advanced inpainting models [12,15].

Different Patch Shapes and Targets. To further evaluate the generality of the proposed TPM, we evaluate it against rectangle adversarial patches and different targets on the ImageNet dataset. We evaluate the performance of adversarial patches within the 4%–8% sizes. We set the L as 70 and S as 80. As shown in Table 3, TPM achieves average robust accuracy above 77% and 75% for square and rectangle adversarial patches, respectively. We randomly select three attack targets for square and rectangle adversarial patches, and the average performance of the three targets in Table 3 demonstrates that TPM maintains robust performance for different attack targets. Our method is effective for different patch shapes and attack targets.

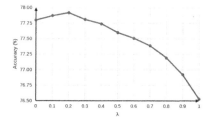

Fig. 3. Robust accuracy varies with different λ on the ImageNet.

Effect of the λ on Prediction. We analyze the effect of the λ on the final prediction and summarize the detailed results in Fig. 3. We choose a 6% adversarial patch on the ImageNet to verify it. As shown in Fig. 3, it can achieve effective performance boosts when λ is approximately 0.2. The reason is that ResNet50-v2 is more sensitive to the noise introduced than the semantics recovered by image inpainting. Thus the influence of noise is greatly reduced while considering the semantics of the restoration. By giving a smaller λ to the inpainted image, it is equivalent to using only a small fraction of the semantics on its inpainted region. So appropriate λ to the model which has a different sensitivity to the noise is important.

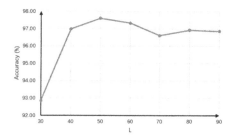

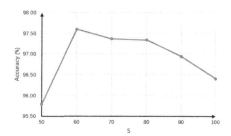

Fig. 4. Robust accuracy varies with different L on the ImageNette.

Fig. 5. Robust accuracy varies with different S on the ImageNette.

Effect of the L and S on Prediction. We analyze the sliding square side length L and mask side length S to the effect of the final prediction. Since the ImageNette dataset is more sensitive to the L and S, we choose it to evaluate. We utilize different L and S to evaluate their average performance on all size patches, respectively. As shown in Fig. 4, L is set 50 that can achieve the best performance. In the Fig. 5, S is set 60 can achieve the best performance. Besides, other sizes also achieve good performance.

Adaptive Attack. The above analysis demonstrated the effectiveness of TPM in defending against white-box adversarial patch attacks. We further evaluate an adaptive attack [2,4,5] that has knowledge about TPM. It can attempt to create an adversarial patch that fools TPM.

TPM relies on the Region Treatment's patch locator to locate the potential adversarial patch. An adaptive attacker may try to reduce the feature salience of the adversarial patch to evade our region's localization. Therefore, we add restriction to the optimization process of the adversarial patch target attack so that the salience of the adversarial patch $(\hat{F}^* (x_j^a))$ is closed to 0 $(\hat{F}_0^*)$ to make it possible to be undetected while the attack succeeds. For a 6% adversarial patch on the ImageNet, its attack success rate drops significantly from 99.05% to 7.36% after adding the above restrictions. Experiments demonstrate that the two optimization tasks of attack success and evasion localization are contradictory to each other. It shows that TPM can effectively inhibit adaptive attacks.

5 Conclusion

In this paper, we propose a Two-stage Prediction Mechanism called TPM for white-box universal adversarial patch defense. TPM uses Region Treatment to remove the potential adversarial patches and Category Prediction to achieve effective prediction. Extensive experiments validate TPM's effect against universal patch attacks. Besides, it can further defend different patch shapes and attack targets, and even adaptive attacks.

Acknowledgements. This work was supported by National Key Research and Development Project (No. 2020AAA0106200), the National Nature Science Foundation of China under Grants (No. 61936005, 61872424), and the Natural Science Foundation of Jiangsu Province (Grants No. BK20200037).

References

1. Brown, T.B., Mané, D., Roy, A., Abadi, M., Gilmer, J.: Adversarial patch. arXiv preprint arXiv:1712.09665 (2017)
2. Carlini, N., et al.: On evaluating adversarial robustness. arXiv preprint arXiv:1902.06705 (2019)
3. Chen, Z., Li, B., Xu, J., Wu, S., Ding, S., Zhang, W.: Towards practical certifiable patch defense with vision transformer. In: CVPR, pp. 15148–15158 (2022)
4. Chen, Z., Dash, P., Pattabiraman, K.: Turning your strength against you: detecting and mitigating robust and universal adversarial patch attack. arXiv preprint arXiv:2108.05075 (2021)
5. Chou, E., Tramer, F., Pellegrino, G.: SentiNet: detecting localized universal attacks against deep learning systems. In: SPW, pp. 48–54. IEEE (2020)
6. Co, K.T., Muñoz-González, L., Kanthan, L., Lupu, E.C.: Real-time detection of practical universal adversarial perturbations. arXiv preprint arXiv:2105.07334 (2021)
7. Deng, J., Dong, W., Socher, R., Li, L.J., Li, K., Fei-Fei, L.: ImageNet: a large-scale hierarchical image database. In: CVPR, pp. 248–255 (2009)

8. DeVries, T., Taylor, G.W.: Improved regularization of convolutional neural networks with cutout. arXiv preprint arXiv:1708.04552 (2017)
9. Hayes, J.: On visible adversarial perturbations & digital watermarking. In: CVPR Workshops, pp. 1597–1604 (2018)
10. He, K., Zhang, X., Ren, S., Sun, J.: Deep residual learning for image recognition. In: CVPR, pp. 770–778 (2016)
11. Li, F., Liu, X., Zhang, X., Li, Q., Sun, K., Li, K.: Detecting localized adversarial examples: a generic approach using critical region analysis. In: IEEE INFOCOM, pp. 1–10 (2021)
12. Lugmayr, A., Danelljan, M., Romero, A., Yu, F., Timofte, R., Van Gool, L.: RePaint: inpainting using denoising diffusion probabilistic models. In: CVPR, pp. 11461–11471 (2022)
13. Naseer, M., Khan, S., Porikli, F.: Local gradients smoothing: Defense against localized adversarial attacks. In: WACV, pp. 1300–1307 (2019)
14. Smilkov, D., Thorat, N., Kim, B., Viégas, F., Wattenberg, M.: SmoothGrad: removing noise by adding noise. arXiv preprint arXiv:1706.03825 (2017)
15. Suvorov, R., et al.: Resolution-robust large mask inpainting with Fourier convolutions. In: CVPR, pp. 2149–2159 (2022)
16. Xiang, C., Bhagoji, A.N., Sehwag, V., Mittal, P.: {PatchGuard}: a provably robust defense against adversarial patches via small receptive fields and masking. In: USENIX Security Symposium, pp. 2237–2254 (2021)
17. Xiang, C., Mahloujifar, S., Mittal, P.: {PatchCleanser}: certifiably robust defense against adversarial patches for any image classifier. In: USENIX Security Symposium, pp. 2065–2082 (2022)
18. Xu, K., Xiao, Y., Zheng, Z., Cai, K., Nevatia, R.: PatchZero: defending against adversarial patch attacks by detecting and zeroing the patch. arXiv preprint arXiv:2207.01795 (2022)
19. Yang, X., Wei, F., Zhang, H., Zhu, J.: Design and interpretation of universal adversarial patches in face detection. In: Vedaldi, A., Bischof, H., Brox, T., Frahm, J.-M. (eds.) ECCV 2020. LNCS, vol. 12362, pp. 174–191. Springer, Cham (2020). https://doi.org/10.1007/978-3-030-58520-4_11
20. Yu, C., et al.: Defending against universal adversarial patches by clipping feature norms. In: ICCV, pp. 16434–16442 (2021)
21. Zhang, Z., Yuan, B., McCoyd, M., Wagner, D.: Clipped BagNet: defending against sticker attacks with clipped bag-of-features. In: SPW, pp. 55–61. IEEE (2020)
22. Zheng, C., Cham, T.J., Cai, J.: Pluralistic image completion. In: CVPR, pp. 1438–1447 (2019)

Surveillance and Remote Sensing

WSAD-Net: Weakly Supervised Anomaly Detection in Untrimmed Surveillance Videos

Peng Wu and Yanning Zhang[✉]

School of Computer Science, Northwestern Polytechnical University, Xi'an, China
ynzhang@nwpu.edu.cn

Abstract. Weakly supervised anomaly detection (WSAD) is a newfangled and challenging task, the goal of which is to detect anomalous activities in untrimmed surveillance videos with no requirement of temporal localization annotations. A few methods have been proposed to detect anomalies under the weakly supervised setting. In order to combat the issue even further, we present a weakly supervised anomaly detector network (WSAD-Net), which is composed of a pre-trained feature extractor and an anomaly-specific subnetwork. To learn the anomaly-specific parameters of WSAD-Net, we design a Classification Loss based on the multiple instance learning (MIL) and two novel losses, namely, Compactness Loss and Magnetism Loss, which play an important role in evaluating the correlation of features. During the test phase, we introduce the Anomaly-specific Temporal Class Activation Sequence (Ano-TCAS) to generate the anomaly score. We evaluate WSAD-Net on two benchmarks, i.e., the UCF-Crime and Live-Videos datasets, and experiments on these two benchmarks show that WSAD-Net outperforms or competes with current state-of-the-art methods.

Keywords: Video Anomaly Detection · Weak Supervision · Untrimmed Surveillance Video · Temporal Class Activation Sequence

1 Introduction

Anomaly detection in videos refers to the task of automatically detecting the anomalous activities, which has received widespread attention along with the rapid increase of online videos and surveillance videos. Owing to the rare occurrence of anomalous events, previous research works [2–6, 14–18] put more focus on the one-class classification, the key of which is to build a normality model using only normal videos. Abnormality can be detected as those activities that obviously deviate from this normality model. However, there are some potential drawbacks in the above mode. First, due to the limited datasets (from several minutes to one hour), overfitting is more likely to happen when the model is enormous. Second, it is difficult or infeasible to build a normality model that takes all possible normal patterns into account.

This work is supported in part by the National Natural Science Foundation of China (NFSC) (No. U19B2037).

To alleviate the aforementioned problems, recently, Sultani *et al.* [1] collected a large-scale dataset by means of Internet, termed as UCF-Crime, which consists of 1900 untrimmed videos with total duration of 128 h. This dataset is very challenging for three reasons: 1) *Untrimmed videos.* The duration of videos ranges from seconds to hours; 2) *Weak labels.* Only video-level labels are provided during the training phase, since frame-wise annotations are expensive and time-consuming, and the boundary between normal and anomalous activities is often ambiguous; 3) *High variance within anomalies.* Unlike prior datasets [16, 17, 20] that regard unseen cars, bikers, throwing papers or some analogous actions as anomalous events, the UCF-Crime dataset covers 13 kinds of real-world anomalies, such as shooting, vandalism and road accidents. Based on this dataset, Sultani *et al.* [1] proposed a multiple instance learning (MIL) based deep ranking network for weakly supervised anomaly detection (WSAD), and obtained the state-of-the-art performance. However, coarse temporal processing of the method in [1] may result in reduced detection granularity. In addition, the method in [1] ignores the correlation of features.

In this paper, we propose a weakly supervised anomaly detector network (WSAD-Net) to automatically detect anomalies with no requirement of frame-wise annotations. The overview of WSAD-Net is shown in Fig. 1. A long untrimmed video is first decomposed into short video clips and clip-level visual features are extracted. All features within the same video are concatenated and pass through Fusion Module to obtain the fusion feature map. Then the feature map is fed into Classifier to generate the anomaly activation. To learn anomaly-specific parameters of WSAD-Net, we first introduce a Classification Loss based on MIL, and further design the Compact Loss and Magnetism Loss to complement Classification Loss. Specifically, it is hard or impossible to build a model to completely cover all anomalous activities due to high variance within anomalies and weak video-level labels. Conversely, there are reasonable grounds to believe that the normal activities or background are supposed to be compact in the feature space and generate lower anomaly confidence. This motivation inspires us to introduce the Compactness Loss to make the feature of normal activities and background be compact, and the Magnetism Loss aims at attracting the features with low anomaly confidence and repelling features with high anomaly confidence in anomalous videos. However, as temporal frame-wise annotations are unknown in training videos, we employ the Anomaly-specific Temporal Class Activation Sequence (Ano-TCAS) to obtain the anomaly score as proxy anomaly confidence.

In summary, our contributions are three-fold:

(1) A principled network called WSAD-Net is proposed, which is the seamless connection between a pre-trained feature extractor and an anomaly-specific subnetwork, for weakly supervised anomaly detection in untrimmed surveillance videos.

(2) The Classification Loss is introduced based on MIL, and the novel Compact Loss and Magnetism Loss are designed to encourage WSAD-Net to better distinguish normal and anomalous activities in the feature space.

(3) Extensive experiments on two challenging benchmarks, i.e., UCF-Crime and Live-Videos, show the superiority of WSAD-Net.

2 Related Work

Anomaly detection [25] in videos is challenging and nontrivial, which can be applied to surveillance, as well as online videos. As mentioned, previous research works [2–6, 14–18] focus on constructing normality models. For example, Cong et al. [15] introduced sparse reconstruction costs over the normal dictionary to measure the regularity of testing samples based on multi-scale histogram of optical flow (MHOF). Mahadevan et al. [20] fitted a Gaussian mixture model to mixture of dynamic textures (MDT). Kartz et al. [14] presented an HMM-based method to detect anomalies using 3D Gaussian distributions of spatiotemporal gradients. The above methods use hand-crafted features that may be not able to handle complex scenes due to their limited representativeness. In the past few years, deep learning has achieved remarkable success in several areas. Appearance-motion-deepNet [18] is the first attempt to use deep learning for anomaly detection, the core of which is to learn features using fully connected autoencoder and utilize one-class SVM to generate anomaly scores. Hasan et al. [6] proposed a fully-convolutional autoencoder to learn the spatiotemporal regularity. In addition, Liu et al. [3] presented a future frame prediction framework that took historical consecutive frames as the input, and predicted the future frame, then used prediction errors to detect abnormal behaviors. Some other works [4, 26] employed the deep auto-encoder to reconstruct normal videos with the help of prototype or memory networks.

Unlike the above methods, WSAD-Net is used for weakly supervised anomaly detection [1, 7, 24, 27, 28] in untrimmed surveillance videos, which devotes oneself to detect anomalies of the real and complex scenario and endeavors to meet the demands of practical applications.

3 WSAD-Net

In this section, we present WSAD-Net for weakly supervised anomaly detection in detail, whose framework is shown in Fig. 1. Consider that we have a training set of n videos $V = \{v_i\}_{i=1}^N$ and the corresponding label set $Y = \{y_i\}_{i=1}^N$, where $y_i \in \{0,1\}$, $y_i = 1$ denotes v_i covers anomalous activities.

3.1 Feature Extractor and Video Sampling

In this paper, we leverage the I3D network [19] pre-trained on the Kinetics dataset as the feature extractor, due to its remarkable performance in activity recognition. Note that, we just use it as the feature extractor without any fine-tuning on our target datasets. Given a video v_i, we first compute the optical flow field f_i using TV-L1 [11], and then divide v_i and f_i into 16-frames clips without overlapping. Finally put these clips into RGB and Optical Flow streams of I3D to extract features individually. We use $\mathbf{X}_i^r$ and $\mathbf{X}_i^o$ to denote the RGB and optical flow features, respectively, both of which are of shape $1024 \times T_i$. Further, we concatenate the RGB and optical flow features as the spatiotemporal feature map of shape $2048 \times T_i$. In this paper, we use T_i to denote the length of v_i.

As mentioned previously, untrimmed videos have large variance in length, from a few seconds to several hours. We use a simple but effective sampling to meet GPU

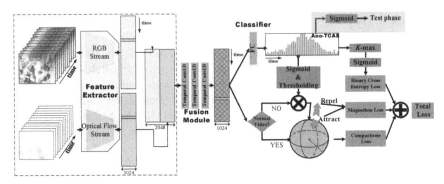

Fig. 1. The framework of WSAD-Net. Given an untrimmed video and the corresponding optical flow, (1) we extract RGB and optical flow features using the pre-trained I3D network; (2) concatenate two modalities and put these into Fusion Module to generate fusion feature maps; (3) one branch: put fusion features into Classifier to generate the Anomaly-specific Temporal Class Activation Sequence (Ano-TCAS) and compute Classification Loss; another branch: use fusion features and Ano-TCAS to compute Compactness Loss and Magnetism Loss; (4) during the test phase, detect anomalies using Ano-TCAS.

memory constraints. Consider a video v_i, we process the entire video if its length T_i is less than the pre-defined length T. However, if the length T_i is greater than T, we uniformly extract from it a segment of length T to represent the whole video.

3.2 Network Architecture

Fusion Model. Given a video v_i, its feature map passes through Fusion Module, which consists of three temporal 1-dimensional (1D) convolution layers in a cascade form. Each temporal convolutional layer has 1024 filters, the first two of which have kernel size 1 in time with stride 1, and are followed by ReLU. The third layer has kernel size 3 in time with padding and stride 1 to aggregate more information over the temporal dimension. We apply Dropout to all temporal convolutional layers. Since anomaly detection in surveillance videos, as an online detection task [8], should timely detect anomalies without delay, we employ the causal convolution that only uses the previous information as the third layer. The output of Fusion Module is the fusion feature map Xi, and the shape of X_i is $1024 \times T_i$.

Classifier. Classifier is a FC layer of 1 node without the bias. The anomaly activation can be represented as follows,

$$A_i = WX_i \tag{1}$$

where the shape of W and A_i are 1×1024 and $1 \times T_i$, respectively, and the anomaly activation represents the abnormality possibility of video clips at each of the temporal instants. In the following section, this activation is used to derive the class activation sequence and compute different loss functions.

3.3 Ano-TCAS

Class activation mapping [23] is an ingenious way to localize the discriminative regions. Similarly, we also derive a 1-dimensional Anomaly-specific Temporal Class Activation Sequence (Ano-TCAS). We denote W^k as the kth element of the weight vector W in Classifier. Given a video v_i, the value of Ano-TCAS at time t can be represented as,

$$A_i^t = \sum_{k=1}^{1024} W^k X_i[k, t] \tag{2}$$

It reveals that $\mathbf{A}_i = \left[A_i^1, A_i^2, ..., A_i^t, ..., A_i^{T_i}\right]$ is the Ano-TCAS, which presents the anomaly-specific information. In addition, we use S_i to denote the anomaly score, which is represented as $sigmoid(\mathbf{A}_i)$.

3.4 Loss Function

In this subsection, we introduce three loss functions in detail, i.e., Classification Loss, Compactness Loss and Magnetism Loss. We vividly illustrate them in Fig. 2.

Classification Loss. Following the principles of MIL [1], we compute the prediction label p_i using the average of K-max activation over the temporal dimension rather than the whole activation. Formally, the predicted label can be represented as follows,

$$p_i = \text{sigmoid}\left(\frac{1}{K_i} \max_{A_i^j \subset M_{Topk}} \sum_j^{K_i} A_i^j\right) \tag{3}$$

where M_{Topk} is the K-max activation, and K_i is defined as T_i/s. The instances corresponding to the K-max activation in the positive bag is most likely to be true positive instances (anomalous). The instances corresponding to the K-max activation in the negative bag is hard instances. We expect these two types of instances to be as far as possible.

Finally, the Classification Loss $\mathcal{L}_{BCE}$ is the binary cross-entropy between the predicted label p_i and ground truth y_i, which is shown as follows,

$$\mathcal{L}_{BCE} = \sum_{i=1}^{N} -y_i \log(p_i) - (1 - y_i) \log(1 - p_i) \tag{4}$$

Compactness Loss. Inspired by prior works [5, 13], for anomaly detection and novelty detection that design compact one-class models to isolate outliers, in this work, the Compactness Loss drives normal video clips to be compact in the feature space and generate small anomaly scores. Based on the above viewpoints, the Compactness Loss is designed as,

$$\mathcal{L}_{COM} = \sum_{i=1}^{N} \mathbb{I}(|y_i - 1|) \sum_{j=1}^{T_i} \|\mathbf{X}_i[:, j] - \mathbf{C}\|_2^2 \tag{5}$$

$$\mathbf{C} = \frac{1}{N_C} \sum_{i=1}^{N} \mathbb{I}(|y_i - 1|) \min_{A_i^j \subset M_{Bottomk}} \sum_{j=1}^{K_i} \|\mathbf{X}_i[:, j]\|_2^2 \tag{6}$$

where C is the center of normal features with the smallest anomaly activations, $M_{Bottomk}$ is the K-min activation, and $N_C = |M_{Bottomk}|$.

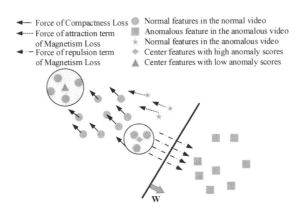

Fig. 2. The illustration of the loss functions (Color figure online)

Magnetism Loss. The goal of Classifier is to effectively discriminate normal and anomalous features. Ideally, we may want the following properties in the learned feature representations X_i. 1) Feature representation of the portion where anomaly occurs in anomalous videos should be different from that of normal videos. 2) Feature representation of normal segments in anomalous videos should be similar (or close) to that of normal videos. We all know the law of magnets: like poles repel; unlike poles attract. Drawing inspiration from this law, we design a novel Magnetism Loss to make features that are most likely to be anomalous be far away from normal features, and make features that are least likely to be anomalous be close to normal features. Following the recent work [9], we use the anomaly score S_i to identify the anomalous portions, since we do not have frame-wise annotations.

First, the repulsion term is defined as follows,

$$\mathcal{L}_{REP} = \frac{1}{N_h} \sum_{i=1}^{N} \mathbb{I}(y_i) \sum_{j=1}^{T_i} \mathbb{I}(S_i^j \geq \tau_h) \max\left(0, \delta^2 - \|\mathbf{X}_i[:,j] - \mathbf{C}_h\|_2^2\right) \quad (7)$$

$$\mathbf{C}_h = \frac{1}{N_{Ch}} \sum_{i=1}^{N} \mathbb{I}(|y_i - 1|) \max_{A_i^j \subset M_{Topk}} \sum_{j=1}^{K_i} \|\mathbf{X}_i[:,j]\|_2^2 \quad (8)$$

where $\mathbf{C}_h$ is the center of normal features but with the highest anomaly activation, M_{Topk} is the K-max activation, and $N_{Ch} = |M_{Topk}|$. τ_h is a predefined threshold, and only features with anomaly scores greater than τ_h are taken into account (N_h is the number of these features). The repulsion term is the hinge loss with a margin parameter of δ.

Then the attraction term is defined as follows,

$$\mathcal{L}_{ATT} = \frac{1}{N_l} \sum_{i=1}^{N} \mathbb{I}(y_i) \sum_{j=1}^{T_i} \mathbb{I}(S_i^j \leq \tau_l) \|\mathbf{X}_i[:,j] - \mathbf{C}\|_2^2 \quad (9)$$

Similarly, τ_l is a predefined threshold, and we only take the features with anomaly score less than τ_l into account (N_l is the number of these features). Finally, we combine the repulsion and attraction terms to form Magnetism Loss, which is represented as,

$$\mathcal{L}_{MAG} = \mathcal{L}_{REP} + \mathcal{L}_{ATT} \quad (10)$$

3.5 Optimization

We add up all the above loss functions to form the total loss function, which is presented as,

$$L_{TOTAL} = L_{BCE} + \alpha L_{COM} + \beta L_{MAG} \qquad (11)$$

We set α and β to 0.0005 to guarantee different loss functions are in the same magnitude, and employ Adam [10] to optimize $\mathcal{L}_{TOTAL}$ with a batch size of 64. For inference, we use the anomaly score S to detect anomalies during the test phase.

4 Experiments

4.1 Datasets and Evaluation Metric

Datasets. *UCF-Crime* dataset [1] is a large-scale dataset that consists of 1610 training videos and 290 test videos. Anomalous videos cover 13 kinds of real-world anomalies, including abuse, arrest, arson, assault, accident, burglary, explosion, fighting, robbery, shooting, stealing, shoplifting, and vandalism. For training videos, only video-level labels are provided. *Live-Videos* (LV) dataset [17] contains 28 realistic sequences. Anomalous events last from a couple of frames to thousands of frames, which includes cars in the wrong-way, crash, fighting, illegal turn, kidnapping, loitering, murder, panic, people clashing, people falling, robbery, trespassing and vandalism.

Evaluation Metric. Following previous works on anomaly detection [1–6], we use frame-level area under the curve (AUC) of receiver operating characteristic (ROC) as the evaluation metric.

4.2 Implementation Details

We train WSAD-Net on the NVIDIA GTX 1080Ti GPU using PyTorch. For the feature extractor, we employ the I3D network that is trained on the Kinetics dataset to extract features from the *global-average-pool* layer. We do not fine-tune the feature extractor. In addition, we train WSAD-Net with an initial learning rate of 0.00003, which is divided by 2 for every 10 epochs. We set τ_h, τ_l, s and δ to 0.9, 0.1, 16, 50, respectively.

4.3 Results

Results on the UCF-Crime Dataset. We compare WSAD-Net with four state-of-the-art methods for anomaly detection. The AUC result is illustrated in Table 1. As we can see from Table 1, WSAD-Net outperforms other state-of-the-art methods by a large margin, which improves the AUC over the classical method in [1] from 75.41% to 83.15%. We also implement the method in [1] using I3D features rather than C3D [12] features used in 1, and obtain the AUC of 80.87%, which is inferior to that of WSAD-Net by approximately 2.3%, which significantly convinces that WSAD-Net performs significantly better than the method in [1] on the UCF-Crime dataset even employing the same features.

Table 1. The AUC comparison on the UCF-Crime dataset.

Method		AUC (%)
Semi-Supervison	Binary classifier	50.00
	Hasan et al. [6]	50.60
	Lu et al. [16]	65.51
Weak Supervison	Sultani et al.[1]	75.41
	Sultani et al. [1]	80.87
	GCN [24]	82.12
	Wu et al. [7]	82.44
	WSAD-Net	**83.15**

Table 2. The AUC comparison on the Live-Videos dataset.

Method		AUC (%)
w / Training	Gunale et al. [22]	39.75
	Lu et al. [16]	49.56
	Biswas et al. [21]	55.58
	Leyva et al. [17]	61.79
wo / Training	WSAD-Net	55.91

Table 3. The AUC of WSAD-Net with different loss functions on the UCF-Crime dataset.

$\mathcal{L}_{BCE}$	$\mathcal{L}_{COM}$	$\mathcal{L}_{MAG}$	AUC (%)
✓	×	×	82.06
✓	✓	✓	83.15

Results on the Live-Videos Dataset. It must be emphasized that we directly use WSAD-Net pre-trained on the UCF-Crime dataset to detect anomalies on the LV dataset, and not fine-tune or train it on the LV dataset. There are two reasons that we do that. First, the UCF-Crime dataset is the only one that is used for weakly supervised anomaly detection so far. Second, the LV dataset is acquired under changing illumination and camera motion, which is extremely challenging and can be utilized to evaluate the generalization capabilities of WSAD-Net. Table 2. demonstrates quantitative results on the LV dataset. It is also easy to notice that WSAD-Net is very competitive even outperforms two out of the four methods. Results on the LV dataset convincingly demonstrate the good generalization capability of WSAD-Net.

Qualitative Results. Figure 3demonstrates the qualitative results on the UCF-Crime dataset. (a), (b), (d) and (e) show the anomalous activities in videos, and (e) and (f) show normal videos. We see that WSAD-Net provides successful and timely detection of those anomalies by generating high anomaly score for the anomalous frames. Particularly, (d) shows an example of burglary in the dark scene, which is very challenging but WSAD-Net still works well. In addition, an interesting observation in (a) is that WSAD-Net produces anomaly scores greater than 0.5 in the middle part of the video, however, no abnormality occurs in the corresponding part of the ground truth. We discover the possible cause in this video: a terrorist holding a submachine gun appears in the surveillance camera. For normal videos, WSAD-Net generates lower anomaly scores that are close to 0. There is a pretty small segment with anomaly scores close to 0.5 in (f) due to a passer-by outside the door, which may be a false alarm. It implies that using networks and weak labels to detect anomalous activities is a big challenge and a long way to go.

4.4 Ablation Studies

In this subsection, we conduct ablation studies to analyze the contributions of several different components, including loss functions, maximum length of sequence T and modalities (different features).

Impact of Loss Functions. We evaluate the performance of WSAD-Net with different loss functions, and the results are reported in Table 3. WSAD-Net with $\mathcal{L}_{BCE}$ as a baseline, achieves an AUC of 82.06%. WSAD-Net employing all loss functions achieves the highest AUC of 83.15%, which clearly demonstrates the significance of Compactness Loss and Magnetism Loss.

Impact of Maximum Length of Sequence T. As mentioned previously, we need to process the entire video at once because we only have video-level labels. In Sect. 3.1, we use a sampling mechanism with a pre-defined length T to meet GPU memory constraints. To choose a reasonable T on the UCF-Crime dataset, we conduct experiments to evaluate the impact of different T. From Fig. 4(a), we can see that in the beginning the AUC improves with an increase of T, and eventually reaches a plateau. Taking the performance

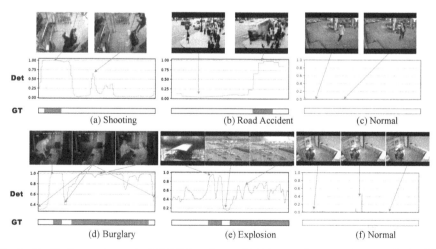

Fig. 3. Qualitative results on the UCF-Crime dataset. **Det** denotes the anomaly score obtained by WSAD-Net, and **GT** denotes the ground truth.

and time consumption into account simultaneously, we choose $T = 200$ as the default setting in this work.

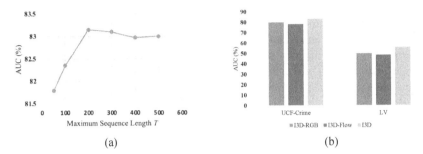

(a)   (b)

Fig. 4. Ablation Studies. (a) The AUC of WSAD-Net with different T on the UCF-Crime dataset. (b) The AUC of WSAD-Net with different modalities on the UCF-Crime and LV datasets.

Impact of Modalities. We also evaluate the impact of different modalities on the UCF-Crime and LV datasets. Figure 4(b) illustrates the effectiveness of each modality and their combination. The RGB modality achieves similar performance to the optical flow modality on both UCF-Crime and LV datasets. Finally, the alliance between RGB and optical flow improves the performance, which indicates the appearance and motion information are complementary in anomaly detection task.

5 Conclusion

In this paper, we propose a weakly supervised anomaly detector network called WSAD-Net to detect anomalies in untrimmed surveillance videos with only video-level labels. We first design a Classification Loss in MIL perspective, and then introduce two novel losses, namely, Compactness Loss and Magnetism Loss, to further improve the performance. Extensive experiments on the UCF-Crime dataset show that WSAD-Net outperforms the state-of-the-art methods by a large margin. Furthermore, we also directly apply WSAD-Net pre-trained on the UCF-Crime dataset to another challenging dataset Live-Videos, and obtain competitive results.

References

1. Sultani, W., Chen, C., Shah, M.: Real-world anomaly detection in surveillance videos. In: Proceedings of the 2018 IEEE Conference on Computer Vision and Pattern Recognition (CVPR), pp. 6479–6488. (2016)
2. Luo, W., Liu, W., Gao, S.: A revisit of sparse coding based anomaly detection in stacked RNN framework. In: Proceedings of the 2017 IEEE Conference on Computer Vision (ICCV), pp. 341–349. (2017)
3. Liu, W., Luo, W., Lian, D., Gao, S.: Future frame prediction for anomaly detection–a new baseline. In: Proceedings of the 2018 IEEE Conference on Computer Vision and Pattern Recognition (CVPR), pp. 6536–6545. (2018)

4. Lv, H., Chen, C., Cui, Z., Xu, C., Li, Y., Yang, J.: Learning normal dynamics in videos with meta prototype network. In: Proceedings of the 2021 IEEE Conference on Computer Vision and Pattern Recognition (CVPR) (2021)
5. Wu, P., Liu, J., Shen, F.: A deep one-class neural network for anomalous event detection in complex scenes. IEEE Trans. Neural Netw. Learn. Syst. **31**(7), 2609–2622 (2020)
6. Hasan, M., Choi, J., Neumann, J., Roy-Chowdhury, A.K., Davis, L.S.: Learning temporal regularity in video sequences. In: Proceedings of the 2016 IEEE Conference on Computer Vision and Pattern Recognition (CVPR), pp. 733–742. (2016)
7. Peng, Wu., Liu, J., Shi, Y., Sun, Y., Shao, F., Zhaoyang, Wu., Yang, Z.: Not only look, but also listen: learning multimodal violence detection under weak supervision. In: Vedaldi, A., Bischof, H., Brox, T., Frahm, J.-M. (eds.) Computer Vision – ECCV 2020: 16th European Conference, Glasgow, UK, August 23–28, 2020, Proceedings, Part XXX, pp. 322–339. Springer International Publishing, Cham (2020). https://doi.org/10.1007/978-3-030-58577-8_20
8. De Geest, R., Gavves, E., Ghodrati, A., Li, Z., Snoek, C., Tuytelaars, T.: Online action detection. In: Leibe, B., Matas, J., Sebe, N., Welling, M. (eds.) Computer Vision – ECCV 2016: 14th European Conference, Amsterdam, The Netherlands, October 11-14, 2016, Proceedings, Part V, pp. 269–284. Springer International Publishing, Cham (2016). https://doi.org/10.1007/978-3-319-46454-1_17
9. Paul, S., Roy, S., Roy-Chowdhury, A.K.: W-TALC: weakly-supervised temporal activity localization and classification. In: Ferrari, V., Hebert, M., Sminchisescu, C., Weiss, Y. (eds.) Computer Vision – ECCV 2018: 15th European Conference, Munich, Germany, September 8-14, 2018, Proceedings, Part IV, pp. 588–607. Springer International Publishing, Cham (2018). https://doi.org/10.1007/978-3-030-01225-0_35
10. Kingma, D.P., Ba, J.: Adam: a method for stochastic optimization. arXiv:1412.6980. Retrieved from https://arxiv.org/abs/1412.6980. (2014)
11. Wedel, A., Pock, T., Zach, C., Bischof, H., Cremers, D.: An improved algorithm for TV-L1 optical flow. In: Proceedings of the International Dagstuhl-Seminar on Statistical and Geometrical Approaches to Visual Motion Analysis, pp. 23–45 (2009)
12. Tran, D., Bourdev, L., Fergus, R., Torresani, L., Paluri, M.: Learning spatiotemporal features with 3d convolutional networks. In: Proceedings of the 2015 IEEE Conference on Computer Vision (ICCV), pp. 4489–4497 (2015)
13. Ruff, L., et al.: Deep one-class classification. In: Proceedings of the 2018 International Conference on Machine Learning (ICML), pp. 4393–4402 (2018)
14. Kratz, L., Nishino, K.: Anomaly detection in extremely crowded scenes using spatio-temporal motion pattern models. In: Proceedings of the 2009 IEEE Conference on Computer Vision and Pattern Recognition (CVPR), pp. 1446–1453 (2009)
15. Cong, Y., Yuan, J., Liu, J.: Sparse reconstruction cost for abnormal event detection. In: Proceedings of the 2011 IEEE Conference on Computer Vision and Pattern Recognition (CVPR), pp. 3449–3456 (2011)
16. Lu, C., Shi, J., Jia, J.: Abnormal event detection at 150 fps in matlab. In: Proceedings of the 2013 IEEE Conference on Computer Vision (ICCV) pp. 2720–2727 (2013)
17. Leyva, R., Sanchez, V., Li, C.-S.: Video anomaly detection with compact feature sets for online performance. IEEE Transactions on Image Processing (TIP), vol. 26(7), pp. 3463–3478 (2017)
18. Xu, D., Ricci, E., Yan, Y., Song, J., Sebe, N.: Learning deep representations of appearance and motion for anomalous event detection. In: Proceedings of the 2015 British Machine Vision Conference (BMVC) (2015)
19. Carreira, J., Zisserman, A.: Quo vadis, action recognition? a new model and the kinetics dataset. In: Proceedings of the 2017 IEEE Conference on Computer Vision and Pattern Recognition (CVPR), pp. 4724–4733 (2017)

20. Mahadevan, V., Li, W., Bhalodia, V., Vasconcelos, N.: Anomaly detection in crowded scenes. In: Proceedings of the 2010 IEEE Conference on Computer Vision and Pattern Recognition (CVPR), pp. 1975–1981 (2010)
21. Biswas, S., Babu, R.V.: Real time anomaly detection in H.264 compressed videos. In: Proceedings of the 2013 National Conference on Computer Vision, Pattern Recognition, Image Processing and Graphics (NCVPRIPG), pp.1–4 (2013)
22. Gunale, K.G., Mukherji, P. Deep learning with a spatiotemporal descriptor of appearance and motion estimation for video anomaly detection. J. Imaging (2018)
23. Zhou, B., Khosla, A., Lapedriza, A., Oliva, A., Torralba, A. Learning deep features for discriminative localization. In: Proceedings of the 2016 IEEE Conference on Computer Vision and Pattern Recognition (CVPR), pp. 2921–2929 (2016)
24. Zhong, J., Li, N., Kong, W., Liu, S., Li, T.H., Li, G.: Graph convolutional label noise cleaner: train a plug-and-play action classifier for anomaly detection. In: Proceedings of the 2019 IEEE Conference on Computer Vision and Pattern Recognition (CVPR), pp. 1237–1246 (2019)
25. Pang, G., Shen, C., Cao, L., van den Hengel, A.: Deep learning for anomaly detection: a review. arXiv: 2007.02500. https://arxiv.org/abs/2007.02500. (2020)
26. Yang, Z., Peng, W., Liu, J., Liu, X.: Dynamic local aggregation network with adaptive clusterer for anomaly detection. In: Avidan, S., Brostow, G., Cissé, M., Farinella, G.M., Hassner, T. (eds.) Computer Vision – ECCV 2022: 17th European Conference, Tel Aviv, Israel, October 23–27, 2022, Proceedings, Part IV, pp. 404–421. Springer Nature Switzerland, Cham (2022). https://doi.org/10.1007/978-3-031-19772-7_24
27. Wu, P., Liu, X., Liu, J.: Weakly supervised audio-visual violence detection. IEEE Trans. Multimedia (TMM) **26**, 1674–1685 (2022)
28. Tian, Y., Pang, G., Chen, Y., Singh, R., Verjans, J.W., Carneiro, G.: Weakly-supervised video anomaly detection with robust temporal feature magnitude learning. In: Proceedings of the 2021 IEEE International Conference on Computer Vision (CVPR), pp. 4975–4986 (2021)

Multi-object Tracking in Remote Sensing Video Based on Motion and Multi-scale Local Cost Volume

Xuqian Zhu and Bin Zhang[✉]

Xi'an Jiaotong University, Xi'an 710054, China
bzhang82@xjtu.edu.cn

Abstract. Multi-object tracking (MOT) in remote sensing videos is significant in many application scenarios. That task in ordinary scenarios has been widely used in vehicle tracking and monitoring. However, due to the peculiarities of remote sensing video, many new challenges will be brought to the task. So many frameworks for ordinary scenarios are inappropriate. In this paper, we propose a novel network called a multi-scale local cost volume network (MLCVNet) that can extract multi-scale features and inter-frame motion information. We use a multi-scale local cost volume module to obtain the object's displacement information between current and historical frames, and the historic features will be mapped into the current features to obtain enhanced features through which objects can be detected and tracked. Some experiments have been conducted on remote sensing videos, which are collected from the Jilin-1 satellite, and the results have demonstrated the effectiveness and robustness of the proposed method. Experimental results show that our method achieves state-of-art performance.

Keywords: multi-object tracking · remote sensing · motion information · local cost volume

1 Instruction

MOT in ordinary videos has received widespread attention and research, and many excellent results have been applied to various scenarios. MOT in remote sensing videos is even more critical in some applications. Remote sensing satellites can easily observe large areas of target regions, track vehicle flow, and support smart city transportation. MOT in remote sensing videos has become an important research topic in remote sensing image processing. However, compared to ordinary videos, remote sensing videos face many new challenges: 1) Low discrimination between objects and the background. 2) High background noise. 3) Small object areas. 4) Lack of detailed features. 5) Cloud cover.

These challenges pose great difficulties to object tracking in remote sensing videos, so we require effective methods to overcome them. In this article, motivated by the TraDeS [1] for MOT in ordinary video, a new MOT framework is proposed, which can be applied to remote sensing videos for tracking tiny objects.

The main contributions of this paper are as follows:

1) We propose a multi-scale local cost volume mechanism that could accurately represent the motion offset of small objects than the baseline.
2) A head representing the direction of object motion is added to the network output head. The detection branch and tracking branch of output heads are connected to the not enhanced current feature and final enhanced feature, respectively.

Our proposed MOT method based on MLCVNet is designed to address some challenges in remote sensing videos. Compared to [1] in remote sensing videos, our MLCV model can more accurately match the same object between previous and current frames while effectively reducing computation. Without introducing extra network branches with excessive computational requirements as in DSFNet [2], the proposed method can meet the real-time tracking needs of multi-object in remote sensing videos while performing well. Detailed network architecture will discuss in Sect. 3.

2   Related Works

The concept of object tracking was proposed by Wax N in the 1960s [3] and was applied to pedestrian tracking. Since then, the field of object tracking has received much attention from researchers, with new theories and research results constantly emerging and being innovated. This article is about multi-object tracking, and the current research status will be briefly described below.

2.1   MOT in Ordinary Video

In the traditional object tracking framework, detection is done by establishing an appearance model to identify the object's identity, including unique features that distinguish different objects and are used for subsequent association tracking. Many of the MOT frameworks that have emerged in recent years are based on deep learning. They are roughly divided into two types of tracking frameworks: tracking-by-detection (TBD) and joint detection and tracking (JDT) [4].

The appearance model of an object can be represented by different object attributes, including color, texture, gradient, motion, and optical flow, to identify the object uniquely. By extracting a class of features or joint features of the object, it is possible to distinguish the object from the background and thus distinguish different objects. Many traditional multi-object tracking frameworks fall into this category [5–7].

Compared to traditional methods, deep learning does not require manual feature extraction and can obtain richer feature representations, often achieving better results. DeepSort [8] improves the Sort [9] method that utilizes deep learning. In the object detection phase, a detection network is used to detect the object. Then the detected object is passed to a re-identification (ReID) appearance feature extraction network for feature extraction, followed by the tracking process. The MOTDT [10] framework fully utilizes the advantages of deep neural networks to address prominent issues in TBD, such as unreliable detection and intra-class occlusion. The detection part in D&T [11] is based on the R-FCN fully convolutional network, and the tracking part incorporates the tracking ideas based on correlation and regression from single-object tracking methods into the front-end detection framework, implementing this multi-object tracking method.

In recent years, more and more research has leaned towards one-stage methods, which only require one network to accomplish object detection and appearance feature extraction simultaneously. JDE [12] proposes a network model that can integrate object detection and ReID tasks into one by incorporating the appearance ReID model into the one-shot detector. FairMOT [13] points out multiple imbalances in general anchor-based methods and proposes an improvement. FairMOT is a tracking method based on the anchor-free feature extraction network DLA [14], which adds a ReID branch on top of the detection task. CenterTrack [15] is an improvement on the CenterNet [16], adding a branch to the detection output branch to reflect the position movement vector of the object between two frames, thus implementing multi-object tracking in one network. TraDeS [1] proposes a new online joint detection and tracking model with tracking features to assist with end-to-end detection tasks. It infers the object tracking offset based on cost volume and then uses it to propagate the object features from a previous moment to improve the current frame's object detection and segmentation tasks.

2.2 MOT in Remote Sensing Video

Currently, some multi-object tracking frameworks based on remote sensing videos have been proposed. Du et al. [17] proposed a specific strategy for constructing a more robust tracker using a kernel correlation filtering (KCF) tracker and a three-frame differencing algorithm. Guo et al. [18] proposed a correlation filter Kalman filter (CFKF) tracker, which is a tracking algorithm based on a fast correlation filter (CF) for satellite video object tracking. Shao et al. [19] proposed a velocity correlation filter (VCF) algorithm to overcome the problem of insufficient brightness and color features of remote sensing video objects. Xuan et al. [20] proposed a new motion estimation (ME) algorithm based on the kernel correlation filtering (KCF) algorithm, which combines Kalman filtering and motion smoothing trajectory to reduce the boundary effects of the kernel correlation filtering algorithm.

He et al. [21] proposed a graph-based multi-task reasoning tracking framework, which models multi-object tracking as a graph feature information fusion process based on message inference. Xiao et al. [2] proposed a two-stream network that integrates object motion information and object appearance information, which the authors refer to as dynamic information and static information, respectively. It was originally used for object detection tasks in remote sensing videos, but its network can also be used for multi-object tracking.

3 Network Architecture

The overall architecture of MLCVNet consists of four main parts, as shown in Fig. 1. During the training process, there are three inputs, the current frame $\mathbf{I}^t$ at time t, the historical frame $\mathbf{I}^{t-\tau}$, and the heatmap $\mathbf{P}^{t-\tau}$ of the historical frame.

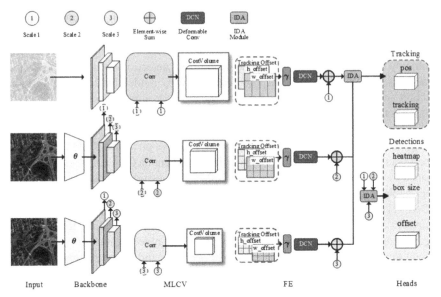

Fig. 1. The detailed network architecture includes a DLA-34 backbone, which extracts three scales of feature maps $\mathbf{f}_s^f$ and $\mathbf{f}_s^{t-\tau}$ from the input frames $\mathbf{I}^t$ and $\mathbf{I}^{t-\tau}$, respectively. These feature maps are then used in a correlation operation to produce local cost volume $\mathbf{C}_s$, which is further processed using a template operation to obtain the offset matrix $\mathbf{O}_s$. The FE module extracts motion transformation features at three scales. The resulting fusion feature is combined with the current feature to obtain an enhanced feature map connected to the output branches to produce the final outputs.

3.1 Multi-scale Local Cost Volume

Firstly, a DLA-34 network was used to extract multi-scale features from the image. The input image size of the backbone is $3 \times H_i \times W_i$. After passing it, $\mathbf{I}^t$ and $\mathbf{I}^{t-\tau}$ get three scales of feature maps, which are $\mathbf{f}_s^f \in \mathbb{R}^{C_s^f \times H_s^f \times W_s^f}$ and $\mathbf{f}_s^{t-\tau}$, respectively. The down-sampling ratios of the feature maps are 2, 4, and 8, denoted as s, where $H_s^f = \frac{H_i}{s}$, $W_s^f = \frac{W_i}{s}$.

The second part is MLCV module. The feature maps $\mathbf{f}_s^t$ and $\mathbf{f}_s^{t-\tau}$ at corresponding scales were first handled by a correlation operation to obtain a local cost volume $\mathbf{C}_s \in \mathbb{R}^{H_s^d \times W_s^d \times H_s^f \times W_s^f}$ between the current frame and the previous frame. Specifically, a correlation operation is performed at each pixel position in the feature map $\mathbf{f}_s^t$, using a correlation kernel $\mathbf{K}_{x,y}^t$ of size $k \times k$ centered at the position (x_f, y_f). Then a search window of size $H_s^d \times W_s^d$ centered at the corresponding position in feature map $\mathbf{f}_s^{t-\tau}$ is slid and correlated, resulting in a vector $\mathbf{C}_{x_f, y_f} \in \mathbb{R}^{H_d \times W_d}$ of length $H_s^d \times W_s^d$, which stores the correlation values of the kernel of the feature $\mathbf{f}_s^t$ and all kernels in the window of the feature $\mathbf{f}_s^{t-\tau}$. This vector reflects the matching degree between the object in the current frame and the possible positions of the object in the previous frame. The process is shown in Fig. 2.

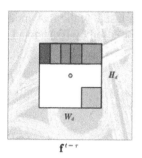
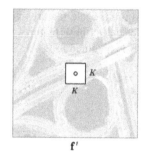
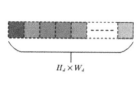

Fig. 2. During the correlation operation, a kernel centered at position (x, y) in feature map $\mathbf{f}^t$ is slid in a search window at the corresponding position in feature map $\mathbf{f}^{t-\tau}$. The kernel $\mathbf{K}^t_{x,y}$ correlates with every kernel $\mathbf{K}^{t-\tau}_{x',y'}$ in the search window, and each pair of kernels produces a value $\mathbf{C}_{x,y,x',y'}$.

If we ignore the difference in the scales s, the process of correlation operation is the same. The value $\mathbf{C}_{x,y,x',y'}$ in the vector is handled by doing an inner product of the two kernel vectors, which is obtained by the following equation:

$$\mathbf{C}_{x,y,x',y'} = \mathbf{K}^t_{x,y}\mathbf{K}^{t-\tau\top}_{x',y'} \tag{1}$$

A maximum value in the vector indicates the highest matching degree between the two kernels because they represent objects' partial features at the corresponding positions in the two frames. So, the highest matching value means these two objects are most likely to match. The complete correlation operation is performed for all positions in frame $\mathbf{f}^t_s$, resulting in a local cost volume $\mathbf{C}$. The operation is expressed as:

$$\mathbf{C} = \mathrm{Corr}\big(\mathbf{f}^t, \mathbf{f}^{t-\tau}, d', k\big) \tag{2}$$

where d' represents the displacement of the search window, $d' = \lfloor \frac{d}{2} \rfloor$, and $d = d' \times 2 + 1$. k is the size of the correlation kernel, and the default value is set to 3.

The local cost volume $\mathbf{C}$ obtained by the correlation operation is a four-dimensional matrix with dimensions $[1, H_d \times W_d, H_f, W_f]$. It needs to be reshaped into dimensions $[1, H_d, W_d, H_f \times W_f]$, and then the maximum value is taken in the second and third dimensions to obtain the maximum cost volume values $\mathbf{C}_H \in \mathbb{R}^{H_f \times W_f \times H_d}$ and $\mathbf{C}_W \in \mathbb{R}^{H_f \times W_f \times W_d}$ of each pixel between feature map $\mathbf{f}^t$ ant the corresponding search window of $\mathbf{f}^{t-\tau}$ in the height and width directions, respectively. Then, using the preset vertical and horizontal offset templates $\mathbf{V} \in \mathbb{R}^{H_f \times W_f \times H_d}$ and $\mathbf{H} \in \mathbb{R}^{H_f \times W_f \times W_d}$, the vectors of the two templates at position (i, j) are denoted as $\mathbf{V}_{i,j} \in \mathbb{R}^{H_d}$ and $\mathbf{H}_{i,j} \in \mathbb{R}^{W_d}$, respectively. By multiplying the values from the softmaxed cost volume in the two directions, the position offset vector $\mathbf{O}_{i,j} = \left[\mathbf{C}^H_{i,j}\mathbf{V}_{i,j}, \mathbf{C}^W_{i,j}\mathbf{H}_{i,j}\right]^\top$ with the maximum matching value from time t to $t - \tau$ at position (i, j) can be obtained, and the tracking offset matrix $\mathbf{O} \in \mathbb{R}^{H_f \times W_f \times 2}$ of all pixels in the feature map can be obtained.

The third part is the feature enhancement module, which is simplification of the MFW module [1], through which the enhanced feature $\widetilde{\mathbf{f}}^t_q$ will be obtained. But our FE model works on multi-scale, and multi-scale features will be fused by the IDA model [14]. After that we get $\widetilde{\mathbf{f}}_s^t$ at three scales, these features will be fused by IDA model at last. The final enhanced feature $\widetilde{\mathbf{f}}^t$ is obtained in Eq. 3.

$$\widetilde{\mathbf{f}}^t = IDA(\mathbf{f}_s^t), \quad s = 2, 4, 8 \tag{3}$$

3.2 Motion Direction Head

The output heads, which includes the detection and tracking branches. The detection branch is similar with [15], while the tracking branch contains a tracking offset head and a pos head. Each head of the detection branch is followed by a convolutional operation after the current time feature $\mathbf{f}^t$ to predict the corresponding information. The tracking offset head and pos head output by directly connecting a convolution to the final enhanced feature $\widetilde{\mathbf{f}}^t$, which are used to predict the position offset of the object, and the motion direction of the object, respectively.

For the tracking branch, in order to learn the position offset of the object more accurately between t and $t - \tau$, some improvements have been made. In the heads of [1], the enhanced feature $\widetilde{\mathbf{f}}^t$ is connected to both the detection branch and the tracking branch, which is detrimental to the learning of the tracking offset head and pos head in the tracking branch. However, in our framework, the enhanced feature is only connected to the tracking branch to ensure that the MLCV and FE modules can better learn the enhanced features for object position offset.

For the pos head, which is used to predict the direction of object motion. Because for remote sensing, the video is captured from a top-down perspective, so the motion of the object in the video is equivalent to moving on a plane. The enhanced feature hides motion information of object within it. Therefore, it is considered to output the direction of object motion in the multi-frames as a header so that the network can learn the object's motion information accurately. Specifically, the ground is roughly divided into eight directions: up, down, left, right, upper right, lower right, lower left, and upper left. That is, each pixel is represented by a vector of length 8. If an object exists in that pixel position, the direction index corresponding to the object's motion direction in that vector is set to 1, and others are set to 0. As shown in Fig. 3, the object relative to the origin of the coordinate system in the right-side figure moves in the upper right direction compared to its position in the left figure.

The size of the pos feature map is $8 \times H_o \times W_o$, where $H_o = H_i/2$, $W_o = W_i/2$. If a real object box $\mathbf{b}^i = \left(x_1^i, y_1^i, x_2^i, y_2^i\right)$ is in the image, with center at the position $\left(c_x^i, c_y^i\right)$. The vector at the position $\left(\tilde{c}_x^i, \tilde{c}_y^i\right) = \left(\left\lfloor \frac{c_x^i}{2} \right\rfloor, \left\lfloor \frac{c_y^i}{2} \right\rfloor\right)$ on the feature represents the motion direction of an object i. For example, in Fig. 4, the motion direction of the object is upper right, and the vector at the corresponding position in the true label of pos is $\mathbf{p}^i = [0, 1, 0, 0, 0, 0, 0, 0]$. The loss function of the motion direction header uses the Mean Squared Error loss, and the loss function is shown in Eq. 4.

$$L_{pos} = \frac{1}{N} \sum_{i=1}^{N} \left(\hat{\mathbf{p}}^i - \mathbf{p}^i\right)^2 \tag{4}$$

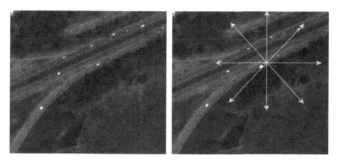

Fig. 3. An example to illustrate the ground truth of pos head, the object relative to the origin of the coordinate system in the right figure moves in the upper right direction compared to its position in the left figure.

where N is the number of objects in the video frames.

The overall loss of network consists of two head branches together, and the total loss function can be obtained by summing up the different branches by assigning certain weights to them.

$$L_{total} = w_1 L_{heat} + w_2 L_{box} + w_3 L_{tr} + w_4 L_{pos} \tag{5}$$

where w_1, w_2, w_3, and w_4 represent weight values for the four losses. L_{heat} and L_{box} are the detection losses as in [15]. L_{tr} is the tracking offset loss as in [1].

4   Experiments

4.1   Datasets and Implementation Details

To validate the performance of the proposed multi-object tracking framework, it is tested on a remote sensing video dataset. The dataset used in this paper is provided by the DSFNet, which proposed a method for object detection in remote sensing images, but the dataset format also supports MOTChallenge multi-object tracking. The videos in the dataset were captured by the Jilin-1 video satellite, and the training set contains 72 videos, while the test set contains 7 videos. During the training process, some image data augmentation techniques are applied, including flipping and color space transformation. The experiment mainly focuses on vehicle-like objects in the video.

Table 1. Detail experimental environments.

Environment	Version
Operate system	Ubuntu18.04
CPU	12-core Intel(R) Xeon(R) Platinum 8255C
GPU	RTX3090 24G
CUDA	10.3
Python	3.8
Pytorch	1.7

The specific experimental environments are shown in Table 1.

To train MLCVNet, we utilized the Adam optimizer with a batch size of 8 and an initial learning rate of 1.25×10^{-4}. The entire network was trained for 30 epochs before termination. In the MLCV module, we used a kernel size of 3×3 when down-sampling by a factor of 2 and a search window size of 7×7. For down-sampling by a factor of 4, the kernel size was set to 3×3, and the search window size was set to 5×5. When down-sampling by a factor of 8, we used a kernel size of 1×1 and a search window size of 3×3.

In order to verify the effectiveness of the method proposed in this thesis, some multi-object tracking frameworks with outstanding performance are selected for comparison, including CenterTrack [15], FairMOT [13], DSFNet [2], and TraDeS [1]. The experimental results are shown in Table 2.

Table 2. Experimental results of each tracking framework on the remote sensing video test set

Method	IDs↓	MT↑	ML↓	FP↓	FN↓	IDF1↑	MOTA↑	FPS↑
CenterTrack	2618	4.4%	47.3%	25.6%	59.6%	24.9%	11.9%	**26**
FairMOT	840	14.8%	25.9%	37.9%	48.4%	42.4%	12.8%	22
TraDeS	1869	21.1%	45.1%	24.4%	53.4%	36.8%	20.2%	16
DSFNet	**740**	**51.9%**	17.6%	**23.3%**	25.4%	70.0%	50.5%	2
MLCVNet	750	50.7%	**13.8%**	24.2%	**24.0%**	**70.7%**	**51.0%**	14

Some frameworks that perform well in regular videos, such as CenterTrack, Fair-MOT, and TraDeS, rely mainly on object appearance features for learning. This leads to poor results in remote sensing videos because of some prominent characteristics of remote sensing videos. The DSFNet framework integrates object motion information and object appearance information, which the authors refer to as dynamic information and static information, respectively. It was originally used for object detection tasks in remote sensing videos, but its network can also be used for multi-object tracking. Therefore, it performs well in the test set, but due to the addition of a motion information branch and the output size of its network being consistent with the original image size, the computational cost of the entire network is very high, resulting in an FPS of only 2 during testing.

Several indicators of MLCVNet have reached the best level, with the MOTA indicator reaching 51.0%, consistent with the [2]. Because the output feature map of the MLCVNet network is down-sampled by 2 times, and the motion branch is not introduced, the computational cost of the overall network is much smaller than that of [2], and its inference speed reaches 14 frames per second. The results are shown in Fig. 4, with one complete result image selected for each framework, and the FPS indicator of each framework is marked in the upper-left corner.

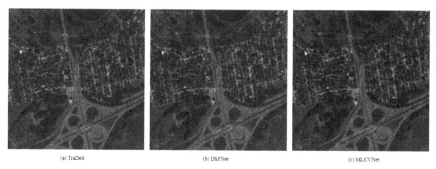

(a) TraDeS   (b) DSFNet   (c) MLCVNet

Fig. 4. Illustration of the FPS results for each framework run on the test set. (b) FPS indicator for DSFNet is only 2. (c) MLCVNet runs at 14 frames per second.

4.2 Ablation Studies

In order to prove the effectiveness of the three improvement schemes proposed in this paper, the ablation experiments are now conducted for these different schemes of the original baseline TraDeS, TraDeS with improved head connection (TraDeS*), improved TraDeS with added MLCV module (TraDeS*+MLCV), improved TraDeS with added MLCV module and pos head (MLCVNet), respectively, and the results of the experiments are shown in Table 3.

Table 3. Experimental results of ablation studies

Method	IDs	MT	ML	FP	FN	IDF1	MOTA
TraDeS	1869	21.1%	45.1%	24.4%	53.4%	36.8%	20.2%
TraDeS*	935	24.3%	35.4%	20.7%	47.7%	40.3%	30.6%
TraDeS*+MLCV	841	55.4%	10.6%	33.4%	23.3%	60.5%	42.5%
MLCVNet	750	50.7%	13.8%	24.2%	24.0%	70.7%	51.0%

From Table 3, it can be seen that both adding the MLCV module, adding the MLCV module and pos head to the baseline have improved accuracy, which fully proves the effectiveness of the MLCV module and pos head.

When adding the pos head to MLCVNet, it is to learn the tracking information of the object more accurately, but it can also serve as an auxiliary branch to learn detection information, which can effectively help learn the heatmap head information and improve the confidence of the learned objects' information. To verify this idea, the confidence information of all objects was extracted from the test set videos before and after adding the pos head to the framework. The confidence values were then divided into intervals of 0.1 within the range of [0, 1). The number of detected objects within each interval was counted and the results were plotted, as shown in Fig. 5.

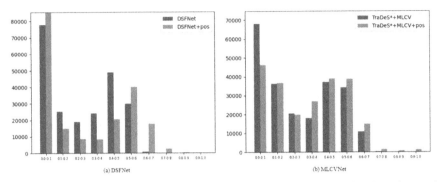

(a) DSFNet   (b) MLCVNet

Fig. 5. The figure shows the change in the distribution of confidence scores of all detection results obtained when the two tracking frameworks run on the test set before and after adding the pos head.

The above figure shows that (a) is the result of testing on DSFNet. After adding the pos branch, the number of low confidence objects in DSFNet has decreased significantly, and more detection objects with confidence scores above 0.5 are output by the framework. Figure 5 (b) is the result of testing on the framework proposed in this paper. By comparing the MLCVNet network with and without the pos branch, it can be seen that the number of low confidence objects has slightly decreased and the number of objects with scores above 0.3 has increased. Although the overall effect is not as obvious as in (a), the overall distribution of confidence scores is also moving towards the high score interval. From the analysis of the results in Fig. 5 (a) and (b), it can be concluded that the pos branch proposed in this paper is effective in helping the network learn detection information of the objects.

5 Conclusion

In this paper, we propose a novel multi-object tracking framework for remote sensing videos based on the TraDeS framework. We make three improvements to address the prominent issues in remote sensing videos and achieve good performance in tracking tiny objects in terms of accuracy and real-time processing. Firstly, we improve the head connection of the framework, enabling the network to learn better tracking and detection information separately. Secondly, the MLCV module utilizes the kernel and local search window mechanism to extract the motion information of small objects in remote sensing videos more accurately. Lastly, we add a pos head to the tracking branch of the network's output head to represent the direction of object motion, which helps the network to learn more accurate object detection information. The results of comparative and ablation experiments show that the proposed method is effective and achieves excellent performance in multi-object tracking for remote sensing videos.

References

1. Wu, J., Cao, J., Song, L., Wang, Y., Yang, M., Yuan, J.: Track to detect and segment: an online multi-object tracker. In: Proceedings of the IEEE/CVF Conference on Computer Vision and Pattern Recognition, pp. 12352–12361 (2021)
2. Xiao, C., et al.: DSFNet: dynamic and static fusion network for moving object detection in satellite videos. IEEE Geosci. Remote Sens. Lett. **19**, 1–5 (2021)
3. Wax, N.: Signal-to-noise improvement and the statistics of track populations. J. Appl. Phys. **26**, 586–595 (1955)
4. Wang, Q., Zheng, Y., Pan, P., Xu, Y.: Multiple object tracking with correlation learning. In: Proceedings of the IEEE/CVF Conference on Computer Vision and Pattern Recognition, pp. 3876–3886 (2021)
5. Ullah, M., Cheikh, F.A., Imran, A.S.: HoG based real-time multi-target tracking in bayesian framework. In: 2016 13th IEEE International Conference on Advanced Video and Signal Based Surveillance (AVSS), pp. 416–422. IEEE (2016)
6. Andriyenko, A., Schindler, K.: Multi-target tracking by continuous energy minimization. In: CVPR 2011, pp. 1265–1272. IEEE (2011)
7. Yin, J., Wang, W., Meng, Q., Yang, R., Shen, J.: A unified object motion and affinity model for online multi-object tracking. In: Proceedings of the IEEE/CVF Conference on Computer Vision and Pattern Recognition, pp. 6768–6777 (2020)
8. Wojke, N., Bewley, A., Paulus, D.: Simple online and realtime tracking with a deep association metric. In: 2017 IEEE International Conference on Image Processing (ICIP), pp. 3645–3649. IEEE (2017)
9. Bewley, A., Ge, Z., Ott, L., Ramos, F., Upcroft, B.: Simple online and realtime tracking. In: 2016 IEEE International Conference on Image Processing (ICIP), pp. 3464–3468. IEEE (2016)
10. Chen, L., Ai, H., Zhuang, Z., Shang, C.: Real-time multiple people tracking with deeply learned candidate selection and person re-identification. In: 2018 IEEE International Conference on Multimedia and Expo (ICME), pp. 1–6. IEEE (2018)
11. Feichtenhofer, C., Pinz, A., Zisserman, A.: Detect to track and track to detect. In: Proceedings of the IEEE International Conference on Computer Vision, pp. 3038–3046 (2017)
12. Wang, Z., Zheng, L., Liu, Y., Li, Y., Wang, S.: Towards real-time multi-object tracking. In: Vedaldi, A., Bischof, H., Brox, T., Frahm, J.-M. (eds.) ECCV 2020. LNCS, vol. 12356, pp. 107–122. Springer, Cham (2020). https://doi.org/10.1007/978-3-030-58621-8_7
13. Zhang, Y., Wang, C., Wang, X., Zeng, W., Liu, W.: FairMOT: on the fairness of detection and re-identification in multiple object tracking. Int. J. Comput. Vision **129**, 3069–3087 (2021)
14. Yu, F., Wang, D., Shelhamer, E., Darrell, T.: Deep layer aggregation. In: Proceedings of the IEEE Conference on Computer Vision and Pattern Recognition, pp. 2403–2412 (2018)
15. Zhou, X., Koltun, V., Krähenbühl, P.: Tracking objects as points. In: Vedaldi, A., Bischof, H., Brox, T., Frahm, J.-M. (eds.) ECCV 2020. LNCS, vol. 12349, pp. 474–490. Springer, Cham (2020). https://doi.org/10.1007/978-3-030-58548-8_28
16. Duan, K., Bai, S., Xie, L., Qi, H., Huang, Q., Tian, Q.: CenterNet: keypoint triplets for object detection. In: Proceedings of the IEEE/CVF International Conference on Computer Vision, pp. 6569–6578 (2019)
17. Du, B., Sun, Y., Cai, S., Wu, C., Du, Q.: Object tracking in satellite videos by fusing the kernel correlation filter and the three-frame-difference algorithm. IEEE Geosci. Remote Sens. Lett. **15**, 168–172 (2017)
18. Guo, Y., Yang, D., Chen, Z.: Object tracking on satellite videos: a correlation filter-based tracking method with trajectory correction by Kalman filter. IEEE J. Sel. Topics Appl. Earth Observ. Remote Sens. **12**, 3538–3551 (2019)

19. Shao, J., Du, B., Wu, C., Zhang, L.: Tracking objects from satellite videos: a velocity feature based correlation filter. IEEE Trans. Geosci. Remote Sens. **57**, 7860–7871 (2019)
20. Xuan, S., Li, S., Han, M., Wan, X., Xia, G.-S.: Object tracking in satellite videos by improved correlation filters with motion estimations. IEEE Trans. Geosci. Remote Sens. **58**, 1074–1086 (2019)
21. He, Q., Sun, X., Yan, Z., Li, B., Fu, K.: Multi-object tracking in satellite videos with graph-based multitask modeling. IEEE Trans. Geosci. Remote Sens. **60**, 1–13 (2022)

Density Map Augmentation-Based Point-to-Point Vehicle Counting and Localization in Remote Sensing Imagery with Limited Resolution

Ziqian Tan[1], Yinong Guo[1], and Chen Wu[1,2(✉)]

[1] State Key Laboratory of Information Engineering in Surveying, Mapping and Remote Sensing, Wuhan University, Wuhan, China
{tan_zq,yinongguo,chen.wu}@whu.edu.cn
[2] Institute of Artificial Intelligence, Wuhan University, Wuhan, China

Abstract. Monitoring traffic flow is of great significance to contemporary urban management and intelligent transportation construction. Among them, satellite remote sensing images are the most easily accessible and cost-effective remote sensing image data sources. However, most high-resolution satellite remote sensing images tend to have only sub-meter (0.5 m–1 m) spatial resolution, which makes vehicle extraction from such images very difficult to be carried out, and there are only a few related research studies. If vehicle counting and localization can be done under such limited-resolution remote sensing images, the application potential and study's value of such images can be greatly explored, and large-scale multi-temporal urban traffic condition analysis can be conducted with low acquisition costs. After the vehicle counting work with limited-resolution remote sensing images is proven to be feasible, this paper will improve the granularity of vehicle extraction tasks and conduct research studies on vehicle counting and localization tasks under this resolution. Combining the existing research studies results on density map counting, this paper designs a density map enhancement module that can be used to enhance the vehicle localization model and proposes an improved model based on the classical point-based keypoint object localization model P2PNet. The effectiveness of the proposed point-based keypoint localization model based on the density map enhancement strategy is verified on the RSVC dataset for the vehicle localization task of limited-resolution remote sensing images.

Keywords: Remote Sensing · Vehicle Counting · Vehicle Localization

1 Introduction

With the advancement of technology and urbanization, the number of vehicles per capita in the world is increasing. Although the increasing number of vehicles facilitates logistics and transportation, it also contributes to increasing traffic congestion and even traffic accidents in cities and towns. To control and solve traffic problems, monitoring traffic flow and grasping vehicle distribution will be the most important preliminary tool, and

H. Lu et al. (Eds.): ICIG 2023, LNCS 14359, pp. 295–307, 2023.
https://doi.org/10.1007/978-3-031-46317-4_24

the key to this is vehicle counting and vehicle localization. Although vehicle localization and density information can be obtained from a variety of data sources, one of the most important data sources, road traffic monitoring data, is often owned only by national governments. This type of data is difficult to share and open due to issues such as public safety and government governance. In contrast, remote sensing images, obtained by remote sensing technology, are characterized by large scale, wide range, and multiple periods, and are very suitable for conducting vehicle object extraction research studies with urban areas as the unit. Among them, remote sensing images that can interpret common vehicle objects must have a high spatial resolution, which is called high-resolution remote sensing images, but at this stage, the most easily acquired satellite remote sensing images that can interpret vehicle objects to have a spatial resolution concentrated in the sub-meter level, mainly 0.5 m–1 m. Although such images are called high-resolution remote sensing images, their spatial resolution is still "limited" compared to vehicle objects within 4 m in length and 2 m in width, so this paper refers to such images as limited-resolution remote sensing images.

Although existing object detection methods have been developed to a certain extent in the field of remote sensing images, most of them can only be applied to images with a high spatial resolution (higher than 0.5 m) or excellent quality, and vehicle objects are characterized by small size, arbitrary direction and dense distribution in remote sensing images, which increases the difficulty of interpreting these objects. Therefore, it is necessary to consider a more efficient method to achieve the task of vehicle counting and localization on limited-resolution remote sensing images. In this paper, considering the difficulty of labeling small-size bounding boxes and the difficulty of extracting small-size object features under the limited-resolution condition, we will not further explore the object detection method, but retreat to investigate the object counting method and object localization method.

In our previous work, we proposed a lightweight dense scene recognition network CSRNet⁻ (Congested Scene Recognition Network Minus) [1], which obtains a visualized density map through a vehicle counting algorithm based on the density map method and also gives feedback on the distribution of vehicles on the image at the visual level. This solves to some extent the problem that the pure counting scheme ignores the vehicle object location information. These works do demonstrate the potential of density map counting methods to be used for vehicle counting tasks in remote sensing images, but there are no typical examples of existing object localization methods that can be directly applied to remote sensing images. Meanwhile, the mainstream object localization methods have their limitations: the pseudo box method is not suitable for small-scale object localization in remote sensing images due to its design idea, while the natural nature of the density-based keypoint localization method also determines that the count results obtained in the density map counting phase and the point extraction localization phase are not matched.

Therefore, this paper proposes to design a set of deep learning algorithm models for vehicle localization applicable to limited-resolution remote sensing images concerning the popular head object localization scheme in the field of crowd counting and conducts an exploratory study on vehicle counting and localization tasks under limited-resolution remote sensing images. The model does not need to feed the specific enclosing bounding box of the vehicle object but only needs to obtain the location of its center point or pseudo box, which can provide further object distribution information compared with the density map counting scheme. At the same time, the intermediate results of the density map are introduced into the model to enhance the information extraction capability of the model and thus improve the localization effect.

2   Related Work

2.1   Object Counting

Object counting is a coarse-grained object recognition task that aims to accomplish the counting of the number of specified objects in a specific area without precisely obtaining the location and size of each object. The main application direction of this task is natural image crowd counting. Like vehicle objects on limited-resolution remote sensing images, head objects in dense crowds are difficult to label with bounding boxes, which makes it difficult to apply object detection methods to crowd counting tasks as well. The mainstream density map counting CNN networks can be broadly classified into multilayer networks and single-layer networks according to the model structure. The former, such as M-CNN [2] and Switch CNN [3], aim to achieve the extraction of objects at different scales using multiple parallel branches, and the latter, such as CSRNet [4] and SANet [5], such models aim to obtain predictive density maps end-to-end using only single-layer networks with methods such as dilated convolution. Currently, single-layer networks have become the mainstream object counting method due to their concise and efficient features, and we improved the classical single-layer object counting network CSRNet in our previous work to propose the lightweight dense scene recognition network CSRNet$^-$ for vehicle counting of vehicle objects on limited-resolution remote sensing images; at this stage, some researchers have also introduced density map-based counting methods into the task of object counting on remote sensing images, for example, Gao et al. established a multi-class object counting aerospace image dataset, and Abozeid et al. examined the feasibility of counting olive trees on satellite images with simple background [6], etc.

2.2   Object Localization

Object localization is a more coarse-grained object recognition task than object counting. Although this type of task also does not need to provide precise size information of the object, it needs to give back information about the center point location of the object. This task is a new task proposed after some progress in research studies in the field of crowd counting and is also very suitable for vehicle object extraction work on limited-resolution remote sensing images. The mainstream object localization methods are divided into two major categories, namely the pseudo box and the keypoint localization. The pseudo box predicts an approximate size by the coordinates of the center point position of the object rather than an enclosing bounding box that closely fits the shape of the object, such as LSC-CNN networks [7]; the keypoint localization networks only need to obtain the predicted coordinates of the center point of the object without feeding the approximate size of the object, and the common ones are density-based keypoint localization and point-based keypoint localization. Among them, the density-based keypoint localization is to generate the predicted density map according to the idea of density map counting first, and then gradually extracts the location coordinates of the predicted points from the predicted density map, such as D2CNet [8], MPS [9], etc.; while the point-based keypoint localization discards the aid of intermediate results such as density map, which can be directly predicted by point-to-point, and solves the problem of mismatch between counting and location results in the density map point extraction method, such as P2PNet [10].

3   Method

We proposed a lightweight dense scene recognition network CSRNet⁻ in our previous work, and it has been demonstrated that the vehicle counting framework of density map and deep learning techniques can be used for vehicle counting in limited-resolution remote sensing images. Therefore, the model proposed in this paper improves the backbone network and feature pyramid module structure of the P2PNet model, while proposing a density map enhancement module to use the density map to assist the model in the extraction of vehicle objects.

3.1   Feature Pyramid Module

The feature pyramid module (FPM) is a design structure that makes a horizontal connection between the encoder and decoder, and it is shown schematically in Fig. 1. This module was designed from the beginning to fuse the feature information of different layers of feature maps in an arithmetic cost-effective way, to combine the small-size object feature information retained in the low-level feature maps with the deep semantic information in the high-level feature maps to enhance the model's ability to extract small-size objects.

This is precisely compatible with the task of extracting small-size vehicle objects under limited-resolution conditions in this paper. For feature maps of adjacent levels but different scales in the backbone network, each feature map is first channel compressed by a 1×1 convolution kernel, and then the smaller-scale feature map is performed a double up-sampling, to unify the size and number of channels of the two feature maps. Finally, the two feature maps are subjected to a pixel-level summation operation to fuse the feature information on both feature maps. The feature pyramid module is applied in the original P2PNet, but only a single fusion is performed on the last two feature maps. However, the feasibility of using this module to fuse multi-layer feature maps will be examined in our model.

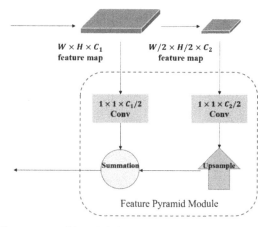

Fig. 1. Feature pyramid module between two adjacent level feature maps

3.2 Density Map Enhancement Module

The density map enhancement module is the core of our improved method, which enhances the model's ability to extract objects by introducing an intermediate result density map to enhance the model's attention to the region containing the vehicle.

The input of the density map enhancement module is the fully encoded feature map in the model, which is called the master feature map (if the feature pyramid module is used, the master feature map is the feature map after all the feature maps of the levels to be fused have been fused using the feature pyramid). The main feature map $F_0(x)$ first passes through a layer of $3 \times 3 \times 256$ dilated convolution kernels with a dilation rate of 2 to obtain the feature map $F(x)$, which is fed to two layers of 3×3 dilated convolution kernels with 128 and 64 channels and a dilation rate of 2, and outputted by a 1×1 single channel convolution kernel to obtain the density map $D(x)$. It can be found that if the original 17-layer VGG-16 backbone network in P2PNet is followed, the process of generating the density map $D(x)$ will go through the same number of convolutional layers as the baseline model CSRNet$^-$ in the previous research studies work, thus ensuring the quality of the density map generation. Next, this density map $D(x)$ will be fused with the feature map $F(x)$. Our goal is to use the density map to enhance the model's attention to dense areas of vehicle objects, so the density map $D(x)$ is first passed through a Sigmoid activation layer to amplify the response values of the pixels attributed to the vehicle objects in the density map to obtain the activated density map $D'(x)$. Then, the fusion is performed using the following equation:

$$F'(x) = F(x) + F(x)D'(x) \tag{1}$$

As a result, we obtain the feature map $F'(x)$ reinforced by the density map, which is sent to the subsequent structure of the network to extract the point information. The schematic diagram of the density map enhancement module is shown in Fig. 2.

It should be noted that the density map $D(x)$ generated in the above process is the same size as the main feature map $F_0(x)$, so for supervised model training, $D(x)$ must first be up-sampled to the same size as the baseline density map $D_{GT}(x)$, denoted as $D_u(x)$. In the experiments of this paper, the loss function generated by the density map in this module will use the L_2 loss:

$$\mathcal{L}_{den} = |D_{GT}(x) - D_u(x)|^2 \tag{2}$$

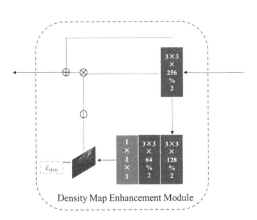

Fig. 2. Density map enhancement module

3.3 Candidate Point Processing

For the enhanced feature map $F'(x)$ obtained by the density map enhancement operation, candidate points need to be laid on it according to the original P2PNet method as the basis for subsequent object prediction points. The idea of laying candidate points is similar to laying candidate boxes in the candidate region proposal network (RPN) in the classical object detection algorithm Faster R-CNN. On each pixel of the reinforcement feature map $F'(x)$, k candidate points are laid out in a grid-like pattern: that is, a single pixel is evenly cut into several grids, and a total of k candidate points are laid out in the center of each grid as evenly as possible. In this way, assuming that the enhanced feature map $F'(x)$ can be scaled back to the size of the input image, the k candidate points will be distributed as evenly as possible within each pixel of the original size feature map.

After laying out the candidate points, the reinforcement feature map $F'(x)$ will be simultaneously input to two parallel branches, the classification head and the regression head, to perform binary classification and coordinate regression on the candidate points. The structure of the classification head is after two convolutional layers of size 3 × 3 and 256 channels, followed by a convolutional layer of size 3 × 3 and 2k channels, where k represents the number of candidate points within each pixel on the reinforcement feature map $F'(x)$ and 2 represents the number of categories. For this task, this is a binary classification, i.e. whether the candidate point is a vehicle object or not. After this series of convolutions, the resulting map is still of the same size as the reinforcement feature map $F'(x)$, while the number of channels is 2k, storing the score of each candidate point in each pixel on the reinforcement feature map $F'(x)$ belonging to the positive or negative class. Finally, this resulting map is also activated by a Sigmoid function to obtain a normalized confidence score. The structure of the regression header is approximately the same as the classification header, but it does not need to be activated by the Sigmoid function, and the number of channels $2k$ in the final result map means that for each pixel on the reinforcement feature map $F'(x)$ there are k candidate points, and each candidate point needs to store the horizontal coordinate offset Δx and the vertical coordinate offset Δy.

As a result, we obtain the classification confidence scores and coordinate regression offsets of all candidate points laid on the reinforcement feature map $F'(x)$. If during the testing phase, we can directly output the coordinates of the predicted points according to the confidence score threshold. If during the training phase, the Hungarian matching algorithm is used to match the candidate points with the anchor points according to the weighted sum of the classification confidence score and coordinate distance difference as the matching criterion, the loss function of classification and regression can be formed to supervise the model training.

Assuming that there are M candidate points and N anchor points, the value of k should be designed in such a way that $M > N$. After the one-to-one matching, there are N candidate points that will be matched with the anchor points, and the set of these points is denoted as:

$$\hat{\mathcal{P}}_{pos} = \left\{\hat{p}_{\xi(i)} | i \in (1, 2, \ldots, N)\right\} \tag{3}$$

The set of the remaining $(M - N)$ candidate points that are not matched are denoted as:

$$\hat{\mathcal{P}}_{neg} = \left\{\hat{p}_{\xi(i)} | i \in (N + 1, N + 2, \ldots, M)\right\} \tag{4}$$

Then the loss function for the classification part will use the Focused Loss:

$$\mathcal{L}_{cls} = -\frac{1}{M}\left(\sum_{I=1}^{N} log\hat{c}_{\xi(i)} + \lambda_1 \sum_{i=N+1}^{M} log\left(1 - \hat{c}_{\xi(i)}\right)\right) \tag{5}$$

where λ_1 is the hyperparameter. The loss function for the coordinate regression part will use the average Euclidean distance between the points on the match and the anchor points as follows:

$$\mathcal{L}_{loc} = \frac{1}{N}\sum_{I=1}^{N} \left\| p_i - \hat{p}_{\xi(i)} \right\|_2^2 \tag{6}$$

3.4 Model Structure

On the limited-resolution remote sensing images, vehicles are small-sized objects, and if too much down-sampling operation is used, it may lead to the loss of some feature information and thus reduce the extraction accuracy. The original P2PNet uses the first 17 layers of VGG-16 (four times max-pooling in total, divided into five major layers) as the backbone network, and only the two feature maps of the last two layers (1/8 and 1/16 size) are fused using the feature pyramid module, but the feature maps at this scale are not best suited for the vehicle localization task in this paper. At the same time, considering that the gain of the dilated convolution is higher for the model to extract vehicle objects according to the CSRNet setup, the last layers in the backbone network can be replaced by the dilated convolution. So, we proposed various sub-models for experiments in these two improvement directions and finally obtained the optimal model structure.

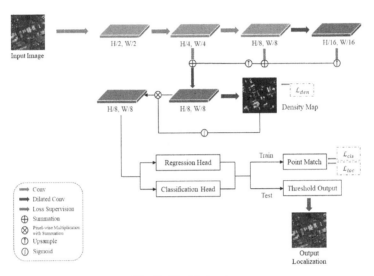

Fig. 3. Model structure

The structure of the final model is shown in Fig. 3. Compared with the original P2PNet structure, the model expands the fusion of the feature pyramid module to fuse the three feature maps of the second, third, and fourth max-pooling layers and outputs the main feature map of 1/4 size at the end of this module to be fed into the density map enhancement module. The loss function during the training period uses the weighted sum of the three loss functions, Eq. (2) density map loss function, Eq. (5) classification loss function, and Eq. (6) coordinate regression loss function as follows:

$$L = \mathcal{L}_{cls} + \lambda_2 \mathcal{L}_{loc} + \lambda_3 \mathcal{L}_{den} \tag{7}$$

where λ_2 and λ_3 are hyperparameters.

4 Experiments

4.1 Dataset and Experimental Configuration

We use the RSVC dataset for our experiments. This dataset, called Remote Sensing Vehicle Counting Dataset, is obtained from a series of operations including down-sampling, cropping, and annotations transformation from the existing DOTA and ITCVD datasets of high-resolution aerospace imagery object detection datasets containing vehicle objects. It has a spatial resolution in the range of 0.5 m to 1 m. And it is a single-point annotations vehicle object dataset that can be used for deep learning training of vehicle counting or localization models for limited-resolution remote sensing images. The parameters of the RSVC dataset are listed in Table 1.

Table 1. RSVC dataset

Parameters	Training Set	Test Set
Numbers of Images	985	133
Maximum Numbers of Vehicles	4826	4496
Minimum Numbers of Vehicles	1	1
Average Numbers of Vehicles	146.384	256.364
Maximum GSD	~1.1 m	
Minimum GSD	~0.5 m	
Maximum Image Size	1024 × 1024	
Minimum Image Size	~200 × 200	

For training and testing on the RSVC dataset, the following benchmark experimental settings are used in this paper: the learning rate of the skeleton network is set to 10^{-5}, the learning rate of the rest of the network is set to 10^{-4}, and the model is trained for 1000 rounds (epoch). For our model, $k = 4$, $\lambda_1 = 0.5$, $\lambda_2 = 0.002$, and $\lambda_3 = 0.1$ are set.

4.2 Comparative Results and Visualization

Following the above experimental configuration, the counting and localization test results for each model on the RSVC dataset can be obtained, as shown in Table 2.

The comparison models for this experiment are some typical models for object counting and localization mentioned above, where CSRNet⁻ is the counting model, only counting accuracy is calculated; two density-based keypoint localization models (D2CNet and MPS), counting accuracy (noted as Model-Count) is calculated by density map counting results, and then counting accuracy (noted as Model-Loc) is calculated by localization point results.

For the accuracy metrics of model counting, three localization metrics, MAE (Mean Absolute Error), MSE (Mean Square Error), and NAE (Normalized Absolute Error) are used. For the accuracy metrics of model localization, three localization metrics, Precision, Recall, and F-1 Score are used. It can be found that the pseudo box method LSC-CNN obtains the optimal recall, but its performance in other accuracy metrics is slightly inferior. As can be seen in the subsequent visualization results display, the pseudo box extracted by this method has a large problem in size; the two density-based keypoint localization methods have poor performance in both counting accuracy and

Table 2. Experimental results

Model	Counting			Localization		
	MAE	MSE	NAE	Precision	Recall	F1-Score
CSRNet⁻	52.7	106.8	0.39	–	–	–
LSC-CNN	55.37	117.69	0.64	0.5513	**0.6142**	0.5394
D2CNet-Count	50.05	105.18	0.56	–	–	–
D2CNet-Loc	73.86	208.81	0.52	0.5163	0.5025	0.4681
MPS-Count	85.09	182.16	0.45	–	–	–
MPS-Loc	72.27	240.87	**0.28**	0.3061	0.3217	0.2967
P2PNet	47.26	106.19	0.35	0.5911	0.5828	0.5568
Ours	**37.68**	**76.25**	0.31	**0.6025**	0.6115	**0.5790**

localization accuracy. And the counting results of such density maps have the problem of mismatching with the final number of extracted points; both the original P2PNet and our model perform better in localization accuracy, and the counting accuracy of P2PNet is comparable to that of the counting model CSRNet⁻, while our proposed model performs significantly better than CSRNet⁻ in counting metrics.

In summary, P2PNet and our model are better in both accuracy of counting and localization, and our model achieves the combined best performance. This not only indicates that the point-based keypoint localization model is more suitable for the task of this paper, but also demonstrates that the improved scheme proposed in this paper can further enhance the counting accuracy of the model in the vehicle localization process. The visualization and positioning results of some images are shown in Fig. 4.

In all these visualization results, our model achieves a relatively good performance. Even in Fig. 4(b), the prediction result of the model is slightly inferior to CSRNet⁻, but it still not only has better visualization and quantitative results but also is the best performer among all localization methods. Meanwhile, these images also demonstrate the adaptability of the proposed method to both the typical distribution and the dense distribution of vehicle objects, and our model exhibits the most stable performance. In addition, it can be found that the pseudo box method LSC-CNN often makes errors in the box size; the two density-based keypoint localization methods perform poorly, especially MPS predicts poorly in the face of a large number of dense vehicle objects scenario in Fig. 4(b). We can also examine some detailed parts of these images, as shown in Fig. 5.

Each image in Fig. 5 is selected with a specific region to zoom in and show details. In Fig. 5(a), the original P2PNet's localization shows a certain degree of offset and the visualization was very messy, even mistakenly detecting the structures on top of buildings as vehicle objects, while our predictions are relatively neater and closer to the ground truth annotation. This indicates that the density map enhancement strategy can strengthen the model's attention to the area where the vehicle object is located, help the model obtain more accurate localization results, and also suppress some false

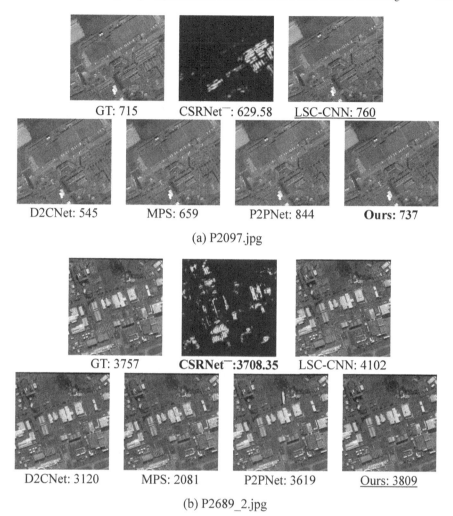

Fig. 4. Localization results for two images of RSVC dataset. (Green points: ground truth (GT); density map: visualization of the counting-only model; green boxes: the pseudo box; red points: prediction results of the keypoint localization). (Color figure online)

detection cases. In Fig. 5(b), the original P2PNet shows more missed detections, while our predictions are more complete. This indicates that enhancing the model's attention with a density map does allow the model to extract more difficult objects and avoid some of the missed detection cases.

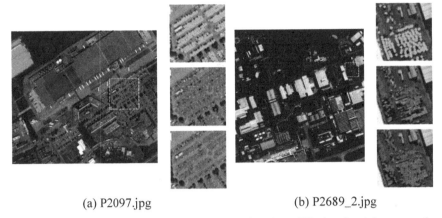

(a) P2097.jpg   (b) P2689_2.jpg

Fig. 5. Details of RSVC image localization results. The enlarged blocks of each image are, from top to bottom, GT annotation, P2PNet prediction results, and our prediction results

5 Conclusion

Limited-resolution remote sensing imagery has strong potential for vehicle extraction and traffic flow monitoring, but there are great vacancies in related studies due to various difficult characteristics of vehicle objects limited to this resolution. In this paper, we propose a series of point-based keypoint localization vehicle localization models based on density map enhancement strategy and conduct simulation experiments on the RSVC dataset to verify the feasibility of vehicle counting and localization work in limited-resolution remote sensing imagery. The results verify that the proposed point-based keypoint localization based on the density map enhancement strategy can achieve satisfactory accuracy in the vehicle localization task of limited-resolution remote sensing images and have considerable application potential.

References

1. Guo, Y., Wu, C., Du, B., Zhang, L.: Density map-based vehicle counting in remote sensing images with limited resolution. ISPRS J. Photogramm. Remote. Sens. **189**, 201–217 (2022)
2. Zhang, Y., Zhou, D., Chen, S., Gao, S., Ma, Y.: Single-image crowd counting via multi-column convolutional neural network. In: IEEE Conference on Computer Vision and Pattern Recognition (CVPR), Las Vegas, NV, USA, pp. 589–597 (2016)
3. Sam, D.B., Surya, S., Babu, R.V.: Switching convolutional neural network for crowd counting. In: IEEE Conference on Computer Vision and Pattern Recognition (CVPR), Honolulu, HI, USA, pp. 4031–4039 (2017)
4. Li, Y., Zhang, X., Chen, D.: CSRNet: dilated convolutional neural networks for understanding the highly congested scenes. In: IEEE/CVF Conference on Computer Vision and Pattern Recognition, Salt Lake City, UT, USA, pp. 1091–1100 (2018)
5. Cao, X., Wang, Z., Zhao, Y., Su, F.: Scale aggregation network for accurate and efficient crowd counting. In: Ferrari, V., Hebert, M., Sminchisescu, C., Weiss, Y. (eds.) Computer Vision-ECCV 2018, LNCS, vol. 11209, pp. 757–773. Springer, Cham (2018)

6. Gao, G., Liu, Q., Wang, Y.: Counting from sky: a large-scale data set for remote sensing object counting and a benchmark method. IEEE Trans. Geosci. Remote Sens. **56**(5), 3642–3655 (2021)
7. Alanazi, R., Elhadad, A., Taloba, A.I., Abd El-Aziz, R.M.: A large-scale dataset and deep learning model for detecting and counting olive trees in satellite imagery. Comput. Intell. Neurosci. **2022**, 1549842–1549849 (2022)
8. Sam, D.B., Peri, S.V., Sundararaman, M.N., Kamath, A., Babu, R.V.: Locate, size, and count: accurately resolving people in dense crowds via detection. IEEE Trans. Pattern Anal. Mach. Intell. **43**(8), 2739–2751 (2021)
9. Zand, M., Damirchi, H., Farley, A., Molahasani, M., Greenspan, M., Etemad, A.: Multiscale crowd counting and localization by multitask point supervision. In: 2022 IEEE International Conference on Acoustics, Speech and Signal Processing (ICASSP), Singapore, pp. 1820–1824 (2022)
10. Song, Q., et al.: Rethinking counting and localization in crowds: a purely point-based framework. In: 2021 IEEE/CVF International Conference on Computer Vision (ICCV), Montreal, QC, Canada, pp. 3345–3354 (2021)

Large Window Attention Based Transformer Network for Change Detection of Remote Sensing Images

Kunfeng Yu[1] (ID), Yuqian Zhang[2] (ID), Bo Hou[3], Tao Xu[1](✉) (ID), Wenshuo Li[1] (ID), Zhen Liu[1] (ID), and Junyuan Zang[1] (ID)

[1] School of Information Science and Engineering, University of Jinan, Jinan 250022, China
xutao@ujn.edu.cn
[2] No. 1 Geological Team of Shandong Provincial Bureau of Geology and Mineral Resources, Jinan 250001, China
[3] Institute of Satellite Technology, Shandong Institute of Industrial Technology, Jinan, China

Abstract. The vision transformer (VIT) is widely used in Image Detection because of their powerful capabilities. The change detection network framework based on transformer proposed in recent years, have achieved good results. However, most transformer network frameworks still have the disadvantage that they are not accurate enough for detecting large targets. Because the large window attention can enhance the network's attention to a wide range of information, it is useful for enhancing the network's ability to detect large targets. Therefore, this paper proposes a Siamese network framework based on large window attention and multi-scale. By adding the large window attention mechanism, the network framework enables it to complete the query of a wider range of context windows with little computational overhead, and we also introduce multi-scale. We experiment this network framework on UJN-CD dataset. Experimental results demonstrate that our proposed method is very efficient compared with the existing methods.

Keywords: Change detection · Transformer · Deep Learning · Remote Sensing Images

1 Introduction

Change Detection (CD), in the task of change detection of remote sensing images, refers to the determination of differences between images acquired at different times in the same geographical area. CD uses two or more different images of the same region to detect regions of change of interest. CD is commonly used in a variety of scenarios, including land use detection, land cover change, urban expansion, environmental surveys, damage assessment, and post-disaster rescue operations.

In recent years, deep learning is widely used in remote sensing image processing because of its powerful feature representation capability. In convolutional neural networks (CNNs), many change detection methods enable change detection frameworks with improved performance by extracting features. The great success of transformer in natural language processing (NLP) has led researchers to apply transformers

H. Lu et al. (Eds.): ICIG 2023, LNCS 14359, pp. 308–319, 2023.
https://doi.org/10.1007/978-3-031-46317-4_25

to various computer vision tasks. Compared to deep convolutional neural networks, these transformer networks have a larger effective receptive field (ERF), which allows the transformer to obtain better context modeling capabilities. However, most existing transformer-based CD networks do not perform well for the large and complex targets. LWAASPP has the ability to improve the recognition of large targets in the network, so we propose our network framework, which enhances the ability of feature acquisition in large regions of the network by introducing LWAASPP. Thus, our framework performs better for large targets.

LWAASPP consists of multiple LWA-Transformers that are improved by adding large window attention modules to the base transformer. In large window attention [1], a uniformly partitioned patch query covers a larger region of contextual patches, while patch in local-window concern queries only itself. Here, the patch in the large window note can capture contextual information of any size, incurring only a small computational overhead caused by the location blending operation. Therefore, the LWAASPP, which consists of a large window attention and multiple scales, is effective in improving the context modeling capability of the network framework.

Thus, the main contributions of this paper are as follows:

We propose a novel CD learning framework for remote sensing images, which enhances the ability of context acquisition by introducing large window attention, improved recognition of complex targets.

Extensive experiments on the UJN-CD dataset show that our framework achieves better performance than most state-of-the-art methods.

2 Related Work

2.1 Technology Research

With the development of remote sensing technology, high resolution remote sensing images are widely used in change detection. In the development of high-resolution remote sensing images, many change detection methods have been proposed. Here, they are usually classified into two categories: traditional methods and deep neural network-based methods.

Traditional change detection methods are usually used to analyze multi-temporal remote sensing images for change detection from the perspective of algebraic operations or feature information, traditional methods focus on the feature information of an image, including more significant features such as shape, texture, and spectrum. Through these features traditional methods are also used in certain scenarios. Traditional methods include image arithmetic algorithm, Change Vector Analysis (CVA), Image Regression, Vegetation Index Difference Method, Principal Component Analysis (PCA), Multivariate Alteration Detection (MAD), Independent Component Analysis (ICA), and so on.

With the development of deep learning techniques, many work to improve the performance of CD by extracting more discriminatory features. For example, Hou et al. [2] took advantage of the depth feature and introduced low-rank analysis to improve the CD results. Meanwhile, some methods transform the CD task into a binary image segmentation task. Therefore, CD can be done in a supervised manner. The authors of [3] proposed a dual attention module. This module captures long-term dependencies from both spatial and channel aspects to enhance the recognition performance of the model. The authors of [4] constructed an attention-based spatio-temporal module to obtain relationships between multi-scale dual-time features and to learn more discriminative features. The authors of [5] constructed a hierarchical feature extraction module to obtain long distance relationships in features by a combination of cross-layer and multi-head methods. The authors of [6] proposed a self-attention module and a relative attention fusion module based on an improved fractal Tanimoto similarity metric, the change information is obtained by combining the dual temporal feature information. The authors of [7] proposed a correlated attention-guided feature fusion neck to obtain object-level CD results, the attention module allows refining features that are relevant to change and suppressing irrelevant features by applying attention mechanisms spatially and on the channels. In recent years, transformer [8] have been applied to many computer vision tasks, such as image classification, object detection, and semantic segmentation. Inspired by this, Li et al. [10] proposed a codec hybrid framework for CD that combines the advantages of Transformer and U-Net. [11] unified a hierarchically structured Transformer encoder with a multilayer perception (MLP) decoder in a Siamese network to efficiently present multi-scale remote details for accurate CD. Chen et al. [12] proposed a bitemporal image transformer (BIT) that can effectively model the context in the time domain of CDs. [13] proposed a hybrid Transformer with token aggregation for remote sensing image CD. Song et al. [14] combined multi-scale Swin-transformer all these approaches show that Transformer can model inter-patch relationships for strong feature representations. However, these methods do not fully utilize the capabilities of transformers in multi-level feature learning.

3   Method

Our network framework is shown in the following figure. First, the input image goes through the convolutional block and sent to the semantic tokenizer to generate tokens. The tokens then undergo a simple concat and are fed into the transformer encoder for encoding. Then the whole tokens are split into two tokens after encoding. The two tokens are fed into the transformer decoder for decoding. Next, the output data is then put into LWAASPP for processing. Finally, the integrated data is subtracted and sent to conv for calculation of the results (Fig. 1).

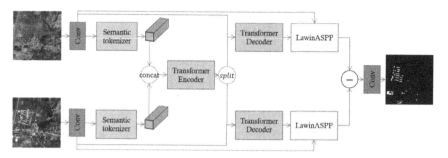

Fig. 1. Our overall network structure

3.1 Semantic Tokenizer

First, as shown in Fig. 2, we put the image features into the Siamese tokenizer, which obtains a semantic token sequence from the image features through a convolutional layer. The semantic token sequence has multiple tagging vectors whose information is extracted from the whole image features.

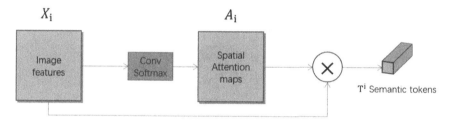

Fig. 2. Semantic tokenizer structure.

Let $X_1, X_2 \in R^{HW \times C}$ be the input dual-time image feature, where H, W and C are the height, width, and channel dimensions of the image feature. Let $T_1, T_2 \in R^{L \times C}$ be two sets of tokens, where L is the size of the set of tokens. Then each semantic token is calculated using the softmax function in the HW dimension to calculate a spatial attention map, and a weighted average sum of pixels is used to calculate a compact set of words of size L, the semantic tokens T_i.

$$T_i = (A_i)^T X_i = (softmax(conv(X_i)))^T X_i, \tag{1}$$

where *conv* denotes the point-wise convolution layer, T_I is computed by the multiplication of A_I and X_i.

3.2 Transformer Encoder

After obtaining the two sets of semantic tokens for the input dual temporal images, we use the transformer encoder to model the context between these tokens. The structure of the Transformer is shown above as shown in Fig. 3.

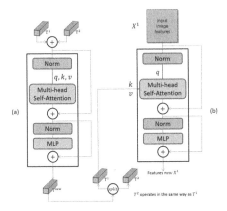

Fig. 3. Transformer encoder (a) and transformer decoder (b).

In the transformer encoder, we concatenate these two sets of tokens into a new token set $T \in R^{2L \times C}$, which is then fed into the transformer encoder. The transformer encoder consists of a multi-headed self-attentive (MSA) and multilayer perceptron (MLP) block of NE layers. And the layer normalization is placed before the MSA/MLP layer.

At each layer l, the input to self-attention is a triple (query Q, key K, value V) computed from the input $T^{(l-1)} \in R^{2L \times C}$:

$$
\begin{aligned}
Q &= T^{(l-1)}W_q^{l-1}, \\
K &= T^{(l-1)}W_k^{l-1}, \\
V &= T^{(l-1)}W_v^{l-1},
\end{aligned}
\tag{2}
$$

where W_q^{l-1}, W_k^{l-1}, $W_v^{l-1} \in R^{C \times d}$ are the learnable parameters of three linear projection layers and d is the channel dimension of the triple. One attention head is formulated as:

$$
Att(Q, \ K, \ V) = softmax\left(\frac{QK^T}{\sqrt{d}}\right)V,
\tag{3}
$$

where $softmax()$ denotes the softmax function operated on the channel dimension. Multihead self-attention is the important part of the transformer encoder. The final values of the MSA are generated by using multiple attention heads in parallel, concatenating all outputs and then projecting to result. Through joint attention information from different position of the said subspace is one of the largest advantages of MSA. Formally,

$$
\begin{aligned}
MSA\left(T^{(l-1)}\right) &= Concat(head_1, ..., head_h)W^O, \\
\text{where } head_j &= Att\left(T^{(l-1)}W_q^j, \ T^{(l-1)}W_k^j, \ T^{(l-1)}W_v^j\right),
\end{aligned}
\tag{4}
$$

where W_q^j, W_k^j, $W_v^j \in R^{C \times d}$, $W^O \in R^{hC \times d}$ are the linear projection matrices, h is the number of attention heads, j is the j-th attention head. The feature map is output after entering a linear transformation layer, a GELU activation layer, and a linear transformation layer, which is the MLP. Formally,

$$\mathrm{MLP}\left(T^{(l-1)}\right) = \mathrm{Linear}\left(\mathrm{GELU}\left(\mathrm{Linear}(T^{(l-1)})\right)\right), \tag{5}$$

Finally, we split T_{new} obtained by Transformer encoder and pass T_i to different transformer decoder.

3.3 Transformer Decoder

First, we integrate the token sequence T_i^{new} obtained from the transformer encode and the original image features X_i into the transformer decode.

The transformer decoder is composed of multiple layers, which are composed of a combination of MA and MLP. The MLP structure is the same as the transformer encoder. Formally, at each layer l, MA is defined as:

$$\begin{aligned} \mathrm{MA}\left(X_i^{(l-1)}, T_i^{new}\right) &= \mathrm{Concat}(\mathrm{head}_1, \ldots, \mathrm{head}_h)W^O, \\ \text{where } \mathrm{head}_j &= \mathrm{Att}\left(X_i^{(l-1)}W_q^j, X_i^{(l-1)}W_k^j, X_i^{(l-1)}W_v^j\right), \end{aligned} \tag{6}$$

where W_q^j, W_k^j, $W_v^j \in R^{C \times d}$, $W^O \in R^{hd \times C}$ are the linear projection matrices, h is the number of attention heads, j is the j-th attention head.

Then the feature maps X_i^{new} are passed into the different LWAASPP respectively.

3.4 Large Window Attention

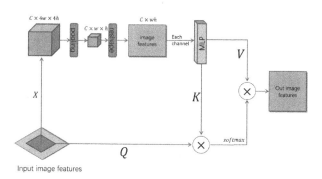

Fig. 4. Large window attention structure

We can divide the whole feature map into multiple identical blocks by large window attention. The current patch can capture more areas as the large window attention moves across the image. For simplicity, the large context patch of the query is denoted as $CP \in R^{Y^2 \times P^2 \times C}$, the query patch is denoted as $QP \in R^{P^2 \times C}$, where Y is the ratio of the context patch size to the query patch size and P^2 is the patch area. We use a multi-head MLP that focuses on the number C of channel,

$$MLP = \{MLP_1, MLP_2, \ldots, MLP_h\}.$$

where h is the number of channels.

As shown in Fig. 4, The feature map X produced by intercepting from the image features with patch size, $\hat{X}$ is obtained by pooling and reshape, $\hat{X}_i$ is fed into the MLP of each channel separately, and then concat to generate K, V, the calculation is:

$$\hat{X} = \text{Reshape}\,(pooling(X)), \tag{7}$$

$$X^{new} = \text{Reshape}\left(\text{concat}\left[MLP_1\left(\hat{X}_1\right); \; MLP_2\left(\hat{X}_2\right); \; \ldots \; MLP_h\left(\hat{X}_h\right)\right]\right), \tag{8}$$

where h is the number of channels. *pooling* denotes the average pooling operation.

Finally, after the product of k and q through softmax, multiply with v to output A. Therefore, the formula is as follows:

$$A = \text{softmax}\left(\frac{(W_q X)(W_k X^{new})^T}{\sqrt{d}}\right)(W_v X^{new}), \tag{9}$$

$$MHA = \text{concat}\,[A_1; A_2; \ldots; A_h]W_{mha} \tag{10}$$

where $W_q, W_k, W_v \in R^{C \times D_h}$ is the learned linear projection matrices, $W_{mha} \in R^{d \times C}$ is the weight of the learned aggregated multiple attention values. d is the embedding dimension.

3.5 LWAASPP

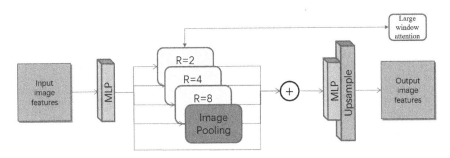

Fig. 5. LWAASPP structure

The LWAASPP module is composed of five parallel routes, including an image pooling layer, an original image input and three large window attention layers. This module has the ability to acquire multi-scale representation. In these three large window attention layers, by adjusting the size of R, the feature map of the acquired image will also change accordingly. The image pool branch uses the global pooling layer to obtain global context information and push it into a linear transformation. Then, the outputs of all routes will be concatenated and then put into the MLP for linear transformation. Finally, an Upsample layer is used to operate on the feature map (Fig. 5).

4 Experimental Results and Analysis

4.1 Datasets

The UJN-CD dataset focuses on architectural changes, the dataset includes 4 satellite images and a pair of fused images, and the area studied in the dataset includes some towns and cities in Shandong Province. The years 2019–2021 are included, while the time gap of each image pair is controlled at about 1 year, and the images are all acquired by the Gaofen-2 satellite with a resolution better than 1 m.

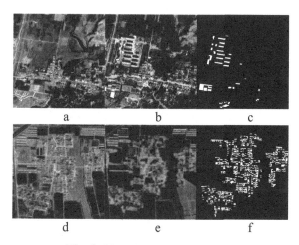

Fig. 6. UJN-CD Dataset examples.

In Fig. 6 a, b, c, are the images and real images of building additions class. d, e, f, are the images and real images of building declines class.

4.2 Implementation Details

Our experiments were conducted on a single NVIDIA GeForce RTX3090, each model used AdamW as the optimizer, the learning rate was set to 0.01, the learning rate was linearly decayed, the experiments used random initialization weights, the batch size was set to 4, the input image size for all networks was 256 * 256, and they were all formed by 1024 * 1024 images are formed after transformation, and a total of 200 iterations are performed.

4.3 Experimental Results

In this experiment we used FC-EF, FC-Siam-Conc, IFNet, SNUNet, BIT mainstream networks for our change detection comparison experiment (Table 1).

Table 1. The performance of different change detection methods in the UJN-CD dataset

Method	Recall	Precision	F1	OA
FC-EF	58.30	81 .59	68.00	99.24
FC-Siam-Conc	65.21	81.39	72.40	99.32
IFNet	62.94	86.55	72.88	99.36
SNUNet	66.62	80.95	73.09	99.32
BIT	67.04	87.76	76.01	99.42
ours	**69.12**	**90.17**	**78.25**	**99.47**

Compared with other experimental networks, our network has a significant advantage in Recall, a 2.08% improvement compared to bit network, and there is also a 2.41% improvement in accuracy. From the overall F1 metrics, our network has a good improvement compared to other network. Therefore, it can be considered that our network is helpful for practical applications.

In Fig. 7, a is the former image, b is the latter image, c is the real label, d is the prediction image of FC-EF, e is the prediction image of FC-Siam-Conc, f is the prediction image of IFNet, and g is the prediction image of SNUNet, h is the prediction map of BIT, i is the prediction map of our network.

For the complex targets in the figure it can be seen that the experimental results of our network have different enhancement effects compared to other networks.

4.4 Ablation Experiments

We conducted ablation experiments on our proposed network framework, and we divided the experiments into three approaches. Finally, it can be seen from the table below that LWAASPP has different levels of improvement in Precision and F1 index compared with the other two types of methods, which proves that LWAASPP has practical effects on CD networks (Table 2).

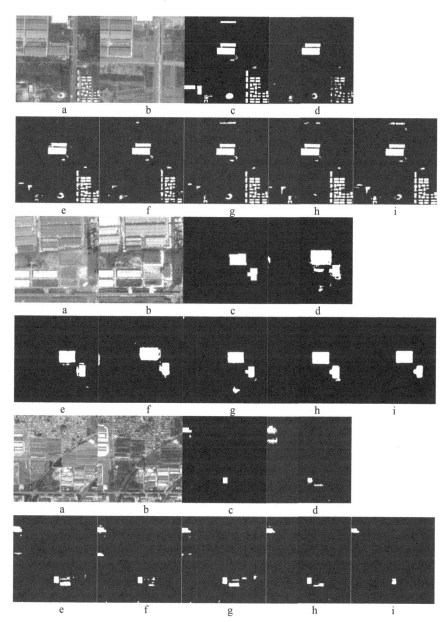

Fig. 7. Comparison of network results on the UJN-CD dataset

Table 2. Results of our network ablation experiments.

Method	Recall	Precision	F1	OA
Transformer	71.08	82.77	75.26	99.41
Transformer + ASPP	70.91	85.96	78.01	99.44
Transformer + LWAASPP	69.12	90.17	78.25	99.47

5   Conclusion

In this work, we propose a new learning framework for change detection in biphasic remote sensing images. Technically, we start with a converter with an Encoder-Decoder structure. Then, we introduce the pyramid structure of the LWAASPP for feature extraction. Finally, we use deep supervised learning with multiple loss functions for model training. Extensive experiments conducted on the UJN-CD benchmark show that our proposed framework exhibits better performance than most state-of-the-art methods. In future work, we will explore more efficient transformer structures to reduce the computational effort.

Acknowledgement. This research was supported by the Shandong Provincial Key Research and Development Program (2018JMRH0102), Science and technology project of Department of Industry and Information Technology of Shandong Province (SJG2103), the Science and Technology Program of University of Jinan (XKY1803, XKY1928, XKY2001).

References

1. Yan, H., Zhang, C., Wu, M.: LWA transformer: improving semantic segmentation transformer with multi-scale representations via large window attention. arXiv e-prints (2022). https://doi.org/10.48550/arXiv.2201.01615
2. Hou, B., Wang, Y., Liu, Q.: Change detection based on deep features and low rank. IEEE Geosci. Remote Sens. Lett. **14**(12), 2418–2422 (2017)
3. Chen, J., et al.: DASNet: dual attentive fully convolutional Siamese networks for change detection of high-resolution satellite images. IEEE J. Sel. Top. Appl. Earth Obs. Remote. Sens. **14**, 1194–1206 (2020)
4. Chen, H., Shi, Z.: A spatial-temporal attention-based method and a new dataset for remote sensing image change detection. Remote Sens. **12**, 1662 (2020)
5. Cheng, H., Wu, H., Zheng, J., Qi, K., Liu, W.: A hierarchical self-attention augmented Laplacian pyramid expanding network for change detection in high-resolution remote sensing images. ISPRS J. Photogramm. Remote Sens. **182**, 52–66 (2021)
6. Diakogiannis, F.I., Waldner, F., Caccetta, P.: Looking for change? Roll the Dice and demand attention. Remote Sens. **13**, 3707 (2021)
7. Song, L., Xia, M., Jin, J., Qian, M., Zhang, Y.: SUACDNet: attentional change detection network based on Siamese U-shaped structure. Int. J. Appl. Earth Obs. Geoinf. **105**, 102597 (2021)

8. Vaswani, A., et al.: Attention is all you need. In: Advances in Neural Information Processing Systems, vol. 30 (2017)
9. Wang, G., Li, B., Zhang, T., Zhang, S.: A network combining a transformer and a convolutional neural network for remote sensing image change detection. Remote Sens. **14**(9), 2228 (2022)
10. Li, Q., Zhong, R., Du, X., Du, Y.: TransUNetCD: a hybrid transformer network for change detection in optical remote-sensing images. IEEE Trans. Geosci. Remote Sens. **60**, 1–19 (2022)
11. Bandara, W.G.C., Patel, V.M.: A transformer-based Siamese network for change detection. arXiv:2201.01293 (2022)
12. Chen, H., Qi, Z., Shi, Z.: Remote sensing image change detection with transformers. IEEE Trans. Geosci. Remote Sens. **60**, 1–14 (2021)
13. Ke, Q., Zhang, P.: Hybrid-TransCD: a hybrid transformer remote sensing image change detection network via token aggregation. ISPRS Int. J. Geo Inf. **11**(4), 263 (2022)
14. Song, F., Zhang, S., Lei, T., Song, Y., Peng, Z.: MSTDSNet-CD: multiscale Swin transformer and deeply supervised network for change detection of the fast-growing urban regions. IEEE Geosci. Remote Sens. Lett. **19**, 1–5 (2022)

U-TEN: An Unsupervised Two-Branch Enhancement Network for Object Detection Under Complex-Light Condition

Xiaolei Luo[1], Xiaoxuan Ma[1], Song Hu[1], Kejun Wu[3], Jiang Tang[1,2], and You Yang[1(✉)]

[1] Huazhong University of Science and Technology, Wuhan 430074, China
yangyou@hust.edu.cn
[2] Optics Valley Laboratory, Wuhan 430074, China
[3] School of Electrical and Electronic Engineering, Nanyang Technological University, Singapore 639798, Singapore

Abstract. The goal of low-light enhancement is to improve the visual quality of dark regions in an image. However, the existing low-light enhancement methods always failed in nighttime traffic surveillance. The reason comes from complex-light instead of low-light, while traditional methods can hardly treat regions with different light conditions. In this paper, in order to solve above challenge, we propose an unsupervised tow-branch complex-light enhancement network (U-TEN) with graph attention network and generative adversarial network to enhance pixels in different regions according to their light conditions. To solve the problem that enhance weights are supposed to varied with regions, we proposed two-branch attention block. It aims to model two kinds of light information interaction. U-TEN can improve the object detection performance under complex-light condition in nighttime traffic surveillance. The proposed U-TEN is verified on ODLS dataset, and the results show that our network improves the object detection average precision by 3.50% on average, and 4.93% in maximum. These results demonstrate the proposed U-TEN has great potential to be used in vision applications of nighttime traffic surveillance.

Keywords: Graph Attention Network · Light condition · Image enhancement

This work was supported in part by the National Key Research and Development Program of China under Grant 2020YFB2103501, in part by the National Natural Science Foundation of China under Grant 61991412, in part by the Major Project of Fundamental Research on Frontier Leading Technology of Jiangsu Province under Grant BK20222006.

H. Lu et al. (Eds.): ICIG 2023, LNCS 14359, pp. 320–331, 2023.
https://doi.org/10.1007/978-3-031-46317-4_26

1   Introduction

As is illustrated in [14,21], Low-light enhancement is always the problem researchers concern about, as it matters the quality of visual information of the image. Typically, objects in low-light images are too dark to be recognized [10,20]. Challenges remain in case of nighttime traffic surveillance, and images may suffer from nonuniformed light conditions. How to improve the visual quality of images and the performance of object detection in such complex-light condition becomes a new paradigm in the community [9,11].

In recent years, learning based methods for low-light image enhancement have witnessed a rapid development. The classical low-light image enhancement networks are almost based on supervised learning. For example, LLNet [17] utilizes a variant of stacked sparse denoising autoencoder [5] to enhance and denoise low-light images. This work inspires the application of end-to-end networks in image low-light enhancement algorithms. Lv *et al.* [18] proposed an end-to-end multi-branch enhancement network. In addition to the aforementioned algorithms, researchers have developed a Multi-Scale Retinex with Color Restoration (MSRCR) [7], which enhances color in the multi-scale Retinex algorithm. Furthermore, some researchers have introduced pyramid network (LPNet) [2] and laplacian pyramid [1] in low-light enhancement network, proposing DSLR [16]. These methods effectively integrate feature representations through commonly used end-to-end network structures. Xu *et al.* [25] proposed a frequency-based decomposition enhancement network based on the contrast formed by image noise in different frequency components. Zhang *et al.* proposed KinD [27] consisting of three sub-networks. One sub-network is used to decompose the input image into illumination and reflection maps, another to restore the decomposed reflection map, and the remaining one to adjust the decomposed illumination map. A deep curve estimation network called Zero-DCE was proposed in [4]. Zero-DCE considers light enhancement as a task of estimating specific curves for image pixel values, taking dark images as input and producing mapping curves as output. These curves are used to adjust the dynamic range of the input at a pixel level to obtain an enhanced image. Additionally, an accelerated and lightweight version called Zero-DCE++ [15] was also proposed. Rizwan *et al.* focus on ill light conditions, and proposed [12,13] to handle it. Ma *et al.* proposed a self-calibrating low-light enhancement network SCI [19] that achieves the goal by establishing a cascade low-light enhancement network with a weight-sharing mechanism. Jin *et al.* proposed a night image enhancement network [6] combining image layer decomposition network and light suppression network. Wu *et al.* propose a Retinex-based deep unfolding network (URetinex-Net [24]), which unfolds an optimization problem into a learnable network to decompose a low-light image into reflectance and illumination layers.

Existing methods for image enhancement primarily address situations where the majority of the scene is relatively dark. And the light transportation is always diffuse reflection. However, light enhancement techniques are often employed in conjunction with numerous high-level vision tasks such as object detection and segmentation. For instance, in a nighttime traffic surveillance, light enhancement technology needs to be combined with object detection techniques. Such a scenario differs significantly from the typical low-light scenarios described above, as there are numerous light sources in this scenario (such as headlights and traffic signals), and specular reflection is quite common. So when using existing light enhancement methods to handle such situation, the bright regions will be enhanced as the dark regions, resulting in excessive illumination in the bright regions. Challenges arise from performing vision tasks on the excessively enhanced images, such as object detection and action recognition. Another challenge is that it is hard to build paired data required in the existing supervised methods, especially in dynamic scenes, where objects are in irregular moving.

In this paper, we proposed a U-TEN network by combining Graph Attention Network [22] (GAT) and Generative Adversarial Network [3] (GAN). It is an unsupervised two-branch network to solve the complex-light enhancement challenge in object detection task. In the proposed network, we design two branch networks for feature extraction under long-range interaction and short-range interaction, respectively. These two types of features are merged with the guidance of SNR-map (Signal to Noise Ratio map). Finally, we train the proposed U-TEN networks on ODLS dataset in unsupervised way, which does not rely on paired data. Experiment results demonstrate the proposed U-TEN achieves better object detection performance than other state-of-the-art methods.

The remaining sections are organized as follows: the first section introduces the problem we concern about and the method we proposed. The second section is in charge of reveal U-TEN we proposed in details. And the corresponding experiment results are shown in the next section. In last section, we conclude the paper and propose future work briefly.

2   The Proposed U-TEN

In this section, we introduce the network we proposed in details. In subsequent sections, the input image and the output image are denoted as $I \in \mathbb{R}^{H \times W \times 3}$ and $I' \in \mathbb{R}^{H \times W \times 3}$. The generator and discriminator are denoted as $G(\cdot)$ and $D(\cdot)$. The encoder and decoder are denoted as $\text{En}(\cdot)$ and $\text{De}(\cdot)$.

In this work, our goal is to enhance the input image which is under complex-light condition to secure the output image have better performances in object detection. The overview of U-TEN are as Fig. 1: firstly we compute the SNR-map of the input image, then feed the encoder with input image to get the intermediate feature $F(F = \text{En}(I))$. Secondly use the two-branch attention block to extract feature from F under long and short range interaction respectively. Then we can get the output feature F_o, then use the decoder to process F' to obtain the final result $I(I = \text{De}(F_o))$. All mentioned above belong to the work process of generator, which aims to generate image under normal light condition. The duty of discriminator is to tell the output of generator from natural normal light image, it can create obstacle for generator to force it to produce results of as higher quality as possible. The whole process doesn't need paired dataset as supervised information provider. The VGG16 network will help constrain I and I' have same content.

2.1   SNR-Map Computation

In nighttime traffic surveillance scenes, there are numerous light sources which can affect the overall illumination of the image. Typically, objects in close proximity to the light source exhibit ideal illumination condition and pixels in corresponding region of image have high signal-to-noise ratio (SNR), whereas areas further away from the light source exhibit lower pixel SNR. The primary objective of enhancing complex-light images is to significantly increase the brightness of low SNR pixels within the aforementioned low SNR area, resulting in higher SNR. For high SNR pixels, the degree of brightness enhancement should be more subtle (as excessive brightness can negatively impact visual effects and subsequent vision tasks).

As there is a lack of images under normal light condition for pairing with the same scene, there is no reference for enhancing low SNR pixels. However, it is worth noting that both low SNR and high SNR pixels are affected by the light source, albeit to varying degrees. In other words, some high SNR image regions can be approximated as being under normal light conditions. By utilizing the image information from these high SNR areas, the problem of lacking light enhancement references for low SNR pixels can be addressed. The purpose of the SNR map is to model the SNR levels in different regions of an image. This is achieved by computing the SNR map, which provides sufficient prior information for the fusion of two-branch features. Therefore, we adopt the following approach to compute the SNR map: Since image noise often manifests as pixels with significant differences in pixel values from the surrounding pixels in a specific region, it can be approximated that the area is affected by image noise when there is a drastic change in pixel values among adjacent pixels. Given the input image I, firstly we compute its gray-scale image I_g, then the corresponding SNR map $S \in \mathbb{R}^{H \times W}$ is defined as follows:

$$\tilde{I}_g = \text{bidenoise}\left(I_g\right), \quad N = \text{abs}\left(I_g - \tilde{I}_g\right), \quad S = \tilde{I}_g/N \qquad (1)$$

The function bidenoise($\cdot$) denotes the bilateral filtering operation for images, aimed at eliminating noise while preserving image details. The function abs($\cdot$) represents an absolute value operation. $N \in \mathbb{R}^{H \times W}$ represents a distribution map of image noise. By dividing the pixel values of each pixel in the gray-scale image $\tilde{I}_g$, after being subjected to bilateral filtering, by the corresponding pixel values in the noise distribution map N, an SNR map for the input image can be obtained.

2.2   Two-Branch Attention Block

In this section, we proposed two branch attention block to extract and merge features from different ranges. As the SNR of pixels in different regions varies, the two-branch attention block includes two distinct feature branch extraction modules: a long-range interaction branch and a short-range interaction branch. The long-range interaction branch primarily addresses the need for pixels in low SNR ratio areas to obtain information from pixels in high SNR ratio areas.

Long-Range Interaction Branch. To ensure the efficient transmission of information, a graph attention network is utilized in this section's algorithm to achieve long-range interaction. The detailed implements are as follows. Given the encoded feature F, we divide it into m patches, which is denoted as $F_i, F_i \in R^{p \times p \times C}, i = \{1, \ldots, m\}$, assumed that $F \in \mathbb{R}^{h \times w \times c}$, so we can got $m = \frac{h}{p} \times \frac{w}{p}$. Before utilizing GAT, it is imperative to construct the graph. Within the algorithms presented in this section, each patch is treated as a node, resulting in a total of m nodes. Furthermore, by resizing F_i we can get the feature for node i, denoted as $\vec{h_i} \in \mathbb{R}^l$, where $l = p \times p \times c$, the definition for nodes within the GAT is established so long. The subsequent tasks involve defining the edges between the nodes. Typically, regions with high SNR and those with SNR have considerable geometric distances in images. Nevertheless, neural network inference is primarily used to understand the distribution of data. Thus, it is essential to reflect the differences in geometric distances onto the data distribution. Due to the substantial content variance between areas of different signal-to-noise ratios, there is also a significant difference in pixel values between two regions. Therefore, the Euclidean distance and Structural Similarity (SSIM) can be utilized to represent this dissimilarity. Regarding any patch F_i represented by a node i, the SSIM value $l_{SSIM}(F_i, F_j)$ for the corresponding patch between node i and any other node j (where $j = 1, 2, \ldots, m$) is first calculated. Then, $1/l_{SSIM}(F_i, F_j)$ is used as the distance between node i and node j, with the distance between nodes

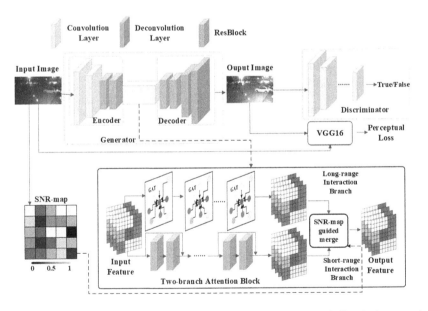

Fig. 1. The overview of U-TEN. U-TEN includes generator and discriminator. And generator can be divided into encoder, decoder and two-branch attention block. The two-branch attention block is designed for feature interaction from two different ranges. It combines graph attention network and resblock.

being closer if the similarity between the patches corresponding to the nodes is lower. Finally, the edges are constructed by selecting the N closest nodes. The display exhibits the information updating process of graph nodes in the attention mechanism. For any given node i, there exists a set of neighboring nodes, represented as $\mathcal{N}(i)$, which are those nodes that have a relationship with node i via an edge. During each update of node i, a correlation coefficient eij is computed between node i and its neighboring node j ($j \in \mathcal{N}(i)$). This computation process involves the features $\vec{h}_i$ of node i and the features $\vec{h}_j$ of node j, as shown in Eq. (3):

$$e_{ij} = a\left(\mathbf{W}\vec{h}_i, \mathbf{W}\vec{h}_j\right) \tag{2}$$

Firstly, the node features are mapped to a high-dimensional space using a weight matrix $\mathbf{W}$. The mapping of node i and node j's features processed by weight matrix $\mathbf{W}$ is concatenated and then mapped to a real number using a single-layer feed forward neural network. After computing the correlation coefficient between node i and its neighboring nodes, the next step is to calculate the attention coefficient α_{ij} between node i and node j:

$$\alpha_{ij} = \frac{\exp\left(\text{LeakyReLU}\left(\vec{\mathbf{a}}^T\left[\mathbf{W}\vec{h}_i\|\mathbf{W}\vec{h}_j\right]\right)\right)}{\sum_{k \in \mathcal{N}_i} \exp\left(\text{LeakyReLU}\left(\vec{\mathbf{a}}^T\left[\mathbf{W}\vec{h}_i\|\mathbf{W}\vec{h}_k\right]\right)\right)} \tag{3}$$

where LeakyReLU($\cdot$) denotes LeakyReLU function, T denotes the transpose operation of matrix, $\|$ denotes concatenation. With α_{ij}, we can calculate the input feature using weighted sum, then node i's updated feature $\vec{h}_i'$ can be obtained as follows:

$$\vec{h}_i' = \sigma\left(\sum_{j \in \mathcal{N}_i} \alpha_{ij} \mathbf{W}\vec{h}_j\right) \tag{4}$$

The block proposed in this section utilizes a multi-head graph attention mechanism. During a single node feature update, multiple branches are utilized to perform graph attention operations. This approach provides the benefit of rendering the extracted features more robust while also enhancing the stability of network training. The node feature output, denoted as $\vec{h}_i'$, after being processed by the multi-headed graph attention mechanism can be calculated using the Eq. (6).

$$\vec{h}_i' = \|_{k=1}^{K} \sigma\left(\sum_{j \in \mathcal{N}_i} \alpha_{ij}^k \mathbf{W}^k \vec{h}_j\right) \tag{5}$$

where K denotes the how many heads we use in multi-head graph attention mechanism, α_{ij}^k denotes the weight matrix of the k-th head. $\sigma(\cdot)$ denotes Sigmoid function. In order to facilitate the fusion of the output features of the short-range interaction branch, the weight matrix $\mathbf{W}_o$ will be used for $\vec{h}_i'$: $\vec{h}_i^f = \mathbf{W}_o\vec{h}_i'$, then we can get the node i's final feature $\vec{h}_i^f$. Resize $\vec{h}_i^f$ to F_{il}, the size of which is as the same as F_i. With all mentioned above, the output of the long-range interaction branch F_l can be produced by gathering all F_{il}.

Short-Range Interaction Branch. For the short-range interaction branch, the convolution operation can fulfill the interaction requirements, as the pixels only need to interact with surrounding neighboring pixels. Moreover, the convolution operation offers the advantages of training stability and relatively small computational cost. Therefore, in the short-range interaction branch, we employs the processing of multiple concatenated residual blocks (ResBlocks) to handle the input feature F, in order to obtain the short-range interaction result F_s. It is worth noting that the residual block does not alter the size of the input feature. This process can be mathematically expressed as follows:

$$F_s = \text{ResBlock}(F)^n \tag{6}$$

We resize the SNR map S to the same size of F and normalize it to S'. Then we can get the outputs of two branches and merge them, the result is denoted as F_o, which is described as:

$$F_o = F_s \times S' + (1 - S') \times F_l \tag{7}$$

Eventually, the output image I' can be calculated as:

$$I' = \text{De}\,(F_o) \tag{8}$$

2.3   Loss Function

Firstly we calculate adversarial loss $\mathcal{L}_{adv}(I, I')$ for adversarial training:

$$\mathcal{L}_{adv}\,(I, I') = \mathbb{E}[\log(D(I))] + \mathbb{E}\,[\log\,(1 - D\,(I'))] \tag{9}$$

where $\mathbb{E}[\cdot]$ denotes mathematical expectation, $\log(D(I))$ denotes the possibility of which I is considered under complex-light condition by discriminator D. $\mathcal{L}_{adv}$ can force generator G to make I''s light condition as close as normal light condition. The next loss function we want to introduce is perceptual loss $\mathcal{L}_{perc}(I, I')$ [8], which use VGG16 network to keep I' has as same content as I.

$$\mathcal{L}_{perc}(I, I') = \|\,\text{VGG16}(I) - \text{VGG16}(I')\|_2 \tag{10}$$

$\mathcal{L}_{perc}(I, I')$ calculate the normalized L2 distance between the features extracted from I and I' respectively by VGG16 network. Actually we use the feature produced by the 3-th, 7-th, 11-th convolution layer of VGG16 network. The whole loss function of our network is:

$$\mathcal{L}_{U-TEN}(I, I') = \mathcal{L}_{perc}(I, I') + \mathcal{L}_{adv}(I, I') \tag{11}$$

3   Experiments Results

3.1   Experimental Settings

In this section, we use ODLS dataset for evaluation, which consists of more than 100K nighttime traffic surveillance images captured in Wuhan University.

It's a objection detection dataset under complex-light condition proposed by ACM Multimedia Asia 2021 officially. The whole dataset includes more than 200 scenes, for the fairness of evaluation, we select 30 scenes whose light condition relatively most complex among all scenes. We built 10 sub-datasets named Par1 Par10, each of them consists of 10 different images in every scene being selected, the number of images for evaluation is $30 \times 10 \times 10 = 3000$. What's more, we use AP (Average Precision) as the evaluation metric of our experiments. Because the goal of our network is to help images under complex-light condition have better performances in object detection, not for better visual equality. We choose 7 state of the art light enhancement methods for comparison with our network. All images they enhanced will be processed by Yolo-v5, the IoU threshold is set to 0.45, the confidence threshold is set to 0.25, the category of detection objects is car. U-TEN takes about 0.337 s for processing one image of ODLS dataset. In Table 1, "Input image" represents the OLDS dataset without being enhanced.

Table 1. The AP of all methods comparison

Sub-dataset	Input image	Retinex-Net [23]	KinD [27]	DSLR [16]	Zero-DCE++ [15]	Zhang *et al.* [26]	SCI [19]	Jin *et al.* [6]	Ours
Part1	0.782	0.771	0.792	0.803	0.782	0.723	0.731	0.779	**0.837**
Part2	0.668	0.654	0.712	0.709	0.691	0.618	0.626	0.680	**0.734**
Part3	0.653	0.643	0.709	0.710	0.712	0.656	0.667	0.705	**0.727**
Part4	0.692	0.701	0.730	0.724	0.711	0.654	0.632	0.717	**0.766**
Part5	0.751	0.763	0.779	0.791	0.772	0.682	0.711	0.776	**0.815**
Part6	0.684	0.704	0.771	0.762	0.759	0.658	0.661	0.728	**0.797**
Part7	0.696	0.682	0.754	0.732	0.757	0.656	0.637	0.763	**0.782**
Part8	0.643	0.631	0.731	0.727	0.737	0.645	0.741	0.729	**0.772**
Part9	0.626	0.691	0.724	**0.765**	0.737	0.623	0.615	0.705	0.757
Part10	0.677	0.664	0.711	0.689	0.698	0.569	0.616	0.642	**0.739**

3.2 Quantitative Comparison and Object Detection Comparison

As we can see from Table 1, our network outperfroms other light enhancement methods in most sub-datasets by 3.50% in average, and 4.93% in maximum. It proves that our network is effective in dealing with complex-light condition, the scene we aim at is very meaningful in practical applications.

The object detection results are shown in Fig. 2 and Fig. 3, we choose 2 scenes for example, our network can help Yolo-v5 detect more cars precisely under complex-light condition. For example, in the left part of image we exhibit, there are four cars, but three of them are in the dark, and the last one is almost covered by its own light. In this situation, our network can make Yolo-v5 recognize all four cars while other light enhancement methods can't. Even for SCI [19] and Zhang *et al.* [26], they enhance all regions of an image, which makes enhanced image too bright to recognize cars. And some comparison algorithms have unsatisfying performance in dealing with this situation. It proves that when the light condition of the scene is complex, the light enhancement method is supposed to set different weight for different image regions.

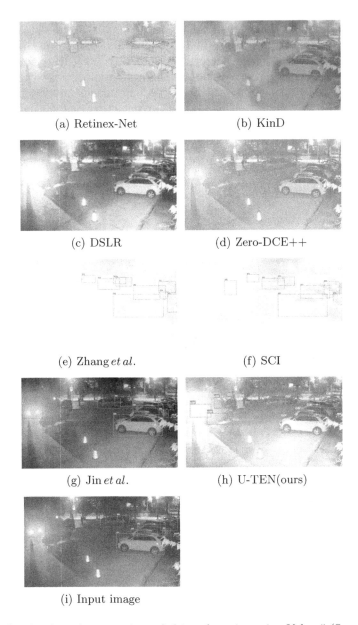

(a) Retinex-Net

(b) KinD

(c) DSLR

(d) Zero-DCE++

(e) Zhang *et al.*

(f) SCI

(g) Jin *et al.*

(h) U-TEN(ours)

(i) Input image

Fig. 2. The visual result comparison of object detection using Yolo-v5 (Scene number is c0033)

(a) Retinex-Net   (b) KinD

(c) DSLR   (d) Zero-DCE++

(e) Zhang *et al.*   (f) SCI

(g) Jin *et al.*   (h) U-TEN(ours)

(i) Input image

Fig. 3. The visual result comparison of object detection using Yolo-v5 (Scene number is c0069)

4   Conclusion

In this paper, we propose U-TEN, a complex-light enhancement network for object detection under complex-light condition. In our method, we use generative adversarial network for unsupervised learning, which solves the difficulty of constructing paired dataset in complex-light scenes, such as nighttime traffic surveillance. Specifically, we proposed a two-branch attention block. It combines the global and local illuminance information. Different enhance weights are assigned/distributed for different image regions according to SNR-map and GAT. Both of them increase the flexibility and robustness of information interaction during complex-light enhancement process. High-level vision tasks, such as object detection is also conducted/performed on enhanced images by using Yolo-v5. Experimental results demonstrate that our network can achieve the highest average precision in object detection on ODLS dataset. Our future work will focus on how to apply our network to nighttime autonomous driving.

References

1. Adelson, E.H., Anderson, C.H., Bergen, J.R., Burt, P.J., Ogden, J.M.: Pyramid methods in image processing. RCA Eng. **29**(6), 33–41 (1984)
2. Fu, X., Liang, B., Huang, Y., Ding, X., Paisley, J.: Lightweight pyramid networks for image deraining. IEEE Trans. Neural Netw. Learn. Syst. **31**(6), 1794–1807 (2019)
3. Goodfellow, I., et al.: Generative adversarial networks, pp. 1–9. ArXiv preprint ArXiv:1406.2661 (2014)
4. Guo, C., et al.: Zero-reference deep curve estimation for low-light image enhancement. In: Proceedings of the IEEE/CVF Conference on Computer Vision and Pattern Recognition, pp. 1780–1789 (2020)
5. Jain, V., Seung, S.: Natural image denoising with convolutional networks. In: Advances in Neural Information Processing Systems, vol. 21 (2008)
6. Jin, Y., Yang, W., Tan, R.T.: Unsupervised night image enhancement: when layer decomposition meets light-effects suppression. In: Avidan, S., Brostow, G., Cissé, M., Farinella, G.M., Hassner, T. (eds.) Computer Vision – ECCV 2022. LNCS, vol. 13697, pp. 404–421. Springer, Cham (2022). https://doi.org/10.1007/978-3-031-19836-6_23
7. Jobson, D.J., Rahman, Z.U., Woodell, G.A.: A multiscale retinex for bridging the gap between color images and the human observation of scenes. IEEE Trans. Image Process. **6**(7), 965–976 (1997)
8. Johnson, J., Alahi, A., Fei-Fei, L.: Perceptual losses for real-time style transfer and super-resolution. In: Leibe, B., Matas, J., Sebe, N., Welling, M. (eds.) ECCV 2016. LNCS, vol. 9906, pp. 694–711. Springer, Cham (2016). https://doi.org/10.1007/978-3-319-46475-6_43
9. Kejun, W., Qiong, L., Yi, W., You, Y.: End-to-end varifocal multiview images coding framework from data acquisition end to vision application end. Opt. Express **31**(7), 11659–11679 (2023)
10. Kejun, W., You, Y., Qiong, L., Xiao-Ping, Z.: Focal stack image compression based on basis-quadtree representation. IEEE Trans. Multimedia (2022). https://doi.org/10.1109/TMM.2022.3169055

11. Kejun, W., You, Y., Qiong, L., Xiaoping, Z.: Gaussian-wiener representation and hierarchical coding scheme for focal stack images. IEEE Trans. Circuits Syst. Video Technol. **32**(2), 523–537 (2022)
12. Khan, R., Yang, Y., Liu, Q., Qaisar, Z.H.: Divide and conquer: ill-light image enhancement via hybrid deep network. Expert Syst. Appl. **182**, 115034 (2021)
13. Khan, R., Yang, Y., Liu, Q., Shen, J., Li, B.: Deep image enhancement for ill light imaging. J. Opt. Soc. Am. A **38**(6), 827–839 (2021)
14. Li, C., et al.: Low-light image and video enhancement using deep learning: a survey. IEEE Trans. Pattern Anal. Mach. Intell. (2021)
15. Li, C., Guo, C., Loy, C.C.: Learning to enhance low-light image via zero-reference deep curve estimation. IEEE Trans. Pattern Anal. Mach. Intell. **44**(8), 4225–4238 (2021)
16. Lim, S., Kim, W.: DSLR: deep stacked Laplacian restorer for low-light image enhancement. IEEE Trans. Multimedia **23**, 4272–4284 (2020)
17. Lore, K.G., Akintayo, A., Sarkar, S.: LLNet: a deep autoencoder approach to natural low-light image enhancement. Pattern Recogn. **61**, 650–662 (2017)
18. Lv, F., Lu, F., Wu, J., Lim, C.: MBLLEN: low-light image/video enhancement using CNNs. In: British Machine Vision Conference, vol. 220, p. 4 (2018)
19. Ma, L., Ma, T., Liu, R., Fan, X., Luo, Z.: Toward fast, flexible, and robust low-light image enhancement. In: Proceedings of the IEEE/CVF Conference on Computer Vision and Pattern Recognition, pp. 5637–5646 (2022)
20. Rashed, H., Ramzy, M., Vaquero, V., El Sallab, A., Sistu, G., Yogamani, S.: Fuse-MODNet: real-time camera and lidar based moving object detection for robust low-light autonomous driving. In: Proceedings of the IEEE/CVF International Conference on Computer Vision Workshops (2019)
21. Rizwan, K., You, Y., Kejun, W., Atif, M., Zahid Hussain, Q., Zhonglong, Z.: A high dynamic range imaging method for short exposure multiview images. Pattern Recogn. **137**, 109344 (2023)
22. Veličković, P., Cucurull, G., Casanova, A., Romero, A., Lio, P., Bengio, Y.: Graph attention networks. ArXiv preprint ArXiv:1710.10903 (2017)
23. Wei, C., Wang, W., Yang, W., Liu, J.: Deep retinex decomposition for low-light enhancement. ArXiv preprint ArXiv:1808.04560 (2018)
24. Wu, W., Weng, J., Zhang, P., Wang, X., Yang, W., Jiang, J.: URetinex-Net: retinex-based deep unfolding network for low-light image enhancement. In: Proceedings of the IEEE/CVF Conference on Computer Vision and Pattern Recognition, pp. 5901–5910 (2022)
25. Xu, K., Yang, X., Yin, B., Lau, R.W.: Learning to restore low-light images via decomposition-and-enhancement. In: Proceedings of the IEEE/CVF Conference on Computer Vision and Pattern Recognition, pp. 2281–2290 (2020)
26. Zhang, F., Shao, Y., Sun, Y., Zhu, K., Gao, C., Sang, N.: Unsupervised low-light image enhancement via histogram equalization prior. ArXiv preprint ArXiv:2112.01766 (2021)
27. Zhang, Y., Zhang, J., Guo, X.: Kindling the darkness: a practical low-light image enhancer. In: Proceedings of the 27th ACM International Conference on Multimedia, pp. 1632–1640 (2019)

Virtual Reality

Design of Virtual Assembly Guidance System Based on Mixed Reality

Haoxin Wu and Nongliang Sun[✉]

College of Electronic Information Engineering, Shandong University of Science and
Technology, Qingdao, China
`nl-jackson@vip.163.com`

Abstract. Mixed reality technology has evolved from virtual reality and enables
the creation of interactive feedback loops between the real and virtual worlds. It
has practical applications in training and industrial manufacturing. This paper proposes a virtual assembly guidance system based on mixed reality technology and
helmets to overcome the challenges of high cost, danger, and difficulty in equipment installation during training and practice. Using Unity 3D and Microsoft's
Hololens 2, the system integrates virtual models with real space to guide operators
in assembling fictitious spaceships. The system improves the existing third-person
perspective scheme of mixed reality, enabling bystanders to watch the virtual-
reality fusion operation process through their mobile phones, thereby overcoming
the exclusivity problem of virtual reality and mixed reality. Results show that the
system's interaction mode is more natural and efficient, while the third-person
perspective function solves the isolation problem of existing virtual assembly
systems. The design is universal and highly useful.

Keywords: Mixed reality · Virtual assembly · Virtual and real fusion ·
Human-computer interaction · Third-person perspective

1 Introduction

Virtual reality technology includes computer graphics, simulation, human-computer
interaction, and other fields of technology to build a three-dimensional environment
that provides a virtual reality experience [1].

In the field of industrial manufacturing, the assembly process has a significant impact
on the quality of products. Installation errors may be caused by operators' non-standard
operation due to the complexity of the mechanical equipment, which may have a large
number of parts. Furthermore, significant safety accidents may occur in the case of some
special equipment [2].

At present, traditional installation guidance mainly relies on two-dimensional information such as pictures and videos, and the assembly process is mainly based on complex
drawings. Compared with the traditional way, mixed reality technology can provide a
more natural, flexible, and powerful platform [3].

© The Author(s), under exclusive license to Springer Nature Switzerland AG 2023
H. Lu et al. (Eds.): ICIG 2023, LNCS 14359, pp. 335–351, 2023.
https://doi.org/10.1007/978-3-031-46317-4_27

In addition, equipment installation is a skill that requires repeated practice. In traditional installation training processes, learning, memory, and actual operation are often disconnected, leading to a gap between theory and practice. These factors are not conducive to the standardization of operator assembly techniques. Mixed reality provides a new display method that combines data information with real-world operation scenes, presenting data in a three-dimensional visual manner. With more specific and intuitive three-dimensional models, operators can more accurately visualize all the details of the parts to be installed, resulting in effective improvements in training, construction, and maintenance [4–6].

Jayaram et al. proposed the concept of a virtual assembly system based on virtual reality and developed a preliminary prototype, which verified the feasibility of virtual assembly. This research was a major breakthrough in virtual assembly technology [7]. Sagardia et al. developed a virtual reality platform that integrates and solves challenging problems in the field of virtual assembly [8]. Joan Sol Roo and Martin Hachet developed a system that integrated multiple mixed reality technologies, allowing users to gradually transition from a pure reality experience to a pure virtual experience and greatly improving the human-computer interaction experience in mixed reality [9]. Mustufa H Abidi et al. designed a semi-immersive virtual assembly simulation system for aircraft turbine engines [10]. The virtual assembly simulation system designed by Noghabaei et al. helps to improve the efficiency of complex system assembly [11]. Nicolas Meier et al. designed a laser-based manual assembly assisted digital twinning system, allowing users to control the digital twinning system through gestures, voice, and other interactive methods [12]. Shang Lei et al. applied augmented reality technology to the teaching of marine engineering specialties and designed and implemented a marine auxiliary engine disassembly and assembly system [13]. Xuhui Zhang et al. developed a maintenance guidance system for mining equipment based on mixed reality, which intuitively presented virtual models, animations, voice prompts, and other information to maintenance personnel [14]. Yixiong Wei et al. have realized the visualization method of virtual and real fusion of third-party perspectives based on network communication and completed the spatial matching between the main perspective and the third-party perspective [15]. In the existing virtual assembly system, there are various breakthroughs in technologies and methods, and they provide valuable references for the further development and improvement of virtual assembly technology. There are still some limitations that need to be addressed. For instance, there is poor integration between virtual and real scenes, and the benefits of the virtual experience are limited to only the operators of the equipment, while it is difficult for multiple individuals to collaborate effectively. Additionally, there may be challenges in creating a seamless and intuitive interface that ensures a high level of user engagement and satisfaction. These limitations may hinder the widespread adoption of virtual assembly systems in industrial settings.

This paper focuses on the application of mixed reality technology in virtual assembly and the development of a virtual assembly guidance system with a third-person perspective based on mixed reality. The development platform is Unity 3D, and Microsoft's Hololens 2 is used as hardware. The logic scheme of the guidance function is designed according to actual needs, and the operators can interact naturally based on the integration of the virtual model with the real space. An improvement is made to the existing third-person perspective scheme of mixed reality, simplifying the operation process and overcoming the monopoly defects in virtual reality and mixed reality. As a result, bystanders without mixed reality devices can also watch the operation process of virtual reality integration through mobile phones. This will improve the efficiency of user design, installation, and other work and provide new ideas for realizing the digital transformation of industry and manufacturing.

2 Overall System Architecture Design

The system architecture is divided into three layers: hardware, SDK, and application, according to system requirements. Figure 1 shows the development framework of the system. The application layer consists of a presentation layer, logic layer, and data layer. The presentation layer contains visual components such as the system scene screen and UI, while the logic layer manages the operation and control of data, and the data layer contains resources such as models, audio, and pictures. The SDK layer acts as a bridge between the application layer and the hardware layer, enabling data transmission between them. The hardware layer comprises the data acquisition module of Hololens 2, which includes cameras, depth sensors, gyroscopes, etc. The underlying hardware is essential for realizing human-computer interaction.

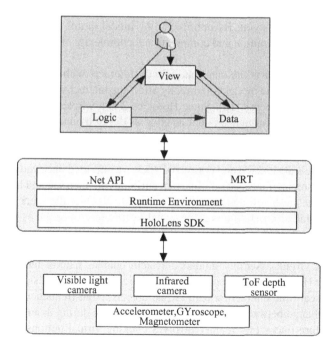

Fig. 1. The development framework of the system

2.1 System Development Process

The system development process consists of three main steps. The first step involves creating 3D models of the equipment components needed for the system. In the second step, the 3D models and material maps are imported into Unity 3D to build the virtual environment. Various features, such as gesture interaction, voice interaction, gaze, and virtual assembly guidance, are designed and implemented in this step. In the third step, the third person perspective function is designed and implemented. This includes the communication among Hololens 2 client, mobile client, and server. Additionally, the acquisition and calibration of mobile phone location, the conversion of model information, and real-time synchronization are also implemented in this step.

2.2 System Function Design

Optimization of the 3D model is important to ensure that the system can run smoothly and provide a good user experience. In particular, the model should be optimized to reduce memory consumption and computational complexity. This is because Hololens 2, as a wireless mobile computing device, has limited computing performance compared to desktop computers.

To optimize the model, it is necessary to reduce the number of polygons in the model, simplify the geometry, and use efficient texture maps. This can be achieved through various techniques such as mesh decimation, LOD (Level of Detail) generation, texture compression, and so on. By optimizing the model in this way, it is possible to reduce the memory consumption and computational complexity of the system, and thus improve its performance.

The component model is the data that directly interacts with users in the system. The production effect of the model will directly affect the interactive experience of users during the installation process [16]. Since Hololens 2 is a wireless mobile computing device, its computing performance is not as good as desktop computers. Therefore, in the process of creating 3D models, we should focus on optimizing the models to reduce memory consumption and computational complexity.

Once the models are created and optimized, they are imported into Unity 3D to build the virtual environment of the system. Relevant attributes are then set, and box colliders, spherical colliders, mesh colliders, and triggers are added. Once the scene is built, it is packaged and installed on Hololens 2 for actual testing to ensure the system can run smoothly. If it gets stuck during testing, further optimization of the models is required. After the test is passed, the next step is human-computer interaction design.

This paper's virtual assembly guidance system enables natural human-computer interaction using Hololens 2 and incorporates voice, gesture, and line of sight interaction, enabling direct real-time interaction with virtual objects. High-frequency and real-time information exchange between the operator and the system during assembly operation is ensured. Gesture interaction mainly involves clicking virtual buttons, rotating, and moving the virtual model. Speech interaction uses Microsoft's cognitive service for UI interface wake-up and hiding. Eye-tracking has been added to Hololens 2, and gaze interaction is mainly used for page turning when reading long documents.

To implement the installation guidance function in the system, it is necessary to complete the interactive system first. The function prompts the position and angle of parts in the form of holographic images. After the user operates the parts, the system judges the position and angle of the model. Simultaneously, considering the installation sequence, the system should verify whether the operated parts are in the installable state and provide corresponding prompts. Successfully installed parts should integrate with other installed parts.

The third-person perspective function of the system is achieved based on real-time communication among Hololens 2, mobile phones, and servers. After connecting with the server, a Hololens 2 device serves as the primary operating device and can connect to multiple mobile phones or Hololens 2 devices as bystander devices to communicate. Since each mixed reality and augmented reality system has its coordinate system during operation, to make the virtual reality fusion scene seen on the mobile phone consistent with the main operating device Hololens 2, it is necessary to coordinate the position information of the model. Vuforia can recognize planar images or 3D objects in real-time based on computer vision technology and obtain the position of images or 3D objects. Once the primary operating device obtains the position information of the bystander device, it can convert the coordinates of the virtual model relative to the primary operating device to the coordinates relative to the bystander device.

3 Realization of Virtual Reality Fusion Scene and Assembly Guidance Function

3.1 Construction of Virtual Reality Fusion Scene

In a mixed reality system, the real world and virtual space have their own spatial coordinate systems. In order to achieve the fusion effect between the virtual scene and the real scene, it is necessary to unify each coordinate system through transformation and accurately place the virtual scene into the real world through coordinate transformation to achieve the effect of virtual-real fusion. The realization of 3D registration involves the transformation of multiple spatial coordinates. To facilitate the description, the relationships among coordinates are established as shown in Fig. 2.

The implementation of 3D registration requires three coordinate transformation matrices, where the transformation matrix from virtual space coordinates to real world coordinates is Vr, the transformation matrix from real world coordinates to Hololens 2 coordinate system is Rh, and the transformation matrix from Hololens 2 spatial coordinates to projection plane coordinates is Hp. The 3D registration process is as follows [17]:

(1) The transformation from virtual space to real space is necessary to determine the position of the virtual object in the real world, and it is represented by a matrix as follows:

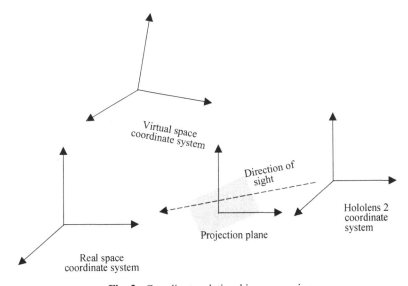

Fig. 2. Coordinate relationships conversion

$$\begin{bmatrix} Xr \\ Yr \\ Zr \\ 1 \end{bmatrix} = Vr \begin{bmatrix} Xv \\ Yv \\ Zv \\ 1 \end{bmatrix} \tag{1}$$

where, Vr is determined by the functions required by the system, so Vr is a known matrix.

The coordinate transformation between real-world coordinates and Hololens 2 coordinates is used to determine the relative relationship between real-world scenes and Hololens 2. The coordinate transformation relationship is obtained by matching the characteristic points of the markers, and it is expressed as a matrix. This matrix represents the relationship between the Hololens 2 coordinate system and the real world, and it changes with the movement of Hololens 2.

$$\begin{bmatrix} Xr' \\ Yr' \\ Zr' \\ 1 \end{bmatrix} = \begin{bmatrix} R & S \\ 0 & 1 \end{bmatrix} \begin{bmatrix} Xr \\ Yr \\ Zr \\ 1 \end{bmatrix} = R_h \begin{bmatrix} Xr \\ Yr \\ Zr \\ 1 \end{bmatrix} \tag{2}$$

where Rh is a 4×4 matrix, R and S represent the mapping relationship between the Hololens 2 coordinate system and the real world, which changes with the movement of

Hololens 2. $S = (s_1, s_2, s_3)$, R is expressed in matrix as:

$$R = \begin{bmatrix} r_{11} & r_{12} & r_{13} \\ r_{21} & r_{22} & r_{23} \\ r_{31} & r_{32} & r_{33} \end{bmatrix} \quad (3)$$

(3) The Hololens 2 spatial coordinates are transformed into the projection plane coordinate system to accurately project the virtual objects onto the real world. This is achieved using the Hololens 2 camera parameters according to the perspective imaging principle, resulting in the transformation matrix Hp. By performing this transformation, users can see the scene of virtual and real fusion in an accurate and seamless way. Together with the transformations from virtual space to real space and from real-world coordinates to Hololens 2 coordinates, the 3D registration process is completed.

Currently, there are several three-dimensional registration technologies, including computer vision-based tracking, sensor-based tracking, and mixed tracking registration. After comparing these methods, we have chosen the computer vision-based tracking method to realize the virtual and real fusion of the system.

Firstly, the real space position of the system is determined. Vuforia's image recognition is used to match and compare the natural feature points of the target image captured by the camera with those of the images uploaded in the target library, as shown in Fig. 3.

Fig. 3. Feature point extraction of the image target

The target image should be rigid, with a matte surface and no backlight. Images that meet Vuforia's requirements are uploaded to the Vuforia server as recognition images. After setting the size of the recognition image in Vuforia according to the size of the recognition image placed in the real scene, a Unity 3D resource package is obtained. This package is imported into the Unity 3D project, and the *Vuforia Behavior* component is added to the *Main Camera* under *MixedRealityPlayspace*, so that the camera in the system has the function of Vuforia image recognition. The target image can be selected by choosing the downloaded database in the settings panel of Image Target, after right-clicking in the Hierarchy menu to select Image Target in *Vuforia Engine*.

After configuring Vuforia and *Image Target*, two images in real space can be recognized. The *Image Target Behavior* component in Image Target provides an event interface when a target image is detected. A custom script is written to enable the system to record the position a and b of each image relative to the system coordinate origin after each image is recognized, and the midpoint position of point a and point b and the direction vector b-a composed by the two points are calculated. An empty object is created in the *Hierarchy* as the parent object of the virtual model in the scene, and the position coordinates of the parent object are set to the midpoint of points a and b. The y-axis direction is consistent with the vector b-a. To make the virtual object more accurately match the real object, the real space is scanned using the scanning function of Hololens 2 before building the system virtual scene. The grid model of the real space is exported to Unity 3D as a reference for placing the model when arranging the scene.

3.2 Implementation of Natural Interaction Function Units

At present, the natural interaction in mixed reality systems mainly includes gesture and voice interaction. While a few systems have gaze interaction, it is usually realized through collision detection of rays emitted by the Hololens 2 device, where the direction of rays corresponds to the user's line of sight and is fixed relative to the device. In this system, we propose a novel gaze interaction mode based on the eye-tracking function of Hololens 2.

Hololens 2 tracks eye movement by measuring the eye's fixation point through the infrared camera at the bridge of the nose, providing an input mode that enables more natural operations through eye fixation. Users must calibrate the device before using gaze interaction. Hololens 2 illuminates the eye through an infrared LED, and the infrared camera obtains the image data of the eye for calculation. After calibration, the positions of the pupil and Purkinje spot are extracted [18]. By fitting a function to the corresponding relationship between the fixation point and the pupil cornea, the eyeball is tracked, and the outgoing ray is equivalent to that emitted from the center of the user's eye.

The outgoing ray intersects with the virtual model. If the ray intersects with the virtual object at point P, with the front tangent plane at point P_1 (x_1, y_1, z_1), and with the back tangent plane at point P_2 (x_2, y_2, z_2), the coordinates of the virtual model P can be expressed as [19]:

$$P = P_1 + E \times M = P_2 - E \times M \tag{4}$$

where E is the unit vector and M is the magnitude. If there are three points A, B, and C on the model, then any other point on the plane can be expressed as a linear combination of these three points and the parameters i and j:

$$P = A + k \times (B - A) + v \times (C - A) \tag{5}$$

$$P_1 + E \times M = (1 - i - j) \times A + i \times B + j \times C \tag{6}$$

where, $k > 0$, $v < 1$, $k + v < 1$.

$$
\begin{aligned}
X_1 + E \times M &= (1 - i - j) \times X_a + i \times X_b + j \times X_c \\
Y_1 + E \times M &= (1 - i - j) \times Y_a + i \times Y_b + j \times Y_c \\
Z_1 + E \times M &= (1 - i - j) \times Z_a + i \times Z_b + j \times Z_c
\end{aligned} \tag{7}
$$

According to the equations, the values of i, j, and M can be calculated, and then the position information of the collision point can be obtained.

The eye gaze interaction designed based on eye tracking in the system can make it easier for users to interact with virtual objects. For example, users may need to consult documentation while installing but may not be able to use gesture interaction when holding other objects or voice interaction for accurate page turning. At such times, eye gaze interaction provides an advantage and enables page scrolling through gaze.

3.3 The Realization of the Third Person Perspective Function

When people use HoloLens 2 to immerse themselves in the wonderful experience brought by the development of science and technology, they often overlook the fact that people without devices cannot share the mixed reality fusion scene due to the limitations of exclusive content and difficulty in sharing. At present, most common virtual assembly systems are operated by one person and lack multi-person collaboration. If the application scene of the system requires multi-person collaboration or the virtual reality fusion scene seen by the operator needs to be painted in real-time to share with others, it is still difficult to meet the requirement using only one device.

Microsoft provides two solutions. One is mixed reality capture, which uses the camera on HoloLens 2 to capture video and superimpose it on the virtual scene. After that, the first-person perspective is transferred to the web, where others can view the perspective by accessing the *HoloLens Device Portal* through the browser, as shown in Fig. 4. In this scheme, the bystander's perspective is limited by the operator and cannot rotate freely. Additionally, this method has low resolution and high delay.

Fig. 4. Microsoft's first solution of third person perspective

Another solution is *Spectator View*, where the main principle is to synchronize the anchor data of the two Hololens devices. The images taken by the camera and the second Hololens device are processed through an algorithm, and a calibration file is generated. The position and angle offset between the HoloLens and the camera are calibrated using the calibration file, and the final synthesized video is transmitted to a two-dimensional screen display, as shown in Fig. 5 [20]. This scheme can transform the 3D scene seen by the users of the Hololens device into a 2D scene and present it on the screen for the audience to understand the mixed reality content. However, this scheme requires two Hololens devices, cameras, acquisition cards, fixed racks, and other devices. The deployment process of the system is complex, and multiple SDKs need to be integrated, which poses constraints and challenges.

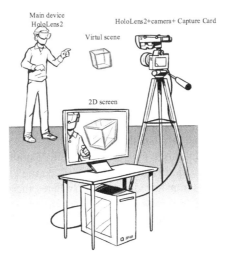

Fig. 5. Microsoft's second solution of third person perspective

The third-person perspective function scheme of our system uses a Hololens 2 as the primary perspective device, with a mobile phone supporting ARCore as the third-person perspective device. The orientation of the third-person perspective device is obtained through Vuforia recognition, and the sharing of virtual and real fusion images is accomplished based on Socket asynchronous communication. To reduce the pressure of data on the network transmission bandwidth and achieve low information synchronization delay between devices, we store all the virtual models used for synchronous display in the scene in the local database. Each client has a copy of virtual model data locally. When the user model status of the main view device changes, modifying the virtual model status data of each device is enough. The network framework does not need to transmit the status data of the entire virtual model during communication but only the position, posture, and other data of the operated parts in the virtual model. Other third-person perspective device users accept the data and update the data locally. The main principle of the third-person perspective function in the system is to use the respective spatial continuous positioning functions of Hololens 2 and ARCore mobile phones to uniformly convert the spatial coordinates of the two devices, and the synchronization of operations between devices is finally achieved, as shown in Fig. 6.

The third-person perspective function module of the system is divided into two parts, the client and the server. The client consists of the Hololens 2 as the main perspective device and a mobile phone supporting ARCore as the third-person perspective

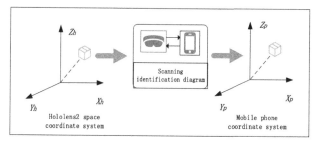

Fig. 6. The synchronization of operations between Hololens 2 and mobile phones

device. The server is the functional module deployed on a computer or cloud server for processing communication data transmission. The implementation process of the third-person perspective function includes opening the server to establish communication connections between devices, obtaining the location information of the third-person perspective device, initializing the calibration, and synchronizing the operation of the main perspective device to the third-person perspective device through network communication.

The third-person perspective function in the system can be divided into three steps. First, the main perspective device is connected to the mobile phone as the third-person perspective device, so that all devices are in the same conversation room. Second, the main perspective device obtains the position and attitude information of the mobile phone, and converts the model space coordinates of the main perspective device into the model space coordinates of the mobile phone according to the position and attitude information of the mobile phone, generates initialization data, and sends it to the mobile phone. The mobile phone calibrates after obtaining the data. Finally, information interaction between users and virtual models, and real-time information synchronization of model state change data between the main perspective device and the third-person perspective device are achieved, as shown in Fig. 7.

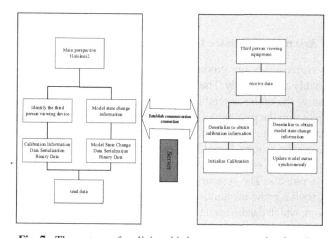

Fig. 7. Three steps of realizing third person perspective function

The third-person perspective device in the system utilizes Android-based mobile phones that support *ARCore*. For ease of development, the Unity 3D development tool is also used to create a new project with Android as the platform in *Build Settings* and to enable support for *ARCore* in *XR Plug-in Management* in system settings. Since all client devices in the system have local virtual model status data, it is only necessary to import the model and material from the Hololens 2 project and make appropriate modifications. As the main view device needs to obtain the position of the mobile phone by scanning the recognition image, the mobile phone terminal should set an image that can be opened and closed as the recognition image. Once the main view device obtains the location information of the mobile phone, it converts the spatial coordinates of the model relative to the main view device into spatial coordinates (x_p, y_p, z_p) relative to the mobile phone and sends them to the mobile phone. However, since this position is the center point of the camera screen, while the mobile phone system's ARCore obtains the position of the camera, the position of the model should be corrected according to the offset of the camera position. The position coordinates of the model relative to the camera are as follows:

$$(x_c, y_c, z_c) = (x_p, y_p, z_p) - (x, 0, z) \tag{8}$$

where x is the distance from the camera in the vertical direction to the center of the mobile phone, which is negative when the camera is above the center, and z is the distance from the camera in the horizontal direction to the center of the mobile phone, and which is positive when the camera is on the right side of the center.

After initialization and calibration, the matching of virtual and real fusion information between devices has been completed. The next step is to achieve real-time synchronization of the model state information between devices. In this paper, all data to be transferred and the method name to be called are stored as *Object-type* data, which are then serialized and sent to the third-party device through the server. Upon receiving the data and deserializing it, the mobile phone will search for the method with the same name in the data within the class that inherits BaseSendOrder, and the other data will be executed as parameters.

3.4 Design of Assembly Guidance Logic

The key to the virtual assembly guidance system is guiding the user to complete the assembly reasonably and correctly. The system needs to design the corresponding assembly logic to control the entire assembly process according to the expected procedure. When the user picks up the part model, a highlighted holographic reminder is displayed at the correct position of the part model in the assembly scene. If the user does not install according to the correct process flow, the system will give a prompt. In addition, the user can view the help document to obtain the correct assembly process information of the current operation process. The system assembly guidance process is shown in Fig. 8.

The MRTK toolkit provides multiple event interfaces at the beginning, during, and after the operation, which can be used to write logic scripts for implementing the assembly guidance function and related additional functions. The model to be assembled is a spacecraft, which is divided into ten parts, including the main frame, engine, window,

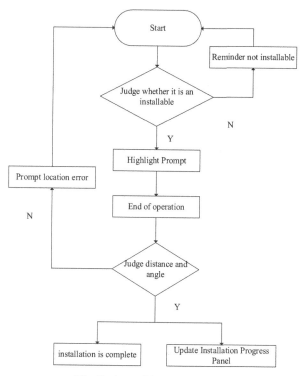

Fig. 8. Assembly guide process

and internal instruments, and each part contains multiple components. The assembly process is designed such that other parts can only be installed after the main frame is installed. During assembly, the part containing the current component is checked to determine whether it can be installed, and if it can, then the previous component is also checked to ensure that it has been installed before. The process is as follows:

(1) The spacecraft model is divided into three levels in the level menu of the Unity 3D project. The first level is an empty object that represents the entire spacecraft and is used to conveniently perform overall movements, rotations, and other operations of the spacecraft during design. The second level is also an empty object that represents all parts of the spacecraft and is used to classify different components. The third level consists of specific component models. The installation judgment logic involves traversing the sub-objects of the second level, where the order of the model in the category represents the order of installation. A tag is set for each model, which is used to obtain the category of the component when scripting.

(2) According to the object-oriented idea, the functions that each component model needs to use, such as whether the component can be installed, and the display and hiding of prompt information, are encapsulated into a management class called AssemblyManager. AssemblyManager is a singleton class that inherits from the MonoBehaviour class, which can be called without instantiation. It is mounted on the empty object at the first level, which is convenient for other scripts to use. Ten collections are created in this class

to store Boolean values of whether components of ten categories are installed correctly. The default Boolean value is false, and the length of each collection is the number of components in each category.

4   Test Results and Analysis

After the system is deployed, it is intended to run in an environment with consistent lighting and appropriate brightness to ensure that users can view the virtual scene without difficulty. The system's operating environment parameters are detailed in Table 1.

Table 1. Operating Environment Parameters

Hololens 2 applications	Mobile applications	Server program
Hololens 2 generation Operating system: Windows holographic operating system SoC: Qualcomm Snapdragon 850 computing platform HPU: second generation customized holographic processing unit Memory: 4 GB Storage: 64 GB	Samsung Galaxy S9 Operating system: Android 10.0 CPU: Qualcomm Snapdragon 845 Memory: 4 GB Storage: 64 GB	Cloud server Operating system: Windows Server 2019 CPU: Intel Xeon Gold 6133 Memory: 4 GB Storage: 80 GB

4.1   System Function Test

The user interface (UI) displayed after the system is activated can be seen in Fig. 9. And Fig. 10 shows the effect of raising one's hand to wake up the hand menu, as well as the implementation of the system components.

Fig. 9. UI interface

The system's memory consumption and frame rate during operation can be seen in Fig. 11. It is evident that the frame rate of the system is maintained between 52–59 fps,

Fig. 10. Hand menu and component display effect

Fig. 11. System memory consumption and frame rate

and the system delay is kept at 10–15 ms, while the peak memory usage does not exceed 50% of the device's memory.

Figure 12 displays the grabbing and clicking gestures of the gesture interaction, as well as the holographic highlighting effect of corresponding operations (Fig. 13).

Fig. 12. Gesture interaction and holographic reminder

Fig. 13. Third person perspective effect and remote user interface

4.2 Test Analysis

The system underwent successful operation tests on both the Hololens 2 and mobile phones, providing accurate guidance and prompts during spacecraft assembly. The system's auxiliary interfaces were displayed and updated correctly, and users were able to interact with the system using gestures, voice commands, and gaze. The mobile phone version of the system provided the same virtual and real fusion effect as the Hololens 2 version and was able to synchronize in real time. Remote users were also able to view the assembly process via the network.

5 Conclusion

This paper aims to address the challenges of difficult equipment installation, high cost, and danger in practical training by designing and implementing a virtual assembly guidance system based on hybrid reality.

The design is built on the Unity 3D development platform and employs the Hololens2 mixed reality head display as the primary hardware. Through coordinate transformation and three-dimensional registration, all coordinate systems are unified, ensuring accurate fusion of the virtual model and real space. The system features human-computer interaction modes, including gesture, voice, and gaze, making the operation process simple, fast, and efficient. The third-person perspective scheme of mixed reality is also improved, allowing bystanders without mixed reality equipment to watch the operation process of virtual-reality fusion through mobile phones, overcoming the exclusivity of virtual reality and mixed reality.

The system uses a fictitious spacecraft as a model to provide users with real-time assembly process guidance. The actual operation results demonstrate that the system can achieve accurate and real-time assembly guidance by providing both first-person and third-person perspectives, enabling users to complete the assembly of the entire spacecraft and achieve the expected goal. The system is also adaptable to other models using the same ideas and processes.

References

1. Yang, Q., Zhong, S.: Research on the development of virtual reality technology in China: review and prospect. Sci. Manage. Res. **38**(05), 20–26 (2020)
2. Zhao, Z.: Research on online quality control method for assembly process of complex mechanical products. Hefei University of Technology, Hefei (2013)
3. Ye, N., Banerjee, P., Banerjee, A., et al.: A comparative study of assembly planning in traditional and virtual environments. IEEE Trans. Syst. Man Cybern. Part C **29**(4), 546–555 (2002)
4. Shan, X., Zhu, M., Li, J., et al.: Research on ship digital assembly process design and simulation technology. Aviat. Manuf. Technol. **465**(21), 57–59 (2014)
5. Boonmee, P., Jantarakongkul, B., Jitngernmadan, P.: VR training environment for electrical vehicle assembly training in EEC. In: 2020-5th International Conference on Information Technology (INCIT 2020), pp. 238–242 (2020)
6. Liu, Y., Tang, Y., Zhao, J., et al.: 5G+ VR industrial technology application. In: 2020 International Conference on virtual reality and visualization (ICVRV 2020), pp. 336–337 (2020)
7. Jayaram, S., Connacher, H.I., Lyons, K.W.: Virtual assembly using virtual reality techniques. Comput. Aided Des. **29**(8), 575–584 (1997)
8. Sagardia, M., Hulin, T., Hertkorn, K., et al.: A platform for bimanual virtual assembly training with haptic feedback in large multi-object environments. In: Proceedings of the 22nd ACM Conference on Virtual Reality Software and Technology, pp. 153–162 (2016)
9. Roo, J.S., Hachet, M.: One reality: augmenting how the physical world is experienced by combining multiple mixed reality modalities. In: Proceedings of the 30th Annual ACM Symposium on User Interface Software and Technology, pp. 787–795 (2017)
10. Abidi, M.H., Al-Ahmari, A.M., Ahmad, A., et al.: Semi-immersive virtual turbine engine simulation system. Int. J. Turbo Jet-Engines **35**(2), 149–160 (2018)
11. Noghabaei, M., Asadi, K., Han, K.: Virtual manipulation in an immersive virtual environment: simulation of virtual assembly. In: ASCE International Conference on Computing in Civil Engineering, pp. 95–102 (2019)
12. Meier, N., Müller-Polyzou, R., Brach, L., et al.: Digital twin support for laser-based assembly assistance. Procedia CIRP **99**(5), 460–465 (2021)
13. Shang, L., Wang, B., Yang, Z., et al.: Research and implementation of ship auxiliary engine disassembly and assembly system based on HoloLens. China Navig. **41**(3), 38–42 (2018)
14. Zhang, X., Zhang, Y., Wang, M., et al.: Mining equipment maintenance guidance system based on hybrid reality. Ind. Mining Autom. **45**(6), 27–31 (2019)
15. Wei, Y., Zhang, Y., Zhang, H., et al.: Research on third-party perspective technology for headworn augmented/hybrid reality devices. Comput. Worker Cheng **47**(6), 284–291 (2021)
16. Zhang, P.: Design and implementation of manufacturing cell simulation system based on unity engine. University of the Chinese Academy of Sciences (Shenyang Institute of Computing Technology, Chinese Academy of Sciences), Shenyang (2018)
17. Chen, X.: Research on robot teaching and reproduction technology based on augmented reality and natural human-computer interaction. South China University of Technology, Guangdong (2018)
18. Zhao, C.: Research and development of steam turbine maintenance auxiliary system based on AR. North China Electric Power University, Beijing (2021)
19. Xing, L.: Printing machine operation training system based on mixed reality. Xi'an University of Technology, Xi'an (2021)
20. Spectator view for Hololens and Hololens 2. https://docs.microsoft.com/en-us/windows/mixedreality/design/spectator-view. Accessed 8 Mar 2022

Blind Omnidirectional Image Quality Assessment Based on Swin Transformer with Scanpath-Oriented

Xufeng Tang[1,2,3], Ping An[1,2,3(✉)], and Chao Yang[1,2,3]

[1] Key Laboratory of Specialty Fiber Optics and Optical Access Networks, Shanghai University, Shanghai 200444, China
anping@shu.edu.cn
[2] Shanghai Institute for Advanced Communication and Data Science, Shanghai University, Shanghai 200444, China
[3] School of Communication and Information Engineering, Shanghai University, Shanghai 200444, China

Abstract. With the emergence of 5th generation mobile communication technology, the demand for Virtual Reality (VR) applications is on the rise worldwide. As one of the technologies related to visual content in VR, the quality evaluation of omnidirectional images has become an important issue. Inspired by the transformer, we propose a novel blind omnidirectional image quality assessment method. Firstly, we predict the path that the human eye follows when viewing omnidirectional images through headsets, and extract the area with the longest gaze duration on the path as the viewport. Then, to consider the intrinsic structural features of each pixel within each viewport, we use the Swin Transformer to extract viewport features. Finally, to establish a general scene perception and accurately evaluate immersive experiences, we construct a spatial viewport map for the entire perceptual scene. The graph structure performs reasoning on the overall relationship based on the spatial perception path. Experimental results demonstrate that our proposed model outperforms the current state-of-the-art Image Quality Assessment metrics, as evidenced by its superior results on two public databases.

Keywords: omnidirectional image · Swin Transformer · natural scene similarity · blind quality assessment

1 Introduction

With the rapid advancement of social productivity and information technology in recent years, human perception of real-world scenes is no longer confined to a limited field of view. This has resulted in a growing global demand for VR applications [1], and the VR industry is presented with new opportunities and

This work was supported in part by the NSFC under Grant 62071287, 61901252, 62020106011, 62171002, and Science and Technology Commission of Shanghai Municipality under Grant 22ZR1424300 and 20DZ2290100.

H. Lu et al. (Eds.): ICIG 2023, LNCS 14359, pp. 352–364, 2023.
https://doi.org/10.1007/978-3-031-46317-4_28

challenges. VR technology has revolutionized traditional media by freeing it from the constraints of traditional screens. With the help of Head Mounted Display (HMD) [2], users can experience a 360° immersive view and watch videos from any angle by simply rotating their heads. As a visual imaging technology, it offers users interactive services that provide an in-depth and immersive experience, making it the most popular technology for displaying vision without any blind spots.

However, compared with traditional images, omnidirectional images (OI) [3] require capturing 360° views and typically demand high resolutions such as 4 K, 8 K, or higher to satisfy users' Quality of Experience (QoE). Therefore, such images are often heavily compressed for transmission and storage purposes [4]. During the process of immersive content acquisition, it is inevitable to encounter image distortion. As a result, it will lead to a degradation in the quality of the final image displayed to the user.

At the same time, visual degradation in VR applications can result in a reduced quality of experience for users. To address this issue, No-Reference Omnidirectional Image Quality Assessment (NR-OIQA) has been developed to enable humans to perceive visual distortion in omnidirectional images and improve the quality of the visual experience. Consequently, designing a feasible objective quality evaluation algorithm for the omnidirectional images holds significant practical and theoretical value.

Based on this, we propose a scanpath-oriented deep learning network for blind omnidirectional image quality assessment. Initially, the scanning path of the omnidirectional image is employed as a reference to derive the trajectory of the human eye's gaze within the head-mounted device. The viewports are extracted based on this trajectory. Secondly, taking into account the fact that existing CNN-based OIQA methods are limited by the receptive field and cannot establish global contextual connections, we employ the Swin Transformer to extract features for judging viewport quality. Finally, to construct a global correlation of viewports based on scanning paths, we use a graph-based approach. Notably, we extract the Natural Scene Statistics (NSS) features from each viewport, which effectively represents the similarity and correlation between viewports.

Our contributions are listed as follows:

- We propose a novel approach for extracting viewports from omnidirectional images by leveraging a model of scanning paths. A graph structure is constructed, which represents the complete viewing path of the omnidirectional image. It enables us to simulate the information interaction among different viewports and model the overall viewing process dynamically.
- We propose employing NSS features to calculate feature similarity and correlation across various viewports, with the objective of constructing an affinity matrix.
- We propose a novel deep learning model that integrates Swin Transformer with the graph structure to predict quality scores for omnidirectional images. This model facilitates both local and global feature interactions within and

across viewports. Our network outperforms existing Full-Reference and No-Reference methods on two benchmark databases.

2   Related Works

In this section, we introduce various methods about No-Reference omnidirectional image quality assessment. Then we make an overview of the recent related works on vision transformers.

2.1   NR-OIQA

NR-OIQA aims to objectively and accurately evaluate visual quality without reference images. Recently, deep learning technologies promote the development of NR-OIQA. Kim et al. [5] proposed a CNN-based adversarial learning method, which is called DeepVR-IQA. They partitioned an omnidirectional image into patches and employed an adversarial network to estimate their local quality and weight. Then the weighted quality scores are aggregated to obtain the final score.

Tian et al. [6] utilized a pseudo-reference viewport and employed spherical convolution to eliminate projection distortion. The final prediction score is obtained by merging the quality scores from two branches.

From the perspective of mitigating geometric distortion, Sun et al. [7] used a multi-channel CNN framework to predict the quality score of omnidirectional images. On this basis, Zhou et al. [8] incorporated a distortion discrimination-assisted network to promote OIQA learning tasks. However, the inherent differences between viewpoints as well as the interactive information between them are being overlooked.

To better illustrate the dependency of various viewports in 360° images, Xu et al. [9] first introduced graph convolutional networks into OIQA and modeled the spatial positional relationship of viewports in omnidirectional images. However, they only consider the spatial position of the viewports in the construction of the graph but ignore its content characteristics. To this end, Fu et al. [10] developed an adaptive hypergraph convolutional network (AHGCN) for NR-OIQA. In addition to the location-based features, the content-based features are also taken into consideration, which are generated based on their content similarity.

While the spatial and content characteristics of viewports are taken into account, the influence of viewport distortion is overlooked. Therefore, we propose to use NSS features sensitive to distortion to construct the correlation between viewports with the Swin Transformer. The NSS features are also used in [11,12], and [13] to achieve high consistency with human perception.

2.2   IQA Based on Swin Transformer

Inspired by the success of the Transformer [14] in various NLP tasks [15], an increasing number of methods based on the Transformer [16] have appeared in CV tasks, including no-reference omnidirectional image quality assessment tasks. Compared to frequently employed CNN models, the Swin Transformer introduces a shifted-window self-attention mechanism that facilitates the establishment of contextual connections. Conversely, CNNs possess restricted receptive fields, which restrict their attention to global features. In the task of IQA, both local and global quality perceptions are critical. Evaluators of image quality are sensitive not only to the quality of the current viewport but also to the previously viewed viewport, as this can affect their overall quality perception. Inspired by this fact, we use the Swin Transformer to establish local information interaction within the viewport. Also, a graph structure is used to construct feature transfer between viewports.

3   Method

In this section, we introduce the proposed OIQA method. Figure 1 illustrates the overall architecture. Our method uses a generative model to extract viewports from 360° images, producing realistic scanpaths. We implement the visual viewport interaction based on human eye perception and generate a perception score.

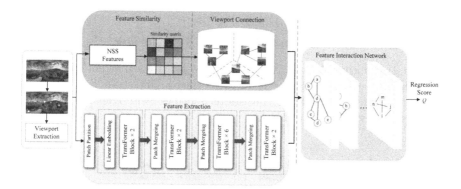

Fig. 1. The architecture of our proposed model. Viewports are firstly extracted from the distorted omnidirectional image in ERP format and input into the feature extraction module. The semantic features will be sent to the feature interaction network together with the extracted relevance matrix and regress the final perception score.

3.1   Viewport Extraction

When a 360° image is viewed in a VR device, the visual content is displayed as a flat section that touches the sphere created by the viewing angle. Also, when evaluating the quality of a 360° image, viewers look around the 360° image from multiple perspectives. Based on this, we employ a technique that mimics the human visual perception process by examining the scanning path data of an omnidirectional image as seen through human eyes. We use the model, which is proposed in [17] to directly process the equirectangular project (ERP) format. The predicted gaze points are shown in Fig. 1 when viewing the omnidirectional image in HMD.

Figure 2 illustrates the process of viewport extraction. We set the viewing angle to 90°, which consists of the FOV of the most popular VR devices. Then, given a distorted omnidirectional image V_d and select N central points to extract viewports. The viewport sets are denoted as $\{V_i\}_{i=1}^{N}$. Then, we obtain N viewports covering the 90° FOVs.

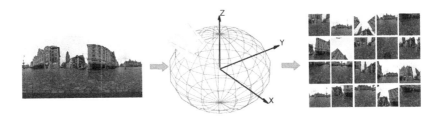

Fig. 2. The process of viewports extraction.

3.2 Graph Nodes Constructed by Swin Transformer

The Swin Transformer utilizes a shifted-window-based local attention computation method to achieve a hierarchical Transformer architecture. So we use it to extract the semantic feature. It consists of multiple Swin Transformer blocks. Figure 3 shows two successive blocks.

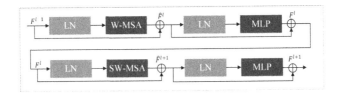

Fig. 3. Swin Transformer Block.

The window-based multi-head self-attention (W-MSA) module and the shifted window-based multi-head self-attention (SW-MSA) module are employed in two consecutive transformer blocks. Prior to every MSA module and MLP layer, a LayerNorm (LN) layer is employed for normalization, and residual connections are applied after each module. Based on such a window division mechanism, continuous Swin Transformer blocks can be calculated as:

$$\hat{F}^l = W\text{-}MSA(LN(F^{l-1})) + F^{l-1}, \tag{1}$$

$$F^l = MLP(LN(\hat{F}^l)) + \hat{F}^l, \tag{2}$$

$$\hat{F}^{l+1} = SW\text{-}MSA(LN(F^l)) + F^l, \tag{3}$$

$$F^{l+1} = MLP(LN(\hat{F}^{l+1})) + \hat{F}^{l+1}, \tag{4}$$

$\hat{F}^l$ and F^l denote the output of the l_{th} block of the (S)W-MSA and MLP, respectively. N viewports $\{V_i\}_{i=1}^{N}$ are sampled and sent to the Swin Transformer. The number of blocks in each stage is 2, 2, 6, 2. We represent the feature of N viewports as $V = \{v_1, v_2, \cdots, v_N\}$. The feature of each viewport represents a node of the graph.

3.3   Graph Edges Constructed by NSS

Considering that the extracted viewport is independent, it cannot simulate the process of viewing the omnidirectional image. Additionally, there exist variations in visual distortions across different viewports. We use NSS features that are crucial to the perceptual quality of OI as the edge of the graph structure to represent the similarity and correlation between different viewports.

To measure the loss of naturalness in viewports, it is necessary to compute the local mean subtracted and contrast normalized (MSCN) coefficients. These coefficients can be used to analyze the statistical features. For each distorted ERP map and viewports, the MSCN coefficients are calculated by:

$$\hat{D}^z(i,j) = \frac{D^z(i,j) - \mu(i,j)}{\sigma(i,j) + C} \tag{5}$$

where i and j represent the spatial coordinates. $\hat{D}^z(i,j)$ means the MSCN coefficients. $\mu(i,j)$ and $\sigma(i,j)$ represent the local mean and the standard deviation.

Then the generalized Gaussian distribution model is employed to model the statistic feature.

Figure 4 shows the difference between the MSCN distribution of different viewports. It is clear that the FOV information exhibits superior features and a greater capacity for expressing noise-related features compared to ERP images.

In order to construct viewports' correlation based on NSS features, we calculate the feature similarity through Eq. (6).

$$s_{i,m} = \frac{g_i \cdot g_m}{\|g_i\|_2 \cdot \|g_m\|_2} \tag{6}$$

where $i, m \in \{1, 2, \cdots, N\}$, and g_i, g_m represent the NSS features of the viewport i and m, respectively. $s_{i,m}$ denotes the natural feature similarity between two viewports on a spherical domain.

Considering that the feature similarity between viewports will change with different distortion types and different distortion levels, we use the average of feature similarities across multiple viewports as the feature similarity threshold.

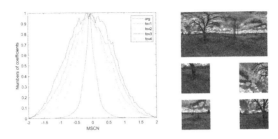

Fig. 4. The MSCN distribution of different viewports and the ERP image.

We calculate N viewports with the most similar NSS features by the following formula:

$$A_{i,m}(v_i, v_m) = \begin{cases} 1, s_{i,m} \geq \text{average}(s_{i,m}) \\ 0, s_{i,m} < \text{average}(s_{i,m}) \end{cases} \tag{7}$$

where $A_{i,m}$ is the affinity matrix representing whether there is information interaction between different viewpoints.

3.4   Quality Prediction

With the representation of the node feature vector $V = \{v_1, v_2, \cdots, v_N\}$ and the affinity matrix A, the perception process based on omnidirectional scanning path is constructed. Each node feature is represented as a 768-dimensional feature vector to input. And then the quality of the omnidirectional images can be predicted by the network, which is composed of 5-layer graph convolutions. The process of interacting and updating the node information can be expressed as:

$$H^{(l+1)} = f\left(BN\left(\hat{A}H^{(l)}W^{(l)}\right)\right) \tag{8}$$

where $\hat{A}$ is the adjacency matrix after normalization. The Softplus activation function $f(\cdot)$ [18] is used with batch normalization $BN(\cdot)$. The resulting feature matrices H^l are obtained by applying activations to the trainable weight matrix W^l. To match the number of hierarchical feature nodes of the Swin Transformer, the output dimension of each layer's feature nodes is 384, 192, 96, 48, 1. We then obtain the score of each viewport and leverage information from each viewport to produce accurate quality score Q.

4   Experimental Results

In this section, we provide an introduction to the databases utilized in our experiments, along with pertinent implementation details. We then compare the performance of our network with other metrics on a single and across databases. Finally, we conduct an ablation study and a cross-database evaluation to demonstrate the robustness and effectiveness of our model.

4.1 Databases

Two databases of omnidirectional images are utilized in the experiment: OIQA Database [19] and CVIQD Database [20].

OIQA Database: The database consists of 16 original images and their corresponding 320 degraded images. The degraded images include JPEG compression (JPEG), JPEG2000 compression (JP2K), Gaussian blur (BLUR), and Gaussian white noise (WN).

CVIQD Database: This database includes 16 reference images and 528 corresponding distorted images. Three encoding techniques are used to compress images, namely JPEG, H.264/AVC, and H.265/HEVC.

4.2 Implementation Details

Our model was executed on an NVIDIA GeForce RTX 3090 GPU with PyTorch. Our model uses Swin-Tiny as the backbone, which is pre-trained on ImageNet [21]. Each viewport image is resized to 256×256 and the batch size is set to 2. We utilize the Adam optimizer. The learning rate is set as 1×10^{-5}. The split ratio of the training set and test set in the database is 8:2. To avoid any overlap between the training and test data, distorted images that correspond to the same reference image have been assigned to the same set. The training loss we use is Mean Square Error (MSE) Loss. The final perception score is generated by predicting the mean score of 20 viewports.

Table 1. Overall performance comparison on CVIQD and OIQA databases. Best performance in bold.

Database		CVIQD			OIQA		
Metric		SROCC	PLCC	RMSE	SROCC	PLCC	RMSE
FR-IQA	PSNR	0.6239	0.7008	9.9599	0.5226	0.5812	1.7005
	SSIM [22]	0.8842	0.9002	6.0793	0.8588	0.8718	1.0238
	CPP-PSNR [23]	0.6265	0.6871	10.1448	0.5149	0.5683	1.7193
	S-PSNR [24]	0.6449	0.7083	9.8564	0.5399	0.5997	1.6721
	MS-SSIM [25]	0.8222	0.8521	7.3072	0.7379	0.7710	1.3308
	WS-PSNR [27]	0.6107	0.6729	10.3283	0.5263	0.5819	1.6994
NR-IQA	BRISQUE [12]	0.8180	0.8376	7.6271	0.8331	0.8424	1.1261
	DB-CNN [26]	0.9308	0.9356	4.9311	0.8653	0.8852	0.9717
	MC360IQA [7]	0.9428	0.9429	4.6506	0.9139	0.9267	0.7854
	VGCN [9]	0.9639	**0.9651**	3.6573	0.9515	0.9584	0.5967
	AHGCN [10]	0.9623	0.9643	3.6990	0.9590	0.9649	0.5487
	proposed	**0.9699**	0.9619	**3.5999**	**0.9702**	**0.9709**	**0.5292**

360

4.3

We
data
Cor
to e
pres
of o
on
met
in
our
acc
0.9(

4.4

dat
em
tes
ing
pe
Tr
po
rel
ser

4.

Vi
ou
vie
of
m(

Printed in the United States
by Baker & Taylor Publisher Services